CONTESTED FEDERALISM

Certainty and Ambiguity in the Canadian Federation

CONTESTED FEDERALISM

Certainty and Ambiguity in the
Canadian Federation

Herman Bakvis • Gerald Baier • Douglas Brown

OXFORD
UNIVERSITY PRESS

OXFORD
UNIVERSITY PRESS

70 Wynford Drive, Don Mills, Ontario M3C 1J9
www.oupcanada.com

Oxford University Press is a department of the University of Oxford.
It furthers the University's objective of excellence in research, scholarship,
and education by publishing worldwide in

Oxford   New York

Auckland   Cape Town   Dar es Salaam   Hong Kong   Karachi
Kuala Lumpur   Madrid   Melbourne   Mexico City   Nairobi
New Delhi   Shanghai   Taipei   Toronto

With offices in

Argentina   Austria   Brazil   Chile   Czech Republic   France   Greece
Guatemala   Hungary   Italy   Japan   Poland   Portugal   Singapore
South Korea   Switzerland   Thailand   Turkey   Ukraine   Vietnam

Oxford is a trade mark of Oxford University Press
in the UK and in certain other countries

Published in Canada
by Oxford University Press

Copyright © Oxford University Press Canada 2009

The moral rights of the author have been asserted

Database right Oxford University Press (maker)

First Published 2009

Library and Archives Canada Cataloguing in Publication

Bakvis, Herman, 1948–
Contested federalism : certainty and ambiguity in the Canadian
federation / Herman Bakvis, Gerald Baier, Doug Brown.

Includes index.
ISBN 978-0-19-542529-1

1. Federal-provincial relations—Canada—Textbooks.   2. Federal
government—Canada—Textbooks.   3. Canada—Politics and government—
Textbooks.   I. Baier, Gerald, 1971–   II. Brown, Douglas M. (Douglas
Mitchell), 1954–   III. Title.

JL27.B39 2009   320.471   C2008-907910-8

Cover image: CSA MOD Art/ Veer Images

This book is printed on permanent acid-free paper ∞.
Printed and bound in Canada.

1 2 3 4 — 12 11 10 09

Contents

List of Tables and Figures

TABLES

FIGURES

Preface

In recent years many fine studies have examined Canadian federalism in relation to the constitution, the courts, democracy, and various aspects of social and economic policy. But there has been no comprehensive critical examination of the federation and its component parts. It has been two decades since the publication of *The Federal Condition in Canada* by Donald Smiley and *Unfulfilled Union* by Garth Stevenson, two classic studies of the main issues at play in the federation in the 1980s. Needless to say, much has happened since then—perhaps too much, and too quickly, for anyone to have been tempted to record it, let alone try to make sense of it all.

Our aim here is to start filling this void by examining the main institutions and processes of the Canadian federation, together with the major policy areas that are currently the subject of debate, negotiation, and decision-making within the various federal–provincial–territorial arenas. Some of our themes are well established—judicial review, executive federalism, the economic union— but we also look at a number of newer issues such as the environmental union, the role of local government in intergovernmental negotiations, and the challenges involved in opening the federation to accommodate Aboriginal aspirations to self-government.

In assessing the state of Canadian federalism we highlight, among other things, the interdependencies between the different orders of government with respect to roles and responsibilities, the gap between citizens' expectations and the formal rules and institutions of federalism, and the unique positions that Quebec and Aboriginal peoples occupy within the federation. In so doing we focus on a theme that we feel connects several of these concerns, namely the inherent tension between the need for flexibility and the need for certainty. As a result of this tension the meaning of Canadian federalism is essentially contested. Is it a simple system of fixed rules and formal procedures? Or is it a more complex matter of informal, pragmatic accommodations and carefully constructed ambiguities? A long habit of cloaking important intergovernmental agreements in ambiguity, we argue, has played a major role in keeping the federation intact. But this approach has its drawbacks, particularly when efforts to reach consensus fail and Ottawa ends up taking unilateral action, effectively centralizing a decision-making process that ought to be decentralized. We have no easy solutions to offer; but we think it is useful to draw attention to the way the competing orders of government interact with each other, as well as the consequences of those interactions.

In bringing this book to completion we faced a number of challenges. Not least of these was the realization that, despite the absence of recent book-length overviews, an enormous amount of material on Canadian federalism, and federalism generally, has been produced over the past decade in the form of theses, specialized studies, and edited collections. Bringing order and perspective to this material while incorporating our own original research was no easy task. A further challenge was the fact that in the midst of this project all three authors changed their home institutions, two of us moving from the east coast to the west and the third from central Canada to the east coast.

We are indebted to several individuals and institutions for the assistance they have given us. The Social Sciences and Humanities Research Council of Canada graciously provided financial support for our research under its 'Federalism and Federations' program. With this support we were able to convene a series of focus groups in Canada and Australia on federalism-related themes and topics ranging from the 'federal spending power' to senate reform. We are grateful to the participants in these sessions—academics, politicians, public servants, and others—for sharing their insights and helping us refine our assumptions and propositions. Throughout the research and writing of the book we relied on the excellent research assistance of Devin Anderson, Katherine Boothe, Erin Crandall, Karen Diepeveen, Penny Frearson, Carmel McCauley, and Shannon Wells. James Boxall, map curator and head of the Map and Geospatial Information Collection at Dalhousie University, kindly produced the map used in Chapter 2. At St Francis Xavier University, we benefited from able research assistance provided by Marianne Gillis, Dr Allison Butler, and Michael MacIsaac.

Early drafts of a number of chapters were first used in an online course on intergovernmental relations developed by Herman Bakvis and delivered through the School of Public Administration at Dalhousie University. We are grateful to the School for its support in preparing this material in its initial stages and to the students for their feedback on the material. Subsequently all three of us used further drafts of various chapters in our regular courses on federalism, Canadian politics, and intergovernmental relations at Dalhousie University, Queen's University, St Francis Xavier University, the University of British Columbia, the University of Victoria, and Yale University. We are grateful to our students for allowing us to use them as sounding boards for our ideas on the best way of tackling the complexities of federalism.

We are grateful to Oxford University Press Canada and its staff for their sustained support over the last four years. Laura McLeod encouraged us to undertake the project and assured us that it was worth doing. Jennifer Charlton kept us on track in submitting and revising the various chapters. Sally Livingston, in her role as copy editor, queried just about every concept, sentence, and paragraph in the manuscript, a process that seemed painful at the time but in the end forced us to write an infinitely better, more accessible and readable book. Janice Evans was both efficient and flexible in managing the final production process, including correcting the page proofs. And Francesca Scalzo constructed a first-rate index.

We are deeply obliged to the numerous scholars who have contributed to the federalism literature. Like the Canadian federation itself, this book covers an enormous amount of ground. Yet each chapter covers only the most prominent features of the topics and debates at hand. Deeper understanding can be reached only by consulting directly the works we cite and exploring what their authors have had to say on the topic at hand. We urge you to do so. By far the largest numbers of citations are from English-language sources—as is appropriate, given our intended readership—but we have attempted to take into account key sources available only in the French language. An excellent point of departure for a rich literature, mainly from Quebec, is Alain-G. Gagnon's edited collection *Le Fédéralisme canadien contemporain: Fondements, traditions, institutions* (2006).

It is not possible here to list everyone who has contributed to this literature, but we would be remiss not to cite those most instrumental in shaping our views on Canadian federalism. For all three of us, Richard Simeon has been variously teacher, mentor, and colleague. The framework for studying Canadian intergovernmental relations that he developed in his classic *Federal–Provincial Diplomacy* (1972) remains extraordinarily useful, and its influence is evident in this book. Harvey Lazar, both when he was in government and in his capacity as director of the Institute of Intergovernmental Relation at Queen's, has always been supportive of our inquiries into Canadian federalism and social policy. He also kindly commented on some of the draft chapters. Peter Aucoin, Kathy Brock, Alan Cairns, the two David Camerons (David M. at Dalhousie University and David R. at the University of Toronto), Steve Dupré, Alain-G. Gagnon, Brian Galligan, David Good, Kathryn Harrison, Evert Lindquist, Peter Meekison, Michael Murphy, John Nethercote, Peter Russell, Campbell Sharman, Julie Simmons, Grace Skogstad, Jennifer Smith, Robert Young, John Warhurst, and Ronald Watts have provided invaluable advice and support over the years in our various academic endeavours, both separately and in connection with this project.

We are indebted to colleagues at six different home universities for their sufferance and their support as we worked to bring this project to a conclusion. Last but not least, we are grateful to our families for support of the kind that only close family members can provide. They are no doubt equally grateful that this project is now complete.

Victoria, Vancouver, Antigonish
November 2008

Introduction

> The distinguishing characteristic of federalism is the peculiar ambivalence of the ends men seek to make it serve. Quite literally an ambivalence: Federalism is always an arrangement pointed in two contrary directions or aimed at securing two contrary ends (Diamond, 1973: 129).

Martin Diamond's observation is as true today as it was nearly four decades ago. The decision to form a federation often has less to do with a desire for union between constituent units—former colonies of an imperial power, for example—than with a distrust of complete union. The understandings reached between the founding units regarding the powers that will be shared—held by a national government—and the powers that they will retain are usually reflected in a federal constitutional 'bargain'. But this bargain itself can become a source of tension and ambivalence, especially with the passage of time. Constitutional documents pronounce on the respective responsibilities of the orders of government, but they rarely have much to say about the institutions that will coordinate the activities of the various governments, or how disputes between them will be resolved.

The Canadian federation is no exception in these respects. In this book we examine the relations among Canada's governments—federal, provincial, local, and Aboriginal—along with the tensions, conflicts, and adaptations they have given rise to. In so doing, we explore both the basic federal and intergovernmental structure—the constitutional and institutional framework—and what we might term federal governance. With respect to the latter, our discussions invariably revolve around the shifting relations between and among government and non-government actors, their interests and policy objectives, the resources available to them, and the strategies they deploy in pursuit of their objectives. Both the objectives and the strategies in many ways reflect a basic tension between the desire for autonomy and the desire to be part of a larger whole, between what Daniel Elazar (1996) has called 'shared rule' and 'self rule'. Thus federalism, particularly in its Canadian form, entails an ongoing contestation of interests, ideas, and identities that sometimes clarifies and sometimes obscures the issues at stake, if only because (as we will argue) ambiguity is often a pre-condition to their resolution.

This ambivalent quality colours many of the debates specific to federations: debates over matters such as the appropriate balance between the national government and regional and local governments, the adjudication of intergovernmental disputes, and even whether federalism is still the appropriate form of governance for the nation in light of changing domestic needs and global conditions. Two other frequent topics of debate are the function of central institutions, such as courts and second chambers, in managing issues affecting the federation as a whole, and the role that federalism plays, or should play, in expanding or limiting democratic rights and freedoms. These themes are relevant to most federations.

Other themes are more specific (though not necessarily unique) to Canada as a federation characterized by distinct regional, cultural, and linguistic differences. Matters related to Quebec's constitutional status, or the possibility of Quebec's secession, appear regularly on the political agenda not only inside Quebec but also in Ottawa, where the Bloc Québécois represents the sovereignist vision, and in the federation as a whole, where federal and provincial leaders spend considerable energy trying to accommodate Quebec's unique demands. More homogeneous nations such as Australia and Germany do not experience the same kinds of tensions, and therefore their federal systems are subject to somewhat fewer and certainly less intense pressures for decentralization. For this reason, we will argue, Canada has been particularly inclined towards ambivalence and ambiguity in its intergovernmental institutions and practices.

Another distinctive feature of the Canadian federation is the emphasis it puts on 'executive federalism', a pattern of interaction in which much of the negotiating required to manage the federation takes place between the executives, elected and unelected, of the main orders of governments (Smiley, 1987; Watts, 1999). The concerns here include the closed, elitist nature of this executive network; the way our parliamentary institutions encourage its dominance by concentrating power in the hands of 'first ministers' (premiers and prime minister) (Savoie, 1999, 2008; White, 2005); and the extent to which this pattern contributes both to the Canadian version of the democratic deficit and to what some believe is an unusually high level of conflict between and among the federal and provincial/territorial governments.

All the above problems, questions, and conundrums come into play at some point or other in our examination of the underpinnings of Canadian federalism. Finally, though, there are two factors that, along with ambiguity, we consider crucial. One is balance. This is not simply a matter of balancing unity and diversity, preserving the autonomy of two or more orders of government, and providing for some rough equality between the constituent units (provinces or states). These are all important, but we believe it is also crucial to find a balance between flexibility and certainty in the norms and rules involved in the governance of the Canadian federation. Federal institutions and processes must be flexible enough to adapt to a rapidly changing domestic and global environment; yet they must also be clear and firm enough to give citizens a sense of certainty. The other factor is the relevance of the basic federal framework to the social, economic, and political conditions in which citizens and political elites find themselves. Earlier writers on federalism (e.g. Wheare, 1963) emphasized that practically all federations have felt the need for a written constitution spelling out, at least in broad terms, the responsibilities and powers of the two (or more) constituent orders of government, the degree of autonomy each is to enjoy, and some basic mechanisms for resolving disputes between them. Even with provisions for judicial interpretation and formal amendment, however, virtually every federal constitution will sooner or later be found lacking in relevance to current conditions. Key constitutional provisions will become outdated, judicial rulings will be found misguided; and amending procedures, typically requiring double majorities, will prove too inflexible to permit essential changes (Smith, 2004; Watts, 2005).

In fact, attempts at constitutional change affecting the balance between the main orders of government are rare in modern federations, and they even more rarely succeed. The double failure of the Meech Lake (1990) and Charlottetown (1992) Accords to amend Canada's constitution illustrates the point. The inevitability that the constitution will become outdated makes it all the more crucial that a federation have a variety of ways—formal and informal—for its governments to reach political understandings and agreements. The need is perhaps especially acute in Canada's case, partly because the distribution of powers between federal and provincial governments in the original 1867 Constitution Act is both detailed and dated, and hence questionable, partly because of the horizontal imbalances between provinces in natural resources and partly because of unresolved regional differences and the ambiguity of Quebec's position in Confederation.

Given the importance, in federations, of intergovernmental coordination, one might expect that any federal constitution would establish the basic institutional framework within which negotiations will take place—specifying the arena(s), for instance, and setting out rules for decision-making. But some constitutions do a better job than others in this respect. The German constitution provides for the direct representation of Länder (state governments) in the second chamber of the parliament, the Bundesrat. And the constitution of the European Union specifies that, to pass, decisions made by Council of the EU require more than a simple majority but less than unanimity. In Canada, however, institutional arrangements for intergovernmental relations are almost non-existent.[1] In the twenty-first century, the absence not only of decision rules to resolve the inevitable intergovernmental disputes, but of formal provisions for interaction between governments, or between government and civil society, raises serious questions about the relevance of Canada's nineteenth-century constitution.

In fact, a number of critics, and not just in Canada, have called for major reform or even questioned the value of federalism itself. In 2008, for instance, when Australia's new Labor government convened a 'summit' on the country's future, a major theme was 'the need to fix federalism to create a modern Australian federation' (Australia, 2008).[2] More than a century earlier, the English constitutional scholar A.V. Dicey—a true believer in the virtues of parliamentary government— was dismayed by the formalization and legal strictures that a federal constitution introduced. In his view, federal law was stiff and uncompromising; it forced governments into narrow roles and constrained the creativity necessary to address public problems (see Dicey, 1959 [1885]). The British political scientist Harold

Laski (1939) believed that federal systems were too fragmented to stand up to the forces of capitalism and deal adequately with the damage wrought by the Great Depression. In the 1960s, in a frequently cited essay, the American William Riker questioned not so much the dysfunctional aspects of federalism as its very relevance; having posed the question 'Does federalism make any difference in the way people are governed?' he supplied the answer himself: 'Hardly any at all' (Riker, 1969: 145).

The Canadian political scientist Roger Gibbins took a rather different view in the late twentieth century. Unlike Laski or Riker, Gibbins expressed no doubt about the value of federalism. Instead, he worried that Canadians no longer see federalism as an 'anchor or point of reference' and that their political identities now 'bear little relationship to formal federal structures' (Gibbins, 1999: 218). Richard Simeon (2006 [1972]), in his classic study of intergovernmental policy-making in Canada, *Federal–Provincial Diplomacy*, noted a significant disjunction between the constitution, which envisions federal and provincial areas of juris-diction as entirely separate (the 'watertight compartments' theory) and actual practice, in which the two orders of government, despite their formal autonomy, are often highly interdependent when it comes to policy-making and program delivery. This interdependence limits what governments can do on their own and means that they must be able to pool or share their autonomy or sovereignty—in other words, to collaborate.

Canadians generally are aware of the shared nature of power and decision-making in many policy fields, if only because they are routinely exposed to the wrangling, complaints, and blame-shifting that seem to come with any sharing of governmental responsibility. The provinces blame the federal government for what they say is the impoverished state of the health care system; the federal government harangues provincial premiers for looking the other way on environmental issues such as climate change, or not doing enough to control the negative effects of their provincial industries. Meanwhile, municipal govern-ments plead for funds to improve the infrastructure and services that they are increasingly told are essential to the prosperity of their cities and regions, and ultimately the country. The squabbling that Canadians witness is in part the outward manifestation of the intergovernmental negotiation that is a constant in a system of shared rule. Experienced observers may dismiss much of the squab-bling as a matter of strategic posturing. Yet at times it can be legitimate to ask, as Gibbins (1999) does, how well contemporary federalism is meeting the needs of urban areas and citizens (especially members of ethnic minorities).

Overall, though—as we argue throughout this book—the system works well. Agreements may sometimes be long in coming, or so clouded in ambiguity that citizens have no idea what has been accomplished on their behalf, but they get made and they make many important things possible. It would be poor social science to specify causes in the absence of more specific evidence. Yet it seems that Canada's above-average performance on a host of global indicators pertaining to educational achievement, health outcomes, economic well-being, and, not least, political stability, among others, has at least not been harmed by federalism; in some areas, perhaps, federalism has even contributed something to that performance. Our particular federal system has its flaws, but we believe some sort of federalism is essential to sustain the political unity that has been the foundation for much of what Canada and Canadians have achieved since 1867.

The institutions and processes of intergovernmental relations are generally pragmatic. Over the years there have been demands for greater formalization of those processes, largely to make them more transparent and increase the opportunities for public input (Skogstad, 2003). But the system has resisted those pressures, even when governments (the primary participants in the federal system) themselves have been the advocates of formalization. As we examine the characteristics of the intergovernmental system in the chapters that follow, this tension between formality and flexibility will become more apparent. The penchant for secrecy characteristic of elites operating within the framework of the intergovernmental system may appear self-serving. Yet it can be argued that a modicum of secrecy, coupled with ambiguity, is necessary if elites are to reach agreement on ways to accommodate the tensions within a divided larger society.[3] In other words, despite the rancour and disputatiousness that sometimes seem the hallmarks of Canada's federal system, the Canadian model is by many important measures peaceful and stable, with governments working quietly behind the scenes on both major and minor issues.

In this book we focus mainly on the relations between the two orders of government formally recognized in Canada's constitution: federal and provincial/territorial. But these are not the only components of the intergovernmental system. Two other components, both of which are now seeking to expand their self-governing capacities, are municipal and Aboriginal governments. Constitutionally, local government is directly controlled by the provinces, which have the power to alter the roles and responsibilities of municipalities at will. Yet municipal governments do have some resources, as well as a certain amount of political and moral authority, that they can use to press their case for greater autonomy. And in recent years, as amalgamation has created larger municipalities with increasingly significant infrastructure needs, provincial and federal governments alike have become interested in the possibility that municipalities might play a more active role in the intergovernmental system. Such a change would be in keeping with the current trend towards what political economists have described as 'glocalization': a double movement of power and influence away from the national level and towards on one hand the global level—with external actors such as Washington or the WTO increasingly playing a part in the framing of domestic policy decisions—and on the other hand the local level (Courchene, 1995a; Hale, 2004).

Meanwhile Canada's Aboriginal peoples continue to seek recognition as full-fledged sovereign entities (Cairns, 2000) with their own place in the intergovernmental system. Some progress is being made, but the pace has been slow. The difficulty of achieving even urgently needed improvements in the management and delivery of basic public services for Aboriginal people, on and off the reserves, is an illustration of the challenges posed by a system of shared rule in areas where both federal and provincial governments have responsibilities. To work effectively, the system requires acceptance of the roles and responsibilities assigned by the constitution, but it also needs cooperation, trust, and collaboration among governmental partners. The failure, so far, to reach agreement on what those roles and responsibilities are has an effect on the intergovernmental system as a whole.

These developments outside the old federal–provincial relationship have led some analysts to focus on what has been called 'multi-level governance' (Hooghe and Marks, 2001; Bache, 2004); we will discuss this concept in Chapter 1. Even so, most of the activity and all the significant relationships in Canada continue to centre on the federal–provincial–territorial nexus. Issues involving other types of government—international, local, Aboriginal—may have significant consequences for intergovernmental relations, but they are still best understood through the prism of federal–provincial relations. The two autonomous orders of government with constitutionally defined powers are the keys to the directions that major public policies take. And the political climate in which they share rights and responsibilities has a definite bearing on the kinds of outcomes that the intergovernmental system produces.

In the chapters that follow we will examine the social, economic, and institutional bases of Canadian federalism, intergovernmental relations and the policy process, the role of the constitution and the courts, and the machinery, institutions, and processes of executive federalism, as well as four crucial policy areas: fiscal federalism, the social union, the economic union, and the environmental union. First, though, we will look at the concept of federalism itself and review some of the principal approaches that have been taken to the subject, with emphasis on the Canadian variants. This review is intended to familiarize readers with the basic assumptions that we make as authors about how federal systems work and are best understood. The perspectives sketched in this brief introduction will become clearer in the context of other efforts to understand the perennial tension in federalism between its demands for certainty and ambiguity.

Chapter 1

Understanding Federalism and Intergovernmental Relations

Federalism is something of a chicken-and-egg phenomenon. Do certain societal or geographical characteristics compel a country to adopt a federal system? Or does the adoption of a federal system allow different cultures and regions to flourish in a way that otherwise would not be possible? In other words, is federalism simply a response to societal differences? Or does federalism itself create more important differences, which then need dedicated intergovernmental institutions to accommodate them? Since one of our central concerns in this book is the structure of intergovernmental relations in Canada, it is worth investigating the origins of that diversity.

For many people, federalism may be defined in terms of the division of powers on the basis of territory or geography rather than function. By dividing authority between two or more orders of government,[1] to provide representation for territorial, religious, linguistic, or ethnic differences in the decision-making structures of the state, federalism essentially creates conditions that may entrench differences over time. The reasons that lead a state to opt for federalism will have some bearing on how much or how little intergovernmental 'relating' is required to promote the development of a stable and responsive state.

This chapter surveys the origins of the federal idea or principle, along with the different schools of thought regarding diversity and societal differences in federal systems. Federal institutions are meant to channel diversity, sometimes to resolve conflicts and sometimes to allow for diversity to be reflected in the decisions made by the state at different levels. Federalism is indeed an '-ism': a set of beliefs about the correct way to organize political life. But it is a complicated one, which must simultaneously maintain unity among the diverse parts and allow those parts to flourish and express their differences in tangible policy choices. Federalism endorses the idea that for purposes of governance, different communities may need some degree of unity without being strictly unified. As an ideology it affirms the appropriateness of two or more governments exercising authority on behalf of a single community and its parts. Canadians may find it easier than others to grasp the idea that federalism is an ideological choice. This is especially clear in Quebec's relations with the rest of Canada. Quebecers who support the Canadian national government or strong(er) ties with the rest of Canada are routinely described as federalists, while those who do not support the federal union are commonly labelled separatists or sovereignists. Both camps are seen as endorsing a particular position loaded with normative ideas about the value of group rights and individual rights or about the need for self-governing at a more local level and ultimately about the very nature of the state and the kinds of collective goals that it might or might not wish to pursue.

Overall, federalism is no less normative an idea. The adoption of a federal system implies a society's preference for a degree of collective unity offset by genuine autonomy for individual regions, with a written constitution and the rule of law to keep the various elements in check. Canada's choice of a federal system indicates an ideological preference for some kind of balance between the concentration of power at the national level (as in a unitary system) and the dispersion of power to the provinces (as in a confederal alliance).

If this ideological dimension is sometimes forgotten, it is because the choice of federalism seems above all to imply that the society has decided to put a certain set of institutional commitments ahead of any commitment to controversial ideas or values. As teachers we are all too aware that federalism in Canada is often seen as a set of dry, boring procedural rules and neutral institutions that the more exciting forces of collective life, such as politics and ideology, have to work *through* if citizens are to realize their social goals or policy preferences. In reality, however, the decision to adopt and maintain a federal system is anything but neutral. It reflects a certain commitment on the part of both the united subunits and the population, a commitment that needs perpetual reinforcement and affirmation—that is why constitutional discussions that question the very basis of federal unity can be so dangerous.

The consequence of choosing federalism is federation. The ideological choice of a federal model leads to certain kinds of observable institutions and rules. The institutions and rules characteristic of federated governments look fairly similar from one federation to the next, but they work differently in different contexts and may have quirks that undermine or exaggerate the intent of the system's designers. That said, federation does appear to have some universal traits that distinguish it from other forms of political organization. The minimum requirements are usually seen as including a written constitution with a division of legislative powers, a constitutional court to serve as umpire when disputes arise between governments, a mechanism for coordination between governments (intergovernmental relations), and representation of subunits in national institutions (Watts, 1999a).

Once again, at the core of federalism is a commitment to organizing political life so as to recognize regional and societal diversity and preserve self-government at a local level. Federalism began as a response to the challenge of governing complicated societies and spaces, and so it remains. Where students of federalism differ is on the relative importance of institutions and societal differences in explaining how federations operate and evolve. This is a perennial question of political science: what matters more to outcomes, the demands and preferences of a political community, or the institutions that those demands and preferences are channelled through?

In this chapter we first survey the origins of the federal idea; we then discuss the differences between two basic perspectives. A discussion of varying Canadian conceptions of the purpose and meaning of our federal system reinforces our point about the ideological character of federalism and reminds us of the contending viewpoints that continue to drive much of the activity in Canadian intergovernmental relations. Finally we discuss the value of bringing a comparative perspective to the examination of intergovernmental relations and institutions, and why we think federalism is indeed an important variable in the kinds of political outcomes that the citizens of federal polities experience.

THE ORIGINS OF FEDERALISM

The idea of federalism is an ancient one. The roots of the contemporary Dutch and Swiss confederacies can be traced back to the medieval period or even earlier (Hueglin, 2003). In North America, the Iroquois nations had formed a confederacy before the first European settlers arrived, and a number of other Aboriginal nations had established power-sharing arrangements (Ladner, 2003). Some of these models may have provided inspiration to the American colonists when they were looking for ways to establish a greater union. What we call federalism today, however, is of much more recent vintage. The plan for the first modern federation was laid out with the drafting of the American constitution in 1787. The advocates of that constitution, particularly the authors of *The Federalist Papers*, essentially co-opted the term 'federal' for a system of government that had never been seen before, even by those with a nominal notion of federalism (Diamond, 1961). In the American constitution, legitimate governing authority was distributed between the federal (national) and state governments, but was not held by either: it remained independent of both orders of government, residing in the constitution and, ultimately, the people. Prior to the final ratification of this document in 1789, the 13 American states were linked together rather loosely under the Articles of Confederation, which was the first arrangement for governing the former British colonies after the Revolution.

Among the notable features of the early American confederation was the absence of an independent central government. In this respect it resembled many earlier federal-style arrangements: the partners to the compact shared some nominal sense of unity, but kept for themselves all governing authority and sovereignty. We now describe these older federations as examples of 'confederal' arrangements. Under such arrangements the collective can do nothing without the unanimous agreement of its component parts. The pre-constitution American union had neither an executive nor a judicial branch; executive tasks were entrusted to committees struck by the Continental Congress. The 1787 US constitution rectified what were seen as major deficiencies, primary among them the absence of an independent federal government with meaningful powers. The creation of such an entity was not without controversy. Self-governing states had little interest in transferring significant power to a distant new national government that provided for, among other things, a directly elected legislature with representation based on population and separate executive and judiciary branches. The rhetorical victory of the Federalists was to claim for their invention, a system of compound sovereignty, the name 'Federal'. Their opponents, who wanted to maintain the dispersed power of the older arrangement, were reduced to the status of Anti-Federalists.

The American constitution has served as the prototype for modern federations. It challenged the idea that collective sovereignty could be realized only in a unitary form. Its invention made it possible for the people of a state to exercise local sovereignty in some matters and to be part of a greater sovereignty at the national level. The independence of the individual governments in such an arrangement was critical. It was the basis for the famous definition of the federal principle put forward by K.C. Wheare in his book *Federal Government*: 'By the federal principle I mean the method of dividing powers so that the general and regional governments are each, within a sphere, coordinate and independent' (Wheare, 1963: 10). The key terms in this definition are 'coordinate' and 'independent'. The former denotes a lack of hierarchy: the two orders of governments are of equal standing. The latter states that neither depends on the other: each is sovereign in its own sphere of jurisdiction.

In this federal context the life of the citizen is also bifurcated. Two orders of government overlap in the same citizen body, and each has a direct relationship with the people (Vernon, 1988). Thus in modern federations such as the US, Canada, and Australia, citizens elect representatives to both the state/provincial and federal legislatures. Deriving government authority from a constitution whose authority in turn is grounded in popular sovereignty freed the national government from the dictates of its component parts. This was not the case with earlier confederal models; in 1775, for example, when the 13 colonial governments sent delegates to the Continental Congress, each state had exactly one vote. We describe such a system as confederal because, although it still has some features of union, the national or union level depends on the parts for its authority. Delegates to Congress under the Articles of Confederation were true delegates, chosen to faithfully transmit the views of the governments they represented. These delegates were selected by the governments—not directly elected by the people. Federalism before 1787 had meant some kind of union government, but one that was in effect created and controlled by the regional governments. The US constitution, in providing for the direct election of members of the House of Representatives, freed those representatives from the instructions of their state governments. The presidency draws its legitimacy from the people as well, but indirectly, through the state-based electoral college, which gives it something of a compound character. Once in office, neither the lower house of the national legislature nor the national executive owes any allegiance to subnational governments. Each order of government, therefore, enjoys an independent source of authority and legitimacy.

Its democratic character was not the only feature that made the American system so revolutionary. Few people in 1787 had any notion of government authority as anything other than unitary. Since the Treaties of Westphalia of 1648, European sovereignty had been considered indivisible, even to the point of suppressing previous federal experience (Hueglin, 1999). In the British parliamentary model to which most of the American colonists were accustomed, the final authority for making and approving laws rested with a single legislature or government. This is still the case in Britain and other unitary systems today: regional or local governments may exist, but they lack the constitutionally protected independent authority, autonomy, and jurisdiction enjoyed by states and provinces in constitutionalized federal systems. Their status and privileges can be altered at will by the national legislature, and decisions rendered by lower-level governments can be nullified by the same legislature. The relationship between Canada's municipal and provincial governments is of this type. In recent years, provincial governments have exercised significant authority over municipalities—changing their responsibilities, for example, and forcing amalgamations. The federal government does not have any equivalent power over the provinces.

The autonomy and dispersion of power we've discussed in these three models—confederal, federal, and unitary—can be placed on a continuum, as in Figure 1.1. These are ideal types, and most systems of government combine elements of each. Federations nominally occupy the middle ground on this continuum, but they also represent a compound of unitary and confederal elements. For example, the second chambers of federations vary in form from mildly to explicitly confederal. In the US, until the 17th Amendment in 1913, members of the national senate were selected by state legislatures rather than directly by the citizens of the states. In Germany, the second chamber of the national legislature, the Bundesrat, is populated by the premiers and senior members of state governments. In these cases, state governments have the capacity to impose direct checks on the power of the federal legislature. Other federations, including the present-day US, elect upper house members directly, and those representatives feel much less loyalty to state governments than they do to state citizens. Within their spheres of jurisdiction, governments can theoretically act as though they were quite unitary. But in practice, national institutions make it possible for regions or regional governments to have a say in what the federal government does. In this respect, it is worth noting that while Canada has a second chamber based on regional representation—the Senate—its members are appointed directly by the federal government and thus lack the legitimacy accorded by either direct election or appointment by provincial governments. Canada stands in contrast to other federations in this respect, and many observers would argue that the Canadian federation is essentially incomplete because of it (King, 1982).

Given the need to balance elements of unitary and confederal decision-making (or centralizing and decentralizing forces, if you prefer), federations generally look to second chambers, although the form of the national executive (a regionally representative cabinet, for example) can also mitigate this tension. A baseline requirement for realizing the federal idea is a written constitution, which can divide power on a territorial basis to ensure the coordinate and independent status of two or more orders of government. To ensure the representation of regions or regional governments in central government decision-making, however, federations typically rely on a body whose members are either elected by the citizens of the various regions or appointed by the regional governments. But these two features do not necessarily provide an accurate or complete picture of how federations function.

It is important to note that the coordinate and independent status emphasized by Wheare is premised on what has been labelled the 'watertight compartments' notion of federalism,[2] in which each government is seen as operating in its own separate sphere, never really overlapping or crossing paths with the other level. This separateness is assumed to be beneficial, just as it is beneficial for a ship with a hole in its hull if the water can be contained in one compartment without flowing into another. This classic notion of independence and autonomy assumed no need for regular interaction between the different orders of government in a federation. Since the early twentieth century, however, experience has suggested that this is an unrealistic assumption. In fact, it was discovered early in

Figure 1.1   Degrees of Centralization in Federal and Confederal Forms

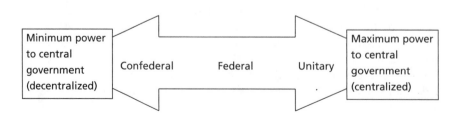

the life of the American federation that extensive cooperation between federal and state governments was necessary for the new nation to develop its infrastructure, allowing the country to develop its full potential, whether it was with respect to education, canals, roads, or railways (Elazar, 1962). It also became evident that the distinct jurisdictional spheres or functions of the two orders of government were soon thoroughly intertwined—a development that led one writer to liken the American federation to a marble cake (Grodzins, 1966). In Canada, at times, somewhat greater efforts were made to maintain a strict division between provincial and national jurisdiction, but here too it became clear, once governments started to do more, that the responsibilities of the two orders could not easily be separated. Thus it is interdependence rather than independence that appears to be the hallmark of modern federalism. And this interdependence of government functions in turn requires considerable interaction between governments on a large variety of administrative and policy issues (Lindquist, 1999). Increasing interdependence does not necessarily mean that one order of government exercises control over the other, though this is one possible outcome. Certainly in Canada we have a high level of autonomy on the part of the constituent units (the federal and provincial governments) coupled with considerable interdependence (Simeon, 2006 [1972]). What this means in practice is that when a policy initiative needs to be moved forward, the two orders of government will usually need to cooperate; conversely, if one government or set of governments refuses to cooperate, the initiative could well be stymied. How governments negotiate, the strategies they use, the objectives they seek to attain in various policy areas, and the constraints under which they operate: these are what intergovernmental relations are largely about.

INSTITUTIONAL AND SOCIETAL VIEWS OF FEDERALISM

The two principal views of federalism differ in their responses to the question we asked at the outset of this chapter. Societal explanations maintain that the root cause of federation is difference, that intergovernmental institutions are created to recognize and accommodate differences, and that those institutions must adapt to meet changing patterns of diversity. From this perspective there would be little need for federalism at all if the differences were to disappear.

Institutional explanations, by contrast, focus on the impact that the particular intergovernmental institutions of a given federation have on the way it accommodates differences or even ensures that differences have the opportunity to flourish. Institutionalists want to know what kinds of institutions are in place and how they operate. In fact, as we shall see, the institutions themselves can contribute to diversity even in a relatively homogeneous population where most people are exposed to the same culture and media influences. Both perspectives acknowledge that federations are complex; where they differ is on the source of the energy that drives the federal system.

Societal accounts of federalism point to societal factors as the reasons for choosing federalism in the first place and see popular attitudes and cultural traits as the main sources of federalism's staying power. Societal influence is most evident in what have come to be called multinational or multiethnic federations, where there are clear differences in the languages people speak or the cultural practices they follow. But important societal differences can also be found in federations that appear more homogeneous. For William Livingston (1956), an early proponent of the society-first view, the distinguishing feature of federations was diversity—economic, cultural, linguistic, religious, climactic—with a geographic or territorial connection. It is this geographic element that distinguishes federal societies from those in which differences may exist—and need governmental accommodation—but are not associated with particular regions. In short, federalism is necessary when you have differences plus geography. Without a geographic connection, what you have is simply a diverse society. The concentration of a particular language group in a particular territory, or vast differences in geography (and therefore in natural resources and economic conditions), will compel a society to organize itself on a territorial basis and allow for the expression and representation of those differences. It is no accident that federations do not fit well into the nation-state model and lack homogeneity in language and culture. It is also no accident that the world's largest states have opted for federalism to accommodate the enormous territorial distinctions within their borders.

For Livingston, the societal differences underlying federalism were the main variables determining how a federal system worked. Institutions—he called them 'instrumentalities'—had to be responsive to societal differences. A federal system in which the instrumentalities were not responsive to societal diversity, in his view, risked serious trouble. Livingston was particularly interested in the mechanisms used by federations to make constitutional change, because the formal alteration of instrumentalities was evidence of the primacy of societal forces in shaping federalism. Livingston's approach was famously criticized by the Canadian political scientist Alan Cairns (1977) as overemphasizing the importance of organic, inherent differences within federations and underestimating the extent to which governments themselves promote diversity in the federal state. While there is no denying that territorially concentrated differences remain in Canada today, equally strong forces serve to unify Canadians—and yet federalism persists. For Cairns and others, provincial governments will always seek to justify their own existence, and if endowed with sufficient powers they will persevere long after their usefulness has passed.

Other scholars have been more inclined to approach federalism as a largely institutional phenomenon. As we have seen, the introduction of federalism required considerable institutional invention. Little surprise, then, that people seeking to understand the impact of a federal system look at the influence of institutions as well as their capacity to accommodate diversity. A focus on institutions was also compatible with the dominant trends in political science in its early development as a discipline. Political science in Canada, and elsewhere, was initially concerned with explaining the minutiae of institutional arrangements and their operations (Smith, 2005). Federalism lends itself to such an analysis because the institutions of different federations vary in the weight they give to uniting and self-governing forces. However, there is some danger in too literal an institutional approach. Canadian scholars, for instance, initially attributed the early decentralization of Canadian federalism almost wholly to a province-favouring interpretation of the division of powers by the Judicial Committee of the Privy Council. Those scholars were later scolded for not acknowledging the influence of Canada's geographic realities, which would inevitably be decentralizing, nor the increase in importance of the subject matters (such as health care and social welfare) that were originally assigned to the provinces at Confederation (Cairns, 1971). In other words, institutional explanations of federalism have to take into account the context in which intergovernmental institutions operate. Decentralization was virtually inevitable in Canada, regardless of what any court might decide on the basis of the constitution. The decentralizing preferences of the courts helped, but the direction of the country's development would almost certainly have been the same in any event.

Institutions created to serve federal systems are not neutral on the question of diversity. The Canadian experience has shown that federal institutions intended to cope with diversity can often reinforce differences between subnational communities. In some provinces the differences in geography, language, or culture are small, but because of the choices made early in their history, and because of the trajectories taken by particular governments, some differences in attitude and perspective came to be so entrenched that they are now cherished. Perhaps the best examples are the divergent directions taken by Alberta and Saskatchewan after they were carved out of the North-West Territories in 1905. Alberta became home to some of the most ideologically conservative governments in Canadian history, while Saskatchewan elected the first socialist government in North America and served as the incubator for many of the earliest efforts to develop a welfare state in Canada, including universal medical care. It is true that the two provinces have had rather different settlement patterns, and that the oil industry has historically been much more important to Alberta's economy than Saskatchewan's. Yet a large part of the difference between them can be attributed to the institutional and policy choices made by governments early in the provinces' history. They owe their existence as separate provinces to nothing more than a decision to draw some arbitrary lines on the map of the former North-West Territories. The ability of provincial executive branches to realize their policy goals—sometimes even when diffuse majorities oppose them—contributes to the strength of the provincial state vis-à-vis the provincial society. What the state wants and what society wants are not always the same thing. The parliamentary system gives the state the upper hand in the articulation of preferences. In a federal system this means that federal diversity reflects diversity in government positions as much as it does organic diversity among provincial societies. So even societal explanations of federalism have to account for the fact that the mere existence of federal institutions and subunit governments is likely to result in some degree of manufactured—as opposed to organic—diversity.

As will be evident throughout the book, we are inclined to give considerable explanatory power to institutions, however changeable they may be. Intergovernmental affairs work the way they do because actors in the system are endowed with certain powers by the institutional structure of parliamentary government in the federal and provincial orders and are constrained by the rules in the constitution and the practices and habits of previous governments.

THE INSTITUTIONS OF FEDERALISM

What are the primary institutions that a student of federalism, particularly Canadian federalism, looks at? The conduct of intergovernmental relations—the way strategies are developed and implemented, and negotiations managed—is structured by several factors. Among the most important of those factors is the institutional framework defining the federation. We have already noted some aspects of this framework, such as the distribution of powers and the nature of regional representation in central institutions such as a second legislative chamber or the federal executive. It is worth elaborating on why this framework is important and the variety of forms it may take.

First, virtually every federation has some kind of written constitution. One of the most important functions of that document is to spell out the distribution of powers. The mere existence of a written constitution speaks to the contractual nature of federalism. Maintaining autonomy seems to require fallback rules that cannot easily be changed to suit current circumstances. Within a written division of powers there are various ways of allocating responsibilities to the different orders of government. Canada is what has sometimes been called a jurisdictional federation. In such cases the constitution includes at least two lists, one defining the powers of the central government, the other the powers of the regional government. Thus in Canada education, local government, the operation of hospitals, and the licensing of physicians are all assigned to provincial jurisdiction, while currency, banking, and national defence are assigned to federal jurisdiction. Other federations enumerate the powers of only one order of government, assuming that the remainder of the legislative sovereignty will reside with the other order.

Some federations have an additional list of 'concurrent powers': areas in which both orders of government have jurisdiction. In Canada agriculture is an example—although in this case the federal government was granted paramountcy (meaning that its laws will prevail in any conflict between federal and provincial laws in this field). Finally, there is a category of power known as 'residual' that covers all matters not already assigned to either federal or provincial/state jurisdiction—in most cases because the founders could not foresee future developments such as advances in technology or (in Canada's case) the nation's assumption of full control over its foreign relations. The residual power can be allocated to one order or the other. In Australia and the US it was assigned to the state governments. In Canada, however, section 91 of the Constitution Act of 1867 assigned this undefined residual power to the federal government. Ironically, though the intention of founders such as John A. Macdonald was to ensure a strong central government (Waite, 1963), Canada became one of the world's more decentralized federations, while the US and especially Australia have evolved in the opposite direction, towards a more centralized model.

Allocating powers on the basis of policy fields, such as education or banking, is not the only way of designing a federal constitution. Another way is to allocate separate powers for the *design* and the *administration* of policy and programs. This model may be described as horizontal or administrative federalism. In the German federation, for example, law-making in most policy fields is the responsibility of the national government; the responsibility for administering policy, however, rests largely with the Länder (state) governments. That tends to mean that within the various substantive policy areas there is a division of labour rather than a division by subject area: the central government designs the general policy framework and the laws necessary to implement it, while the states implement and administer the laws written at the national level. It is worth stressing that in Germany the state governments are represented directly in the federal second chamber (the Bundesrat). In this body, state governments are in a position to shape the relevant legislation that will be administered by these state governments.

In Canada there is only one area where horizontal federalism prevails: in the field of justice. Ottawa is responsible for the legal framework governing the justice system, largely encompassed in the federal criminal code. The provinces in turn have the primary responsibility for the administration of justice, such as policing and the management of the court system. Here it is worth noting that the provinces—unlike the German Länder—do not have any direct input in the formulation of laws in this policy area. They can put pressure on Ottawa to revise a law (e.g., to amend the Young Offenders Act to make it more punitive for particular crimes), but—unlike their German counterparts—they have no opportunity to block or veto such legislation. In the US, senators (two per state) are elected directly by the people rather than appointed by state governments. Nevertheless, they frequently act on behalf of their states' values and interests in the Senate, effectively giving state governments and state-based interests the opportunity to shape national legislation (this sort of activity is facilitated by the fact that party discipline in the US Congress as a whole is much weaker than in Canada). In Germany and the US alike, the representation of regional interests in central institutions—also known as *intra*state federalism, *intra* being Latin for 'within'—reflects the confederal elements that we referred to earlier. Canada, by contrast, is largely lacking in formal opportunities for this kind of representation.

Despite the bi-cameral structure of the federal parliament, regional interests are much more likely to be conveyed to the centre by provincial governments, which make their representations directly to the federal government. Most intergovernmental interaction in Canada, therefore, takes place between governments rather than within central institutions (as is the case in Germany especially). For this reason Canada is more accurately described as an *inter*state federation—*inter* meaning 'between' (Smiley and Watts, 1985).

With respect to the distribution of powers, there is one additional set of powers that is critical: this is the power to tax, raise revenue, and/or regulate and own revenue sources. Wheare, concerned as he was with the autonomy of governments in a federal system, pointed out that without adequate fiscal resources to meet its constitutional responsibilities, the legislative autonomy claimed by any one government is effectively meaningless. Furthermore, if a government is responsible for delivering policies but depends for the funding on another order of government that attaches conditions to those funds, then the implementing government can hardly be said to be fully in control of that field. In Australia the centralization of financial arrangements is one of the primary sources of the central government's relative strength when compared to Canada (Brown, 2002a). Revenues and responsibilities are regularly out of sync in federations, and Canada is certainly no exception. Because of this mismatch between revenue and responsibilities, much if not most of the intergovernmental activity that takes place in Canada concerns the financing of programs delivered by provincial governments—including those crucial to the well-being of most Canadians, such as health care, education, and social assistance.

There are some additional institutional features worth highlighting. If federations were to conform to Wheare's dictum, they would need to be ever vigilant about the boundaries between their constitutionally assigned responsibilities. Yet even when the component governments are inclined to be more relaxed about their interconnectedness and interdependence, there will still be occasions when their interests collide and they demand clarity from the constitution. For instance, even the kinds of programs and services that citizens in a democracy come to expect and demand can be a poor fit for a decades-old division of powers. To use a Canadian example, do labour market training programs fall under the heading of education (a provincial responsibility) or economic management (an area where the federal government can claim to have a role)? Many such disputes can be resolved through negotiation. But not all of them can. In the latter case it is not uncommon for the result to be a stalemate; alternatively, the courts may be asked to adjudicate. In short, every federation needs a constitutional court to adjudicate or arbitrate disputes over jurisdiction and interpretation of the federal compact.

The role played by this court—known in Canada and the US as the Supreme Court and in Australia as the High Court—is critical in two respects: in helping to maintain a balance of power between the national and regional governments, and thus in the federation as a whole; and in serving as an arena in which disputes between governments can be resolved. The courts are not the only, or necessarily the most desirable, arena for settling disagreements, but they are in keeping with the spirit of federalism as a system that insists on preserving some baseline of autonomy for its component governments, even when they acknowledge that much of what they do requires cooperation or collaboration with one another.

The courts are not always neutral bystanders. One advantage of approaching federalism from the institutional angle is that it allows us to isolate some of the effects that individual institutions might have on the way a federation evolves. Certainly a constitutional court can alter the balance between the two orders of government by subtly, or not so subtly, reinterpreting jurisdictional powers. Another way in which the balance of powers can be redefined is through a constitutionally entrenched amending procedure—something that most, though not all, federations have (Canada did not acquire its formal amending procedure until 1982). The use of such mechanisms is relatively rare, in part because the threshold for successful change is so high. However, *de facto* changes have taken place as a result of judicial decisions. Most change occurs at the level of informal rules, norms, and understandings agreed to by the two orders of government and shaped to a considerable degree by public opinion, usually as a consequence of negotiations and interactions between elected and unelected officials—in other words, as a product of intergovernmental relations. These kinds of informal rules and norms often have a kind of opaque quality, which may be conducive to resolving problems in the short to medium run but may prove deleterious down the road, especially if the actual practice of federalism falls seriously out of sync with the formal rules of the federation.

Finally, there are some features of Canada's parliamentary democracy that are not part of the federal arrangement as such, but nonetheless have a powerful impact on the nature of federalism and the conduct of intergovernmental relations. As we noted in our discussion of intra- versus interstate federalism, the weakness of party discipline in the US makes it relatively easy for state interests and state governments (as well as other interests, of course) to influence legislative decision-making. This feature reflects the checks and balances built into the US system as a function of the separation of powers doctrine. The consequence is that at both the national and the state level, power tends to be dispersed. The US president does not sit in the legislature and is rarely in a position to push through a legislative agenda without challenge, even when both houses of Congress are under the control of the president's party. In Canada the concentration of authority in the government, whether federal or provincial, is much greater, reflecting the historical role of the Crown (Smith, 1995).

Indeed, some analysts would argue that this concentration of power has become even more pronounced since the 1990s (Savoie, 1999; Simpson, 2001). This state of affairs can be attributed in good part to the parliamentary democracy model, originally borrowed from the UK, and the way it has evolved in Canada. This model allows—indeed, encourages—executive dominance of the legislature, whether federal or provincial. By convention, the prime minister (or premier) and cabinet ministers are all also members of the federal Parliament (or provincial legislature). Fully supported by a competent and professional civil service, the first minister and cabinet set the legislative agenda and, by enforcing party discipline within the legislature (whether House of Commons and Senate, or provincial legislative assembly) can usually ensure the successful passage of this agenda. The executive, in turn, is dominated by a single individual: the prime minister or premier. The fact that party leaders in Canada are typically selected by the general membership of their parties, either in a direct vote or a convention, means that first ministers often have considerable leverage over their parliamentary members and cabinet ministers. With powerful central agencies, and government departments organized on a hierarchical basis, the prime minister has available a wide variety of mechanisms to ensure that power remains concentrated within a relatively small circle of key advisers, ministers, and senior civil servants (Savoie, 1999). The same is true at the provincial level. Though a minority government may temper the pattern somewhat, Stephen Harper's lack of a majority in the House of Commons has done little to weaken the centralization of power in the prime ministership. The ability of powerful governments—federal and provincial alike—to concentrate their resources behind their first minister can result in dramatic and often personalized confrontations between governments.

EXECUTIVE FEDERALISM

Among the institutions of Canadian federalism, none has more influence on policy outcomes and the shape of intergovernmental relations than the fact of executive federalism. Executive dominance means that most of the interaction in Canada's federal system takes place between executives, whether at the political or the permanent bureaucratic level.[3] As Ronald Watts suggests, executive federalism captures 'the predominant role of governmental executives (ministers and their officials) in intergovernmental relations in parliamentary federations where responsible first ministers and cabinet ministers tend to predominate within both levels of government' (Watts, 1999a: 58) The fact that executive federalism is the norm reinforces the government-to-government nature of relations between the federal and provincial orders and makes it difficult to form regionally based legislative coalitions that cut across governmental jurisdictions.

Executive federalism works in two reasonably distinct ways. On an everyday basis, the bulk of intergovernmental interaction is carried out by 'officials' on each side: permanent public servants. For example, federal finance officials work with their provincial counterparts to implement federal transfers to the provinces; federal and provincial forestry bureaucrats cooperate on harvesting and stumpage policies that will have ramifications for international trade; and educational administrators work to ensure that academic standards and university admissions policies are comparable across provinces. Without all these interactions at the functional level, governments could unwittingly compete, either undermining or duplicating one another's efforts. The complexity of policy delivery means that neither order of government can achieve its goals without cooperating to take advantage of the experience and opportunities offered by the other.

A more familiar form of executive federalism, perhaps, is the one that operates at the 'summit' level. Cabinet ministers, as the political heads of their departments, can work together to establish policies and approaches that will be implemented by their officials. This is also a more contentious form of executive federalism, however, as it serves as a forum for the expression of political differences. Since the people involved are more prominent, it also attracts more attention both from the media and from citizens who expect solutions to persistent intergovernmental coordination problems. At the peak of the hierarchy are interactions between first ministers. The federal prime minister and provincial premiers potentially have the power to set directions without the consent or even the knowledge of departments and ministers, and their interactions have the highest public profile. At this level, the personalities of the politicians involved become critical variables in negotiations. If a prime minister and a premier take a strong dislike to each other, this can affect a whole range of issues between the two governments.

From the viewpoint of effective intergovernmental governance, this system has advantages and disadvantages. In later chapters we will discuss different ideas about what 'effective' means in the context of debates over democracy and legitimacy. What we can say here is that the limited number of actors involved in executive federalism sometimes makes it easier to reach agreement. On the other hand, personality issues can become amplified and the system generally can encourage a competitive approach. In particular, there may be a tendency to link several discrete issues in a single package for debate and negotiation, making agreement more difficult to reach than is usually the case with the smaller, more manageable issues handled at lower levels. This is not to say that under executive federalism intergovernmental agreement is always difficult to achieve or that conflict is inevitable. In fact, Canada's stability—despite awesome challenges of geography, language, and regional economic disparities—suggests that the federal system might be doing something right. The elite accommodation that executive federalism allows is essentially good for stability; but it may not be good for the transparency of decision-making or accountability to the electorate (concerns that we will discuss in later chapters). It might also be said that a certain amount of competition between governments can be healthy. Indeed, some theorists of federalism have cited competition between governments as one of the normative advantages of federation over unitary government (Breton, 1985). Much as a separation of powers within any given order of government results in a more responsive (if not efficient) system, competition between federal subunits can also make them more responsive to popular demands. But competition also has the potential to be detrimental to the public interest, especially if provinces get into what has been described as a 'race to the bottom'. If competition for jobs and investment leads provinces to lower taxes and regulatory hurdles, or to decrease the generosity of their social welfare standards to avoid becoming 'welfare magnets', the result may be an overall deterioration in public goods and services. Although the extent of this problem in Canada is unclear, governments certainly point to competition as a reason for the unpopular choices they sometimes make (Harrison, 2006a).

This inherent tendency within the Canadian system towards competition between governments, fuelled in part by the adversarial norms typical of Westminster systems, is at odds with some of the important principles of federalism. Essentially, modern-day federalism prefers consensus-based decision-making, since in a well-balanced federation neither order of government would be in a position to dominate the other and each would require some minimum of cooperation or tolerance from the other in order to deliver its programs effectively. This accommodative capacity of executive federalism is the practice of elites from opposing factions or communities in society reaching compromises in the face of dissent at the societal level.[4] In Canada these opposing communities are often, though not always, represented by provincial political elites, especially the heads of provincial governments. The role of Canadian political elites has been seen as crucial, both in the striking of the original Confederation package and in maintaining the stability of the federation over time (McRae, 1974). To preserve the overall stability of the system, leaders will often strike agreements on the quiet that are contrary to the wishes of their own followers.

Three prime examples of elite accommodation on contentious issues are the agreements reached regarding Medicare and the Canada Pension Plan (CPP) in the 1960s and the Meech Lake constitutional accord in 1987. The two latter cases both represented efforts to create a unique space for Quebec within the federation, the CPP by allowing the creation of a separate Quebec Pension Plan and Meech Lake by giving constitutional recognition to Quebec's status as a distinct society within Canada.

But Meech Lake also illustrated the limitations of elite accommodation and executive federalism. The agreement reached by the federal prime minister and the ten provincial premiers ultimately collapsed when two provincial legislatures failed to ratify the amendments within the required time frame largely because of negative public sentiment outside Quebec and pressure from constituencies such as women and aboriginal people. While many opposed Meech for substantive reasons—such as concern that it would compromise the operation of the Charter of Rights and Freedoms—most also disapproved of the exclusive and secretive process by which the accord was negotiated. Since that time in particular, executive federalism has come under challenge, especially from those who believe that the intergovernmental process should be not only more transparent but open to a broader range of actors, including non-government actors such as public advocacy groups. The ongoing desire to increase the power of federal and provincial legislatures vis-à-vis the cabinet, and the prospect of subjecting inter-governmental agreements to legislative review, are also likely to serve as constraints on executive federalism in the future.

These developments are generally seen as consistent with good democratic practice. But they may also undermine the more traditional forms of elite accommodation and the benefits they offer with respect to national unity. Elite accommodation depends in part on secrecy and lack of transparency, while executive federalism also benefits from a general lack of procedural and decision-making rules that allow for compromise and a shrugging acceptance of difference that has helped Quebec attain a certain *de facto* recognition of its special status. The 2004 Health Care Accord, signed by the federal and provincial governments, included a codicil explicitly endorsing the idea of asymmetry in federal–provincial relations; this effectively allowed Quebec or other provinces to opt out of the general terms agreed to by the other provinces and make its own arrangements with the federal government. (We will return to this subject at several points in later chapters.) Regardless of whether intergovernmental relations are elite accommodation or broader agreements, a workable federalism requires the generation of trust ties, mutual respect and understanding, and a willingness to accept that decisions should be based on mutual consent (Dupré, 1988). The exception to this rule is the court system, which, like parliament, is based on adversarial norms and legal certainties. This arena, as we shall see, produces results that are not always predictable and are often quite unsatisfactory for all parties concerned. Whereas the norm in intergovernmental negotiation is compromise, court proceedings are often zero-sum games, producing winner-take-all results.

COMPETING CANADIAN CONCEPTIONS OF FEDERALISM

Related to the notion of accommodation we have just discussed, but perhaps more revealing of the ideological character of federalism, are the different conceptions of federalism held by Canadians. More specifically, there are different accounts of the compromise that created Confederation and the kind of accommodation that Canadian federalism is meant to represent. In this case, the differences centre on what federalism was meant to protect and promote, and what the Canadian federation should be in the long term.

According to one vision, Canadian federalism represents a compact between two nations. In the 1860s the majority of political forces in British North America supported unification of the colonies for military, economic, and political reasons. Many of the Fathers of Confederation would have preferred a more unitary form of government for the proposed union, but the differences in culture, governance traditions, and legal systems between Lower and Upper Canada (the future Quebec and Ontario) were so pronounced as to require a federal form. In this compact, Quebec became the centre of French Canada (though it retained an influential anglophone minority), while the other partners in the compact together constituted English Canada. The 'two nations' interpretation of the Canadian compromise persisted as a kind of national myth through much of the twentieth century as Canada gradually gave fuller expression to its bilingual and bicultural character, going so far as to designate both French and English as official languages. For advocates of the 'two nations' theory, federalism in Canada must operate accordingly. The division of powers must be sensitive to issues around language, culture, and education, allowing the provinces, particularly Quebec, the flexibility necessary to protect and preserve local distinctiveness.

Perhaps more important, the two-nations vision assumes that Quebec is not a province like the others. Thus, according to its proponents, major national policies or constitutional changes require the agreement of both parties to the two-nations compact. It was on these grounds that Quebec refused to sign the 1982 constitution that established Canada's own amending formula and introduced the Charter of Rights. Major constitutional change without the consent of one of the partners to the federal compact was unthinkable to Quebec elites. A two-nations theory of federalism is thus more likely than other models to support a classical interpretation of federalism.

The two-nations compact was meant to serve a functional purpose, with the constitution essentially serving as a contract between the dominant majority and the national minority provincially concentrated in Quebec. A territorially concentrated minority seeking the protection of a federal state is less likely than the national majority to tolerate blurred jurisdictional lines and efforts by the national level to interfere in the fields assigned to provincial governments. However, the two-nations compact theory is undermined by the notion that Quebec does not necessarily represent all the French-speaking people in Canada. For many advocates of a bilingual and bicultural Canada, the existence of French communities outside Quebec and a significant anglophone minority (not to mention First Nations) inside Quebec weakens the Quebec claim to nationhood. Supporting such minority language communities has been a priority of Canada's federal government, particularly under Prime Minister Trudeau, who sought to delegitimize Quebec's claim to speak for all of French Canada. Finally, and significantly, the two-nations theory does not reflect the presence of other national communities within Canada, most notably the Aboriginal peoples. Some have therefore adopted a broader vision of federal diversity that embraces at least three national identities (Taylor, 1991; Kymlicka, 1998).

An alternative version of the compact theory is that Canadian federalism is a compact not of nations but of provinces. In this view, Quebec was not the only province with an identity too distinctive to allow for a unitary form of government: the differences among the English-speaking provinces also warranted a federal system. The provincial-compact theory conceives of the provinces as equal partners in the Confederation compromise. Different provinces may have joined Confederation under different circumstances and to some degree on different terms, but they are still seen as the primary building block of the federal society. Advocates of this interpretation of the compact theory, for whom the constitution was created by the constituent units, naturally call for unanimity on constitutional change. Another hallmark of the provincial-compact view is hostility to nationwide goals on the grounds that such goals ignore provincial differences and marginalize provincial cultures. For provincial-compact believers, the growth of the federal government and the substitution of national projects for provincial ones is the biggest threat to their conception of the federation. Opponents of the Charter of Rights and Freedoms argued that the pan-Canadian identity it promoted would ultimately make it difficult for provincial governments to express their distinctive identities through their policy choices. The provincial-compact theory is reinforced by the practice of executive federalism, which privileges the premiers above all other representatives of provincial societies.

The third vision of federalism in Canada rejects both 'compact' views in favour of the realist proposition that the original act of union was simply that: a piece of legislation enacted by the British Parliament. The BNA Act of 1867 clearly reflected the preferences of a strong coalition of pro-union forces in British North America, but it was not the product of an explicit treaty. The federal Parliament of Canada inherited Britain's job of maintaining unity, and now represents much more than the sum of the constituent parts. The dominance of the federal government was demonstrated in the 1982 patriation of the constitution without the consent of all the provinces and in the face of active opposition from Quebec. Of those who accept this vision, many acknowledge that the Confederation compromise was premised on the protection of local governance for a number of somewhat distinct political societies; but they believe that modern technology, communications, and transportation have made those communities less critical to good government and good outcomes and that the federal system should evolve accordingly.

COMPARATIVE FEDERALISM AND MULTILEVEL GOVERNANCE

We would be remiss if we were to end this chapter without noting another aspect of our approach to the topic of federalism both generally and in the remainder of this book. Increasingly, students of federalism tend to set their discussions of federalism, even within a single country, in a comparative context. We are likewise inclined. The discussion of Canadian intergovernmental relations in this book is informed by comparisons with the experience of other federations. For example, we know that the structure of parliamentary institutions at both the national and the provincial level results in a form of intergovernmentalism that is shared by other parliamentary federations. We also know that weaknesses in the present intergovernmental system might be addressed through institutional changes inspired by the practices of other federations. Examples are peppered throughout the chapters that follow. Not every feature of one federation will be suitable for another, but there are similarities in the problems that all federations are trying to address.

One by-product of this comparative research is an expansion of what now qualifies as federal. Few scholars today are as strict as K.C. Wheare was, a generation ago, about the kinds of arrangements that qualify as 'federal'. For example, Wheare refused even to recognize Canada as a federation on the grounds that Ottawa's control of the residual powers, along with the powers of reservation and disallowance (which theoretically allow it to overturn any provincial legislation) violated the federal principle. The fact that those powers had fallen into disuse (today they may be considered effectively dead) led Wheare to identify Canada as federal in practice if not in law—hence his term 'quasi-federal'. Today our notions of what makes a system 'federal' are much more relaxed. New federal-type systems such as those in Spain, Belgium, and South Africa are helping to redefine the terms of federalism and federation, both of which are becoming more elastic. Another major experiment in formalized power-sharing and pooled sovereignty is the evolving European Union. Having started out in 1951 as an international treaty among a few European countries with rudimentary common institutions, it has evolved into a powerful hybrid, somewhere between a confederal system and a federation. In the process the member states have achieved significant political and economic integration.

As a result of all these developments, notions of what qualifies as federal have become less strict, and our terminology has changed. The label 'federal' may still be reserved, much as it was by Wheare, for systems that faithfully preserve the autonomy of individual orders of government within a constitutionally allocated legislative sphere. But there are many systems in which collective and local governance is significant, even if those collective and local governments do not enjoy federal-style autonomy. These are generally referred to as multilevel systems of governance. The term is meant to capture significant developments in local government as well as the increased relevance of transnational decision-making bodies, whether formal and deeply integrated entities such as the European Union or more dispersed but still influential organizations such as trade and tariff agreements.

Multilevel governance may be defined as a situation in which power and authority are shared, sometimes in relationships established by constitutional law or treaty, sometimes in more informal working arrangements. In this shared governance, decision-making is effectively delegated, depending on the case, downwards to decentralized government agencies, upwards to supranational agencies, or outwards to private or other civil-society agents—or to all or to a combination of all the above! In all cases the scope and mechanisms of public policy extend beyond the central state. And in all cases policy outcomes are achieved that can no longer (or never could) be achieved by a single government on its own.[5] In the Canadian context, multilevel governance can be external in the sense that it includes either the continental region of North America or the global community into which the Canadian society and economy are becoming increasingly integrated. Or it can be domestic, including local governments, Aboriginal governments, and civil-society actors of various kinds. In areas such as public health (e.g., in the case of SARS) it can stretch from local to global. A second new development is encompassed by the word 'governance' itself, which implies that governing is being done, but not necessarily by governments alone, and is often not structured by constitutional and legalized power-sharing, but rather by less formal, more limited forms of power-sharing.

Thus multilevel governance is important for two reasons. First, insofar as multilevel systems resemble federations, they may have some worth for institutional comparison. The institutions that systems like the European Union have developed to make and legitimate policies, and the arrangements they have put in place to cope with complexity and overlap in jurisdictions and policies, might all be useful for our investigation of how Canada currently pursues similar goals. Likewise, the experience of resolving disputes among partners to trade agreements can tell us much about the potential or the limitations of pacts that do not provide for collective autonomy. Second, multilevel governance is relevant to the following chapters because Canada, like almost every other state, is party to supranational agreements that have characteristics of multilevel governance. How federal systems interact with supranational decision-making bodies is particularly interesting because allocations of authority within the federation may limit the national government's ability to pursue policies at the international level, while supranational agreements may restrict the autonomy of subunits even in areas of their exclusive constitutional jurisdiction. Moreover, Canada's diversity does not wholly respect provincial boundaries, and there are a number of challenges for local governance below the level of provinces that require some thinking about multilevel regimes. Aboriginal self-government presents another multilevel challenge for Canada, and the distinct needs and goals of the country's urban regions demonstrate that two autonomous orders of government may not be enough for the realization of self-government in this country.

WHY STUDY FEDERALISM?

Intellectual curiosity is ample reason for studying federalism. The lack of a single unified governance arrangement and the need for government units to negotiate and work together on the basis of consent make federalism both interesting and qualitatively different from other governmental and constitutional forms. How federal arrangements come into being, how they evolve, and why they persist are intriguing questions in their own right. At one point in the last century, when central government roles were expanding rapidly during the rise of the welfare state, some observers predicted that federalism would simply fade away (Laski, 1939). The reasons why it has in fact flourished, despite industrialization, globalization, and other developments, have sparked considerable discussion. At a minimum, most observers now agree that federalism has enormous staying power, even if they disagree on whether it makes for effective government and policy-making.

That staying power raises the practical question of whether federalism actually does make a difference. Would the type and nature of government services be qualitatively different in the absence of a federal system? Would particular policies have had different outcomes if only one government had been involved? Would the quality of health care in Canada, for example, be better, or worse, or at least different if the federal government had sole jurisdiction in this area? These questions are worth asking because they force us to think about the impact of intergovernmental relationships when we examine particular policy initiatives and the way federal structures and the intergovernmental process shape outcomes.

William Riker (1969) argued that federalism makes no difference whatsoever. Pairing federations with economically and culturally similar unitary systems— New Zealand and Australia, Britain and the US, for example—he noted that from an ordinary citizen's perspective it probably made little difference whether the system was federal or unitary, since the type and quality of services they would receive would likely be very similar. Furthermore, there was little difference between a federal and unitary system in terms of government spending in different policy areas.

Other writers, however, have seen things differently. Vincent Ostrom (1973), in a celebrated critique of Riker, notes that focusing strictly on levels of output is misleading. Federalism, according to Ostrom, allows particular communities to tailor their government services and their political lives much more closely to their specific needs. Citizens in one state or province, for example, may prefer to have fewer government services and pay lower taxes than those in other jurisdictions, or vice versa. Furthermore, federalism makes it possible to bring political accountability much closer to the people. A minister in Victoria, for example, who is accountable to the provincial legislature is much more meaningful to British Columbians in terms of access, transparency, and accountability than a minister based in Ottawa who is responsible for the same policy area but for the country as a whole.

Richard Vernon (1988) makes a similar point. Citing *The Federalist Papers* and James Madison's notion of the compound republic, he notes that different orders of government can act as checks on one another. He refers to Alexander Hamilton's notion that competition between two orders of government will make them more responsive to citizen preferences and demands. And he argues that the fixed boundaries and rules required by federalism help to protect minority rights and wishes against the excesses of majority rule. In the framework of a federal system, a group that exists as a minority in the nation as a whole can constitute a majority in the context of a state or province. If the regional government has jurisdiction over matters deemed crucial to the well-being of that national minority—education, for example—then federalism can make an important difference to that particular group.

Both Ostrom and Vernon stress that federalism also makes for a more complicated democracy, one that is probably less efficient and much more demanding of citizens than other types, though ultimately much more rewarding in terms of citizens' capacity to influence government decisions that affect them. In the absence of citizen engagement, or even basic citizen knowledge of how the system functions and affects government decision-making, federalism may not fully serve public interests. Particularly in Canada, the elite-centred nature of federalism and the secrecy surrounding intergovernmental processes suggest that federalism may not be fulfilling the promises claimed for it. Research suggests that citizens do have a hard time identifying who specifically is responsible for the policies that they live with (Cutler, 2004).

Therefore the question 'Does federalism make a difference and in what way?' is an important one with respect both to specific policy areas and to the longer-term issues that will face the Canadian nation-state in the future. In this chapter we have looked at the basic architecture of federal systems and some of the crucial concepts and questions that we will examine more closely in subsequent chapters. Now that we have set the stage, we can briefly review the antecedents of the Canadian federation and the main factors—social, economic, and political—that have shaped its evolution over 140 years.

Chapter 2

The Economic, Social, and Institutional Bases of Canadian Federalism

How federations come into being and how they evolve over time are important questions. Looking into them helps us understand how the legacies of previous political events, decisions, and institutions, as well as the socio-economic make-up of society, bear on the present and the dilemmas they pose for the future. In this chapter we identify the critical socio-economic, political, and institutional underpinnings of the Canadian federalism and the factors that have shaped its development. In the course of this examination three main themes emerge.

First is the asymmetry that underlies the Canadian federation. The largely French-speaking province of Quebec has over the years made strong claims for a special and, at times, separate status vis-à-vis the rest of Canada. Over time a number of political practices and accommodations have evolved in recognition of this *de facto* asymmetry, despite the absence of formal recognition in the written constitution and the fact that at times other provinces too have asked for special treatment, if not status, in recognition of their own unique characteristics. The second theme is the awkward fit between the formal jurisdictions assigned to the two main orders of government, federal and provincial, and the realities of present-day social and economic life. Even though a number of major policy fields, including health care and education, belong to the provinces, the federal government uses its constitutional 'spending power' (see Chapter 4) to play a role in those fields, partly because this is what citizens expect and partly for reasons of its own political and institutional self-interest. Finally, the third theme is the legacy of parliamentary institutions and executive federalism, which appears to limit both the opportunities for citizens to shape and participate directly in the making of public policy and, more generally, their capacity to exercise control over their political representatives.

ORIGINS

In the previous chapter we discussed the rationale behind the adoption of a federal rather than a confederal or unitary form of government. Although there may be compelling reasons for choosing one form over another, the actual choice is usually determined by a variety of factors. Furthermore, once a formal federal arrangement is in place, subsequent developments may take it in a variety of directions. Both Australia and the US were intended to be fairly decentralized federations. Instead, they evolved into relatively centralized ones, especially Australia. Canada, by contrast, was intended to be a highly centralized federation, with provinces representing little more than overgrown municipalities, at least in the eyes of John A. Macdonald. As we have seen, K.C. Wheare (1963: 19) labelled Canada's constitution 'quasi-federal' since Ottawa had been assigned not only the residual powers but also the powers of disallowance and reservation. Over time, however, both powers fell into disuse, while judicial interpretation restricted the meaning of the residual powers, so that Canada, contrary to the intentions of at least some of the Founding Fathers, evolved into quite a decentralized federation.

As we noted in the previous chapter, some writers on federalism attribute both the choice of a federal form of governance and its character as it develops over time primarily to social and geographical factors. William Livingston (1952, 1956), for example, argued that federalism was largely a product of the society existing at the time. Other analysts, however, place the primary emphasis on the institutional framework. Foremost among these is the political scientist Alan Cairns. According to Cairns (1977: 698–9), 'federalism, at least in the Canadian case, is a function not of societies but of the constitution, and more importantly of the governments that work the constitution.' William Riker (1964), on the other hand, is much more inclined to emphasize political factors. He maintains that the US, Canada, and Australia were above all the products of the recession of empire. When colonies left the British Empire, whether through revolt or with Britain's approval (even encouragement), they needed to provide for defence and access to larger markets—necessities that until then had been supplied by the mother country.

Which perspective does more for our understanding is a question to which there is no clear answer. The following review of some of the major points in Canada's development makes it clear that certain features of the 1867 constitution reflected the separate interests of the French- and English-speaking populations—first and foremost, of course, the creation of the separate provinces of Ontario and Quebec out of the United Province of Canada, in which Canada East and Canada West had lived together for more than 25 years. In some instances the Canadian constitution has perhaps taken us into unanticipated directions. Jurisdiction over natural resources has empowered a number of provinces and altered the dynamics of Canadian federalism in ways not anticipated by the Fathers of Confederation. Most developments seem to reflect some interaction between constitutional, political, and social factors. In part, the Canadian federation can be seen as the product of three empires—French, British, and American—each of which left a distinct legacy. The French legacy, obviously, is the francophone population and culture concentrated in Quebec but also present elsewhere. From Britain we inherited a set of political institutions that includes the Constitution Act of 1867 and the Westminster parliamentary model. Finally, the American influence can be seen in a variety of areas, but may be most evident in Canadians' expectation that as citizens they should be able to interact with government, despite the top-down form of representative democracy established by our constitutional make-up.

ECONOMY AND GEOGRAPHY

One way of seeing how Canada's geography and economy have interacted with various social and political factors is to look at a map of North America (see Figure 2.1) and note the way the northern part of the continent came to be colonized by France and Britain. For France, the St Lawrence was the main entry point into the North American interior, with trading routes eventually extending down the Ohio Valley, while British settlers concentrated on the Atlantic seaboard, using rivers such as the Hudson as their entry points into the interior.

As a result of these geographic factors, two competing trading routes developed. Conflict between the rival empires came to an end with France giving way to Britain after the latter had wrested away both its territory and its trading routes, first the Acadian peninsula and then, in 1760, New France itself. By 1783, however, Britain itself was forced to recognize the new republican nation composed of the former 13 American colonies. Thus Britain in turn was forced to give way, and ended up ceding most of the Ohio valley.

Once the remaining British American colonies, including Quebec, had refused to join the 13 American colonies in revolt, their distinctive character was bolstered by the arrival of the Loyalists and affirmed by the War of 1812. Subsequent treaties between Britain and the US confirmed the boundaries of 1783 and, beyond the Great Lakes, set the 49th parallel as the boundary all the way to the Oregon Country. In effect, these boundaries confirmed the presence of two separate economic and political systems.

What remained of the British North American west fell under the control of the Hudson's Bay Company. At the same time, in the St Lawrence River basin, trade in furs came to be replaced by trade in timber, grain, potash, and manufactured goods from the mother country. In the latter half of the nineteenth century the transcontinental railway lines constructed in the US were replicated

Figure 2.1   Map of North America

SOURCE: Map and Geospatial Information Collection, Dalhousie University.

in Canada by the Canadian Pacific Railway, again reinforcing the pattern of dual economic–trading systems. Created out of the purchase of the North-West Territories and Rupert's Land from the Hudson's Bay Company in 1870 and the ceding of the Arctic Islands by Britain to Canada in 1880, the Canadian north has been only sporadically involved in the development of the Canadian federation.[1] As Frances Abele (1987: 311) has pointed out, for several decades after this purchase 'the federal state was preoccupied with national consolidation south of the 60th parallel.' It was only with the discovery of valuable minerals, such as gold in the Yukon in the late 1890s, or when fears emerged that the US had designs on Canadian territory in the north, that authorities in Ottawa felt the need to create an administrative apparatus, beginning with the territorial government of the Yukon, or to strike treaties with the indigenous population. Otherwise Canada had little incentive to integrate the north into the federation either economically or politically until the Second World War. Then the strategic importance of the north, both militarily and with respect to valuable mineral and energy deposits, became apparent. Later in the post-war period the need to recognize and accommodate the aspirations of Canada's Inuit people became evident, a need that was partially met by the creation of the Territory of Nunavut in 1999 by dividing the former Northwest Territories. Eighty-five per cent of Nunavut's population is Inuit, ensuring that the indigenous people play the primary role in shaping the publicly elected government.

All three territorial governments are publicly elected and exercise powers comparable to those held by the provinces, except that—because of their limited fiscal capacities and the heavy administrative costs associated with small populations spread over vast territories—they are much more heavily dependent on Ottawa for financial support. In part because their political development took place much later and followed a different trajectory, the style of governance in the three territories is somewhat different from the one practised in the rest of the country. Political parties play a much less important role and government legislation is much more likely to be developed and adopted on the basis of consensus (Cameron and White, 1995). Since the 1990s, as a result of the Charlottetown Accord process, the three territorial governments have participated in the various conferences of first ministers, premiers, and ministers. As we will see in Chapter 6, the consensus-based approach of territorial governments, together with their policy preferences on issues like climate change, has to some degree altered the character of these conferences.

Particularly since the advent of the Free Trade Agreement (FTA) in 1989 and the North American Free Trade Agreement (NAFTA) in 1994, the focus has been on north–south trade flows and linkages. Yet it is worth recalling that—except during a brief period of reciprocity between the US and British North America from 1854 to 1866—the predominant trading pattern in Canada has been east–west. The National Policy introduced by Sir John A. Macdonald in 1879 had as its aim the opening up of the west through trade and immigration, the construction of the CPR, and tariff protection for local manufacturing. Thus east–west economic linkages were actively fostered well into the second half of the twentieth century. These east–west ties are still important for many Canadians, and their governments. Even though, economically, Canada and its regions have become increasingly integrated into the North American economy as a whole—more than 80 per cent of our international trade is now with the US—we are still linked from east to west by our Canada-wide social safety net, the continuing importance of interprovincial trade, and, to a lesser extent, unique Canadian cultural institutions such as the CBC. Indeed, Courchene and Telmer (1998) have described our social programs as playing much the same role as the nineteenth-century CPR in linking the country together. Still, while our geography provides us with a common land mass, it also serves to attenuate linkages, if only because there is so much of it. As

Mackenzie King is reported to have said just before the Second World War, when the storm clouds were gathering over Europe, 'If some countries have too much history, then Canada has too much geography.'

Now let us return to our map, and note the vast expanse of thinly populated territory that separates the main population centres of southern Ontario and Manitoba north of lakes Huron and Superior. As anyone who has driven that stretch of the Trans-Canada Highway can testify, the endless kilometres of muskeg and granite are interrupted only by the occasional moose, bear, or mining town. In many ways, this terrain represents not only a physical but also a psychological and cultural barrier. By contrast, directly to the south of the lakes lies the heavily populated agricultural belt of the US mid-west.

The barrier that is the Canadian Shield also played a role in the settlement of the Canadian west. In the US, settlers gradually fanned out from the eastern seaboard through the midwest and beyond, but in Canada the settlers who populated the west either moved north from the US or travelled directly there after arriving as immigrants, first from the UK and later from eastern Europe. There was little to tie these people to the traditional political culture of eastern and central Canada. It is not surprising, therefore, that the old two-party system never really took hold in western Canada, a region that has tended to spawn sizeable protest parties. The party system in the US has served to create a more unified and centralized federation, linking state parties with the national parties. In Canada, however, the party system has played a much more limited role in this respect. Indeed, at the provincial level Alberta spawned the United Farmers of Alberta in the 1920s and the Social Credit party in the 1930s, both of which made opposition to Ottawa and its basically central Canadian policies a mainstay of their election platforms and governing philosophy.

The Rocky Mountains have also been said to serve as a barrier, rendering British Columbia much more distinctive, as a society and a polity, than it might otherwise be. Still others have referred to the Ottawa Valley as a major demarcation line.[2] The five provinces to the east tend to lag behind the rest of the country economically; all five have depended on the federal government for equalization to compensate for the below-average fiscal capacities of their governments. In addition, especially in the Atlantic region, political practices have followed a more traditional format, with more reliance on patronage and government grants as means of developing electoral support, and the traditional two-party system is still largely intact— whereas in the west that system never really took root at all.

Provincial boundaries can reinforce geographic factors: the accidents of history have left the three Maritime provinces small in terms of territory, with no room for expansion. Quebec, Ontario, and Manitoba, however, started out small and grew large with additions from territory owned by the federal government, whereas Saskatchewan and Alberta were carved out directly from federal territory. Whether arbitrary or natural, provincial boundaries have a major effect in determining not only settlement patterns but provincial wealth, since each province owns and controls the natural resources within its borders.

Overall, Canada's economic make-up has been determined by its land mass, topography, and waterways. The country is heavily dependent on the production and export of basic commodities such as pulp, paper, lumber, energy, and various metals. In every province, even highly industrialized Ontario, these sectors represent a significant proportion of the total economic activity, and in British Columbia and Alberta they are the dominant sectors by far. The same is true of the three territories (Yukon, NWT, and Nunavut). Much of the trade in these commodities involves exports to other countries, above all the United States. In 2007 more than 76 per cent of Canada's exports went to the US, a proportion that was only 55 per cent two decades earlier.

Matters involving trade, both interprovincial and Canada–US, and economic development provide lots of fodder for intergovernmental debate (Hale, 2004). How should Canada handle trade disputes with the US? (Recent examples include softwood lumber and BSE, or 'mad cow' disease.) What can be done to reduce the remaining barriers to interprovincial trade? What role should the provinces play in the crafting of international trade agreements? These are some of the issues currently on the intergovernmental agenda.

Together, Canada's geography and economic life mean that transportation is another central theme. In fact, transportation in the form of railways was one of the driving forces behind Confederation, for under the Constitution Act of 1867 the federal government was to assume the public debt of each province when it joined the federal union. Both New Brunswick and Nova Scotia had gone heavily into debt subsidizing the construction of railways intended to link them with markets in central Canada and the US. Prince Edward Island, however, was virtually debt-free in 1867, and at first it declined the offer; but in 1871 it embarked on its own railway project, and by 1873 it too was ready to join Confederation. Of course, it was largely on the strength of the promised transcontinental railway that British Columbia was enticed into joining Canada in 1871 (the CPR itself was not completed until 1885).

Transportation issues have frequently given rise to political discontent. Over the years, freight rates were a particular problem for manufacturers in the Maritimes and prairie farmers. The high rates charged to transport grain were among the most important factors in the electoral success of protest parties: the Progressives in Manitoba, the United Farmers and Social Credit in Alberta, and the Co-operative Commonwealth Federation (CCF) in Saskatchewan. In some cases the governments formed by these parties found themselves in confrontation with Ottawa (over the printing of money in the case of Alberta); in others they introduced innovations that Ottawa eventually adopted (medicare in the case of Saskatchewan).

More generally, the west's greater vulnerability to international markets, the economic cycle, and climatic conditions, combined with perceived inequities in Ottawa's policies vis-à-vis the region, has traditionally led to tensions between the western provinces and the federal government. Although the arrival of free trade, beginning in 1989, effectively removed issues such as protective tariffs from the agenda and promoted north–south economic linkages, legacies from the past still make the western provinces sensitive to matters involving energy, transportation, and trade. When the US, for example, introduces substantial subsidies for agricultural producers, Ottawa is expected to provide remedies.

The opening up of the west through immigration, the provision of infrastructure by both federal and provincial governments, and the fostering of a domestic economy through tariffs and other measures, meant that the creation of a transcontinental economy 'was as much a political as an economic achievement' (Simeon and Robinson, 1990: 28). The federal government played a particularly active role in the early years—the era of the National Policy and the building of the transcontinental railway. It was Ottawa's liberal use of the declaratory and disallowance powers to take over provincial undertakings and overturn provincial legislation in this period that led Wheare to conclude that Canadian federalism was less than complete. After 1896, however, Ottawa took a more conciliatory approach in its relations with the provinces, helping to usher in what we might call the era of classical federalism, when governments really did try to maintain separate jurisdictions and the courts supported the 'watertight compartments' approach to judicial interpretation.

In part, this development was a consequence of the position taken by Wilfrid Laurier's Liberal government, elected in 1896, which promised explicit recognition of provincial rights after its Conservative predecessor attempted to use remedial legislation to deal with the Manitoba Schools Crisis.[3] It was also the result, in part, of decisions by the Judicial Committee of the Privy Council (JCPC) of the United Kingdom, Canada's final court of appeal until 1950, that reflected a narrow interpretation of the 'peace, order, and good government' clause in the 1867 Constitution Act (see Chapter 4) and a more generous one of provincial jurisdiction over property and civil rights. Crucially, however, these interpretations also reflected changing economic imperatives.

By the turn of the twentieth century, natural resource extraction, steel production, and other manufacturing meant that provincial governments were playing a more important role in providing infrastructure such as roads and hydroelectric power. As well, since natural resources were owned by the provinces, forestry and mining companies increasingly needed to interact with provincial governments, making the latter more influential actors in the economic development process. Meanwhile, the urban growth that came with industrialization was also increasing the importance of the provinces, since municipal government was another area under provincial jurisdiction. The balance of power between federal and provincial governments was definitely beginning to shift towards the latter.

The Great Depression severely strained the finances of all provincial governments, pushing Saskatchewan and Alberta to the verge of bankruptcy. But this did not necessarily spell increased power for the federal government. The Conservative government of R.B. Bennett was only a late convert to the type of intervention introduced by the Roosevelt administration in the US. And even when the Bennett government did propose some New Deal–style measures, a number of them were rejected by the JCPC as going beyond federal jurisdiction.

The Rowell–Sirois Royal Commission on Dominion–Provincial Relations, struck in 1938 to look at the financial implications of the Depression, did recommend some major changes to the distribution of powers, and a greater centralization of fiscal power in Ottawa, along with what we would now call equalization grants. However, that report was not released until 1940, and its recommendations were vigorously opposed by the three largest and richest provinces (Smiley, 1978).

It was not until the arrival of the Second World War that the exigencies of a wartime economy shifted the balance back towards Ottawa. Among other things, a 'tax rental' agreement was put in place under which the federal government effectively took over a number of important tax fields, such as income tax, and then remitted a portion back to the provinces. After the war, it once again became evident that additional east–west infrastructure linkages were required—such as a cross-Canada highway network and a pipeline system to transport oil and natural gas from the western provinces to central Canadian markets. Also, the social and economic devastation of the 1930s served as a major impetus to put in place a basic social safety net. This area was largely under provincial jurisdiction, but it was clear that Ottawa had both the will and the financial wherewithal to make it happen. Federal funding for post-secondary education was made available both to returning veterans and directly to universities. A Royal Commission on Arts and Letters (the Massey Commission) laid the groundwork for a more active federal role in the nation's educational and cultural activities: in addition to funding the government-owned CBC as a counterweight to American television programming, in 1957 Ottawa created the Canada Council for the Arts (Black, 1975).

Support in the form of federal–provincial shared-cost agreements provided financing for the Trans-Canada Highway system, social assistance, and a variety of hospital and medical programs that ultimately became part of the full-scale medicare system introduced as a federal–provincial shared-cost program in all provinces in 1968. This was the era of cooperative federalism, when officials at both federal and provincial levels worked closely together to develop programs, whether the Trans-Canada Highway or labour market training programs (Dupré et al., 1973). In effect, these officials constituted policy communities of like-minded individuals who played a critical role in both initiating and implementing joint federal–provincial programs. Although provinces like Ontario and Alberta did not agree with the continuation of the tax rental agreements in the post-war period, they were happy to participate in a variety of federal programs. Quebec, however, did not always welcome federal funding. Among other things, Quebec ordered its universities not to accept direct funding from Ottawa, and for some time it refused to accept money available under the federally imposed tax rental agreements, arguing that such funds represented a federal intrusion in provincial jurisdiction.

This period of cooperative federalism was facilitated by Supreme Court decisions that made it possible for one government to delegate authority to an agency of another order of government under particular circumstances and provided a more liberal interpretation of the 'peace, order, and good government' clause. Changing political and economic circumstances, along with the growing capacity of provincial governments to manage their political and economic affairs, made the post-war era of cooperative federalism relatively short-lived. During the 1960s Quebec, in particular, became more sophisticated in its demands for 'opting out' arrangements, based largely on what it considered its unique position in confederation. On the economic front, perhaps the most important development was the first oil shock, which came in 1973 when, as a result of actions initiated by OPEC on behalf of oil-producing states, the world market for energy was radically altered and energy prices rose dramatically. Since energy in the form of oil, natural gas, and hydroelectric power is under provincial jurisdiction, this altered the balance not just between Ottawa and the provinces but also between provinces themselves, making some—notably Alberta, with its vast oil and gas reserves, and Quebec, with its hydro power—substantially better off than others (Doern and Toner, 1985). It ushered in a period of what has been labelled competitive federalism, which extended throughout the 1980s into the 1990s.

Efforts by the federal government, with the support of Ontario, to impose made-in-Canada pricing for oil and natural gas made for battles that were at times extremely bitter. The natural resource amendment, section 92A of the 1982 Constitution Act, effectively saw the federal government concede primary control over natural resources to the provinces.

The imbalanced resource endowments of the provinces also strained the financial resources of the federal government, since Ottawa, through the Equalization Program introduced in 1957, was committed to raising the fiscal capacity of the have-not provinces to a level that would allow them to deliver basic public services comparable to those in the country as a whole. Despite efforts to control increases in provincial entitlements—by reducing the weight of energy revenues in the equalization formula; using a five-provinces standard that excluded Alberta, rather than a national average; and capping increases in social welfare transfers to the better-off provinces—Ottawa's deficit continued to grow.

Finally, in 1995 the federal government reduced its overall transfers to the provinces and at the same time, under the rubric of 'program review', began systematically withdrawing from a number of program areas in the name of reducing overlap and duplication. Although it was keen to maintain a strong presence in areas such as health care, it was willing to give the provinces more flexibility and authority in areas such as social assistance and the environment—in part because it recognized that it was now providing much less funding to the provinces than it had done in the past.

By the close of the 1990s Ottawa and the provinces did reach a rapprochement of sorts. Several provinces put forward the idea of committing themselves to the idea of a Canadian 'social union' in recognition of both the importance of the social safety net and the primary responsibility of the provinces in this regard. In

1999 Ottawa and all the provinces except Quebec signed the Social Union Framework Agreement (SUFA), committing them to put more funding into areas such as health care and closer collaboration on future initiatives in the social policy field. (SUFA is explored in greater detail in Chapter 10.) At the time many argued that Canada was entering a new area of 'collaborative federalism'. Subsequently, however, skepticism grew over the fact that Ottawa and the provinces made little progress in resolving their differences over how best to reform the health care system. Furthermore, although Quebec had refused to sign the agreement, it remained eligible for the benefits available to all the other provinces and territories. Quebec's unique position in confederation and the profound role it has played in shaping the behaviour of all provinces require closer discussion.

QUEBEC

Those who see institutional factors as more important than societal differences often point to Alberta and Saskatchewan as examples. Carved out of a single whole—the North-West Territories—in 1905, over time they have evolved into distinctly different political cultures. Alberta in 1935 elected a populist right-wing party—Social Credit—that was to continue in power for more than 35 years. Saskatchewan, by contrast, in 1944 became the first jurisdiction in North America to elect a social-democratic government; under the leadership of T.C. Douglas, the CCF introduced government-run automobile insurance and pioneered medicare. By drawing a few strokes on a map and endowing the two freshly minted entities with constitutional and political authority, the government of Canada spawned two highly distinct entities.

On the other hand, there is no denying that one of the most significant influences on both the creation and the functioning of the Canadian federation has been the French factor in North America. It was the persistence of two separate social and political communities during the period of the United Province of Canada (1841–67), despite the best efforts of Lord Durham to fuse them, that demanded a new federal arrangement in which Quebec (Canada East) would be recognized as a separate entity. And it was the particular needs of Quebec—to protect its civil code and to secure control of education, health care, and related matters—that directly shaped the distribution of powers in the 1867 Constitution Act.

In the last century, particularly since the transformation of Quebec society that took place in 1960s under the name of the Quiet Revolution, the Canadian federation has been profoundly affected by developments in Quebec. Many Quebecers, even among those who do not support the movement for sovereignty, consider their society to be more akin to a nation than a province like the others—'nation' here meaning a body of people closely connected by heritage and language, who form a relatively complete society without necessarily having (or even demanding) the status of a separate sovereign state.[4] It was in this sense that the word 'nation' was used in the 2006 House of Commons' resolution affirming that 'the Québécois form a nation within a united Canada'.[5]

As we saw in Chapter 1, the 'two nations' conception of the Canadian constitution has been a staple in political and juridical thinking in Quebec since Confederation (Black, 1975). But it is also worth noting that nationalist sentiment in Quebec has changed over the years. That sentiment had a firmly religious basis, with the Roman Catholic Church and Quebec elites feeling that Quebec had a very special mission, effectively since 1789 representing the last bastion of French Catholicism in the world. Furthermore, Britain, through the Quebec Act of 1774, among other pieces of legislation, was willing to afford the Church and associated institutions, such as schools and hospitals, a measure of protection in Quebec to a degree not available elsewhere and certainly not in Britain itself.

In addition, well into the twentieth century, many notable French-Canadian nationalists—Henri Bourassa is one who comes to mind—saw nothing contradictory in claiming to be at once a strong Quebec nationalist and a loyal Canadian (Cook, 1972). They believed that confederation was essentially a partnership between two peoples, French and English, and that Quebec, as the homeland of the French-speaking population, had a special responsibility for safeguarding that community's values. The French language was important, of course, but in a sense it was seen as secondary, a necessary protection for a set of values that centred on the Church. This perspective manifested itself in a kind of institutional self-segregation in areas such as schooling and health care; people were encouraged to enter professions such as law and medicine and to avoid occupations that would expose them to secular, materialist values.

On the other hand, the influence of the Church has in some respects been exaggerated. The Church itself was far from monolithic. In the 1890s, for instance, many parish priests openly supported Laurier and the Liberals, even though the Catholic hierarchy was still firmly committed to the Conservative party. And although it was true that the Church-dominated educational system neglected subjects such as commerce and engineering, it was also the case that English-speaking elites were predominant in most important sectors of Quebec's economy, especially at the higher levels, making it difficult for francophones to pursue careers in those areas without abandoning their language and culture.

What changed with the Quiet Revolution, beginning in 1960 with the election of the Jean Lesage government, was that Quebec nationalism became much more outward-looking. As well, certain strands of Quebec nationalism took a decidedly sovereignist or separatist turn. Among the most important factors contributing to the Quiet Revolution were the dramatic changes taking place in the Church itself under Pope John XXIII, including a new emphasis on ecumenicalism and movement towards more liberal attitudes on social and moral issues. A decline in recruitment into the priesthood had already been evident in the 1950s, and in the next decade increasing numbers of priests and nuns began leaving the Church, with the result that many Church-run institutions no longer had the human resources to keep operating. Thus Quebecers increasingly looked to the rapidly expanding state for services and career opportunities that until then had been provided almost exclusively by the Church. Meanwhile the classical colleges, most of which were run by religious orders, were gradually replaced by a modern secondary and post-secondary educational system.

The nationalization of privately owned power companies led to the creation of Hydro-Québec, which for the first time provided significant opportunities for young Quebec engineers to practise their profession in a largely francophone setting. Hydro-Québec was to become the largest single element in Quebec's economic development, culminating in the completion of the huge James Bay project in the 1970s.

Developments on the political front were equally dramatic. The election of the Lesage Liberals spelled the end of the Union Nationale era. Long-time Union Nationale premier Maurice Duplessis upheld the traditional concept of water-tight compartments in order to keep federal intrusions at a minimum. And in response to the federal government's Massey Commission, Duplessis struck his own Royal Commission to Inquire into Constitutional Problems, known as the Tremblay Commission after its chair (Kwavnick, 1973). Though ostensibly focused primarily on fiscal issues, the Tremblay Commission provided nothing less than a thorough restatement of the raison d'être for the Quebec state, emphasizing time-honoured Catholic values and the need for a highly defensive posture to protect them.

The Lesage government, by contrast, went on the offensive, demanding that Ottawa not only withdraw from Quebec jurisdictions but provide compensation for the funds that it would have spent in Quebec through joint programs in which Quebec had sometimes refused to participate. More generally, Lesage argued that the challenge facing Quebecers was not survival but self-assertion as a people. By now Quebec intellectuals were much less inclined to think of Confederation as a compact between either provinces or 'founding nations'. Rather, they were increasingly referring to the inherent right of nations to self-determination. In addition to expanding and modernizing its administrative capacity, and bringing under the public-sector umbrella matters that had formerly been the preserve of the Church, such as health care and education, the Quebec government was deliberately building up its capacity to manage federal–provincial relations. The case of the Canada Pension Plan and Quebec's alternative proposal, cited earlier, was one such example.

No less important than these developments inside Quebec were the responses from elsewhere in Canada. First, on a practical level, most of the other governments, federal and provincial, were surprised not only by the scale and type of the new Quebec's demands, but also by the sophistication with which Quebec was pursuing its external agenda. The capacity of the Quebec government to provide detailed analysis of various proposals, supported by a large team of experts in various fields, made a profound impression. Soon provinces such as Ontario, along with the federal government, were creating dedicated central agencies for the management of intergovernmental relations. In other words, simple emulation of Quebec's approach to intergovernmental relations altered the basic dynamics of federalism. No longer were political executives content to leave intergovernmental relations to unelected officials in line departments. Furthermore, even smaller provinces recognized the need for greater in-house expertise if they were going to negotiate effectively. On another level, Ottawa and many of the other provinces were initially prepared to be accommodating. Ontario in particular played the role of conciliator, stressing the importance of flexibility and understanding in response to Quebec's aspirations. The acceptance of the Quebec Pension Plan in the 1960s symbolized a tacit if not active recognition that Quebec was, in some important respects, different from other provinces. This tacit acceptance of asymmetrical federalism began to fade by the late 1960s. Nonetheless, Ottawa's initial responses to Quebec's demands during the period of the Quiet Revolution are worth noting (Smiley, 1987: 134–41):

- Opting-out arrangements: Quebec could opt out of cost-shared programs and, at the same time, receive funding or more tax room for comparable programs without being required either to provide matching funds or to meet other conditions.
- Constitutional review and reform: This began in earnest in 1967, continued throughout the 1970s, and culminated with the patriation of the constitution and the introduction of the Charter in 1982.
- Reform of the public service: Launched in 1963, the Royal Commission on Bilingualism and Biculturalism was tasked with examining how to ensure that federal public servants could communicate effectively within the federal government in either of Canada's two official languages, that citizens could do the same in their dealings with the federal government, and that the linguistic and cultural values of both language groups would be reflected in public-service recruitment and training.
- Enhancement of the francophone presence at the highest political level in Ottawa, specifically in cabinet, to better reflect the country's linguistic duality.

The opting-out arrangements were in theory available to all provinces, but—consistent with the tacit acceptance of asymmetrical federalism where Quebec was concerned—in practice it was understood that only Quebec would take advantage of those arrangements. Efforts to find a suitable formula for amending the constitution had been under way for a number of years, but they took on a greater urgency during the 1960s. Discussions of constitutional reform were extended to include the possibility of introducing a charter of rights and giving explicit recognition to Quebec's unique position in confederation.

Constitutional reform would be the major federal–provincial issue from the late 1960s to the early 1990s (Russell, 2004). Over that time it came to be a matter of considerable importance to all governments and a host of citizen groups, as well as Aboriginal peoples, but the initial impetus for it came out of direct concern for Quebec and its place in confederation.

The recommendations of the Bilingualism and Bicultural (B and B) Commission had wide-ranging effects, most specifically in the form of the Official Languages Act of 1969. This act expanded the conditions under which citizens could expect service in either of Canada's two official languages and set requirements for competence in both languages for senior public servants. Among other things, the Commission pointed out that francophones were underrepresented in the federal public service at all levels but particularly at the highest levels; that the instruments and approaches used in public-service recruitment favoured the use of the English language; and that at the political level francophones tended to be allocated portfolios such as Justice and Public Works rather than Finance or Industry. Even before the Commission reported in 1967, the Liberal government of Lester B. Pearson had begun taking steps to change the face of the federal government, especially vis-à-vis francophone citizens: initiatives ranged from renaming federal bodies (Trans-Canada Airlines became Air Canada) to recruiting notable Quebecers directly into the federal cabinet (among them Pierre Trudeau). Perhaps most significant, in 1965 Parliament adopted the maple leaf design as the national flag. The B and B Commission also legitimized the idea that Canada had two founding cultures, French and English, and that the differences between them extended beyond language. It was at this point, however, that the federal government stopped short. Whereas the Pearson government had been sympathetic to the notion of two cultures and supportive of special treatment for Quebec, the Trudeau government was neither.

Trudeau drew a sharp distinction between language and culture, accepting the importance of the former but rejecting the legitimacy of the latter, at least the notion that culture was linked directly to language. Trudeau's austere vision continues to shape the federal government's policy with respect both to Quebec and to Canadian federalism in general, although the Progressive Conservative government under Brian Mulroney (1984–93) and more recently the Conservative government under Stephen Harper have been more amenable to special status for Quebec. Essentially, Trudeau argued that all governments, federal and provincial, were responsible for promoting linguistic duality throughout the country, and rejected the notion that Quebec, home to the majority of francophones in Canada, should have special powers and status. Furthermore, according to Trudeau, 'the term biculturalism does not accurately depict our society; the word multiculturalism is more precise in this respect' (quoted in McRoberts, 2003).

Trudeau's emphasis on multiculturalism served to downplay Quebec's uniqueness, but it also recognized a very real change in the demographic composition of Canada as a whole. Since 1945 Canada's immigration policy had been gradually liberalized, with the result that the population outside Quebec was becoming increasingly heterogeneous (Quebec also experienced significant immigration into the Montreal area, but the majority of its new arrivals came from southern Europe). Arguing that bilingualism was the responsibility of all governments across the country, and that Quebec's unique culture was just one of several unique cultures in Canada, the federal government challenged the rationale behind the dualist vision. Thus Ottawa actively worked to promote bilingualism throughout the nation and equal treatment for all provinces, regardless of language. Inside Quebec, meanwhile, the emphasis shifted from French–English dualism to French primacy, with legislation restricting access to English education, requiring French-only commercial signs, and promoting the use of French as the language of work (McRoberts, 2003). Ottawa in its turn became equally hard-nosed about rejecting Quebec's claims to special status—especially when the Liberals were in power

The conflict between these competing visions set the stage for the election of the first Parti Québécois (PQ) government in 1976, constitutional patriation despite the Quebec government's opposition in 1982, and two provincial referenda, the most recent of which, in 1995, saw the prospect of sovereignty rejected by only the slimmest of margins. Efforts by the Conservative government of Brian Mulroney to bring Quebec into the constitutional fold ended in failure, with the collapse of the Meech Lake Accord in 1990 and the rejection of the Charlottetown Accord in a nation-wide referendum in 1992. Although support for sovereignty among Quebec voters[6] has fluctuated between 33 and 55 per cent over the past 15 years (Leger, 2008; CROP, 2008), there is evidence to suggest that hard-core sovereignists likely represent only about 21 per cent of the Quebec population (Aubin, 2005). In 2007 and 2008 support appears to have settled at around 38 per cent. At times when more than 50 per cent of Quebec voters have indicated a willingness to vote 'Yes', they have typically included a number of federalists who—unhappy with the constitutional status quo or in response to specific events—have done so in order to send a message to Ottawa and the rest of the country. Even if outright sovereignty would likely be unacceptable to the majority of Quebec voters, there are relatively few who find the status quo acceptable. Only among anglophones and some allophones in Quebec would there be any significant support for the current arrangement.

Gagnon and Iacovino (2007: 159) have drawn a distinction between de facto and de jure special status for Quebec, noting that at the de facto level Quebec has in fact made several important gains and obtained concessions, including many achieved during the Trudeau period.[7] The frustration lies in the fact that those gains have not received appropriate legal or symbolic recognition—within the constitution, for example. This strategy of working to make incremental gains, referred to as étapisme, continues. For example, Quebec refused to sign the Social Union Framework Agreement (SUFA) in 1999 and still considers the Constitution Act of 1982 to lack legitimacy. But it was able nevertheless to reach an understanding with Ottawa that would allow it to receive the additional funding for health care that Ottawa made available through SUFA.

What emerged was a pattern that Roger Gibbins (1999) has described as '9-1-1 federalism': Ottawa reaches agreement with the nine provinces and comes to a separate understanding with Quebec. Often this separate understanding takes the form of agreement to disagree. Nonetheless, the extent to which the two sides have been able to reach quiet, informal consensus on major issues is often quite surprising. For example, Quebec today appears willing to accept money from federal infrastructure programs and funding for research chairs at Quebec universities—arrangements that would likely have been unacceptable to the Duplessis government in the 1950s (Bakvis, 2008). As well, despite Quebec's refusal to sign SUFA, Ottawa and Quebec have shared remarkably similar perspectives on medicare and social policy—at least when the Liberals held power in Ottawa.

It is not with Quebec but with Alberta and Ontario that Ottawa has had profound disagreements on issues such as equalization and private provision of health care. Nevertheless, the gap between *de jure* and *de facto* asymmetrical federalism remains. And since the salience of that gap depends as much on emotion as anything else, events that might be seen outside Quebec as relatively benign could still be enough to trigger a surge of support for the sovereignty option among Quebecers. Thus the evidence of kickbacks to the federal Liberal party revealed at the Gomery inquiry into federal sponsorship programs in Quebec set off a wave of revulsion in Quebec that in the spring of 2005 temporarily pushed support for the sovereignty option to well over 50 per cent (Léger, 2008).

Overall, it was the Quebec agenda that drove the constitutional reform process throughout the 1970s and '80s. By the early 1990s, however, the failure of the Meech Lake and Charlottetown accords made it clear that constitutional reform was no longer primarily a Quebec issue. Especially in Ontario, BC, and Alberta, population growth, fuelled in good part by immigration, made issues associated with multiculturalism and the needs of large urban areas much more salient. These issues, which continue to grow in importance, have much less to do with territory than with groups and communities dispersed across the country, and they have made the local level of government much more relevant (Gibbins, 1999). Nonetheless, both Meech Lake and Charlottetown drove home the point that significant constitutional change is unlikely to occur unless due consideration is given to Canada's third founding people, whose presence was rarely even acknowledged until a little over two decades ago.

ABORIGINAL PEOPLES

We suggested above that in the case of Quebec there is *de facto* if not *de jure* recognition of asymmetry. For Canada's Aboriginal peoples the case might be described as the reverse. Both the 1867 and 1982 Constitution Acts give explicit recognition to the unique position of Aboriginal peoples in Canada, the former by stipulating federal jurisdiction over 'Indians and Lands reserved for the Indians', the latter by giving the courts the power to expand on the interpretation of various Aboriginal rights.

The federal Parliament has acquitted these obligations primarily through the Indian Act, which has undergone a number of incarnations since it was first passed in 1876. The Indian Act provides the basic and detailed framework for the provision of governmental services to Aboriginal people who meet its definition of Indian status. The Indian Act places responsibility for so-called status (or registered) Indians and their reserves in the hands of the federal cabinet, and in addition to providing for services to Aboriginal populations it establishes the forms and procedures for band management and governance, including the requirements and mechanisms for the election of band councils. Further, as stipulated in section 91(24) of the 1867 Act, the federal government has been responsible since Confederation for negotiating treaties with First Nations. Unquestionably, the federal government has taken the lead in legislative matters involving Canada's Aboriginal peoples.

Aboriginal and non-Aboriginal perspectives clash over the consequences of section 91(24) for the relationship between Aboriginal people and the Canadian state. From the Aboriginal perspective, that clause merely signified that the federal Crown would be responsible for the continuing management of the nation-to-nation relationship symbolized by treaties. In practice, however, the Indian Act appears to have been driven by more paternalistic concerns. In fact, it was a central element in the longstanding effort (now officially abandoned) to assimilate Aboriginal people into Canadian society. The band council, for example, which serves as the vehicle for whatever self-administration Aboriginal communities have had until now, was an institution imposed by the Indian Act with little regard for pre-existing forms of social organization or governance in these once autonomous communities.

In Quebec, the recognition that other political arrangements might be possible or desirable came in the 1960s with the Quiet Revolution. A similar recognition was sparked among Aboriginal peoples by the release in 1969 of the federal government's White Paper on Indian Policy, which was explicitly designed to assimilate Aboriginal populations. Guided by Trudeau's basic belief in the primacy of the individual over the community, the government proposed that special Indian status be eliminated altogether. This would mean dismantling the Indian Act together with its bureaucratic machinery. Although this would have put an end to the paternalism of the existing system, under which bands were administered and overseen by federal public servants, the idea of eliminating all special consideration for Aboriginal people seemed at odds with the obligations established under treaties.[8]

More than any previous event, the release of the government's proposals galvanized the Aboriginal community. Notwithstanding the paternalism of the band system and the often dire living conditions on reserves, Aboriginal peoples were not prepared to see their special status removed from the constitution. Nor were they prepared to see themselves assimilated into the general population. The White Paper was withdrawn and a long process, still ongoing, was put in motion to negotiate issues germane to the Native community—issues ranging from land claims to the status of Aboriginals as nations.

As Abele and Prince (2002) point out, relations between Canadian governments and Aboriginal peoples involve three levels of activity:

- At the highest level: first ministers' conferences on constitutional matters,
  Supreme Court decisions, and comprehensive land claims;
- At the middle level: financial transfer arrangements, self-government, and
  program transfers, among other things;
- On the ground: internal constitutions, local capacity-building, relations
  between Aboriginal and provincial/municipal governments on matters
  such as provision of services.

Relations, therefore, tend to be multiple, and at any one time an Aboriginal
band may be actively involved in negotiations with other bands, other types of
organizations, and various levels of government. The 1982 Constitution Act
provided explicit recognition of pre-existing treaty rights and also outlined a
process for resolving outstanding constitutional matters involving Aboriginal
people, including first and foremost the issue of self-government.

A significant proportion of the Aboriginal community envisions self-government as meaning that bands would interact with other governments on a nation-
to-nation basis, status, or at least would have a status approximating that of
provincial governments. But casting these desires in the form of concrete
proposals acceptable to all parties has proven to be extraordinarily difficult. And
while a certain amount of progress has been made at the middle and lower levels,
failure to reach a consensus on matters of high politics has limited what can be
achieved on more practical matters, not least because provincial governments are
extremely reluctant to make commitments in the absence of firm understandings
on the implications of land claims made in different provinces.

What compounds these difficulties is the fact that the Aboriginal population—
less than 4 per cent of Canada's population as a whole—is widely dispersed across
the country, with the highest concentrations in Manitoba and Saskatchewan.
More than half of Canada's Aboriginal people live off-reserve in urban areas, and
many of their problems and needs are quite different from those of people living
on reserves. The nature of the relations between Aboriginal people and provincial
governments also varies, depending on whether a treaty was ever negotiated or
signed with the Crown. Aboriginal people in most parts of BC, for example, never
signed treaties, which has made land claims a much more contentious and
complicated issue. An additional problem is the fact there is no single identifiable
leadership within the Aboriginal community. The Assembly of First Nations
(AFN), despite its claims, represents only a minority of Aboriginal peoples, and
then only indirectly, through their band chiefs. Thus the AFN has only limited
moral or legal authority to speak on behalf of the national Aboriginal community.

The high point for the Aboriginal community and the AFN as players in the intergovernmental process likely came in 1992, in the drafting of the Charlottetown
Accord. The leader of the AFN, Ovide Mercredi, took part on an equal footing with

the various first ministers as they hammered out an agreement they hoped would be accepted not only by Aboriginal people but also by Canadians as a whole. The document they produced was ultimately rejected by both the Aboriginal community and Canadians in general (though it did pass with slim majorities in Ontario and three of the Atlantic provinces, and among the Inuit). Thereafter the whole constitutional process was in effect put into the deep freeze by the Liberal government that came to power under Jean Chrétien in 1993. The recommendations of the Royal Commission on Aboriginal Peoples—appointed in 1991 by the Mulroney government—would have seen the relationship between Aboriginal people and the rest of Canada move to a nation-to-nation, government-to-government level; but they were effectively rejected by the Chrétien government. While the short-lived Liberal government under Paul Martin appeared open to broadening negotiations with Aboriginal people, the Conservative government under Stephen Harper has been much more cautious. Overall, the Harper government has taken a low-key approach, striking agreements with individual band councils on service devolution agreements under which the communities would take on more direct responsibility for managing their own affairs. Meanwhile, responsibility for Native affairs has been spread over several federal departments and is no longer concentrated in the Department of Indian and Northern Affairs. The Department of Fisheries and Oceans, for example, in response to Supreme Court decisions concerning Aboriginal fishing rights, has now negotiated a series of agreements with individual bands on licensing and financial arrangements intended to give those rights more meaningful expression. At the same time land claim negotiations are continuing.

Land claims represent only one of the areas in which provinces have a direct interest. Most provinces have created special agencies or departments with responsibility for Aboriginal matters. Similarly, municipalities through service agreements with band councils or by virtue of the fact that they have large populations of Native people residing within their boundaries deal directly with federal agencies as well as with native people themselves. As Abele and Prince (2002: 233) point out, 'Aboriginal communities and governments constitute a significant network of institutional arrangements' that, within the intergovernmental context, cannot simply be ignored, whether at the level of high politics or at the level of on-the-ground administration.

SUMMARY

Geography, the legacies of empire both French and British, the presence of Aboriginal peoples, the waves of immigration from the late nineteenth century onward, and the proximity of the United States—a country with eight times our population and ten times our GDP—have all left their imprint on the Canadian federation. To be sure, Canada's constitutional and institutional arrangements have helped to shape the way Canadian federalism has functioned over the years.

And those arrangements largely continue to define the setting, arenas, and actors that constitute the Canadian intergovernmental system today.

But a good part of the original Constitution Act also reflected the sociological reality of Canada in 1867. Provincial jurisdiction over education and social and health needs, for example, was a major concern of the largely Catholic, French-speaking population of Lower Canada. Linguistic duality has continued to be a major feature of the Canadian polity, and is directly reflected in the fact that Quebec has its own pension plan and blood collection agency, separate from the standard Canadian versions. Geographic distance and significant immigration from a variety of non-English-speaking countries starting in the late nineteenth century helped infuse the Canadian west with quite a different political character, which has also had a profound influence on its position in confederation. Post-war immigration changed Canada's make-up even further, altering the character of major urban centres and giving rise to a set of demands for services that do not fit comfortably into the traditional federal framework. At times, all these linguistic and regional divisions appear to be fault lines that, under the right circumstances, could well open up into unbridgeable chasms, though so far this has never quite come to pass.

Exploring the interaction between social forces and federal institutions reveals significant disparities between the vision of federalism set out in 1867 and the practice of federalism in Canada today. The original Constitution Act may have reflected the societal norms and values and socio-economic conditions that prevailed in 1867, but the passage of time has made many of its provisions anachronistic. First, there is now an enormous gulf between the constitutional principle of provincial equality in relation to the federal government and the asymmetrical nature of the arrangements made to accommodate Quebec in practice. Second, there is an equally enormous gulf between the formal respon-sibilities and jurisdictions of the two orders of government as laid out in the constitution and the practical realities—in particular, what has come to be expected of Ottawa with respect to the costly responsibilities assigned to provin-cial governments. Ottawa has become intimately involved in these areas of provincial jurisdiction—albeit primarily as financier and with perhaps only modest influence—largely through the use of the federal spending power. How the general imbalance between constitutional jurisdiction and political reality is reconciled in the context of federal–provincial negotiation is a frequent theme throughout this book.

Finally, a third disparity (often referred to as the 'democratic deficit') is the one that exists between the traditions of parliamentary democracy and the expecta-tions of citizens that they should be able influence policy and restrain executive power. The cornerstone of parliamentary democracy is the nineteenth-century notion of representative and responsible government—a notion appropriate to an era of strong political parties and limited citizen participation in political life (Sharman, 1990). Executive federalism is in large part rooted in this Westminster-style parliamentary government.

Among the most important societal changes over the past three decades has been a general increase in the numbers of well-educated, critically minded citizens. These people are much less deferential than their predecessors, and less accepting of the secretive and elitist nature of contemporary executive federalism. As will become evident in later chapters, executive federalism is still alive and well in many respects, despite warnings that its death is imminent. Nonetheless, changes in the environment in which executive federalism operates put considerable strain both on the actors directly involved in intergovernmental bargaining and on the system as a whole. In particular, the *de facto* understandings surrounding Quebec's position in confederation largely reflect the views of intergovernmental elites, not the general public. The '9-1-1' federalism exemplified by SUFA, the 2004 Health Care Accord (which included a codicil explicitly endorsing asymmetry for Quebec), and the 2006 House of Commons Resolution recognizing the Québécois as 'a nation within a united Canada' are all examples of such *de facto* understandings. They are also products of the elite accommodation that is still part of modern-day executive federalism.

Chapter 3

Intergovernmental Relations and the Policy Process: A Framework

One of the defining characteristics of a federation is that its component governments—both national and regional—are at one and the same time autonomous and interdependent (Simeon, 2006 [1972]). Governments may well have the constitutional authority to act in areas under their jurisdiction, and they may have the administrative capacity to do so; but invariably their responsibilities are intertwined with those of other governments, in the same policy area or in related areas. Whatever the field—transportation, education, health care—governments generally find that they cannot operate solely on their own. How governments manage their interdependencies in the policy process is the focus of this chapter. We develop a framework that identifies the crucial elements in the policy formulation and negotiation processes—strategies and tactics, political resources and arenas—and outline the major theoretical frameworks that have been used to gain insight into policy formulation.

Ideally, problems associated with interdependency are handled on the basis of consensus, since none of the governments involved is in a position to dictate what another should do in its sphere of jurisdiction. Although the federal government may use various tactics to persuade or pressure one or more provincial or territorial governments to do its bidding, the latter are under no legal obligation to comply.

In some respects relations between states or provinces and their national governments resemble those between countries in the international system, where world organizations such as the United Nations ultimately lack sovereignty over individual nation-states. Much of the activity in international relations consists of nations seeking to influence one another and work out mutually acceptable arrangements for managing common interests and resolving disputes over matters such as trade, security, and communications without resorting to brute force. Nation-states have an array of diplomatic instruments that they can deploy to persuade other nation-states to behave in particular ways, or simply to protect themselves from the depredations of larger states.[1]

This conception of international diplomacy is central to one of the classic works on Canadian intergovernmental relations. Richard Simeon's *Federal–Provincial Diplomacy* (2006 [1972]) was considered revolutionary when it was first published. Likening relations between Ottawa and the provinces to those between independent states in the international arena, Simeon applied concepts from the international relations literature to three Canadian cases, the most interesting of which was the negotiation of the Canada Pension Plan. In 1963–4 the newly elected Pearson government was strongly committed to its election promise of 'pensions for all'—a publicly financed pension scheme. A good portion of the relevant jurisdiction, however, was in provincial hands. Here was a classic example of a policy scheme that depended on collaboration between the two levels of government for successful implementation. The end results were the Canada Pension Plan, a separate Quebec Pension Plan, and some excellent lessons on the conduct of negotiations and the nature of federalism.

The notion of the constituent units as semi-autonomous states is not new. William Riker (1964), for example, argued that federations such as Canada, Australia, and the United States were effectively products of the recession of empire. When the British Empire withdrew—as a consequence of revolt in the case of the original 13 American colonies and by mutual consent in the cases of Australia and Canada—its assorted former possessions needed to find their own ways of providing for economic and military security. In each case the individual colonies could conceivably have functioned on their own, had it not been for their military and economic vulnerability. Federal arrangements allowed them to preserve a degree of autonomy under the umbrella of the larger physical and governmental entity formed by the aggregation of several component units. Although Riker was concerned with the origins of federations and Simeon with policy-making and intergovernmental relations in contemporary federations, both focused on motives and the processes of negotiation between those units.

In recent years, the efforts of the European Union and its efforts to achieve not only economic but also (to some degree) political integration have often given rise to questions about the lessons that federalism might offer with respect to the design of institutions and, especially, an overall constitution (Baier, 2005). Although the EU has acquired more and more of the trappings of a federal structure, it still lacks some of the core features of federalism—most notably a single government directly elected by citizens. Nonetheless, the EU—like the Canadian federation—is an entity in which interstate bargaining and coalition-building are among the principal activities. The EU's Council of Ministers reinvented intergovernmental decision-making in 1986, when it adopted qualified majority voting rules. Since that time the European member-states have been able to collectively reach binding decisions on many matters without unanimous consent. This has greatly facilitated decision-making. Many Canadians have taken notice of this European innovation.

Thus the framework developed originally by Simeon—focused on governments' capacity to pursue their individual goals and interests through negotiation, and the factors that determine both the conduct of such negotiations and their ultimate outcomes—remains highly relevant to the study of intergovernmental relations. While the balance among and between the provinces (and territories) and Ottawa has shifted somewhat over the years, the basic dynamics of the relationship have not. At the same time, more recent work on bargaining and diplomacy between states, along with research into the more general processes of negotiation, strategizing, and policy-making (without reference to federalism or the international arena), has helped to enrich this basic framework. Contributions from economics and political science in the field of game theory, for example, and in the field of policy analysis, add a more rigorous dimension to investigations into why some negotiations succeed while others fail (Considine, 2005; Flanagan, 1998; Scharpf, 1997).

THE INTERGOVERNMENTAL FRAMEWORK

Essentially, the framework identifies a range of critical factors necessary in order to understand a given set of negotiations and ultimate outcomes. They include the following: actors; working rules; issues; interests, goals, and objectives; strategies and tactics; resources; arenas; interactions; and outcomes. Further additions and refinements are possible, depending on the subject at hand, but let us focus a little more closely on each of these basic categories:

Actors

In this book we use the term 'actors' mainly to refer to governments—federal, provincial, territorial, Aboriginal, and local. There are other actors, however, such as interest groups, citizen groups, and Aboriginal organizations that are considered governmental for some purposes but not for others. Furthermore, it would be misleading to think of any government as a single actor, since within each one there may be several conflicting views on various issues, including the optimum position to take vis-à-vis other governments. And while in this book we stress that Canadian governments—federal, provincial and territorial—tend to be characterized by the concentration of power at the centre, this centralization is not absolute. Central agencies such as the Privy Council Office (PCO) in Ottawa play an important role in managing the overall intergovernmental agenda, but the sheer volume and complexity of the intergovernmental issues that arise means that many of them must be handled by various agencies and line departments. This in turn may affect the way an issue is handled. The result arrived at by a line department negotiating with its counterparts in other governments may be quite different from the result that would have been produced if the same issue had been handled by a central agency. This *intra*governmental dimension, as we will see, can have an important impact on intergovernmental relations.[2]

Working Rules

The working rules of intergovernmental relations are the institutional conventions that guide the behaviour of governments in these relationships (Painter, 1991; Brown, 2002b; cf. Ostrom, 1990). First, the participants in executive federalism jealously control membership in their exclusive club. In the past, meetings were usually confined to the 'constituent' governments of the federation—the ten provinces and the federal government—but since the mid-1980s the territorial governments have also been included for almost all purposes. On occasion the governments also meet with national Aboriginal organizations and municipal bodies such as the Federation of Canadian Municipalities, but only by invitation and in somewhat separate processes, not as a matter of right. Second, as a result of the relative autonomy of our provinces and the Westminster principles of responsible government and accountability, our government participants prefer to retain as much independence and flexibility as possible when it comes to intergovernmental cooperation. Thus so far there has been no constitutional commitment to meet, no formal joint process for agreement on agendas, or any legally entrenched set of rules about when and whether to cooperate at all. Third, and following from the last point, the decision-making process remains rudimentary, usually limited to consensus agreement. No votes are taken, and any one government can choose to opt out or stand aside from the consensus. Typically intergovernmental agreements are not binding in any legal sense. There are many examples of newly elected governments that have reneged on the political commitments of their predecessors. And no government wishes to be placed in a position where they could be 'out-voted' by a majority, even a super-majority, of the others. In other words, intergovernmental institutions are not legislative assemblies.

Thus what is actually achieved by intergovernmental relations can be quite limited. Rarely will governments agree on a binding regulatory process. Somewhat more frequently they may commit themselves to joint spending initiatives. Much more commonly, however, after the exchange of information and mutual argument of positions, all that will be released is a general statement of intent, principles, or objectives.

Issues

The issues addressed in intergovernmental negotiations run the gamut from simple administrative matters—recognition of drivers' licences between provinces, for example—to constitutional amendments. Different issues can affect or engage the attention of different provinces in different ways; language policy, for instance, is clearly a much more important issue for some provinces than for others. Issues can enter the intergovernmental hopper when one government wishes to implement a new initiative (as in the case of the Canada Pension Plan, introduced by the newly elected Liberal government in 1963), or when a private individual, society, or company simply challenges the jurisdiction, and hence the authority, of a government to enact a particular piece of legislation. Issues vary in their scope and the extent to which they are likely to become divisive. Some issues may be easily resolved by permitting all actors to obtain their goals; but this is not always possible. In the last part of this chapter we will look at the various characteristics of issues in relation to policy-making (for example, monetary issues compared with symbolic ones) and how these characteristics affect the way they are handled and resolved, as well as the notion of agenda-setting.[3]

Interests, Goals, and Objectives

Each government in a federation will have a set of interests relating to a wide variety of issues. Not all of these interests may be obvious; nor will they necessarily be consistent. As we noted in Chapter 2, the particular interests of any province or territory will reflect a unique combination of geographic, ecological, economic, social, cultural, and political factors. In the case of the federal government, there is a general sense of the interests of Canada as a whole. This calculation of interest, in turn, can lead to the formulation of specific objectives in relation to the issue at hand. Our use of 'may' and 'can' here is deliberate, for some governments are better equipped than others to formulate policy that reflects their interests—or even to recognize what their interests really are. This 'policy capacity' is a reflection of various factors, including individual personnel.

Some interests are relatively constant: all provincial governments would like Ottawa to increase health care transfers, for example. But other interests vary from province to province. Especially with newly emerging issues, governments may not be aware of what is at stake until well into the negotiations, or until public opinion alerts governments to potential controversy.[4] Once a government has determined what its interests are in any given matter, it will need to formulate its goals and objectives. These may be as simple as protecting the status quo in that area or limiting the impact of a change proposed by the federal government. Keep in mind that most governments have a variety of departments and agencies, each with vested interests that may be affected by any given issue; hence it may be difficult to develop a single coherent position. This is particularly true if outside interest and pressure groups are involved, since these groups could challenge any position that the government might take. Awareness by the general public may also make a government cautious about proceeding.

In short, a government must not only be able to identify its interests and formulate its objectives; it also has to be willing to act on its interests. Then it needs to think about how to proceed in its dealings with other governments.

Strategies and Tactics

Once a government has decided what it wants out of any given set of intergovernmental negotiations—that is, its objectives—it must decide what kind of strategy to use in pursuit of them. Developing a strategy means choosing which arenas to work through (the courts, ministerial meetings, public opinion), whether to use public means or quiet diplomacy, and whether or not to link the issue in question with other issues. Success depends on choosing a strategy appropriate to the issue. One of the key elements to be decided is the type of alliance or coalition with other governments that would be most effective. For example, would a province be better off working with the federal government on a one-to-one basis? Or should it aim for a united front with one or more other provinces in order to put maximum pressure on Ottawa? In the case of the federal government, should it pursue a multilateral strategy? Or should it target specific provinces for initial bilateral agreements that can then be used as templates for the remaining provinces?

Resources

The amount and type of resources that a government has on hand or can mobilize is another critical variable. In this connection it is worth remembering that the provinces and territories vary enormously in size, wealth, and social make-up. Table 3.1 summarizes the basic socio-economic features of the provinces and territories, including population, GDP per capita, and proportion of revenue that comes from Ottawa in the form of fiscal transfers.

The figures in the table make the differences between the larger and smaller provinces and territories very clear. British Columbia, Alberta, Ontario, and Quebec together account for more than 80 per cent of the national population and more than 85 per cent of the economy (even though Quebec has below-average GDP and fiscal capacity). Not surprisingly, these provinces can devote more resources to the management of intergovernmental relations than their smaller, poorer counterparts can.

In general, for instance, the wealthier provinces have more fiscal resources to invest in developing other critical resources, such as expertise and the capacity to use it. They also tend be in a better position to say 'no' to the federal government, since they have the resources to provide a cushion. On the other hand, Quebec—despite its limited fiscal capacity—has for several years been one of the more sophisticated players in the intergovernmental arena. One reason for Quebec's success in achieving its own pension plan was its willingness to spend considerable resources on preparing for the negotiations, so that it was able to propose a scheme that was in many respects much more refined than the one proposed by the federal government.

It is true that Quebec is Canada's second largest province, but size is not everything. For a large province to throw its weight around can be counter-productive, particularly if citizens sees such behaviour as contrary to basic values such as

Table 3.1   Provinces and Territories: Basic Socio-Economic Features, 2007

	Population	Provincial revenue from federal transfers (%)	Unemployment rate	GDP per capita	Average weekly earnings ($)
Canada	31,241,030	18.1	6.1	38,495	770.82
Newfoundland and Labrador	500,610	32.2	12.5	35,243	714.65
Prince Edward Island	134,205	39.7	9.6	28,106	628.90
Nova Scotia	903,090	35.8	8.2	30,883	673.38
New Brunswick	719,650	40.4	8.9	29,900	707.93
Quebec	7,435,900	18.6	7.5	33,856	725.29
Ontario	12,028,895	15.8	6.4	40,346	803.46
Manitoba	1,133,510	34.7	4.2	32,708	701.93
Saskatchewan	953,850	17.1	4.1	36,749	724.03
Alberta	3,256,355	10.5	3.6	54,075	835.52
British Columbia	4,074,385	16.2	4.5	35,041	761.01
Yukon Territory	30,195	71.0	—	—	882.47
Northwest Territories	41,055	75.2	—	—	1,004.63
Nunavut	29,325	93.0	—	—	948.68

SOURCES: Fiscal Reference Tables, September 2007 (Ottawa: Department of Finance, 2007); Earnings, average weekly, by province and territory, 2007 (Ottawa: Statistics Canada, 31 March 2008); Economic indicators, by province and territory, 13 June 2008 (Ottawa: Statistics Canada, 2008).

fairness or willingness to share. By the same token, smaller provinces can use their size or relative poverty to their advantage by invoking those values. Furthermore, effective preparation and strategizing do not necessarily depend on financial resources. Frank McKenna, the long-time premier of New Brunswick (1987–97), was considered particularly astute both in surrounding himself with talented individuals and in networking and negotiating with other governments. More recently, Premiers Danny Williams of Newfoundland and Labrador and John Hamm of Nova Scotia, after a long battle with Ottawa over equalization and the clawback of offshore energy royalties, succeeded in negotiating bilateral offshore revenue accords with the Martin government in 2005. Although financial resources are naturally paramount in pursuing intergovernmental objectives, there are other assets that governments can tap. Among them is public opinion. Premiers have been known to call elections with the specific aim of claiming a mandate, and thus legitimacy, to pursue some objective with Ottawa. They have also been known to use their influence with voters as a lever in negotiations with the federal government. It was in this way that Premier Williams was able to extract a promise from Prime Minister Martin regarding the offshore issue in the run-up to the federal election of 2004, and the fact that the Liberals lost their majority status in that election allowed him to continue applying pressure until the deal was done.

Finally, legal jurisdiction is another important resource, and lack of jurisdiction can be a serious constraint. The best-known example involves health care—a matter assigned to provincial jurisdiction. In order to have any influence in this area Ottawa has to rely almost exclusively on its spending power,[5] backed by its considerable fiscal resources. The government with constitutional jurisdiction over an area clearly has the high ground in negotiations. Keep in mind, however, that for many issues jurisdictional boundaries are not at all clear-cut.

Arenas

Sometimes governments do not have much choice about the arena within which an issue is handled. If, for example, an organization or corporation decides to challenge the validity of a law on the grounds that it was passed by a legislature that lacked the jurisdictional authority to do so, the government in question will have to go to court to defend the validity of its legislation. In such cases other governments may enter the fray as well, perhaps taking the side of the litigant, both to protect their interests in that particular case and to defend the broader principle of which it is an example.

However the arena for intergovernmental interactions is determined, it can have a considerable impact on the outcome. The courts, for example, by virtue of their adversarial nature, require that each party to the dispute present its side, and only its side, of the argument in the best possible way. Even a well-articulated and legally defensible argument, however, will not necessarily help in portraying the government in question as flexible or willing to compromise. Thus a hard-nosed legal position may not play well in the court of public opinion. Furthermore, legal decisions are not always predictable, and they may have long-term consequences that governments will eventually regret. It is quite possible for a government to win a case, but on grounds so narrow as to restrict rather than expand its jurisdiction—the classic case of winning the battle but losing the war.

Meetings of officials largely escape the public scrutiny that court proceedings attract and are therefore much more conducive to quiet negotiation and compromise. Even the settings in which meetings take place can be important. It is often said, for example, that first ministers' meetings (those involving the prime minister and premiers) tend to be much more productive when they are held over breakfast or dinner. To the extent that the parties involved in a negotiation have a choice, the arena in which they will meet can be a major strategic consideration.

Subsequent chapters will examine in greater detail different arenas: the courts, first ministers' and ministerial conferences, meetings of officials, and a variety of other settings and organizations, such as intergovernmental affairs agencies. It will become evident that Canadian intergovernmental relations are characterized by a relatively low level of institutionalization. We will, however, look at some of the more formal bodies, such as the Council of Atlantic Premiers (formerly the Council of Maritime Premiers) and the recently created Council of the Federation, made up of the ten provincial premiers and three territorial premiers and based on the longstanding annual premiers' conference.

Interactions

We tend to think of interactions between governments as consisting mainly of negotiations, but there are actually quite a number of activities that come under that heading. Furthermore, the lead up to any set of negotiations usually involves several stages, including plenty of preparatory work. Indeed, the most frequent activities are those in which officials from different governments meet to exchange information, to prepare data in standardized formats, or to assemble information about matters on which there is general agreement. Thus long before there is a meeting of ministers, several meetings of officials will already have taken place. Consultations over the phone, brief meetings in hallways, exchanges of data or information, long discussions on 'Team Canada' missions to foreign parts—any of these can count as intergovernmental interactions. Some of these dealings may produce agreement; others may not. The nature of the settings or arenas, the types of individuals involved (sometimes they will come from similar backgrounds, sometimes they will not), the presence or absence of what J. Stefan Dupré (1988) has called 'trust ties', can all help account for particular outcomes. Equally important is the basic nature of these interactions. One-on-one interactions—those involving just two governments—are quite different from those in which several governments are involved. It is also important to note that the nature of interactions can vary significantly: some are essentially unilateral, with one party directly asserting its will over the other, while others are of a more mutual character, with expectations of bargaining and compromise.

Outcomes

The end product of a set of negotiations can take several forms, including agreement to disagree, or the absence of any agreement at all. In analyzing a set of negotiations it is frequently difficult to identify a specific outcome or to predict the longer-term consequences. For purposes of analysis it is often necessary to assume sufficient clarity as to what the issue is as well as the conclusion of the negotiation process, even if the end result of that process appears to be less than definitive. In our discussion of public policy we will elaborate on outcomes, as distinct from simple outputs. We will also discuss the instruments used to deliver whatever policies are agreed on, because those instruments can play a major role in shaping the ultimate results.

POLICY THEORIES AND OUTCOMES

A key question raised early in this book was whether federalism matters. Does it make a difference? The question is certainly relevant when we examine the policy outcomes of programs or frameworks adopted or agreed to by governments. One way of addressing this issue is to compare the policy outcomes produced by federal and non-federal systems in the same policy areas. This is a rather crude approach, however, and it is unlikely to produce meaningful results because federalism is only one in a host of factors that need to be taken into account. Furthermore, as has been pointed out by Keith Banting (1987) and Paul Pierson (1995), two well-known scholars of social policy, it is not federalism in general but a particular type of federation, with particular features, that combines with other variables to determine outcomes. Thus Pierson points out how many more actors are involved in the US, with its 50 states and its congressional system, compared to Canada, with its 13 constituent units (three of them territories), and notes that the difference in numbers clearly produces a different dynamic in the way policies are handled. For example, a bargaining session is likely to be more effective with a dozen representatives sitting around the table than with fifty. It is equally important to take particular characteristics into account when studying intergovernmental relations in a single country. In the Canadian context, for example, one might ask whether the particular arena in which negotiations were conducted had any effect on the way the issue was handled—whether it increased or decreased the number of actors involved, for instance.

Before tackling the question of how the structure and dynamics of federalism affect policy outcomes, it is important to clarify what we mean by public policy. At its simplest, public policy can be defined as a body of laws or regulations, courses of action or inaction, or budgetary decisions in different program areas, formulated and implemented by governments. Of the many broad theoretical frameworks that have been used to explain choices in the area of public policy, six of the more prominent ones focus on institutions; 'rational choice' theory; socio-economic factors; policy networks, communities, and groups; ideas and political philosophy; and poststructural theory.

Neo-institutionalism

Central to the *neo-institutional* (or path dependency) paradigm is the idea that institutions serve both to structure social and political relationships and to socialize those working within them into the values, norms, and practices pertaining to policies and programs. Under the right conditions, the particular framework adopted in an emerging area may come to play a major role in the future development of that area. The QWERTY keyboard, for example, is not the best or most efficient keyboard available, but because it was the first to be widely used in typewriters, it became so entrenched that superior layouts arriving later were incapable of dislodging it. The development of the Canadian medicare system can be understood in much the same way. Having been accepted as the operating model in the 1960s, it has proven very difficult to alter, even in minor ways, despite some obvious flaws.

Institutional theory helps us understand how policies are sustained over time, and why they can be difficult to change. It is attractive because it argues that both ideas and history matter. Given the number of institutions involved in federalism and intergovernmental relations, the appeal of the neo-institutional model is obvious. It is not very useful, however, in accounting for policy change. While those working from a neo-institutional perspective can and do explain change, they usually do so on a post-facto basis, citing factors that lie outside the institutional model, such as power shifts or a changing balance of forces. Unfortunately, such factors are not very good at predicting what might happen in the future, or at identifying elements that, if they were to be altered, would lead to particular changes.

Rational Choice

Rational choice theory, which some consider to be a subset of neo-institutionalism, sees actors, including individual citizens, as utility maximizers who seek the outcomes that best fit their preferences and whose behaviour is constrained and channelled by rules and institutions (often understood as bundles of negotiated rules). It holds human behaviour itself to be relatively predictable; thus variations in outcomes depend on the rules and institutions through which human behaviour is channelled, and change depends on changes in those rules.

One very useful contribution of rational choice theory is that it highlights what has been called the collective action problem: the fact that collective action may be beneficial for society as a whole, or a good portion of society, but also disadvantageous to many individuals; and conversely, action that is beneficial for many individuals may not be so for the collectivity (Olson, 1971). In identifying the paradoxes associated with collective action, rational choice theory shows how certain rules and institutions of federalism (such as a requirement of unanimity, or consensus) can block collective action. If major players believe that their ability to protect their interests or exercise leverage proportionate to their size will be limited, the perceived legitimacy of the federal arrangements will suffer. Will a rich and powerful province such as Alberta or Ontario always have to water down its interests for the sake of the whole? Will Quebec find itself facing opposition from anglophone provinces when it seeks to defend its autonomy? Heard and Swartz (1997) have shown how the constitutional amending formula introduced in 1996 served to widen the disparities between provinces with respect to their capacity to initiate and/or veto constitutional change, increasing the capacity of the larger provinces and diminishing that of the smaller provinces.

One of the more prominent items in the rational choice toolbox is game theory, which can be used to analyze both specific policy disputes and broader issues of constitutional design. Games such as the prisoner's dilemma can be used to show that the payoff from non-cooperation is often greater than the payoff from cooperation. Similarly, Patrick James (1993) used a sequential gaming model—in which the participants shift strategies as they move through different stages of negotiations—to analyze the energy wars of 1980–1 between Alberta and Ottawa. James argued that, contrary to conventional wisdom, the critical factor determining the outcome was not the personalities involved, but rather the strategic structure of intergovernmental negotiations. Fritz Scharpf (1988), in a classic study of German federalism, points to the 'joint decision-making trap', a case where the numerous veto points inherent in the German federal system can lead to policy paralysis.

The rational choice approach has been critiqued on several grounds, beginning with its assumption that all behaviour can ultimately be reduced to individual preferences. Critics maintain that this assumption leaves little room for collective values, altruism, or the simple fact that people do not always behave in a rational fashion. Another criticism is that rational choice models tend to be highly formalistic, often far removed from the empirical world. Thus while a formal model of a particular situation might suggest that there is no incentive for any of the participants to come to agreement, we know that agreements have been reached in similar circumstances—quite possibly because the participants hold values that transcend individual preferences. Thus, for example, members of the political elite may come to an agreement simply because the absence of an agreement could be catastrophic for the polity as a whole. In fact, it is on this assumption that the elite accommodation model (Lijphart, 1977, 1999) is based.

As well, a variation on the rational choice theme called 'public choice' theory has been criticized for its ideological slant. Adherents of public choice are often strong proponents of federalism—or decentralization—because they believe that increasing the number of jurisdictions or levels of government increases the likelihood that individuals will be able to maximize their preferences across a range of issues.[6] According to this view, multiple and overlapping jurisdiction provides greater flexibility by allowing for the emergence of more defined communities of interest, each of which will develop the package of public goods that best fits its needs and preferences. This kind of decentralization is said to be much more effective in dealing with common resource problems than more centralized arrangements. Unfortunately, public choice theory tends to assume that boundaries and jurisdictions can be altered to suit shifting needs and interests—whereas the boundaries and jurisdictions in federations have typically been fixed since the eighteenth or nineteenth century. Thus Canada's constitution has not been amended to take into account the increasing responsibilities of large municipal governments. In other words, the federal principle of independent and autonomous governments has not been extended to the local government sphere.

Nonetheless, rational choice theory and its variants can be enormously useful for some purposes, helping us not only to analyze institutional frameworks but to understand why some strategies work and others fail.

Socio-Economic Theories

There are many theories that see social and economic factors as the prime determinants of change in public policy. Power is an important consideration, but it is power stemming from the structure of economic and social relationships. Institutions and organizations are seen as peripheral or simply as instruments involved in implementing those policies necessary to allow the inherent logic of those relationships to unfold. The Marxist paradigm is probably the best example: capitalism requires that the state perform certain functions in order to allow capital accumulation to take place and, ultimately, ensure the hegemony of the capitalist class.

A well-known criticism of this highly deterministic approach is the fact that public policies can vary widely from one capitalist country to another, despite the similarities in their economic systems. Why is it that some have generous social support systems while others do not? As a way of explaining these differences, as well as to account for the example of governments that help save capitalism from itself, the concept of the autonomy of the state is introduced by Marxist theorists. This type of explanation, however, appears to enhance the status of institutional and leadership factors.

Another deterministic model comes from the literature on political development, which often suggests that developing countries need to reach a particular stage of economic development before democratic institutions can take hold. In reality, however, it often seems that countries at a similar stage of economic development are at quite different stages with respect to democratic development. Other theories focus on socio-economic indices (GDP per capita, literacy rates, etc.) as background factors, which then serve as the basic constraints or pressures that decision-makers need to address (Hofferbert, 1974). Still other theories focus less on gradual developments and more on socio-economic events that alter the balance between competing groups or coalitions.

Within the general category of theories explaining public policy by reference to socio-economic factors, the literature on globalization is particularly insightful. David R. Cameron (1978, 1986), for example, noted that in the developed world smaller countries tended to spend much more of their GDP on social programs than larger countries did. He attributed this pattern to the fact that these smaller countries were much more dependent on international trade than larger countries (Katzenstein, 1985). The more open the country's economy was to global trade, the less freedom the government had to manage or shape the economy. In such cases the only way for the government to protect the popula-tion from the vicissitudes of the international economy was by providing a generous social safety net. In effect, Cameron identified a significant constraint on the options available to political leaders in certain countries. Given that Canada, like many other smaller nations, is highly dependent on international trade, this factor is likely to constrain decision-makers at both the federal and the provincial level.

Finally, society-based theory, particularly what might be termed neo-Marxist analysis, has made influential contributions to the study of the history and dynamics of Canadian federalism and the explanation of intergovernmental relations. However, it has been more successful at examining large social and economic forces and longer-term trends than specific policy choices and outcomes.[7]

Network Theory

Policy networks, policy communities, and advocacy groups have been the subject of extensive research by students of public policy interested in the interactions between individuals or organizations and the state. The study of pressure groups (now generally known as advocacy groups[8]) has a long tradition, especially in the study of American politics, where policy outputs have often been seen as the outcome of the jousting between different groups competing for the attention of decision-makers. This jousting has been understood in a variety of ways. Political scientists such as A.F. Bentley (1967) and Robert Dahl (1967) see the interactions among groups in the form of competitive behaviour; by contrast, others, such as Theodore Lowi (1979), tend to see less competition and more cartels or monop-olistic behaviour, with certain groups dominating whole sectors, including the government agencies responsible for regulating those sectors. In Canada, Paul Pross (1992) has used the notion of policy communities to analyze government policy-making. In his model, a policy community consists of the specialized government agencies and the key interest groups in a particular policy field, who work together—to develop government regulations and appropriate means for their implementation, for example—in an institutionalized pattern of interac-tion. Interest-dominated intergovernmental relationships are especially prom-inent in resource fields such as agriculture, fisheries, mining, and forestry.[9]

The notion of policy networks originated in Europe, where until the 1980s it was common for state-sanctioned bodies representing private interests to play an active role in government policy-making and implementation. Today this system, known as corporatism, has been largely replaced by one in which the linkages between organizations and governments are much more fluid. It was in the course of investigating these linkages that analysts developed network theory. In the UK intergovernmental relations—between municipal councils and the centre—have been analyzed primarily from within a network perspective (Rhodes, 1996). Some theorists maintain that, with the revolution in information technologies, networks have now taken on a life of their own, challenging traditional forms of political and bureaucratic authority and cutting across formal governmental boundaries. Some believe that quasi-formal and informal networks play a crucial role in managing the interdependencies of governments and the activities within them; these theorists often refer to 'horizontal management' or 'joined-up government'. In Canada, therefore, students of intergovernmental relations have examined a variety of intergovernmental activities from a network or 'horizontal management' perspective, particularly activities at the local level involving a variety of federal, provincial, and local agencies (Bourgault, 2002; Bakvis and Juillet, 2004). Some of the literature on multilevel governance introduced in Chapter 1 is also rooted in the study of networks of interaction.

Policy networks, much like institutions, are said to structure behaviour and exercise influence by encouraging some interests and activities and discouraging others. At the same time network analysis, much like neo-institutional theory, has been criticized on the grounds that it cannot explain why certain policies are adopted or how policies change. Even if it is used only as a metaphor, however, the network concept is very useful for identifying linkages among and between individuals and organizations and understanding how they interact.

Ideas and Political Philosophy

Most of the theories outlined above are concerned with the exercise of influence, whether by institutions, groups, social forces, or individuals. From this point of view ideas are secondary. Yet policy-making is fundamentally an intellectual exercise, about applying ideas to societal problems (Bakvis, 2000). Ideas can range from the specific to the broad and visionary. And they can be shown to have influence. The foundations of the national medicare scheme implemented in 1966 were the ideas about publicly funded medical care first developed by the CCF government of Saskatchewan (Naylor, 1986; Taylor, 1978). Similarly, Pierre Trudeau's vision of a single Canadian identity that could be realized in both of Canada's official languages shaped federal government policy for more than three decades, while the ideas about sovereignty articulated by René Lévesque, among others, continue to shape the demands that Quebec places on the Canadian federation.

Ideas do not have to be grand or visionary in order to have an impact on the conduct of intergovernmental relations. Disciplinary orientations can be important: a major rift developed in the area of labour market training around 1970, for instance, when the policy developers on the federal side were mainly economists while their counterparts on the provincial side were mainly educators (Dupré et al., 1973). Management philosophies can have an impact as well: in the 1990s, a public sector philosophy known as the New Public Management (NPM), which recommended practices such as outsourcing for the sake of efficiency (Aucoin, 1995), had ramifications for federal–provincial relations when some governments adopted NPM values and others did not (Bakvis, 1996).

Ideas can have important consequences at every stage, from policy design through to policy choice of instruments and delivery mechanisms. Equally important is the agenda-setting that marks the start of the policy cycle (Howlett and Ramesh, 2003). A well-crafted policy idea that captures the imagination of both decision-makers and the attentive public can set the stage for discussion. Policy entrepreneurs at universities and (especially) think-tanks can help set things in motion. Royal commissions can also play important roles in bringing new ideas into the public realm (Bradford, 1998). Often it is not enough to develop and place an idea on the public agenda: to gain support for that idea, it may also be necessary to suggest alternatives and then rule them out. While factors other than the quality of the idea or superiority of the argumentation can determine which particular ideas win out, the particular merits of a proposal are still important. Here again, the debate over the Canada Pension Plan is a good example. The reason the final outcome was two separate pension schemes, one for Quebec and one for the rest of Canada, was not simply that Quebec had the power to get what it wanted, but that Quebec's plan was in many respects superior to the federal scheme. Quebec political leaders and officials had done their homework and presented a proposal that was well thought out and carefully costed.

Thus the capacity to generate, analyze, and manage ideas is a crucial part of a government's overall policy capacity—and a strong policy capacity is one of the more important resources available to governments during intergovernmental negotiations. The other important function served by ideas is legitimation. Ideas can help to persuade the public that a particular proposal is justified—and public support is helpful if not essential in order to move a policy forward. In short, an idea or set of ideas can provide the justification or reassurance that the government is moving in the right direction. Legitimation can also be important within the policy community itself, since what must be accepted is not simply a set of policies but also the conceptual apparatus surrounding it (e.g., relevant standards and appropriate tests) (Wilson, 1998).

Ideas, like institutions, rarely have an impact on their own. Additional factors—leadership, resonance (either for the general public or for a specific policy community), a particularly urgent problem that must be addressed—are usually necessary in order for ideas to gain traction.

Poststructural Theory

So far, poststructural theory has not been widely used in the study of intergovernmental relations, but it has made significant inroads into the literature on policy analysis, public administration, and international relations.[10] Rejecting the claims to objectivity of the standard 'scientific' approach, poststructuralism sees the world primarily through a subjective lens. Its primary tools are social deconstruction and discourse analysis, in which the assumption is that 'words, concepts, and definitions do not have a single timeless meaning but reflect a specific context of time, gender, class, and other factors that filter these concepts for the writer and reader alike' (Gillroy, 1997: 164). Knowledge, therefore, is largely experiential and relational, generated through interactions among individuals. Essentially the task of the researcher is to deconstruct the discourse or narrative that structures the meanings that actors attach to actions.

Poststructural theory is criticized for its subjectivity and relativism. Yet it can be well suited to the analysis of intergovernmental policy-making, where so many variables come into play that it is difficult to tease out cause and effect. Our understanding of intergovernmental processes often depends on detailed descriptions of developments and events—that is, the narratives created to explain how national programs came to be adopted. Furthermore, when two governments first begin to explore an area in which they might work together, federal officials will usually argue that no meaningful discussions can take place until agreement is reached on language and definitions—an opening gambit that provincial officials tend to interpret (and resent) as a move to control the agenda. On matters that Ottawa and the provinces tend to see in quite different lights (e.g., transfer payments), each side will try hard to persuade citizens that its definition of the problem is the correct one. In such cases a poststructuralist approach can be used to deconstruct the competing narratives, revealing the assumptions behind them and the power relations inherent in them.

The six theories outlined above are not mutually exclusive. Most analysts use elements from several or even all of them. To the extent that one theory tends to predominate, it is neo-institutionalism, though it should be emphasized that not everyone who uses this general framework would identify it as such. Because institutions figure so prominently in federal systems, they naturally play a major part in most analyses of federalism. Invariably, however, it is necessary to refer to other variables.

ANALYZING POLICY CHARACTERISTICS IN INTERGOVERNMENTAL RELATIONS

All the factors discussed so far—institutions, resources, and ideas—help to shape the outcomes of intergovernmental policy-making. The subject matter and nature of policy fields also come into play: some policy issues are by nature easier to resolve than others. It is important, therefore, that we briefly review some of the concepts used in the policy formulation and analysis literature bearing on characteristics of different types of policies. The key points to be kept in mind are these:

- identification of policy field
- problem definition and policy agendas
- outcomes and endpoints
- rational versus incremental change

- distributive versus redistributive factors
- choice of policy instruments.

Identifying a Policy Field

First, for purposes of analysis we need to identify and define the policy field in question. This is especially important for federal systems, in which respect for jurisdictional boundaries is such a fundamental principle. In many instances this is relatively straightforward; fields such as pensions, transportation, and health care are all readily identifiable. At the other extreme, however, are areas in which there are no explicit government programs or policies at present. To take a hypothetical example, suppose someone decides that a policy is needed concerning extraterrestrial life. This issue would not be on the policy horizon of most governments; but it might well be relevant for certain government activities. In that case it would be up to the analyst to define the subject matter and explain the links to existing fields of government activity. This approach can be useful when, for example, a new policy field has emerged in one or more other countries and seems likely to become an issue for one or more Canadian governments as well. The importance of identifying new policy fields becomes obvious when we think of new reproductive technologies or the new forms of communication and commerce that have developed in recent years: in all these cases, at least some of the governments in power at the time were not at all clear about what their roles or responsibilities might be.

Defining the Problem and the Policy Agenda

Policies are formulated and implemented in order to deal with some issue or problem on the public agenda. How and why that issue has ended up on the agenda, how and in what way it has come to be defined as a problem requiring the attention of governments, are all important questions to ask when seeking to understand the actions of governments.[11] Sometimes it is governments themselves that come to recognize that an issue requires attention; sometimes it takes a crisis to identify a problem (as in the case of water quality); and sometimes political rivals, pressure groups, or think tanks will succeed in placing a policy item on the public agenda. These same entities often play a role in defining the nature of the problem that needs to be addressed. In a federation, defining problems and placing them on the policy agenda are part and parcel of the intergovernmental process. Persuading fellow first ministers that there is indeed a serious problem is the first step towards reaching one's objectives.

Defining the Outcomes and Endpoints of Intergovernmental Relations

As well, it is important to think about the point at which the analysis of a particular intergovernmental process should stop. In the case of negotiations that conclude with an agreement, that agreement might seem to offer an obvious stopping point. An analysis taking this tack might not be wholly satisfactory, however, insofar as it would not take into account the substantive impact of the agreement on the policy area in question. An agreement between two governments may meet the objectives of those governments, but to the detriment of certain groups or constituencies. During the 1990s, for example, the provinces and the government of Canada arrived at what is known as the Harmonization Accord, under which provincial environmental protection agencies became the principal players with respect to environmental problems, leaving the federal government to play a more limited role. This harmonized, collaborative approach certainly reduced federal–provincial tensions and conflicts, but many environmental groups have argued that the result has been an inadequate environmental management regime. Thus it is not enough to look at the immediate outcome or product of an intergovernmental process (e.g., an agreement or a court decision): the longer-term consequences must also be examined.

Rational versus Incremental Change

An idealized model of the intergovernmental policy process has all participants carefully examining the problem at hand and weighing various alternatives, then reaching a rational decision on the basis of full information. This approach is often described as *rational-deductive* or *synoptic*, since it starts from first principles based on extensive knowledge and on the basis of those principles determines specific courses of action. Ideally, a decision made in this way would resolve all outstanding issues, and the resulting policy will often represent a significant departure from the previous policy. The reality tends to be quite different. For example, it is often the case that not all the elements required for an ideal policy are amenable to change. There may be considerable resistance to certain changes for reasons that lie outside the policy area itself. More often than not, therefore, the scope of the agreed-on policy change will be reduced and the actual change will be *incremental*, without any sharp break from the past. These incremental changes can often be uncoordinated (Howlett and Ramesh, 2003).

However messy and unpredictable the policy-making process tends to be, at times governments will attempt to make large-scale change based on extensive planning and research. Such efforts may well come to naught, but the simple fact that the effort was made can have some beneficial effect. The Canada Round of constitutional negotiations in 1990–2 is a good example. At the end of the day no constitutional amendments were achieved, but the process itself effectively managed a crisis in national unity.

A variety of factors may help to determine whether or not agreement is possible. Among other things, it may make it more difficult for governments to come to agreement both on fundamental principles and on details. On the other hand, governments may deliberately choose to make incremental changes on the assumption that these will be easier to achieve, even if it means that the quality of the resulting programs is satisficing rather than maximizing. This approach is reflected in the way governments tend to avoid wholesale change in their fiscal arrangements, preferring to make many small changes from year to year. In short, the approach that governments take towards the formulation of policy can have a distinct impact on the final result.

Another important variable is the scope of the proposed outcome. The broader the scope, the more interests will be involved, not only within governments but outside them, making agreement more difficult to reach. On the other hand, reducing the scope by breaking the issue into several discrete entities may make it more manageable and more amenable to agreement. There is institutional turf to be considered as well. For example, a council of Agriculture ministers may be comfortable dealing with issues related to agricultural supply management through marketing boards, but may not want to take direction from ministers of Trade on the broader implications for the Canadian economic union.

Thus it should be kept in mind that some actors are less amenable than others to approaches that would change the scope of a decision. For example, First Nations leaders are more likely than government actors to refer to first principles or the need for constitutional change. Quebec also is more likely than other provinces to insist on principles. Within governments, central agencies may also prefer a more comprehensive approach, which invariably tends to broaden the scope of an issue.

Distributive versus Redistributive Outcomes

One factor affecting the tractability or intractability of an intergovernmental negotiation is the extent to which the policy in question is expected to produce winners and losers. In game-theory terms, outcomes are described as either positive-sum (distributive) or zero-sum (redistributive). Disputes over the former are generally considered more amenable to resolution. If some parties to a negotiation perceive that they stand to lose by the outcome, they will naturally refuse to agree. In the absence of agreement, the consequence is likely to be unilateral action. The National Energy Program (NEP) of the early 1980s is a good example: as imposed by Ottawa, a made-in-Canada domestic price for oil and natural gas, well below the world price, represented a significant loss of revenues, and control, for the oil-producing western provinces—and a net benefit for the consuming provinces, mainly in eastern Canada. The issue still reverberates in the west, colouring any negotiations involving energy between Ottawa and the producing provinces (Doern and Toner, 1985).

In general, governments try to avoid zero-sum outcomes, preferring to transform the issue so as to produce a positive-sum result. But it is not unheard of for a government to pursue a zero-sum outcome if it thinks it will be the winner. The most obvious example is Quebec, which often seeks a redistributive result so as to set itself apart from the other provinces. In some cases this desire can be satisfied with minimal redistributive effect; sometimes it is the symbolism that matters most. The positive- versus zero-sum distinction is useful for understanding the circumstances under which disputes between governments are resolved and the ease with which they are resolved. It is also an important tool in devising strategies for dealing with tricky issues. A contentious issue may be defused if all the parties involved can consider themselves to be winners. The bigger the pie, the easier it is to divide up and distribute. At the same time, there are some issues that by their nature are bound to create winners and losers. The allocation of fishing quotas between different provinces would be an example, though even here there may be opportunities for trade-offs involving different species. One cannot help noting how efforts to avoid zero-sum solutions by making ever-bigger pies (allowable catches, for instance) contribute to the overexploitation of resources.

Finally, it is important to remember that court decisions too can very easily create winners and losers, often in ways that are not predictable. Thus any government contemplating using the courts as a venue for resolving a dispute must take into consideration the risk of a major loss.

Choice of Policy Instruments

Also important to consider in the study of public policy are the types of instruments available to government (Howlett and Ramesh, 2003; Peters and Hoornebeek, 2005). The tools and means available determine both the feasibility of a given policy or program and the ultimate success of the program. Using a blunt instrument—scattering a lot of money to a broad set of interests, for instance—may have far more in the way of unintended consequences than is desirable. There are four main categories of policy instrument:

1. *Actual program delivery*: government administers the program and provides goods or services through its own agents;
2. *Regulation*: a particular kind of service in which government establishes and applies rules and regulations designed to control or direct the activities of citizens, groups, and corporations;
3. *Expenditure*: governments transfer monetary resources directly to individuals, groups, corporations, or other governments in order to influence their behaviour or achieve certain objectives; and
4. *Taxation*: although the main purpose of the tax system is to collect revenues, government can use the tax system to create incentives or disincentives or to redistribute financial resources.

In a federal context, instrument choice often depends on jurisdiction. Under the constitution health care and education are provincial responsibilities: thus Ottawa is not permitted to deliver such services directly. Yet on a number of grounds the federal government believes that it must play a role in theses areas. The main instrument at its disposal for this purpose is expenditure or, more precisely, what the constitution refers to as its spending power: that is, its right to spend money on whatever classes of subjects it chooses. It can use this spending power to transfer funding to provincial governments for programs such as health care, with the proviso that the recipient governments structure their programs in certain ways (e.g., by banning extra-billing by doctors). It can transfer money directly to individuals (e.g., by offering scholarships for post-secondary education).

The tax system can also be used to achieve social policy objectives. The national child benefit, for example, is a joint federal–provincial program under which the federal government delivers benefits to the 'working poor' directly through the income tax system, while provincial governments provide additional benefits.

Finally, there are some matters in which both orders of government may use the same instrument in the same field. Ottawa and the provinces are equally entitled to establish funding programs for cultural groups or to subsidize struggling industries. In these cases the key political decision for either government may not be the choice of the instrument itself so much as whether to use it cooperatively or competitively with other governments in the system.

In short, instrument choice affects both the types of policies adopted and the manner in which they are implemented. Insofar as federalism restricts the numbers and types of instruments available to the different levels of government, clearly it constitutes an important variable. Studying a policy problem and possible solutions where both levels are involved invariably also means looking at the kinds of instruments available and how they might be combined.

SUMMARY

In this chapter we have outlined an actor-centred framework that highlights the settings and arenas within which federal, provincial, and territorial governments identify their interests and formulate their objectives, which they then pursue using a variety of stratagems. We have also noted important conditional factors, such as the resources available to governments and the different forms they can take—some tangible (money), others less so (public opinion, policy capacity). We have also reviewed some of the theories that have been applied to policy-making. Highlighting different aspects of the policy process, they also provide different perspectives on the structure and dynamics of federalism and intergovernmental relations, and help us understand the forces propelling governments in one direction or another.

Together, the concepts outlined in this chapter constitute essential background material for any research into policy-making where two or more governments are involved. We turn now to the constitution: the rules that define the fundamental relationships between governments and other actors in the Canadian federation.

Chapter 4

The Constitution and Constitutional Change

Intergovernmental relations are in large part a response to the constitutional relationship between the provincial and federal governments. The constitution serves as a blueprint for the assignment of governmental responsibilities and entitlements. Constitutionally defined jurisdiction, perhaps more than any other structural factor, determines the relative weights of the resources available to each order of government in its interactions with one another. With some notable exceptions, constitutional resources are generally quite stable. Provinces can grow and shrink in population or economic might (both of which constitute resources in the intergovernmental game), and they may have more or less influence on the leaders the national legislature and government; but their constitutional resources remain fairly static. By specifying the procedures that would be required to alter those resources in the future, a constitution gives the deceptive impression that it would be easy to change. In Canada's case no clear formal procedures existed in the written constitution until the major amendments of 1982. Even since then, the original 1867 constitution has proven rather durable. Although constitutional issues have been a perennial preoccupation of the intergovernmental elite for much of Canada's history, the constitution itself, with some exceptions, has not been easily altered.

The constitution allocates legislative authority. For the federal and provincial governments alike, the scope of possible activity is limited to what the constitution permits their respective legislatures to do. If a government wants to embark on an ambitious new social program, or grant permission for a large-scale resource-extraction project, it has to have the legislative authority to make the necessary laws. Otherwise it will be obliged to work cooperatively with the government that does have that authority. Legislative jurisdiction matters to intergovernmental relations because it defines the kinds of issues which will be hardest fought in the intergovernmental arena and the degree of influence that governments can have over one another's interests.

At the same time jurisdiction can represent a substantial burden for a government with limited financial resources. The vertical fiscal imbalance that is characteristic of Canadian federalism (discussed at length in Chapters 8 and 9) is largely a product of the fact that the constitution assigned the provinces more legislative jurisdiction than fiscal capacity. Historically, the federal government has tried to use its spending power to help the provinces acquit their responsibilities. Constitutionally this power is one of the federal government's most important assets, allowing it to play a creative role in areas over which the provinces have exclusive law-making control.

That Canada has a federal constitution is a result of the sociological, economic, and geographical factors discussed in Chapter 2. But the kind of federal constitution Canada has also reflects the lessons learned from pre-Confederation constitutional history and other nations' experience with federalism. The legacy of imperial arrangements and the Confederation-era experience of other federations, in particular the United States during its civil war, shaped important features of the constitution that governments and citizens still encounter today (Smith, 1988; Smith, 1995). The same influences also account for the dominance of the executive level in Canadian intergovernmental relations. Although federal practice might be advertised as flexible and responsive, federal constitutions are reasonably fixed in character. This gives governmental actors a degree of certainty about the arrangements of the federation, and lets citizens know which government to hold accountable for particular aspects of public policy, good or bad (Trudeau, 1968). Even so, every constitution requires interpretation and adjustment from time to time. In most federations interpretation is provided by the innovative practices of governmental actors and by the authoritative readings of the legal language of the constitution by high courts (Baier, 2006). Formal adjustment through the alteration of constitutional text is usually provided for in a constitutional amendment procedure that gives some role to the subunits and central government in the development and approval of constitutional changes.

This chapter outlines the constitutional blueprint that informs present-day intergovernmental relations in Canada and explains some of the social and philosophical underpinnings of the choices made at the time of Confederation. While the evolution of the constitution through interpretation will be addressed in Chapter 5, this chapter includes a discussion of constitutional change, both achieved and otherwise, as it relates to the key jurisdictions affecting intergovernmental relations.

CANADA'S CONSTITUTIONAL DEVELOPMENT

The Canadian constitution is perhaps not an ideal federal constitution. For starters, it is a mix of written and unwritten elements. The Constitution of the United States of America is much more codified and consequently even revered as a single, cohesive document. In the United Kingdom, unwritten rules and traditions play a more substantial role than any single document or charter. The Canadian constitution is a conscious amalgam of these two traditions. Although matters such as the exercise of legislative and executive power were spelled out in the British North America (now Constitution) Act, 1867, there was already an understanding that the institutions of government would work differently in practice. The unwritten elements of the constitution are referred to as conventions and the Canadian constitutional system relies heavily on them. Conventions are traditions and rules that are not legally binding, but are enforced in the political sphere. That is to say, the only sanction for violating a convention is a political one (Heard, 1991). For example, the prime minister will generally respect the convention of appointing ministers to his or her cabinet in a way that represents all the provinces and regions of the country. A prime minister who failed to do so could not be legally penalized for ignoring this convention. Come election time, however, the prime minister's party might not fare so well in an unrepresented region. This would be an example of a political sanction.

Conventions are important in constitutional law because they serve to modify elements of the written constitution. This is especially true of the institution of responsible government, or the relationship between the executive and legislative branches of both provincial and federal governments. The Constitution Act, 1867, pledges Canada to a constitution 'similar in principle' to that of the United Kingdom. With that simple phrase, the traditions of parliamentary government, particularly the reliance on convention to govern the behaviour of political actors, was imported wholesale into the Canadian constitutional order. The executive power in the written constitution is assigned to the governor general, who serves as the Crown's representative for Canada at the national level. Similar provisions exist for the provinces in the form of the lieutenant governors, who, though appointed by the federal government, represent the Crown proper—not the federal Crown[1]—and therefore enjoy considerable autonomy with respect to Ottawa.

On paper these offices appear to be very powerful. However, their occupants are instructed to exercise their authority only on the advice of a cabinet chosen from the elected branch. Thus, in practice, representatives of the Crown understand such advice amounts to an order or instruction. The selection of the advisory cabinet is also a matter of convention: the role of providing advice to the Crown goes to the group or party most likely to enjoy the confidence of the legislative chamber. Even though none of these practices is clearly stipulated by the written constitution, they have enormous import for the practice of Canadian federalism.

Because the cabinet secures its legitimacy by holding the confidence of the elected house, it is able to implement its programs and policies quite efficiently. This is particularly true when the advisers come from a party that has the majority of seats in the legislature and through strong party discipline can expect to maintain majority support. Under these circumstances the executive becomes extraordinarily free to direct the state and government policy in a direction commensurate with its goals. Since this is true for all governments in the Canadian system, it is executives, not legislatures, that have the greatest say in what the public sector does. Not coincidentally, if there are coordination problems between governments, the executives of each order become the main conduits for their resolution. In short, the responsible government model is the primary reason why executive federalism has become the dominant mode of intergovernmental interaction and accommodation in Canada. In this case the unwritten elements of the constitution may have as much influence on the shape and nature of the federal system as the written elements. This arrangement stands in contrast to the standard account of federal constitutionalism.

The written components of Canada's constitution still have some role to play, of course. Probably the most familiar of those components are what is often referred to as entrenched constitutional law, beginning with the Constitution Act, 1867, and its successor, the Constitution Act, 1982. Of the less-well-known pieces of Canada's entrenched constitutional law, some predate Confederation (e.g., orders from the imperial Crown and laws of the imperial parliament such as the Royal Proclamation, 1763, or the Act of Union) and others were ratified after as amendments (e.g., the various Terms of Union under which individual provinces entered the Union, the Statute of Westminster, 1931, and the Bill of Rights, 1960).

A second category of written constitutional law consists of ordinary statutes. These pieces of legislation deal with matters such as the electoral franchise, the creation of courts, and even human rights standards. Theoretically these elements of the constitution are the most malleable, since they can be replaced by a simple act of the legislature that created them. Together, these statutes make up a significant portion of what we might refer to as constitutional law. Some are recognized as a part of the written constitution (by section 52 of the Constitution Act, 1982) and others have such a status simply by the nature of their subject matter.

For the purposes of this chapter our focus will be on entrenched constitutional law, in particular the Constitution Acts of 1867 and 1982. It is entrenched law that is most formally relevant to the organization of the federal system. Conventions and ordinary statutes may play a critical role in the operation of the federal system, but they do not directly affect the apportioning of actual legal jurisdiction (and hence resources). Moreover, entrenched constitutional law also is responsible for some of the formal institutions of the federation, including the Senate and the constitutional amending formula.

Pre-Confederation Documents

Canada's constitutional history closely reflects its status as a colony in the British Empire. Both the 1867 and 1982 Acts were simple statutes of the United Kingdom's parliament. Those acts are still in operation today, but since their patriation in 1982 have become wholly Canadian documents. Other imperial statutes and documents are no longer in effect, but in their time gave critical direction to the nature and substance of the present Canadian constitution. The most important of those documents are discussed below.

The earliest Canadian constitutional document is generally recognized to be the Royal Proclamation, 1763, which today is commonly cited as the first document to recognize the rights of Canada's Aboriginal peoples. In addition to pledging the protection of the Crown to the Aboriginal people in their dealings with Europeans, the proclamation imposed British law over the former territory of New France, abolishing the practice of the French civil law in the new colony of 'Quebec'—an area roughly consisting of the French-settled areas along the St Lawrence River. The proclamation also provided for a representative assembly, although no such body ever had the opportunity to meet.

Nine years later, the Quebec Act, 1774, expanded 'Quebec' to include much of what was later to be the province of Ontario. Importantly, it also restored the practice of the French civil law, at least until such time as the colony itself should choose to discontinue it, and provided freedom of worship for Roman Catholics in the colony. One other significant respect in which the Quebec Act differed from the 1763 document was that it failed to provide for an elected assembly, instead creating an appointed legislative council to advise the governor—a precursor to modern responsible government without the democratic foundation of an elected legislature.

The most immediate constitutional consequence of the American Revolution for Canada was the adoption of the Constitutional Act, 1791. The numerous Loyalists who repaired to the Maritimes and the colony of Quebec had bristled at some of the restrictions inherent in the governance structures provided by the Quebec Act, particularly the institution of an appointed council; the American dissenters were loyal to the Crown, but had become accustomed to electing a representative assembly and exercising some degree of control over their own community's affairs. The new act divided the colony of Quebec into Upper and Lower Canada and provided for elected assemblies in each of these colonies.

After the rebellions of the 1830s, Lord Durham was sent to British North America to assess the state of the colonies. His famous report advised the adoption of responsible government and the reunification of Upper and Lower Canada in order to integrate and eventually assimilate the French-speaking population into the now larger English-speaking population. These recommendations were institutionalized by the Act of Union, 1840, which—motivated by the need to give greater self-governing powers to the colonies—provided for a representative assembly. With continued pressure for greater self-government from the colonists themselves, responsible government was achieved within a decade.

As we have noted before, responsible government is central to the way that Canadian federalism has evolved. In January 1848 Nova Scotia became the first colony to dismiss its legislative council for failing to maintain the confidence of the elected assembly. Two other colonies followed suit within the same year: United Canada in March and New Brunswick in December (Smith, 1999). The achievement of responsible government did not come from a change in the written constitutional law, but from a change in the way that colonial governors interpreted their powers under the conventions of responsible government. While colonial law still gave the governor the ultimate legal power, the evolution of responsible government left the provision of advice to the governor in the hands of a delegation that held the confidence of the elected assembly.

CONFEDERATION AND THE BRITISH NORTH AMERICA ACT, 1867

The British North America (BNA) Act (renamed the Constitution Act, 1867, in 1982) brought federalism to Canada. It united some (but not all) of the colonies of British North America, laid out a federal constitutional framework assigning different powers of legislation to the federal and provincial orders, and outlined the basic institutions of parliament. Among the latter was the Senate of Canada, an institution intended to serve as a forum for the representation of regional interests at the national level.

From the viewpoint of intergovernmental relations, an important feature of the BNA Act was its pledge that Canada would have a constitution 'similar in principle to that of the United Kingdom'. This simple phrase transferred to the new Dominion government the majority of conventions and traditions of parliamentary government already in practice in the colonies. With those traditions came a logic that led to the eventual dominance of executives in both the national and provincial orders of government. It was this early pledge of British-style parliamentarism, in preference to congressional/presidential or other forms of government, which created the structures that ensure executive dominance. Executive federalism, with all its democratic deficiencies, is the result not so much of the choice to implement federalism, as of the commitment to maintain a dominant parliamentary executive.

Nevertheless, perhaps the most significant feature of the BNA Act for intergovernmental relations was the division of powers contained largely in sections 91 and 92. Unlike many other federal constitutions, the BNA Act provides lists of legislative responsibilities for both the federal and provincial levels of government. Most other constitutional federations have enumerated the powers of one level of government and left the remainder or residue to the other. This was the American practice, later emulated by the Australians, who rejected the Canadian form. Still, any division of powers has to account for the unforeseen. The American and Australian form presumes to do so by leaving whatever is not enumerated to the states, which as colonies had unitary legislative power—that is to say that all matters open to a legislature could be enacted by that government. The Canadian model did not presume to cover every eventuality, but also sought to give greater clarity to what powers specifically belonged to each of the two orders of government. Thus section 91 of the Constitution Act lists 28 legislative responsibilities for the federal Parliament, including postal service, national defence, the regulation of trade and commerce, and the criminal law. Parliament is also assigned a general power to make laws for the 'peace, order, and good government' of the country. This provision (often referred to as the POGG clause) has been generally understood to afford the federal government the capacity to legislate in areas beyond the 28 powers enumerated in section 91, including areas not otherwise identified by the constitution. In practice, as we will see in Chapter 5, this capacity has been interpreted much less expansively than the generality of the power involved would seem to suggest. Section 92 lists 16 matters in which the power to legislate is reserved for the provinces, among them municipalities, property and civil rights, and public lands, as well as the (now substantial) files of health and education.

The original BNA Act also specifies two categories of concurrent legislation, in which both the federal parliament and the provincial legislatures are entitled to act. Immigration and agriculture are recognized as areas of joint jurisdiction with the proviso that federal legislation will be paramount in the event of conflict. This 'paramountcy' rule ensures that concurrent jurisdiction does not result in deadlock, with different governments' laws cancelling one another out. Finally, the power to write criminal law is assigned to the federal government (hence the nationally uniform Criminal Code), but the enforcement of that law is left to the provinces. Several other features of the BNA Act are also relevant to the form and substance of the federal system, among them the clauses establishing the Senate, providing for the eventual creation of what would become the federal courts, including the Supreme Court of Canada, and making the federal executive responsible for the appointment of the members of all superior courts in the provinces.

The Character of the BNA Act

Scholars generally agree that the Confederation agreement was intended to create a strong national government with relatively weak provincial counterparts. Three provisions are commonly cited in support of this belief. The scope of federal powers, including the seemingly wide reserve powers provided under the POGG clause, is usually seen as the strongest evidence for centralist intent. The Fathers of Confederation believed that they had remedied the singular weakness of the American federation by granting the reserve powers through POGG to the national (hence unifying) government rather than the governments of the various subunits. At the time of Confederation the United States was still reeling from the Civil War—a disaster that many people believed could have been avoided if the American federation had not been so tilted towards the autonomy of the states. For the Canadians, secession of one or more subunits was conceivable only in a system as decentralized as the American one. By granting the residual power to the national government, the Fathers thought they had eliminated the very premise on which the idea of secession had been conceived.

The national parliament's powers of reservation and disallowance have also been seen as evidence of centralist intent. In effect, both of these powers amounted to vetoes over provincial legislation. Reservation allowed the federally appointed lieutenant governor of any province to withhold royal assent from legislation passed by that province until the act had been reviewed and approved by the federal executive. Disallowance went even further, permitting the federal parliament to nullify provincial legislation outright even after royal assent had been granted. Reminiscent of the restrictions under which the British North American colonies had operated as part of the British Empire, these provisions implied a hierarchy among Canadian governments that was antithetical to most formulations of federalism. The powers of reservation and disallowance may be taken as proof that some Fathers of Confederation were less than willing to give the provinces true autonomy. Whereas American federalism somewhat reluctantly turned power over to a central government, the Canadian version seemed to take the Empire as its model. One could argue that some oversight was necessary to ensure that provincial legislatures stayed within their constitutional jurisdiction. By the mid-1880s, however, Ottawa recognized that its ability to exercise its oversight power was limited. For the federal government to overrule a decision of a duly elected legislature was to risk its own political future. Moreover, supervising provincial legislatures was becoming an administrative burden for the federal parliament. The creation of the Supreme Court and its assumption of the power of judicial review over questions of constitutional jurisdiction can be traced to the political difficulties that Ottawa faced in its efforts to maintain a kind of colonial control over the provinces (Smith, 1983).

Finally, the matters assigned to the provinces were assumed to be less important than those assigned to the Parliament of Canada. Federal specialists often quote John A. Macdonald's claim that the Confederation settlement had 'given the General Legislature all the great subjects of legislation' and 'expressly declared that all subjects of general interest not distinctly and exclusively conferred upon the local governments and local legislatures, [should] be conferred upon the General Government and Legislature'; in so doing, he said, 'we have . . . avoided that great source of weakness which has been the cause of the disruption of the United States'—namely, the states' rights problem (Waite, 1963). Today many of the matters assigned to provincial legislatures—public health, education, municipal affairs—have become central to the mission of the modern state, but at the time of Confederation they were genuinely minor concerns, involving services that were rarely provided by government and never on a large scale. That such matters would become so important was beyond the foresight of Confederation's drafters.

CONSTITUTIONAL CHANGE

Many of the constitutional changes that, over time, increased the status of the provinces were the result of judicial interpretation. Those developments will be considered in detail in the next chapter. Here we will simply note that judicial review may be considered a mechanism for informal or incremental constitutional change. In giving practical meaning to the provisions of a constitution, courts may effectively thwart its authors' intentions, or at the very least, change the expectations of governments and citizens about 'who should do what' in a federation. There are certainly many who would argue that judicial interpretation has fundamentally altered the Canadian constitution, taking it in directions that the Fathers never intended. At the very least, the courts played a part in slowly tipping important jurisdictional questions to the provinces (Laskin, 1947; Scott, 1951; Stevenson, 1989). Because judicial review proceeds slowly, little by little, the changes it brings about often go largely unnoticed. Formal amendment procedures generally command much more public attention and debate, sometimes even requiring public consent via referendum (as was the case in 1992).

There are times when formal constitutional change is necessary. In Canada such change has often been the product of the national government's efforts to expand its responsibilities or recover jurisdictional space lost as a result of judicial review. In the 1930s, for example, when the federal government was seeking to introduce various welfare-state programs, the JCPC objected, arguing that parliament lacked the jurisdiction to implement programs to help the unemployed. In order to gain that jurisdiction it was necessary for the federal government to initiate an actual change to the constitution rather than just a change to an understanding of the constitution's provisions.

Most federal constitutions specify the formula to be used for any future amendment, but no such provision was included in Canada's 1867 constitution. Although Macdonald and others were confident that they had in fact anticipated every potential problem, this was not the reason behind the omission. Rather, the Fathers had simply failed to agree on a formula—and the fact that the power to amend the BNA Act remained with the imperial parliament allowed them to set the issue aside for later consideration. Thus any government seeking a specific constitutional change first had to address the lack of an amending formula.

Changes made prior to the 1930s had focused mainly on central government institutions and the creation or admission of new provinces. They had done little or nothing to directly change the power of the provinces or to increase the power of the national government vis-à-vis the provinces. Since Canada's constitution was effectively an act of the Imperial Parliament at Westminster, passed at the request of the colonies, any changes would have to follow the same pattern. This practice was mandated by the Statute of Westminster, 1931, under which the British parliament was permitted to make laws for former colonies only at the latter's request. What would constitute a legitimate request from Canada, however, was not clear. A simple request from the national parliament would have sufficed if Canada had had a unitary system of government. But this was not the case. Because its system was federal, any attempt at constitutional change would have to take the provinces into account, particularly where the substance of the change would affect provincial powers.

It was only in the 1930s, when the need for new powers to address the consequences of the Great Depression became urgent, that the challenge of altering the division of powers in sections 91 and 92 was taken up. Ultimately the federal government secured the unanimous agreement of the provinces to a number of changes, which it was then able to present to the British parliament with a high degree of legitimacy. The need for provincial consent in such cases was never formalized. However, subsequent changes granting the federal parliament special legislative powers (for unemployment insurance in 1940, old age pensions in 1951, and supplementary benefits to old age pensions in 1963) all proceeded only with the unanimous approval of the provinces.

According to James Hurley (1996), by the time Ottawa and nine of the ten provinces finally agreed to a domestic amending formula in 1982, at least 13 earlier efforts to that end had failed. The main points of dispute in those negotiations involved the precise requirements for determining provincial consent to fundamental constitutional change. The question of Quebec's special status as the only majority French-speaking province aside, the wide variations in size and population among the provinces made a wholly majoritarian amending formula unsuitable, but concessions for the older and smaller provinces also seemed unfair, given the growth of the western provinces since Confederation. Proposals varied among the following: (1) unanimity, which would have recognized a sort of provincial equality; (2) a weighted majority giving some consideration to population, but also recognizing the need to provide some protection to the smaller provinces; and (3) mechanisms that would recognize the binational nature of the country by giving some form of veto to Quebec. Various proposals tried to accommodate the provinces' differing interests, but none seemed likely to secure sufficient agreement.

The difficulty of finding an acceptable amending formula was evident in the process that eventually led to the adoption of the Constitution Act of 1982. After an initial threat to unilaterally submit changes to Westminster for approval, the federal government gave in to provincial pressure (and a Supreme Court ruling in the Patriation Reference) and sought 'substantial provincial consent' for its proposal, which in addition to giving complete control over future change to Canadian governments alone, would also entrench a bill of rights. The final deal had the consent of all provinces except Quebec, which challenged the constitutionality of the document in the Supreme Court. The province argued that the Court's own standard of 'substantial provincial consent' and Quebec's historical place in confederation entitled it to a veto over constitutional change. The Court did not agree and the amendment plan proceeded, leading to the patriation of a new constitution that was accepted by every province except Quebec.

The 1982 Amending Formulae and Beyond

The Constitution Act, 1982, patriated the constitutional amendment process so that Canada would no longer depend on the UK for alterations to its fundamental law. The long-standing problem of provincial unanimity was resolved with an amending formula under which unanimity is required only for the most important changes to the constitution. In effect, the 1982 formula is really five separate formulae. The simplest changes are covered in sections 44 and 45, which deal with changes to the federal legislature or executive and the provincial constitutions respectively. Such changes can be made by the relevant legislature acting alone. A slightly more complicated procedure is contemplated in section 43. Changes affecting one or more, but not all, provinces, or language rights within any of the provinces, require the approval of the provinces concerned and the federal government only. Such changes have been relatively straightforward since 1982 and account for the bulk of constitutional changes realized since 1982. In 1993, for instance, the terms of union for Prince Edward Island were changed to remove the requirement for subsidized ferry service to the province after the construction of the Confederation Bridge provided a fixed link to the mainland. Similarly, in 1997 and 1998 the provisions for denominational schools in Quebec and Newfoundland were changed using this procedure.

The two remaining formulae are reserved for more significant constitutional changes. The so-called general amending formula in section 38 would be required in cases involving subjects such as the division of powers, the electoral system, some changes to the Supreme Court, the addition of new provinces or transformation of territories into provinces, and some elements of Senate and House of Commons representation. The latter three categories of change are singled out in section 42 of the constitution as requiring the use of the general amending formula. While such changes are alterations to the structure of federal institutions alone and therefore would seem to qualify for coverage under section 44, those kinds of changes invoke important provincial interests that can be protected by provincial participation in their change. The general formula allows a change to be made if the federal parliament and the legislatures of at least seven provinces representing, in aggregate, more than half of the national population agree. The formula does not offer a veto to any one province, but in effect it does allow regional groupings of provinces (western and Atlantic) to block change as well as the most populous provinces as their support is mathematically required for the amendment hurdles to be reached. Finally, section 41 identifies a number of constitutional changes that would require the unanimous consent of the provinces, including any alteration in the role of the Crown; any reduction in the number of a province's MPs that would leave it with fewer representatives in the House than in the Senate; and changes in the composition of the Supreme Court or the constitutional status of the two official languages, as well as alterations to the amending procedures themselves.

Changes in the Division of Powers

The 1982 constitution did not substantially change the division of legislative powers. In what was mainly a concession to the resource-rich western provinces, section 92A was added to the constitution, conferring on the provincial legislatures the right to develop and regulate non-renewable natural resources and to raise revenues from their extraction through any means or mode of taxation. This section went some way towards resolving the conflicts with Ottawa that arose over the regulation and pricing of non-renewable natural resources following the federal government's adoption of the National Energy Program in 1980.

The amending formula aside, perhaps the most significant aspect of the 1982 constitutional changes for federalism was the fact that the Charter of Rights and Freedoms applied equally to the federal and provincial legislatures and governments. F.L. Morton argued that the Charter had the potential to homogenize provincial policies by applying universal rights standards to areas where the provinces may have significant differences in their policies (Russell, 1983; Morton, 1995). It seems fairly clear that this was what Prime Minister Trudeau intended, believing as he did in the superiority of universal liberal guarantees like those in the Charter over the particular preferences of individual groups or provinces (Clarkson and McCall, 1990). It has even been suggested that the Charter was intended to give the national government the symbolic resources to compete with the provinces for the loyalty of citizens. According to this theory, by creating a generation of 'Charter Canadians', aware of their universal rights and equipped with the legal mechanisms to protect those rights against provincial majorities, Trudeau hoped that the Charter might lead citizens to transfer their psychological attachments from their provincial communities to a national identity centred around rights. The validity of this theory is still hotly debated by constitutional analysts, but provincial legislatures are certainly aware that the laws they make must be consistent with the protections provided by the Charter (Cairns, 1992; Laforest, 1995). In that way the Charter is no less effective a limit on legislative activity than is the division of powers.

Attempted Amendments after 1982

Because Quebec had refused to accept the 1982 constitution, securing its agreement became a priority for the federal government of Brian Mulroney, elected in 1984. Three years later, after the Liberal government of Robert Bourassa had replaced the PQ in Quebec City, Mulroney succeeded in persuading all ten provincial premiers to sign the Meech Lake Accord: a set of constitutional amendments that met Quebec's minimum demands, including increased legislative power for all the provinces regarding immigration and a greater role for all provinces in the appointment of senators and Supreme Court justices. In addition, the Accord promised Quebec a veto over future constitutional change and, most controversially, recognition as a distinct society in a preamble to the constitution.

The nature of these terms (particularly the veto, which was effectively a change to the amending formula and a guarantee of three seats on the Supreme Court for Quebec) meant that adoption of the Accord would require unanimous consent as outlined in section 41 of the Constitution Act, 1982: not only the federal parliament but all provincial legislatures would have to pass resolutions adopting the constitutional change. Furthermore, once a resolution to amend the constitution has been passed by one legislature, section 39 imposes a time limit of three years for all the other legislatures to pass their own resolutions. The first province to adopt the Meech Lake Accord was Quebec, in June 1987. Several other provinces soon followed suit. Manitoba and Newfoundland, however, changed governments before their legislatures had a chance to vote on the proposed changes, and the new governments decided to reopen the issue for debate. Despite last-minute efforts to salvage the Accord, it failed to secure the necessary legislative support and thus expired in June 1990.

After the Meech Lake failure there was still substantial support in Quebec for sovereignty or at the very least greater autonomy within the federation. Bourassa's Liberals bought time by passing a law committing the government to either holding a referendum on sovereignty within two years or bringing to a referendum new proposals for constitutional reform to meet Quebec's traditional demands. This led to a second round of constitutional negotiations that culminated in the Charlottetown Accord, reached in August 1992 and put to a Canada-wide referendum in October of that year.

The architects of the Charlottetown agreement were keenly aware that the Meech Lake process had been deservedly criticized as elite-dominated and more focused on the concerns of governments than of citizens. The Charlottetown process consequently was much more inclusive, and although it offered Quebec many of the same changes proposed in the Meech Lake Accord, it added considerably more to the reform package. If Meech Lake was the 'Quebec round' of constitutional reform, aimed at making Quebec a full partner in the post-1982 constitution, Charlottetown was to be the 'Canada round', meeting Quebec's demands but also taking into account demands from other parts of Canadian society: thus the Accord included proposals for Senate reform, Aboriginal self-government, and even changes to the House of Commons. Governments hoped that the referendum would secure a majority in each province and thus fulfil the unanimity requirement. But in the end only four provinces voted to accept the Accord, one of them—Ontario—by the slimmest of margins. Thus the second round of mega-constitutional change also ended in failure (Russell, 2004).

POST-CHARLOTTETOWN CONSTITUTIONAL POLITICS

The Federal Spending Power

In the years since Charlottetown, governments have been wary of comprehensive constitutional change. Only small changes have been made to the constitution since 1992, almost all of them on the initiative of the provinces directly concerned. Although Stephen Harper relaunched the debate over Senate reform soon after his election in 2006, no government since 1992 has proposed even beginning discussions of constitutional amendment. In fact, Prime Minister Harper made it clear that it was in order to avoid any formal constitutional change that his government chose to seek incremental reforms to the Senate rather than a Charlottetown-style overhaul (Harper, 2006). In short, the focus of intergovernmental relations shifted away from the constitution after 1992. Since that time, much of the intergovernmental activity in Canada has been centred on constraining the use of the federal spending power.

New students of intergovernmental relations in Canada may be forgiven if they are puzzled to find that the list of federal powers in section 91 of the constitution makes no reference to 'spending power'. According to Peter Hogg (2005), the federal spending power is not explicit; rather, it is *inferred* from the constitutional power granted to the federal parliament to raise revenue by whatever means it chooses (in the language of the constitution, by 'any mode or system of taxation'). For Hogg, and for generations of free-spending federal governments, the corollary of the revenue power is the power to spend the revenue collected wherever the federal government wishes—regardless of legislative jurisdiction. When provinces (particularly Quebec) protest that the power to raise revenue does not imply a power to spend, supporters of the spending power reply that Ottawa may condition provincial priorities, but ultimately the provinces are free to refuse the money. The provinces retain their autonomy because they are not truly compelled to participate in the program.

The fiscal reality of Canadian federalism, as other chapters explain in detail, is that the provinces do not have revenue-raising capacities commensurate with their legislative obligations. Hence their freedom to choose is not always as great as defenders of the spending power suggest. The spending power gives the federal government a way to exploit the fiscal-capacity gap. Some of the most expensive public services provided to Canadians—education, welfare, health care—are the responsibility of provincial governments. Yet the provincial taxation power is more limited than that of the federal parliament. In essence the provinces are required to share the most important revenue sources—income and consumption taxes—with the federal government. The result has been that much of what gets done by the provinces, especially the poorer provinces, is paid for from federal revenues.[2] Although today such funding comes with many fewer conditions than it did in the past, some of it still has at least nominal strings attached. The federal government has routinely seen fit to use the power of its purse to promote its goals for the country. Provinces have often been offered funding for new programs on the condition that they meet certain federal standards. Generally, once programs are established for shared funding they become regularized and the provinces are given considerable latitude to implement policy as they see fit. But that does not mean that provinces can rely on Ottawa to uphold its commitments indefinitely.

During the fiscally challenging 1990s, when the federal government needed to balance its books, it did so in part by reducing its transfers to the provinces. As we will see in Chapter 10, on the 'social union', the federal cuts forced the provinces to rationalize some parts of their health care systems, reduce social benefits, and raise university tuitions in order to keep their own books in order. The cutback era demonstrated that federal spending power can mean effective control over matters of provincial jurisdiction. However, the Supreme Court has ruled that it is not strictly an invasion of provincial responsibilities, since the provinces have always been free to reject the funds (*Reference Re: Canada Assistance Plan*, 1991). In response to this uncertainty, the provinces demanded that the federal government establish clearer rules for the use of the federal spending power in the future.

Without explicitly engaging the constitutional file, the two orders of government negotiated a protocol for new social programs initiated by Ottawa. The Social Union Framework Agreement (SUFA) was designed to give the provinces more input into federal spending. An unusual document, SUFA is more than a garden-variety intergovernmental agreement, but it does not amount to a constitutional restriction on the activity of either order of government. The overall strategy was to address some of the outstanding intergovernmental issues raised in the constitutional battles of the late 1980s and early 1990s without actually changing the constitution. Governments have not been especially faithful to the terms of the agreement—perhaps not surprising, given the absence of any legal obligation—and Quebec never fully committed to the project. Consequently, SUFA has not been a resounding success (Noël et al., 2003). The attempt to deal with the spending power in this quasi-constitutional manner having failed, the provinces in recent years have shifted their attention to bringing provincial revenues more in line with provincial responsibilities by addressing what has become known as the 'fiscal imbalance'. In its 2007 Speech from the Throne, the Harper government promised a new, perhaps constitutional, solution to limit the spending power in the future, but no proposal is presently active.

Constitutional Change Redux

Quebec secession

The most significant changes to Canada's federal constitution were undoubtedly those made in 1982. Those changes were motivated in large part by the threat that without them Quebec might leave the federation. Quebec is not the only province to have reconsidered its commitment to the union; in the early years of Confederation secessionist sentiment was strongest in the Maritime provinces. In modern times, however, threats of secession have come almost exclusively from Quebec.

The Parti Québécois has long been committed to independence for Quebec. Since the federal constitution provides no mechanism for a province to secede, the PQ has been obliged to seek ways of showing that popular support for independence is sufficient to justify initiating such a process. In 1980 the PQ government held a referendum on a proposal for a sort of soft independence that they called 'sovereignty association', which would have kept some ties to Canada, but essentially was intended to put the province on the road to sovereign nationhood. That proposal was rejected by roughly 60 per cent of the voters. Nevertheless, during the campaign leading up to the referendum Prime Minister Trudeau pledged that a 'No' vote in the referendum would not be a vote for the status quo. In effect, Trudeau offered Quebecers—and all Canadians—a new constitution if the referendum failed.

The relative strength of the movement for independence thus presented not just a threat but also an opportunity to revisit some of the basic terms of Canada's constitutional structure. Trudeau was able to use the threat of secession to persuade other provinces that the basic constitutional bargain needed updating, and he capitalized on popular support for other possible changes—notably the inclusion of a bill of rights—to keep the premiers at the negotiating table. The eventual product of that process, the Constitution Act, 1982, as we have seen, failed to satisfy the Quebec legislature, and the result was another decade of efforts to blunt the force of arguments for separation and bring Quebec into the constitution.

That the Charlottetown Accord was put to a nationwide referendum was also motivated by the continuing threat of Quebec secession. As we noted above, Quebec premier Robert Bourassa had committed his government to holding another referendum, either on secession or on a new constitutional proposal, after the failure of the Meech Lake Accord. Since Quebec was going to vote on the proposed changes, other provinces wanted a similar opportunity. When the Charlottetown Accord was rejected, the PQ was returned to power with the promise that it would once again take the question of Quebec's relationship with Canada to the Quebec electorate. It held a referendum in 1995 on a vague proposal for a new relationship with the rest of Canada; once again the goal might not necessarily have been complete independence, but there was no doubt that the future of the Canadian state was at stake. Support for the secessionist proposal was much greater in 1995 than it had been in 1980, falling just short of a majority.

The close result obliged the Liberal government of Jean Chrétien to consider new strategies. 'Plan A' was to appease Quebec by meeting at least some of its outstanding constitutional demands and thereby demonstrating that federalism could work. 'Plan B' was to prepare for contesting a future sovereignty vote. One element of the Plan B strategy was to clarify the legal implications of a move towards secession by Quebec or any other province. To this end the federal government asked the Supreme Court of Canada for its opinion on whether Quebec had the right, under Canadian constitutional law or international law, to secede from the federation. In its 1998 decision, *Reference Re: The Secession of Quebec*, the Court essentially replied that no province had the right to unilateral secession. At the same time, however, it suggested that if a province could demonstrate that secession was in fact the democratic will of the people, then the rest of the federation would have a moral obligation to negotiate such an arrangement in good faith (1998; Schneiderman, 1999). The Court further suggested that such a will could be demonstrated by securing a 'clear majority' of voters in support of a 'clear question' in a referendum—though as Gagnon and Erk (2002: 326) note, in failing to specify what might constitute a 'clear question' or a 'clear majority', the decision included 'a fair degree of studied ambiguity'. Two years after the Court's ruling, in 2002, the federal Parliament passed the Clarity Act, which provided for Parliament to have a role in determining whether a question and result were clear, and setting out the conditions under which the federal government would negotiate the secession of a province from Canada.

Federalists and secessionists alike initially declared the Supreme Court's judgment to represent a victory for their side. Although the latter eventually contested some aspects of the ruling, and in particular the Clarity Act, Plan B tactics have served to define the parameters within which secession by a constituent unit could be considered. Some observers have even suggested that the Reference decision amounts to a constitutional amendment itself. In outlining a process through which a province might secede under terms consistent both with other constitutional principles and with the standards of international law, the Supreme Court made more transparent what had been an extremely murky discourse of competing scenarios for the future, particularly in the years immediately before and after the 1995 referendum (Young, 1999; Choudry and Howse, 2000). Now that the implications of secession are better understood, the prospect of another referendum on secession has in fact receded. Quebec's nationalist parties have stated that a third referendum will not be held until 'winning conditions' are in place—that is, until they can expect a majority of voters to support secession.

The 'regional veto'

Another outstanding constitutional issue since patriation has been the role of the provinces in approving constitutional change. Following the 1982 amendments, Quebec continued to argue that its unique status entitled it to a veto over constitutional change. The parts of the constitution that can only be changed with the unanimous consent of the provinces effectively give every province a veto. The Meech Lake and Charlottetown accords seemed to prove that comprehensive constitutional change would almost always require unanimity from the provinces. But the general amending formula still allows changes to go ahead without the approval of as many as three provinces. In the present amending formula, the only government with the guaranteed power to veto constitutional change is the federal parliament, whose consent is required for all amendments except those to provincial constitutions. As part of its 'Plan A' strategy the Liberal government in Ottawa passed legislation providing for Ottawa to 'lend' its veto to any one of five 'regions'—Quebec, Ontario, British Columbia, the prairie provinces, and the Atlantic provinces—in the event that that region did not consent to a particular amendment. This statute, the Act Respecting Constitutional Amendments, 1996, was one of several non-constitutional measures designed to demonstrate that the federation was in fact flexible enough to accommodate Quebec's needs. The fact that it was not entrenched in the constitution, and could therefore be rescinded by a simple parliamentary majority, might have made it meaningless for Quebec nationalists, but the 'regional veto' did seem to satisfy some segments of the Quebec public.

Quebec as a 'nation'

Appealing to Quebec voters has been no less important for Stephen Harper's Conservative government than for his Liberal predecessors. Lacking a parliamentary majority, and well aware of the national reluctance to reopen the constitution, Harper too has tried to accommodate Quebec without disturbing the constitutional status quo. Thus in the fall of 2006, the Harper government initiated a parliamentary recognition of the Québécois as a nation within Canada. In the spirit of the once controversial distinct society clause, this parliamentary resolution was designed to recognize the differential status of Quebec within Canada. Whether it amounted to a grant of new or different powers for the province is unclear. What the recognition did do was continue the post-Charlottetown tradition of taking reversible action on constitutional questions and avoiding formal amendment.

SUMMARY

This chapter illustrates the importance of constitutional structure to the conduct of intergovernmental relations. The constitution provides governments and citizens with a blueprint for the distribution of power within the federation. That plan is subject to ongoing adjustment, and is not necessarily the best guide to 'who does what', but it does provide a baseline from which governments can work. Constitutional jurisdiction and control of revenue sources are precious assets in any intergovernmental system—bargaining chips that can be used in the negotiating struggles that characterize intergovernmental relations—and they are allotted by the constitution. As we have seen, the constitution itself is also an important subject matter for intergovernmental relations. Constitution-making and Constitution-changing in Canada have almost always been the exclusive preserve of governments. Despite the pressure exerted on governments to open up and consult more widely on constitutional issues, since the failure of the Charlottetown Accord decision-making in that area is once again in the hands of government.

At times it seems as though governments have spent almost as much time discussing the rules of the federalism game as they have spent playing it. The meaning and form of the Canadian federal system are constantly under pressure, contested by different parts of the federation. For William Livingston, as we saw in Chapter 1, the institutions that constitutions establish were simple 'instrumentalities': mere reflections of pre-existing diversities within the federation. Thus when those diversities change, the instrumentalities will be pressured to change as well. A federation that lacks the capacity to change instrumentalities will experience increasing tension as the pressure for recognition of new diversities builds. Canada's federal experience suggests that institutions are not as neutral as Livingston suggested—but that only makes the process of altering them all the more likely to become the focus of the nation's doubts, fears, and jealousies.

That said, the Canadian constitution has proven remarkably durable. It is one of only a few constitutions in the world to have lasted more than a century—and to have survived substantial revision in that time. For all the constitutional self-doubt that Canada has experienced since 1982, the federal system keeps clicking along. Indeed, an important part of Canada's constitutional culture may be the ability to live with some uncertainty or lack of specificity (Thomas, 1997). All this suggests a certain tension between the formal, legalistic characteristics of federalism as a form of government, the more pragmatic model of parliamentary government, and the particular challenges that arise in a multinational society with numerous competing visions of what constitutes the ideal Canadian political community.

Chapter 5

Judicial Review and Dispute Resolution

As the preceding chapter suggests, formal alteration of Canada's constitution is by no means easy. The difficulty of constitutional change is an indication of the difficulty of intergovernmental negotiation—and of the degree to which the federation depends on it to manage tensions and policy-making. The simple fact that eleven governments must agree to any substantive amendment makes change difficult. Throw in the need for public consultation and in some cases popular approval through a referendum and the constitution seems even more resistant to major alteration. The dynamics of negotiation and compromise in intergovernmental relations do not easily lend themselves to the kind of definitive resolution necessary for changing the country's supreme law. Provincial premiers and federal prime ministers alike tend to stake out symbolic positions and points of principle that make compromise all but impossible. Fighting over money for social programs or regional development seems easy by comparison. After all, a dollar can be broken down into pennies and distributed more or less equally. It is not so easy to provide every province or region with an equal share of dignity, or to reconcile completely different visions of the purpose of the federation (Dupré, 1988).

Because the constitution itself cannot easily be adapted to new circumstances, the responsibility for ensuring effective operation of the federal system falls heavily on intergovernmental relations. The main vehicles of intergovernmental relations are negotiations between members of the executive branches of the federal and provincial governments—first ministers, cabinet ministers, and senior bureaucrats—conducted at formal meetings and even in more mundane or ceremonial interactions. Lower-level bureaucrats and officials also work out compromises and approaches that require intergovernmental negotiation, often in the course of delivering programs and services. As a federation, Canada is not unique in having difficulties with constitutional change. Consequently, whether by accident or by design, federations have developed more incremental ways of adjusting their constitutional arrangements without formally amending them. Although the resulting adjustments may not be permanent, the fact that they occupy a middle ground between formal amendment and handshake-style informality of intergovernmental relations may in itself offer certain advantages.

The primary mechanism of incremental change is judicial review. In democracies, the main function of courts is adjudicative: to settle disputes between contending parties. In the simple act of resolving a dispute, a court can give more definitive or authoritative meaning both to a particular legislative provision and to the constitution that governs the law-making process. In other words, dispute resolution itself requires interpretation and elaboration of the meaning of constitutional provisions. Judicial review holds a particular law or government action up to the standard of the constitution and in the event of a conflict may find some or all of that law or action to be unconstitutional. In federations judicial review takes on the added question of appropriate jurisdiction. Legislation and government action can be ruled either *intra* or *ultra vires*—that is, within or outside the constitutional mandate of the order of government enacting the legislation. Judicial review is commonly initiated by governments challenging one or another's apparent invasion of what they see to be their legislative jurisdiction.

Legal challenges to the constitutionality of legislation represent an alternative front in intergovernmental relations (Russell, 1985). This is especially true in Canada because of the reference power that governments have inferred from the constitution. A provincial government may refer questions of constitutionality to its highest court, and the federal government may do the same with the Supreme Court of Canada. Authoritative decisions on the meaning of constitutional powers help to shape the envelope of activities in which governments can legitimately engage. When the constitutionality of a legislature's actions is in doubt, the government whose authority has been questioned can refer the matter to its highest court for a definitive ruling. The reference procedure is thus a kind of fast track for constitutional review.

Governments are not the only bodies that can initiate the judicial review process, however. Citizens accused of breaking a law can contest the constitutionality of that law by arguing that the government responsible for the law lacked the jurisdictional authority to legislate in that area. This approach was famously used against the Duplessis regime in Quebec in what were Canada's earliest civil rights cases (Scott, 1959). Similarly, companies subject to regulation by either order of government may challenge the legislative authority of that government to impose rules or sanctions on them. When the federal government began to play a much more active role in regulating the economy and society in the 1930s, companies whose interests were affected turned to the courts to enforce constitutional limitations on those incursions. In the United States as well as Canada, jurisdictional limitations became the principal constitutional grounds cited in legal arguments against regulation. Such challenges were initially quite successful in hampering government activity. Constitutional amendments and changes in courts and their approaches were necessary before federal governments in both countries were able to play a more active role in social and economic policy.

Judicial review is a unique type of intergovernmental activity because in the courts, unlike other forums of intergovernmental relations, decision-making is based on legal rather than political arguments. That is not to say that there are no politics involved in the decision to take an issue to court, or that judges are wholly apolitical in the way they function. Nonetheless, moving an intergovernmental conflict into court introduces a whole new set of variables and incentives for the governments involved to consider. First, the stakes in judicial review are relatively high. The rulings of Canada's Supreme Court, as authoritative interpretations of the constitution's text, are really no less binding than constitutional amendments. As we noted in Chapter 4, the *Reference Re: The Secession of Quebec* has essentially amended the amending formula of the constitution by clarifying the legal procedures that would be required for a province to leave the federation. Most intergovernmental agreements can easily be altered to adjust to new conditions or concerns. Constitutional interpretation is more lasting, and its results are much more 'zero-sum'. Jurisdiction is a difficult thing to divide. Courts generally prefer to award their decisions to one party or another, so a court's ruling rarely allows for compromise between contending interpretations of the constitution. Jurisdiction in any particular area belongs to one government or the other. In practice governments can and do agree to compromise, but legal interpretation of the constitution does not allow for much sharing. Second, courts are obliged to respect the results of prior cases and in most cases to be bound by such precedents. The doctrine of *stare decisis* obliges courts to abide by the findings of higher courts and the judgments in previous cases. While there is always room for new interpretations of constitutional language and even moderate reinterpretations of earlier cases, judges have a much narrower compass for decision-making than politicians do (Hogg, 2005). The adversarial nature of legal argument and the need to articulate a single interpretation of the constitution, one that fits within the parameters of previous interpretations, limits the creativity of judges when they address constitutional issues. Likewise, governments may think twice before taking a jurisdictional dispute to court. A positive result may mean total victory, but a negative one would mean a total loss or a complete concession of jurisdiction to the other order of government.

As a consequence governments use legal resources strategically. When they feel that they have a strong claim to jurisdiction based on past judicial rulings, they are much more likely to take a bold position and risk taking the dispute to court. A strong legal claim also gives a government a stronger position in negotiations. For example, if the Supreme Court has supported a provincial government's claim to jurisdiction, this is likely to strengthen the province's position in negotiations with Ottawa regarding a shared program that the federal government has previously claimed some legislative authority over. On the other hand, it may be in the strategic interest of a government to take a jurisdictional claim to court even if its chances of winning are slim. In the early part of this decade, several provinces opposed to the federal government's firearms registry challenged the federal authority in that area. Even though most legal experts believed that the claimants' case was weak, the provinces in question had strong constituencies hostile to the legislation—constituencies that the governments in question hoped to appease by exhausting the legal avenues available to frustrate the federal plan. Unsurprisingly, in the *Reference Re: Firearms Act (Canada)*, 1998, the Supreme Court ruled in favour of the federal government under the auspices of its criminal law power. The scope of the powers outlined in the constitution has been fleshed out by government initiatives and the approval or disapproval arrived at through judicial review. Governments, both provincial and federal, have pushed the envelope of their respective powers to the limits they think are acceptable. It has fallen to the courts to tell them when they have exceeded their legitimate jurisdiction or to confirm the appropriateness of their judgment (Smith, 1983). In Canada's early history the task of authoritative interpretation was left to the Judicial Committee of the Privy Council—a colonial holdover composed not of Canadian judges but of Law Lords belonging to the upper house of the British parliament. The JCPC remained Canada's highest court long after Confederation, hearing its last Canadian appeals in 1949. Because it was the JCPC that adjudicated Canada's earliest constitutional challenges, its influence on the interpretation of the constitution's provisions regarding the powers exercised by the provincial and federal legislatures has been profound. In addition, the JCPC affirmed the decentralizing direction in which Canadian federalism was independently evolving, thereby reinforcing what was naturally happening in the federation (Cairns, 1971). Since the end of the JCPC era the final arbiter of Canadian federalism and intergovernmental relations has been the Supreme Court of Canada. By interpreting and defining the scope and limits of legislative powers in the constitution, Canada's courts continue to play an important role in intergovernmental relations.

Increasingly, however, Canada's court system is not the only site of dispute resolution between governments. Mindful of the courts' broad interpretive power and the finality of their decisions regarding the relative powers of provincial and federal legislatures, Canada's governments have become increasingly wary of submitting their disputes for judicial review. For either party in an intergovernmental dispute, the risk of losing is substantial enough that both sides often prefer to avoid legal confrontation if at all possible. Periods of intergovernmental disharmony will still see governments resort to formal challenges in the courts, but in recent years a number of parallel institutions have been developed to resolve disputes. These institutions and their implications for intergovernmental relations are discussed in the latter part of this chapter.

JUDICIAL REVIEW AND THE DIVISION OF POWERS

Among the powers listed in the Constitution Act, 1867, are three that have been substantially influenced by judicial interpretation: (1) the preamble to section 91, the POGG clause, which grants the federal parliament the power to implement laws for the general welfare of the country; (2) the provinces' general power over property and civil rights; and (3) the federal power over trade and commerce. Courts have differed over time in their treatment of these three provisions, but cumulatively their interpretations are in large part responsible for the relatively decentralized nature of Canadian federalism. Legislatures have been conditioned to a significant degree by the permissiveness or lack thereof that courts have shown when testing the limits of their jurisdictional spheres.

The JCPC Era

Critics of the JCPC have generally blamed it for the limited powers of the federal government (Cairns, 1971; Laskin, 1947; Scott, 1989). In retrospect, it was perhaps rash to attribute the direction in which Canadian federalism evolved entirely to the Law Lords. That said, however, the success of the provinces in expanding their jurisdiction in the rulings of the JCPC, often at the expense of the federal government, certainly did not disappoint those who favoured a provincially dominated federal system.

The JCPC made its decentralist influence felt mainly by giving narrow interpretations to the federal POGG and trade and commerce powers and expansive ones to the provincial powers over property and civil rights. In so doing, the JCPC has been seen as contradicting the intentions of the Fathers of Confederation. The Fathers, it is argued, sought to create a more centralized union of the provinces. Why the JCPC would undermine that intention is not quite clear. What can be said is that its findings in favour of the provinces were not out of step with the way the provinces were evolving in the late nineteenth and early twentieth centuries.

Bora Laskin, one of the more eminent constitutional scholars and jurists of the last century, described the POGG clause as 'the favourite whipping boy of constitutional commentators' (Laskin, 1947). Critics such as Laskin pointed to what they thought was the JCPC's misinterpretation of POGG as the primary culprit for Canadian federalism's misdirection. A more generous interpretation would certainly have represented a potential threat to provincial autonomy, since POGG is by nature so general that it could be applied to just about any subject of legislation. It has often been remarked that the challenge of POGG is not to decide what it includes, but to figure out what its limitations are. The JCPC erred on the side of more limitations.

POGG is found in the preamble of section 91, the clause that enumerates the powers of the federal parliament. Theoretically, it could be interpreted in either of two ways. A more centralist view would see POGG as a general grant of power, with the enumerated powers of the federal parliament in section 91 serving simply as examples of how the general power might be exercised. Thus to promote peace, order, and good government, the federal parliament can make laws related to weights and measures, as in section 91(17), or fisheries, as in section 91(12), but is not limited to those headings of legislation alone. In other words, the list of 28 powers accorded the federal parliament in section 91 is not meant to be exhaustive, but merely to illustrate the scope of the federal power. The Privy Council supported this vision of POGG for a short period following Confederation. In a series of decisions the committee endorsed a 'two-compart-ment' theory according to which federal jurisdiction consisted of POGG and the list of matters enumerated in section 91, and provincial jurisdiction consisted of the section 92 matters. Not many years later, POGG came to be understood as one of three compartments in the constitution. In that instance, the section 91 list and the section 92 list made up the main compartments for the federal and provincial legislatures respectively and POGG existed as a third compartment—an extra grant to the federal parliament for use in extraordinary circumstances.[1]

Extraordinary circumstances, in the collective mind of the JCPC, basically came to mean national emergencies. Justifications based on the POGG power were available to the federal government, but only in cases where it could be proven that, for the sake of a nation-wide crisis, provincial autonomy had to be overridden. The JCPC's first opportunity to define the emergency power came with *In Re: Board of Commerce Act*, 1922, in which the Lords did not support the broad powers incorporated in the federal anti-profiteering legislation before them, but hinted that a more dire form of extraordinary circumstances might actually qualify for a POGG justification. A year later, in *Fort Frances Pulp & Power Co. v. Manitoba Free Press* (1923), they found such a situation. However, the JCPC narrowed the scope of emergency two years later in *Toronto Electric Commissioners v. Snider* (1925), which critics would later ridicule for justifying an earlier decision (in *Russell v. the Queen*, 1882, which imposed a temperance regime) on the grounds that drunkenness had reached 'emergency' proportions in the Dominion.

The JCPC briefly indicated that potential justification for federal legislation under POGG outside of emergencies might exist in *Re: Regulation and Control of Aeronautics in Canada* (1932). The Committee upheld legislation creating a national regime for the control of air travel and safety under section 132—the so-called Empire treaties clause. The real reason for seeking such control was that the federal government needed it in order to fulfil the terms of an international treaty. But the Committee hinted that a subject like aeronautics might also be considered a matter of national interest that could be handled under the POGG power. The reference *Re: Regulation and Control of Radio Communication in Canada*, A.C. 304 (1932) gave similar hope to centralists.

In that case a treaty implementation power was accorded to parliament on the basis of a national interest alone. The apparent potential for increased central government activity in the name of the national interest encouraged the govern-ment of R.B. Bennett to commit Canada to uphold international standards on a number of matters such as labour regulation in the hope of adding them to the list of policy areas under federal jurisdiction (Saywell, 2002). The POGG power did not fare well, however, when these efforts were constitutionally tested. With respect to the 'Bennett New Deal' legislation, designed to help Canadians cope with the dire economic and social conditions of the Great Depression, the JCPC refused to recognize any emergency justification.[2] It also rejected the federal government's argument that unemployment insurance was a matter of national concern (*Employment and Social Insurance Reference*, 1937). Establishing that power would ultimately require a constitutional amendment.

The JCPC's hostility to expansive readings of federal powers spurred an effort by the federal government to amend the constitution and encouraged demands for reform of a system in which the final court of appeal for Canadians was the Privy Council of Great Britain. Furthermore, that the federal government should have to prove the existence of an emergency before it could exercise the POGG powers made a mockery of the centralists' belief that POGG was a comprehensive residual power. Despite its rejection of the Bennett New Deal legislation, in its last days as Canada's court the JCPC changed course a little and expanded the POGG category to include matters of national concern or dimensions. One of the last major cases to be heard by the JCPC opened up a space for POGG that did not depend on the existence of an emergency. In *Attorney General of Ontario v. Canada Temperance Federation* (1946) the JCPC refuted much of its earlier POGG jurisprudence and created a national concern 'branch' or justification (in addition to an emergency branch) for POGG.

Overall, however, the JCPC was much more generous in its interpretation of provincial powers. Its rulings significantly expanded the scope of the provinces' property and civil rights power, usually at the expense of the federal power over trade and commerce. In *Citizens Insurance Co. v. Parsons* (1881), the JCPC found that the regulation of fire insurance was not within the scope of the federal trade and commerce power, but rather a provincial matter under the heading of property and civil rights. It even went so far as to suggest that the federal power over trade and commerce did not include general commercial relations within the provinces and was effectively limited to the regulation of trade with other nations, interprovincial trade, and 'the general regulation of trade affecting the whole Dominion' (*Citizens Insurance Co. v. Parsons*, 1881). A quarter-century later, in *Attorney General of Canada v. Attorney General of Alberta* (1916), the federal power with respect to trade was even more narrowly interpreted as 'essentially an auxiliary power incapable of serving on its own as a primary source of legislative capacity'. A similar approach was used to place the power over matters such as industrial disputes in the property and civil rights category. By the end of the JCPC era the scope of provincial jurisdiction was much broader than the founders seem to have envisioned, while the federal government faced very strong limitations on its presumed powers under the general POGG power.

All of this happened in a period when the scope of government activity was increasing and the ambitions of the federal government in particular were very broad. The federal government has recognized from a very early stage that its range of activity is limited by restrictive interpretations of the constitution. Thus the system of intergovernmental relations that exists today is in important respects a consequence of the JCPC's narrow interpretation of some federal powers. Since the federal government was not allowed free rein to intervene in the economy, it was unable to create employment and social programs on a broad scale, as its American counterpart did. Instead, Ottawa was compelled to co-operate and negotiate with the provinces.

The Supreme Court Era

The federal parliament's luck seemed to change in 1949, when the Supreme Court of Canada replaced the JCPC as the final arbiter of disputes for the federation. The Supreme Court quickly expanded the notion of national concern first suggested in the *Canada Temperance* case and began to define a broader scope for the POGG power. Added to the POGG list of matters under federal control were aeronautics (in *Johannesson v. West St. Paul*, 1952), atomic energy (in *Pronto Uranium Mines, Ltd. v. O.L.R.B.*, 1956), a national capital region (in *Munro v. National Capital Commission*, 1966), and seabed natural resources (in *Re: Offshore Mineral Rights of B.C.*, 1967). Nevertheless, the Court was moderate in its approach. Although it put an end to the trend towards aggressive decentralization, it did not attempt to reverse direction and move towards centralization, as many legal commentators had hoped that a wholly domestic court would (Laskin, 1951).

This difference in approach can be attributed in part to the nature of the questions that the Supreme Court has been asked to rule on. For example, the JCPC was never asked to rule on the practice known as delegation, in which one order of government lends its legislative power to another—either because it lacks the interest or capacity to deal with the matter in question, or because the other order makes it an offer it cannot refuse. This practice of delegating power could potentially allow both orders of government to use negotiated agreements to skirt the constitutional division of powers. Thus even though, as we have seen, incremental change through bilateral and multilateral agreements is in some ways the trademark of Canadian federalism, the Supreme Court has not been an unalloyed booster of such arrangements. The Court forbade a cooperative scheme put together by the Nova Scotia and federal governments in the so-called interdelegation case of 1951 (*Attorney General of Nova Scotia v. Attorney General of Canada*, 1951), but it did permit a slightly different form of delegation to pass a year later. In *PEI Potato Marketing Board v. H.B. Willis* (1952), the federal parliament was permitted to delegate responsibility to an administrative board created by the provincial legislature, without having to transfer any law-making power to the legislature itself.

Andre Bzdera (1993) argues that an institution appointed by the federal government and based in Ottawa (Supreme Court justices are obliged to live in the National Capital Region during their appointment) is likely to be biased in favour of the national government. On the whole, however, commentators generally describe the Supreme Court's approach to the division of powers as balanced (Hogg, 1979; Baier 2002, 2008). Conflicting reasoning in some of the Supreme Court's rulings on the division of powers suggests that the balance has sometimes required significant contortions on the part of Supreme Court justices. The *Reference Re: Anti-Inflation Act*, which tested the constitutionality of federal wage- and price-control legislation passed in 1976, offers an almost painful example of the Court's efforts to avoid favouring one order of government over the other (Russell, 1977). It also suggests how the different perspectives represented by individual members of the Court can sometimes have the effect of cancelling each other out. The federal government had hoped for a strong endorsement of its policies from a court led by a chief justice who was a noted centralist, but what it got was a welter of opinions and dissents that scarcely managed to uphold the act. A bare majority on the Court endorsed the legislation on the grounds that rampant inflation constituted a national emergency. Part of the reason the Court had been reluctant to accept 'national concern' arguments in support of POGG in the past had always been the seemingly potential limitlessness of such reasoning. If routine matters could be promoted to the status of 'national concern', expansionist central governments would be encouraged to define any number of areas in those terms. The 'national emergency' doctrine represented a less risky option for the Court. Thus even though the *Anti-Inflation* decision ultimately defended the federal government's intervention, it limited the scope for future use of the 'national concern' justification.

With *Anti-Inflation* as the precedent, the Supreme Court began a tradition of somewhat ambivalent jurisprudence in questions involving federalism. Many observers consequently believed that judicial review was of limited importance for the politics of Canadian federalism (Monahan, 1984; Weiler, 1974). By taking the middle ground, the Court had merely endorsed the model of Canadian federalism already in operation. Instead of reshaping it, judicial review simply mirrored the existing system. Some critics even suggested that, in framing its endorsement of the status quo in legalistic terms, the Court was essentially acting in a political manner, pretending that its decisions were based only on what the law demanded (Russell, 1977). Governments appeared to accept this critique and became less interested in litigating their conflicts. Although governments always reserve the option of challenging each other in court, the use of judicial review to work out kinks in the federal system became less frequent because governments were increasingly uncertain about the results and more comfortable negotiating with one another to achieve mutually acceptable outcomes.

The Supreme Court's influence never disappeared, however, and events led the Court to revisit POGG questions in a series of cases through the 1990s. In several cases concerning environmental jurisdiction, the Court had the opportunity to expand the 'national concern' doctrine *R. v. Crown Zellerbach Canada Ltd.* (1988), the Court developed what has become known as the 'provincial inability' test, referring to situations in which the inability of a province to act in some particular area might have adverse effects on other provinces. In instances where provincial inability might be shown to exist, there was potential for the expansion of federal power. In a number of cases since *Crown Zellerbach*, the Court has shied away from any significant expansion of the federal parliament's jurisdiction under POGG (Baier, 1998). It has, however, expanded the federal power in the area of criminal law by including under that rubric matters such as toxic dumping (*R. v. Hydro-Québec*, 1997). The Court further emphasized the scope of the criminal law when it upheld the national firearms registry despite vehement provincial opposition, in *Reference Re: Firearms Act (Canada)*, 1998.

Another potentially important area of federal jurisdiction is trade and commerce. Like POGG, the trade and commerce clause has considerable potential for expansion of federal responsibilities. In the United States, the federal legislature's jurisdiction over commerce has been quite generously interpreted to allow a very wide range of regulatory and program activities. The JCPC never gave much scope to Ottawa's power in that area, preferring to emphasize the provincial property and civil rights category. But the Supreme Court has flirted with expanding the federal trade and commerce power in cases of national interest. International trade is generally recognized as falling under federal control, and the federal government has proceeded accordingly, though it has regularly involved or consulted the provinces in negotiations involving provincially regulated industries (such as forestry) or industries with particular regional concentrations (such as fisheries).

What has been controversial is the prospect that the trade and commerce power might be used to justify federal regulation of internal trade among the provinces. In the relevant cases, the Court has insisted that the power be used only for general purposes, not targeted at a specific industry or activity. The test to be applied in such cases is similar to the 'provincial inability' test: for example, Ottawa might be justified in imposing a general regulation in cases where one province's failure to regulate might have negative consequences for other provinces or for the federation as a whole. Federal anti-combines legislation designed to curb anti-competitive and monopolistic corporate behaviour was upheld under the trade and commerce heading in *General Motors of Canada v. City National Leasing* (1989), in which the Court implied that the federal parliament needed to be able to regulate the national market because provinces might not always do their best to ensure an open market throughout the country.

This latter point has been reflected in the positions that the federal government has taken in negotiations over the economic union. Although the federal authority in this area is still untested, there is reason to believe that Ottawa could be considerably more aggressive in its regulation of trade and commerce and still survive a legal challenge. Thus whenever the provinces have been lackadaisical about negotiating the removal of internal trade barriers, the federal government has not hesitated to threaten unilateral action under the trade and commerce power (Brown, 2002b). Recent federal proposals for a national securities regulator have been grounded in the belief that there is ample room in the trade and commerce power to justify such an exercise. The Court's interpretation of the trade and commerce power is actually an excellent example of the indirect effect that judicial review can have on intergovernmental relations. The real impact of the Court's decisions on the character of Canadian federalism can be seen not in the changing extent of federal power but rather in the way that governments interpret those decisions and conduct themselves.

This is especially apparent in the case of the Charter of Rights. Many observers have maintained that the Charter was designed to override Canada's federal character and impose national standards on the provinces, homogenizing much of their public policy (Morton, 1995; Russell, 1983). In Canada, unlike some other federations, the rights guarantees in the national constitution apply not just to federal laws and activities but to provincial ones as well. Prime Minister Trudeau, the chief architect of the Charter, seemed intent on establishing a sense of national community, based on national values that the legal guarantees set out in the Charter would impose across the country. Those with a less centralist bent feared that the enforcement of those standards by the Supreme Court would prevent the provinces from realizing their diverse preferences in public policy (Morton, 1995). Other observers have found that the Supreme Court's Charter jurisprudence has probably not been as homogenizing as skeptics predicted, though there is controversy about the proper way to measure the effects of the Charter on legislative diversity. Numbers alone don't always tell the whole story. Advocates of the Charter point out that the most frequent loser under the Charter is the federal government, not the provinces. But given the scope of federal activities that is not necessarily surprising. It is not clear that Canadian federalism has become more centralized since 1982, or that provincial legislatures have been unduly restricted in the choices they have made (Kelly, 2001, 2008; Kelly and Murphy, 2005). To borrow from James Kelly and Michael Murphy, the Supreme Court has become something of a 'meta-actor' in Canadian federalism. By interpreting the Charter and the division of powers in the ways that it does, the Supreme Court does have some effect on the framework in which intergovernmental relations are conducted. But judicial review seldom determines the final shape of policy outcomes. Ultimately, governments act in an environment that is conditioned by the Supreme Court, but it is up to governments to decide what they will make of the judiciary's findings (Baier, 2006).

The Limits and Potential of Judicial Review

The limitations of judicial review in the context of intergovernmental relations were illustrated in the early 1990s, when the federal government made some (now modest-seeming) cuts to provincial transfers. The main target was the Canada Assistance Plan (CAP), which paid 50 per cent of the cost of provincial social assistance and welfare programs. In the past the program provided that transfers would increase in tandem with provincial spending on social assistance, but in 1990 Ottawa decided that the so-called 'have' provinces—Alberta, British Columbia, and Ontario—should receive increases of no more than 5 per cent per annum, regardless of how much their spending increased. When this 'cap on CAP' was enacted, rising costs soon ensured that the federal contributions in those provinces amounted to considerably less than 50 per cent.[3]

The British Columbia government referred the legislation, The Government Expenditures Restraint Act, to the BC Court of Appeal, asking whether parliament had the authority to limit its obligations under the CAP without the consent of the provinces affected. The Court of Appeal found that such a change did indeed require provincial consent, but the Supreme Court of Canada in (*Reference Re: Canada Assistance Plan [B.C.]*, 1991) overruled the BC decision, largely on the grounds that to do otherwise would compromise the sovereignty of parliament. Any sanctions against the federal government for reneging on its commitments, the Court found, would have to be political, not legal.

In its unanimous judgment, the Court ruled decisively that parliament, not cabinet, is responsible for the design of intergovernmental agreements. So even if a prime minister makes a promise to the provinces, the authority to back up that promise in actual spending and legislation lies with parliament, not the executive. If parliament wishes to alter the provisions of a commitment to the provinces (such as the CAP), a previous pattern of cost-sharing or even a promise from the federal government cannot be binding. Similarly, the Court argued that a province's legitimate expectation of funds could not override parliamentary sovereignty by requiring that transfers continue regardless of the wishes of parliament. The logic of parliamentary sovereignty means that no parliament can bind the law-making authority of a future parliament through the passing of an ordinary statute. Financial commitments like those contained in the CAP can be made, but it is well within the authority of a future parliament to change those commitments when circumstances change. Intergovernmental agreements by their nature must rest on these impermanent foundations.

The Court may not have intended to discourage provincial governments from seeking judicial resolution of intergovernmental disputes, but its (quite proper) decision to defer to parliament on the changes to the CAP offered them little hope. Intergovernmental agreements, according to the Court's reasoning, are essentially political commitments, outside the authority of the judiciary. While legislation such as the CAP may create obligations to the other governments, those obligations are only as lasting as the legislation itself. If parliament or a provincial legislature wants to change a law there is little the courts can do to stop them, even if other governments have come to rely on the programs that the old law created. The CAP case has had serious implications for the political use of legal resources in intergovernmental relations because it demonstrated that there are real limits to the usefulness of judicial review as a remedy in a significant share of intergovernmental disputes.

The CAP case has provoked observers to think more carefully about how effectively intergovernmental agreements can be legally enforced. Governments often have to pressure one another to live up to the terms of an agreement (internal enforcement), but citizens and others also have an interest in governments living up to the terms of an agreement (external enforcement) (Swinton, 1995). If the courts are not able or willing to help enforce informal commitments between governments, a major route for accountability and legitimacy in the federal system may be blocked off. In short, enforcement of intergovernmental agreements appears to be a political matter, and that generally means that governments can ignore their obligations if they feel that the political cost of doing so will not be severe.

DISPUTE RESOLUTION

Jurisdictional conflicts are not unusual in a federation. The country's high court can serve as an umpire in such cases, impartially applying the constitution (or its reading of the constitution) to resolve the dispute. But jurisdiction is not the only thing that federal and provincial governments disagree about. Historically, in Canada, disagreements about financial commitments or even ambitious new programs to regulate the economy or society have sometimes been massaged into disputes over jurisdiction, but not all conflicts are amenable to settlement on the basis of the constitutional division of powers.

In recent years, for example, some media commentators have suggested that the premiers of Nova Scotia and Newfoundland and Labrador could take legal action to compel the federal government to live up to its obligations under accords reached with those provinces for the development of offshore oil and gas resources, and Lorne Calvert, the former premier of Saskatchewan, began legal proceedings against Ottawa regarding the Equalization Program (Galloway, 2007; Galloway and Alphonso, 2007). Should these matters end up in the courts, the division of powers offers little guidance to judges. Cooperative programs and agreements, by their nature, are relatively untroubled by strict constitutional categories, so looking to the constitution as a guide for enforcement will not be all that helpful. From a practical point of view, as we have already noted (and will note again) elsewhere in this book, strict observance of constitutional jurisdiction would make it impossible for the federation to function. If the constitutional division of powers can be seen as a contractual arrangement between governments establishing who will do what to deliver services to their citizens, judicial review might be conceived as a means of enforcing that contract and clarifying its terms for the signatories. Intergovernmental agreements can be seen in a similar contractual light, although the degree of formality involved varies widely: from a simple handshake agreement to a specific financial commitment to a full-blown accord with multiple chapters and institutionalization of offices and staff. These are contracts of different kind from the constitution; nevertheless, they too occasionally need clarification or enforcement. Since the courts, as we saw with the CAP case, have declined that role, other means of dispute resolution have been required, including in some cases provisions internal to intergovernmental agreements themselves. The role of such provisions should not be overstated, however: negotiation is still the principal method of dispute resolution. One reason is that formal dispute-resolution mechanisms by nature require governments to give up some of the bargaining room they have traditionally used to advance their interests.

Informal negotiations are sometimes conducted in the full glare of the national media. Among present-day premiers, Danny Williams of Newfoundland and Labrador is well known for his skill at using the latter in his battles with Ottawa: placing advertisements asking 'Steve' to be fairer to Newfoundland and Labrador, calling the prime minister to task on talk shows, walking out of first ministers' meetings, and even lowering the Canadian flag to half-staff at provincial government buildings. Williams is hardly the first Canadian premier to stage publicity stunts; all first ministers must make some effort to court public opinion. We should not overestimate either the frequency or the impact of such efforts. Much more often, disputes between the two orders of government are dealt with in private, through quiet accommodation on the part of officials and advisers. Examples discussed elsewhere in this book, such as the negotiation of the Millennium Scholarship fund and Labour Market Training agreements, are just the proverbial tip of the iceberg. Every day, Canadian governments resolve disputes over their respective roles in joint and collaborative programs through simple discussion.

That said, not all matters lend themselves to the behind-the-scenes approach. When governments differ substantially in their views, compromise may not be possible. Even when they can find room for agreement, they may want stronger guarantees of one another's obligations in the future than can be assured by handshakes or goodwill. Recent examples such as the Agreement on Internal Trade (AIT) and the Social Union Framework Agreement suggest more in the way of abstract commitment than concrete obligation, but however flexible they may be, such agreements are nonetheless contractual in nature, and contracts often need enforcing.

Canadian governments since the 1960s have become accustomed to making relatively informal arrangements with one another, and the flexibility of those arrangements has left something of a vacuum for enforcement. As the Supreme Court made clear in the *Canada Assistance Plan Reference*, a court cannot prevent a legislature from operating within the scope of its constitutional powers. The consequences for reneging on intergovernmental commitments are more often political than legal, and are generally diffuse rather than specific. Hence governments may see little need to be especially faithful to such agreements. In recent years, some corners of intergovernmental relations have become a little more formalized or institutionalized, and mechanisms for the resolution of disputes have increasingly been incorporated into agreements themselves. Thus recent intergovernmental structures have included quasi-judicial mechanisms for the resolution of disputes between the parties. The Agreement on Internal Trade, for example, has a chapter devoted to provisions for dispute resolution in the event of a complaint that some jurisdiction has created trade barriers contrary to the agreement. Despite criticisms, those provisions have been used to resolve several significant disputes. The Social Union Framework Agreement proposed a model of dispute resolution that included more formal reporting of disputes between the federal and provincial governments, and outlined various collaborative procedures to resolve them. The Social Union model has also been proposed as a method of dispute resolution in intergovernmental conflicts over health care. In correspondence with the Alberta government in the 1990s, the then federal minister of Health, Anne McClellan, pledged to use informal dispute procedures based on the SUFA model. In general, though, the SUFA provisions have hardly been used at all. In the AIT and SUFA, ad hoc tribunals or panels must be appointed to hear the cases of the governments involved, but in no case does the tribunal or panel have the authority to ensure that governments abide by their rulings.

Despite their relative formality, the new approach to dispute resolution suggests that the old habits of negotiation and compromise between governments die hard. The new procedures are specified in writing, but they are still relatively informal, preferring compromise and behind-the-scenes dispute avoidance. Ultimately they seek to preserve a certain amount of discretion for governments, perhaps to avoid the zero-sum results associated with legal rulings. Though a court may be balanced over time in its treatment of different orders of government, individual cases and hence individual policy outcomes cannot be balanced the same way. As Douglas Brown (2002b) notes, many (if not all) of the governments that negotiated the Agreement on Internal Trade were reluctant to hand over too much authority to an independent secretariat to settle disputes. The Council of the Federation, a cooperative organization of the provinces designed both to communicate provincial concerns to Ottawa and to promote greater cooperation among the provinces, has highlighted the improvement of dispute resolution procedures in the AIT as a priority. The Council has gone so far as to recognize that its own member governments have probably given themselves too much discretion to decide how disputes would be handled and rulings implemented. In addition, there are numerous delays and opportunities for renegotiation built into the AIT dispute process. If disputes are settled by a tribunal, it remains up to the violating government to voluntarily comply with the ruling. Some provinces, such as Alberta, have been enthusiastic supporters of the processes of dispute resolution and have tried to lend the AIT legitimacy by abiding by the tribunals' decisions. Other provinces, such as Quebec, have been less enthusiastic, or at least less prompt to comply with rulings or even properly acquit their responsibilities under the dispute procedures (COF, 2004). In short, while the intergovernmental apparatus has experimented with ways of making agreements more enforceable, these efforts are still at an early stage. Federal theory relies on judicial review to maintain constitutional supremacy and keep governments accountable to the constitutional order. Non-judicial mechanisms for solving disagreements are less final and authoritative, even if they do offer some of the other advantages of more formal mechanisms.

SUMMARY

The activism of the JCPC in promoting decentralization, and the more conscious efforts of the Supreme Court of Canada to balance power between provincial and federal governments, indicate that neutrality is not always a trademark of the judicial function in a federation. Some Canadian legal scholars have suggested that the Court's role in federalism is illegitimate and cannot be justified in the present democratic age (Monahan, 1987; Weiler, 1974): the judiciary, they argue, makes decisions on political grounds behind the veil of an artificial impartiality and is immune from the standards of accountability that political actors in a democracy should be subject to. The merits and demerits of this argument are beyond the scope of this chapter. Nevertheless, the CAP case gives us some idea of the limitations of judicial review in the present age of Canadian federalism.

If the role of judicial review in Canadian federalism is less central today than it was in the past, this has little to do with the perceived legitimacy of the judiciary as an actor in federal–provincial relations. Rather, it is a reflection of the prevalence of cooperative and collaborative intergovernmental agreements that circumvent constitutional niceties such as jurisdiction. The Court occasionally proves its relevance with a case like the *Reference Re: Firearms* or *Hydro-Québec*, and it certainly affects federalism through its enforcement of standards in the Charter of Rights and Freedoms. It is in the role of interpreter of the division of powers or umpire in disputes over what is legitimate federal or provincial activity that the Court's importance has decreased since Confederation.

The consequences of this development for the federation are open to debate. The essential accountability concern is not whether the Supreme Court is properly accountable to the electorate, but whether it is still capable of enforcing governments' accountability for properly exercising their constitutional jurisdiction. In the increasingly complex world of intergovernmental relations it is increasingly difficult for citizens to know who is really supposed to be doing what and whose feet they should hold to the flame if they are unhappy. The decreasing profile of the judiciary as umpire and enforcer of responsibilities can only serve to make the lines of accountability even more obscure.

Chapter 6

Executive Federalism: Sites and Settings, Councils and Conferences

The Canadian federal model is premised on distinct federal and provincial juris-dictions—watertight compartments, in the classic metaphor—which are spelled out in the constitution and subject to both reinforcement and redefinition by court decisions. Yet the realities of modern policy-making and program financing are such that the two orders of government are increasingly interde-pendent. Intergovernmental coordination and collaboration demand flexibility and a willingness to bypass some of the rigidities of the constitutional frame-work. They also imply a need for institutions and a set of agreed-upon rules to manage such interactions. Here, though, a further paradox becomes evident. Intergovernmental institutions such as first ministers' conferences and minister-ial councils generally serve a dual purpose, giving different governments the opportunity both to interact, which ideally should lead to increased trust, and to protect their own jurisdictions, which typically sets them against one another.

These are not the only features of the Canadian intergovernmental system that can be seen as problematic. As we have noted in earlier chapters, the main elements are hierarchically organized: three rather narrow, hierarchical pyramids (representing the federal, provincial, and territorial governments), each of which is dominated by its executive level. If the system as a whole is to function in a reasonably collaborative fashion, the spirit of cooperation must begin at the top, with the prime minister and the 13 premiers. As we shall see in this chapter, however, that spirit is often lacking—with the result that the system does not function as well as it should, not only at the top but at lower levels as well. The key question for many observers is how to improve the system's capacity to develop trust ties among first ministers, ministers, and those below them.

Papillon and Simeon (2004: 132) recommend making the first ministers' conference a regular part of the parliamentary and legislative process, adopting a firmer set of decision rules, and working to promote openness and transparency. Harvey Lazar, on the other hand, implies that the relative absence of institution-alization is one of the strengths of the Canadian system: in his view, the system works precisely because of what he calls its ambiguity: 'Ambiguity was the midwife of Canada's birth. And ambiguity remains central to the Canadian politics of today' (Lazar, 2004: 4; see also Tuohy, 1992; Gagnon and Erk, 2002).

Neither in this chapter nor in the next, on the management and reform of executive federalism, will we attempt to decide between these opposing views. We will simply elucidate some of the unwritten rules and regularities that exist and outline some of the institutional practices that, in conjunction with other factors, either promote or hinder the generation of trust ties, for example. The present chapter will examine the various institutions that make up the intergovernmental system—first ministers' conferences and meetings, the Council of the Federation (COF), ministerial councils, meetings of officials—as well as the tensions between them. We will review briefly the different sites, the formal structures, and the forces that determine how these institutions function. Then Chapter 7 will examine the broader bureaucratic and political trends for the management of intergovernmental relations, the influence of the 'New Public Management' philosophy, the role of political parties, professional norms, and some of the structures and processes internal to governments—what we refer to as the *intra*governmental dimension. Veteran observer of intergovernmental relations J. Stefan Dupré (1988) has noted that this particular dimension has important implications for the conduct of intergovernmental relations. The next chapter also assesses some of the challenges facing executive federalism. Even though the most important issues affecting Canadians involve the intergovernmental process, it is largely a closed process, becoming visible in a significant way only at times of major crises. As a consequence, questions have arisen about the system's openness, transparency, and accountability, as well as its overall effectiveness.

FORUMS

The original 1867 Constitution Act made no provision for intergovernmental relations. Nor did the JCPC in its early efforts at judicial interpretation. Indeed, many of the JCPC's decisions implied that interaction between governments should be limited—essentially, that each order should stick to its own watertight compartment. When interaction did occur, it was often in the courts. Liberal Prime Minister Wilfrid Laurier, elected in 1896 on a platform that included respect for provincial rights, began the tradition of the first ministers' conference in 1906, although it would be 12 years before the next such meeting took place. In fact, the 1906 meeting was called only after persistent badgering from the premiers. In the meantime the provincial premiers, led by Quebec, had already held meetings among themselves, without the federal prime minister, in 1887 and 1902.[1] It was only in the 1930s that the FMC became a regular event, allowing governments to coordinate their responses to the crises associated with the Great Depression.

Things changed dramatically with the establishment of the welfare state after 1945. With Ottawa providing considerable portions of both the financing and the leadership, but lacking the constitutional authority to impose new initiatives on the provinces, a high level of intergovernmental coordination was required. At the same time, the new levels of taxation required to support these initiatives necessitated cooperation. The result was a dramatic increase in the frequency of meetings, primarily of officials, and the rise of what Donald Smiley (1987) termed 'executive federalism'.

In examining the institutions and processes involved in intergovernmental relations, it is again worth stressing the fluidity of the rules and norms and the generally low level of institutionalization in the Canadian system. While there is the Canadian Intergovernmental Conference Secretariat (CICS), created in 1973 and based in Ottawa, it has a relatively small staff and provides only limited administrative support. It sets up meetings, distributes conference material, and maintains a valuable archive, but it plays no role in the drafting or shaping of that material.[2] By contrast, the European Union, which many see as a federation in the making, has a secretariat numbering in the thousands. The secretariat for the Council of Australian Governments (COAG) also appears to play a more active role, providing support for the various ministerial councils among other things.[3] In Canada, the most institutionalized forum for intergovernmental relations— the Council of Atlantic Premiers (previously the Council of Maritime Premiers)—is a regional body, serving a population of less than two million, with a staff that is responsible not only for logistics but also for the conduct of research and analysis in support of the Council's deliberations.

First Ministers' Conferences and First Ministers' Meetings (FMCs/FMMs)

The pre-eminent body, the one that sits at the top of the intergovernmental pyramid, is the First Ministers' Conference, also known more formally as the Federal–Provincial Plenary Conference. It traces its origins to the 1906 meeting convened by Laurier under the title 'Conference of the Representatives of the Government of Canada and the Various Provinces'. One more conference was held under that label, in 1918. The next conference, in 1927, was called 'Dominion–Provincial'. In 1950 'Dominion' was replaced by 'Federal'. The term 'First Ministers' Conference' came into use in 1974, after a provision in the ill-fated Victoria Charter of 1971 called for annual meetings of 'first ministers'.[4]

By the early 1990s, however, the 'First Ministers' Conference' had become closely associated with constitutional wrangling, especially over the failed Meech Lake Accord, and since then the preferred term has been the less formal 'First

Ministers' Meeting' (FMM). All meetings held under Jean Chrétien's stewardship were FMMs. This format reached a new level of informality when the about-to-be-anointed prime minister, Paul Martin, held a session with the premiers over breakfast at the time of the Grey Cup in November 2003.

We begin here by describing the formal process that became established in the 1970s and 1980s, when constitutional issues emerged as a major concern. Even though this type of full-blown intergovernmental summit is now rare, political scientists and the media still tend to consider it the 'classic' model. The FMC is convened by the prime minister, who has considerable scope for setting the agenda, and is attended by all ten provincial premiers as well as the leaders of the three territories. While it is the PM's prerogative to convene a conference, a certain amount of game-playing on the part of the other first ministers typically takes place beforehand; for instance, various premiers may have called for a conference to deal with some putative crisis. The federal government in turn may want to portray itself as not caving in to unseemly provincial posturing.

The core of each delegation consists of the first minister, two to three ministers, and a support group of officials. Some of the latter will come from the first minister's personal advisory staff or office; some will be specialists in intergovernmental affairs; and some will represent the relevant ministries or departments (if the issues to be discussed are economic, for instance, some officials will be drawn from the various finance or treasury departments). In the 1970s and 1980s FMCs usually took place in the conference centre in Ottawa across from the Château Laurier Hotel, where the PM, as the chair, would sit at the mid-point of a horseshoe-shaped table. Arrayed behind each first minister will be the various members of his or her delegation, ready to whisper information or advice into his or her ear. At the beginning of each meeting, each first minister will make an opening public statement. Then the first ministers move into closed sessions, in which discussion can be wide-ranging and at times quite heated. On the other hand, some premiers who have been described as models of decorum and understanding in the private sessions may let fly outside the meeting, in front of the press, chastising Ottawa or other provincial governments for public consumption back home (Simeon, 2006 [1972]: 235).

In general the FMC is more a forum for discussion than for decision-making. Only under exceptional circumstances, as during the constitutional negotiations of the 1980s, do the participants agree on a specific proposal or set of proposals. Votes are rarely held and few clear-cut decisions are taken. Conferences generally last two or three days, at the end of which a communiqué is issued, put together by officials from both orders of government to summarize whatever consensus may have emerged. Following the opening statements, sessions take place in private, and there is no public record of discussions. FMCs are nonetheless covered extensively by the media. First ministers and others are buttonholed as they leave the meetings, and some may hold impromptu press conferences. The number of advisers involved means that leaks are inevitable, if not on the actual substance of the discussions, then at least regarding the tone or atmosphere.

Sometimes leakage is part of a calculated strategy. The governments involved may also employ 'spin doctors' to work the press room with an eye to getting their own position or version of events across to the public via the news media.

The main sessions take place during the day, but those held over dinner or breakfast are often the most valuable. These tend to be much less formal and— since they are usually attended only by the first ministers themselves, they provide opportunities for persuasion that are not available in the regular sessions, where advisers are constantly whispering cautions in ears. The informality of these meetings, the relative absence of constraints, and the small number of people involved allow an adroit PM to develop a consensus or understanding in a way that might be impossible in a larger group. Brian Mulroney was famous for his skill in working a room and bringing otherwise recalcitrant first ministers on-side, his many years as a labour lawyer putting him in good stead; the Meech Lake Accord was said to be the fruit of one such effort. Even though actual agreements are rarely made at FMCs, the discussions begun there can lead to further, more concrete discussions at ministerial meetings and from there to agreements.

As Papillon and Simeon (2004) note, FMMs are less formal and more private than FMCs. In the 1990s they reflected the style of the then-new Chrétien government, as well as a general desire among the participants for greater collaboration and a more low-key approach to resolving intergovernmental issues. No doubt there was also a desire to take first ministers' sessions out of the glare of media attention and make them less accessible to outside actors. Given the spectacular failures of both the Meech Lake and Charlottetown accords, this reaction against full-blown summitry was not surprising. Nevertheless, some of the FMMs held during the 1990s were not very different from old-fashioned FMCs.

Today an FMM is now most likely to be scheduled as the culmination of a long process that started elsewhere, usually in a ministerial council. For example, the Social Union Framework Agreement (SUFA) was developed in part in discussions among provincial governments at annual premiers' conferences starting in 1995. It was then further developed at federal–provincial meetings of ministers of justice and social policy. Finally, in February 1999, when ministers had taken the file as far as possible, the PM called a First Ministers' Meeting and sat down with the premiers to make the final compromises. Although Quebec did not sign it, the agreement was carefully structured so that Quebec could receive the extra health care funding that was part of the SUFA package. In its scale and attendant publicity the SUFA meeting closely resembled a traditional FMC. Though FMMs, like FMCs, are not frequent, and concrete results even more rare, they are still very important; no major change or new policy that cuts across jurisdictional boundaries is likely to be accepted without the involvement of first ministers.

A variant of the FMM, introduced by Jean Chrétien during his tenure as prime minister, was the 'Team Canada' trade mission. Though ostensibly focused on trade rather than federal–provincial issues, these missions—like the informal breakfasts and dinners associated with FMMs and FMCs—allowed for free-flowing discussion across a wide range of issues. The success of these missions—half a dozen of them between 1994 and 2002—as trade promotion exercises is unclear, but as opportunities to promote understanding between federal and provincial governments and tackle problematic issues they were highly productive.

Paul Martin, in his short tenure as prime minister, held no fewer than four FMMs, including a major one on health care in November 2004, as well as an elaborate conference in November 2005 at which first ministers and Aboriginal leaders signed the Kelowna Accord. By contrast, Stephen Harper, in the 32 months of his first government, held one brief, informal dinner meeting with the premiers shortly after taking office and another more formal session, again over dinner, in January 2008. Shortly after the October 2008 federal election, Prime Minister Harper convened a three-hour luncheon meeting with the premiers to deal with the fallout of the firestorm sweeping world financial markets. He made a promise to hold further meetings in the near future. Up to that point, his philosophy of 'open federalism' notwithstanding, Harper had shown little interest in bringing the premiers together as a group, preferring to deal with them individually, either by e-mail or in one-on-one sessions. There have also been signs that he believes it is possible to introduce and implement major initiatives without the participation of other first ministers, either individually or collectively. If this continues to be his strategy, the era when the first ministers' forum was 'the centrepiece . . . of the machinery of intergovernmental relations in Canada' (Papillon and Simeon, 2004: 113) will be compromised. On the other hand, if his promise of further meetings subsequent to his November 2008 first ministers' luncheon holds, we may see a more informal and possibly collaborative pattern take shape.

Premiers and the Council of the Federation

The Council of the Federation, previously known as the Annual Premiers' Conference (APC), consists of all first ministers except the federal prime minister. The first provincial premiers' conference was convened in 1887 by the premier of Quebec, two decades before Laurier hosted the first FMC. The premiers' conference continued to meet sporadically until 1960 when—largely at the instigation of the newly elected Quebec premier, Jean Lesage—it became an annual event. In 2003 the APC took a monumental leap forward, at least by the standards of Canadian intergovernmental relations, remaking itself into the Council of the Federation, with a steering committee composed of provincial deputies, a secretariat, and a provision for the striking of ad hoc committees of ministers to examine specific topics. Again, the premier of Quebec, in this case Jean Charest, was the prime instigator. The Founding Agreement of the COF commits the premiers and territorial leaders to a regular summer meeting and at least one additional meeting every year.

The COF is the only senior national intergovernmental body that meets on a regular basis, though two regional groups (the Council of Atlantic Premiers and the Western Premiers' Conference) also meet regularly. The annual gathering in

July or August, hosted on a rotating basis by one of the premiers (who also serves as council chair for the year), attracts considerable media attention. It has also become somewhat predictable, however. At one stage the annual event focused mainly on interprovincial issues such as securities regulation, interprovincial trucking, or consumer legislation, and though neither the prime minister nor any federal ministers would attend, there was usually a federal observer. In the late 1980s, however, things changed. The federal observer was no longer welcome to sit in on meetings, and the focus (at least the media's focus) shifted to federal–provincial issues. Especially with concerns such as health care and fiscal transfers, the premiers tended to join forces and issue statements about the need for Ottawa to be more responsive in dealing with these matters. In the jaundiced eyes of some observers these demands were becoming too ritualized to have much impact either on Ottawa or on the general public. On the other hand, the fact that the leaders of the three territories, including Nunavut (created in 1999), now attend the meetings as well has given the council a much stronger sense of urgency about issues such as the impact of climate change on Aboriginal people in the north.

Over the years a number of premiers have used their conferences as forums in which to air, and garner support for, issues of particular relevance to themselves or their provinces. These efforts have rarely succeeded, however. In 1996, for example, Premier Mike Harris of Ontario tried to promote the idea that the provinces should take primary responsibility for setting national standards in the social policy area and become less dependent on Ottawa for the financing of social programs.[5] But premiers from have-not provinces proved decidedly lukewarm to the idea, fearing further reductions in federal funding. A few years later, BC's Glen Clark failed to persuade his fellow premiers to exert collective pressure on Ottawa to take more decisive action on the US–Canada dispute over salmon fisheries. John Hamm of Nova Scotia was similarly unsuccessful in 2001, when he sought support for his efforts to protect the province's offshore oil revenues against the clawback provisions of the Equalization Program, although the issue did gain momentum a few years later, after Newfoundland took up the cause (both provinces obtained significant concessions from the Paul Martin government in 2005).[6] The following year, when Ralph Klein of Alberta called on the other premiers to join him in opposing Ottawa's signing of the Kyoto protocol on global warming, his appeal was publicly rejected by a significant proportion of the other premiers, including all three territorial leaders (McCarthy, 2002).

Even if the APCs were less effective than they might have been, however, it was discussion among the premiers in the mid-1990s, in the aftermath of Ottawa's drastic cuts in fiscal transfers to the provinces, that eventually led to the Social Union Framework Agreement. As with FMMs, much of the work was done by ministerial subcommittees and committees of officials. But the essential idea of a framework agreement on the social union can be attributed to the premiers themselves.

The question remains whether the COF represents a significant improvement. It has often been suggested that the premiers missed a valuable opportunity at the time of its creation, in 2003. Some have argued that the council should have been furnished with a set of decision rules akin to those used by the European Union. Others have suggested that the new body should have included the federal government, or been designed to serve as a replacement for the Senate. Both the idea and the name of the council date back to the constitutional discussions of the late 1970s and early 1980s, when such a body was envisioned as either a replacement for the Senate or a variation on the German Bundesrat (a body composed of all state premiers and an integral part of the German parliament, in which it constitutes the second chamber). It was the Bundesrat model that the Task Force on Canadian Unity (Pépin–Robarts) had in mind in 1979 when it proposed what it also called a Council of the Federation.[7] In 1980 the Quebec Liberal Party under leader Claude Ryan proposed the creation of a special intergovernmental body to be called the Federal Council: separate from the federal parliament, though the federal government would be a full participant, this council would have included among its decision rules a regional veto. In the fall of 1980, after a constitutional patriation resolution was tabled in parliament, the Standing Senate Committee on Legal and Constitutional Affairs proposed a Federal–Provincial Council playing a coordinating role.

More recently it was the Quebec government—in particular the Liberal premier, Jean Charest, and his minister of Intergovernmental Relations, Benoît Pelletier—that pressed hardest for the creation of a new intergovernmental institution. The model announced by the premiers in late 2003, however, remained purely confederal, with no role for Ottawa except as respondent to the claims put forward by the premiers. In short, the new council would operate much as the old premiers' conference had. But there was more to it than that. In 2003 Jean Charest, freshly elected as premier of Quebec, was the leader of a non-sovereignist but nonetheless Quebec-first Liberal party. Thus his agenda included two issues of special importance to Quebec: dealing with the fiscal imbalance and asymmetrical federalism. Accordingly, the newly formed council soon launched a special task force to review fiscal federalism, and in 2004 it endorsed a special arrangement between Ottawa and Quebec with respect to health care, which exempted Quebec from certain conditions and affirmed its unique position in confederation (Maioni, 2008). The symbolic value of the latter was in many ways more important than the exemptions themselves, signalling the premiers' unanimous recognition of Quebec's distinct status.

The creators and supporters of the COF publicly stated that the new body, with regular and more frequent meetings, and institutional support in the form of a secretariat working not only for the COF itself but also for various subcommittees, would strengthen the premiers' position in relation to Ottawa, by facilitating the development of a strong consensus on issues. Whereas in the past the premiers had had to negotiate among themselves as well as with Ottawa, the COF or its representatives would now negotiate directly with the federal government;

thus a multilateral process would be transformed into a bilateral one between a collective and a single entity. At a later stage, under this optimistic scenario, COF might come to occupy a position comparable to that of the German Bundesrat, perhaps even displacing the present Senate—though this would require a constitutional amendment. The possibility was also raised that at some stage Ottawa might come to play a formal role within the COF, albeit on terms defined principally by the COF rather than Ottawa. With sufficient discipline and commitment it is conceivable that the COF could displace the FMC/FMM and perhaps even Ottawa from atop the intergovernmental pyramid.[8] With the promise of stronger leadership and greater institutionalization than had been possible with either the Annual Premiers' Conference or the FMC/FMM, hopes were high. In brief, a number of people believed that the provinces now had an opportunity to take collective control of the intergovernmental agenda and gain a long-term strategic advantage vis-à-vis Ottawa. For the COF to be effective in the way many hoped, however, it would need to adopt a set of decision rules capable of ensuring ample support for the council's decisions but at the same time guaranteeing adequate protection for significant minority opinion—without requiring the unrealistically high threshold of unanimity (Brown, 2003a). But no such rules were ever adopted. Instead, the norm was 'consensus', which for all intents and purposes meant 'unanimity'. Given the likelihood that at least one province or territory would be off-side at any particular time, the lack of a more realistic decision-making process was bound to spell trouble sooner or later.

The crucial test arrived with the fiscal imbalance issue—one of the two main items on Charest's agenda. Matters began promisingly enough. A blue-ribbon panel was commissioned by the COF to examine the issue and make recommendations. Fiscal federalism proved to be dangerous terrain on which to prove the COF's mettle, however. One problem was the zero-sum nature of the issue: any new arrangement was bound to produce losers as well as winners. Another problem (as we shall see in Chapters 8 and 9) was the Martin government's decision to make special agreements with two provinces (Nova Scotia and Newfoundland and Labrador), exempting them from the equalization clawbacks that other resource-producing provinces were subject to. In the end, the panel's recommendations—outlined in the Gagné–Stein Report (Gagné and Stein, 2006)—received only lukewarm support from most provinces and were rejected outright by at least three. A meeting of the COF scheduled to discuss Gagné–Stein was abruptly cancelled, as several provinces felt that the rifts among them were too great to bridge. In brief, the COF, which had initially seemed to represent a significant development in Canadian intergovernmental relations, now looked a lot less promising. On one level, the COF's failure to deliver suggests a failure of provincial leadership. On another level, it suggests a general lack of interest in promoting regularization and institutionalization of intergovernmental relations. More critically, perhaps, at times the interests of the provinces are simply so distinctive that no tinkering with rules can easily overcome them (Lazar, 2003).

Ministerial Councils

For insight into intergovernmental relations in Canada there may be no better source than the website of the Canadian Intergovernmental Conference Secretariat. First Ministers' Meetings take place only every couple of years, and the premiers themselves meet only once or twice a year, but ministerial meetings are held almost weekly. A simple click on 'Conference Information' on the CICS website[9] will produce a list of almost all the major intergovernmental meetings held since 1997. In any given month there will be roughly half a dozen ministerial meetings on subjects that range from fisheries to senior citizens. The only meetings not listed are conferences involving ministers of finance and provincial treasurers; these are the most important because they deal with fiscal and financing issues that affect all policy areas.[10] They also tend to attract the most media attention. Relatively few deals or agreements are struck at intergovernmental meetings. Typically, reports will be reviewed, discussions will take place, and commitments will be made to examine various issues further and to work towards developing consensus on matters deemed important to Canadians.

Ministerial councils are noteworthy in four further respects. First, it is at the ministerial council level that much of the real work is accomplished. Though capped at the end by a meeting of the first ministers, most of the actual development work that went into the making of SUFA was conducted at the level of officials operating under the auspices of the Council of Social Union Ministers.[11] Second, ministerial councils tend to be much more institutionalized than FMC/FMMs, with full-time secretariats and regularly scheduled meetings.[12] Third, it is in these bodies that one is most likely to find a significant level of trust among both ministers and officials. Finally, it is in ministerial councils that interaction with civil society (in the form of public interest groups, trade associations, and other stakeholders with a significant interest in the outcomes of intergovernmental negotiations) is most likely to occur.

The Canadian Council of Forest Ministers (CCFM), for example, conducts much of its work through the National Forest Strategy Coalition (NFSC), which has overseen the development of three national forest strategies since 1985. The NFSC, significantly, comprises not only the ministers of the provinces and territories, as well as the federal government, but also industry organizations, and conservation and Aboriginal groups. According to Julie Simmons (2008), its significance lies in the fact that the signatories to the accords that accompany the national forest strategies include both ministers and non-government representatives; further, the accords contain up to 100 separate 'commitments to action' and are the result of a broadly based deliberative process. The 2003–8 accord had 63 signatories, though these did not include the provinces of Quebec, Manitoba, and Alberta.

Simmons also points out that the Canadian Council of Ministers of Environment (CCME) routinely involves non-governmental actors in policy development. With a full-time secretariat, a multi-year business plan, a publications program, and formalized task groups, it is 'the most institutionalized of all the intergovernmental bodies' (Simmons, 2008: 367). Like the CCFM, the CCME has produced a number of accords, though not all its efforts have been successful. Winfield and Macdonald (2008) argue that little progress has been made in the area of developing standards for handling toxic substances, for example. They also point to the example of the 1998 Canada-Wide Harmonization Accord, which they note was heavily criticized by environmental non-governmental organizations, academics, and the Parliamentary Standing Committee on Environment and Sustainable Development for, among other things, the apparent abandonment of Ottawa's regulatory role in the environmental field.

In brief, a number of ministerial councils are part of and sometimes central to distinct policy communities. As Simmons (2005, 2008) has noted, the character of these communities varies: some councils work closely with non-governmental stakeholders, developing trust ties between government and civil society, while others do not.

Ministerial councils can be federal–provincial–territorial or interprovincial–territorial. Some are limited to a subset of ministers (e.g., the Atlantic Council of Fisheries and Aquaculture Ministers). One of the more important committees is the Council of Ministers of Education of Canada (CMEC), which deals with an area officially under the exclusive jurisdiction of the provinces, although the federal government has a significant interest in it, especially at the post-secondary level. The federal minister is rarely invited to attend, and is never present for the normal business of the meeting. In other areas provincial and territorial ministers may meet by themselves. The wide range of the services that the provinces are responsible for delivering means that provinces and territories must meet frequently to ensure coordination in areas such as the administration of justice, transportation, and health care.

It is important to keep in mind, however, that whatever consensus or non-consensus emerges at the level of ministerial councils and associated bodies can easily be overridden by developments at the broader political level. In the case of the 1998 Harmonization Accord on the environment, for instance, the federal government at the highest level decided that the need for an agreement with the provinces overrode strong misgivings on the part of the federal department of the environment and even the minister herself (Winfield and Macdonald, 2008). As we will see in the next chapter, the tensions between central agencies and departments and agencies can be greater than between those departments and their counterparts in other governments.

How best to measure the effectiveness of intergovernmental bodies, whether FMMs or ministerial councils, remains an open question. Whether or not a formal agreement is achieved is not necessarily the most appropriate standard for judging their success. Maintaining good communication and ensuring a common understanding of the issues at hand is an important consideration. Furthermore, the communiqués issued at the end of conferences or meetings (which can be found on the CICS's website) often indicate implicit if not explicit agreement on various matters through phrases such as: 'Ministers expressed support for this [federal] legislation'; 'ministers commended the federal minister's recent decision', or '[the federal] Minister agreed to take the matter of . . . costs . . . to his Cabinet colleagues later this year.' Meetings that indicate support for a federal activity, or that eventually lead to a new or revised piece of federal or provincial legislation, can be seen as evidence of both progress and collaboration. Conversely, failure to issue a post-conference communiqué can be seen as evidence of a significant impasse. In fact, the drafting of the communiqué takes up a fair amount of the participants' time. Outside observers who know how to parse communiqués often find them useful as indicators of the progress being made, the participants' commitment or consensus, and the direction in which a policy area may be heading.

Meetings of Officials

The CICS site also lists meetings of deputy ministers, both federal–provincial and interprovincial. It is often possible to discern patterns in those listings: meetings of ministers are often preceded by meetings of their deputies, though on occasion the sets of meetings will overlap. Essentially, officials do the preparatory work, and in this way play an important role in shaping both the agenda for and the tenor of the discussions. Among other things, officials will draft reports on outstanding issues in various policy domains; collect and standardize the necessary data, and more generally develop a common set of tools and concepts to facilitate discussion on the part of the ministers and/or deputies—if the process is working well. The officials whose work supports these meetings are below the level of deputies themselves; they typically meet on their own, and are in constant communication with one another by phone and e-mail. Meetings of officials, in fact, are the most frequent intergovernmental events. As in the case of cabinet meetings or the management of departments, ministers would be effectively paralyzed without the support that officials provide. This is not to say that ministers lack power or the capacity to give direction: simply that they are not in a position to manage the minutiae of the issues that intergovernmental meetings are called to discuss.

An equally crucial responsibility of officials is to arrange for consultations with non-government actors. We noted above that ministerial councils have now begun to develop connections with non-government stakeholders, as well as third governments such as municipalities and First Nations. Exercises in consultation with these parties can be quite elaborate and require considerable resources to manage properly, especially if they are to be perceived as legitimate by the relevant policy communities and interested observers. Although the arrangements may be outsourced, either to specialized consulting firms or to 'think tanks' with interests and expertise in the policy area in question, the overall process and the key participants continue to be officials from federal and provincial line departments involved in the particular sector.[13]

The increase in consultative exercises is generally seen as a positive development, but it can still give rise to misgivings among governments, officials, and politicians. First, many officials fear losing control of a process that they believe still works best when conducted in secret. Second, governments may use consultative mechanisms as a way of gaining broader community support for their positions, or of bringing pressure to bear on other governments. For example, in 2005, when the Liberal government of Paul Martin negotiated a series of bilateral agreements with the provinces and territories on child care and early childhood learning, a condition attached to most of the agreements was that the provincial governments involved must undertake consultations with their stakeholders. Some of the provincial governments suspected that this was simply a ploy on Ottawa's part to allow various public interest groups, whose views were likely to be aligned with the federal government's aspirations, an opportunity to determine the shape of the programs that the provinces would deliver.

On the whole, it is at the level of officials that ties between governments are closest and communication best. Meetings may be numerous, but the total number of people involved in intergovernmental relations is relatively small. Particularly when Ottawa launches a new program, the officials involved will be in constant touch with each other, sharing information and perspectives. When, as is increasingly the case, Ottawa proceeds on a bilateral basis, negotiating agreements with each province individually, provincial governments are understandably anxious to know what their counterparts are asking for, receiving, or not receiving. Provincial officials are usually quite frank with one another, especially if they have developed close working relations over the years. But they are never totally frank; some crucial information is always withheld, if only because decisions are imminent, or because cabinet confidences may be involved. Even with well-established relationships and a common sense of Canadian loyalty, a certain amount of diplomatic protocol may be required to keep the lines of communication open, but secrets safe, when conflicting interests are at stake.

Officials, especially senior officials, likely exercised more power several decades ago, during the era of cooperative federalism, mainly because political leaders were less engaged in the intergovernmental process and more willing to let officials in line departments handle the arcane details of road construction or tax administration. In many instances, what ministers and premiers were most interested in was the fact that they could construct roads and schools with Ottawa paying 50 per cent of the costs. It was left to officials on both the federal and provincial sides to negotiate the technical details—which permitted officials to shape programs according to their own ideas of appropriate standards and priorities. As we noted in Chapter 2, all this began to change during the 1960s, when Quebec set out to create an infrastructure that simultaneously gave ministers, and especially the premier, more say in policy-making and allowed them to bring more sophisticated expertise to bear on the issues at hand. Even before Quebec introduced these innovations, certain provinces were coming to realize that they needed the expertise not only of engineers but of economists and lawyers who were familiar with the broader framework within which federal–provincial agreements were reached and who knew how to gain maximum advantage.

Even though the involvement of officials has increased over time, the relationship between these officials and the political leadership has grown more complex, including the involvement of central agencies, so that political leaders are now in a much better position to provide direction. This evolution has resulted in greater complexity and uncertainty, as well as more tension within governments—a point that will be examined in the next chapter.

Regional Bodies

We have already noted that many meetings involve subsets of representatives from the 14 federal, provincial, and territorial governments. We have also noted that Ottawa is increasingly likely to pursue national objectives by way of separate agreements with each of the provinces. Nevertheless, there are also interprovincial meetings and bodies with a distinct regional mandate, such as the Council of Atlantic Premiers (known as the Council of Maritime Premiers until 2000, when Newfoundland and Labrador joined), and the Western Premiers' Conference. There are also frequent meetings of Ontario and Quebec first ministers, ministers, and officials to discuss a broad range of bilateral issues, though without regular councils or conferences.

The Council of Atlantic Premiers enjoys a much higher degree of institutionalization than just about any other intergovernmental body in Canada. Born out of a recommendation of the federally sponsored Deutsch Commission on Maritime Union in 1970,[14] the original Council of Maritime Premiers was formed in 1971 with a legal mandate to foster cooperation among the three maritime governments and a permanent secretariat based in Halifax. Some hoped that the CMP would be a step towards a more complete union of the three provinces; others suspected that it was largely a symbolic gesture on the part of the three premiers, intended to stave off such a possibility. In any event, it has served as an umbrella and an enabler for a number of regional administrative agencies and policy activities, in addition to providing support for regularly scheduled quarterly meetings among the region's premiers. It has direct responsibility for managing a number of administrative agencies providing services to either the three Maritime provinces or all four Atlantic provinces, including the Maritime Provinces Higher Education Commission (MPHEC), Atlantic Provinces Education Foundation, and Maritime Provinces Harness Racing Commission. In the past it has also had responsibility for the Maritime Municipal Training and Development Board and the Land Registration Information System.[15]

As long as the Council's activities have been low-key and non-controversial, it has been relatively successful. Higher-profile issues, however, soon make its limitations apparent. Agreement is particularly elusive when the issue at hand may create losers as well as winners. Thus in the late 1970s an initiative entitled the Maritime Energy Corporation proved to be relatively short-lived, despite the promise of federal funding and overall lower electricity costs for consumers. In 2004, when the New Brunswick government applied to the National Energy

Board for a 'made in Canada' price on natural gas from Nova Scotia's offshore operations, Nova Scotia objected on the grounds that this would hamper the development of those operations and reduce its own royalties. In many respects the Council of Atlantic Premiers would have been the ideal venue in which to raise the issue and to try to reach some kind of accommodation. But there is no evidence of any such effort. Similarly, the Council appears to have played no role at all in resolving a bitter boundary dispute between Newfoundland and Labrador and Nova Scotia over the division of the offshore Laurentian sub-basin lying between the two provinces (Baier and Groarke, 2003).

In administrative matters some of the agencies operating under the aegis of the Council of Atlantic Premiers, such as the Maritime Municipal Training and Development Board, have been abolished. Others have come to play a more limited role. The MPHEC, for example, used to recommend funding levels for all maritime post-secondary institutions, in addition to making recommendations on proposals for new PSE degrees and programs. This arrangement ended in 1989, when the government of Nova Scotia set up its own Higher Education Council to evaluate the province's PSE institutions and recommend appropriate funding levels.

The Council of Maritime Premiers was most active in the early 1990s. At the time all three Maritime premiers were relatively new and keen to undertake new initiatives such as the Atlantic Procurement Agreement of 1992, under which the four governments agreed to eliminate discrimination in government procurement contracts for goods, services, and construction originating within the Atlantic region.[16] Though largely superseded by the national Agreement on Internal Trade three years later, at the time it was seen as a significant step towards the reduction of trade barriers and parochialism more generally in the Atlantic region. Since then CAP has taken a rather lower profile, though it has achieved considerable cooperation on matters with lower stakes; the Atlantic Insurance Harmonization Project, aimed at developing common legislative standards, is one example.

The annual Western Premiers Conference (WPC) is similar to the Council of Atlantic Premiers, except that it lacks a permanent secretariat. The seven governments involved take turns hosting and providing administrative support for the event. Just as the Council of Maritime Premiers was first launched in response to Ottawa's suggestion (via the Deutsch Commission) that the three provinces consider closer cooperation if not amalgamation, the WPC arose out of a special Western Economic Opportunities Conference in 1973 organized by Ottawa. The western premiers were sufficiently pleased with the results that they decided to meet on a regular basis. The conference now includes the three territorial leaders as well as the four western premiers.

Like the Council of Atlantic Premiers, the WPC has difficulty dealing with matters in which the interests of the various members are not the same. Thus the Western Energy Grid, like the Maritime Energy Corporation, proved to be a short-lived affair: Alberta feared that its coal-fired plants might be in jeopardy if the proposed grid made Manitoba hydro power more widely available. The premiers have been more likely to agree on a decision that is in everyone's interest (e.g., new funding for a veterinary college serving all western provinces), or when it comes to criticizing Ottawa (e.g., on the softwood lumber dispute with the US or health care funding).[17] Here again, a regional organization can contribute to the quiet resolution of some problems through the sharing of information and the commissioning of studies on specific western issues. One area where both the WPC and Council of Atlantic Premiers play interesting roles is in relations with the US, specifically with neighbouring states. The CAP has a primary role in organizing the Annual Conference of the New England Governors and the Eastern Canadian Premiers (which includes Quebec). Since September 2001, border issues involving trade access and security have been prominent both in this conference and in the annual joint sessions of the WPC and the Western Governors' Association (which take place during the WPC Conference).

SUMMARY

Interdependence in different policy and program areas necessitates practices and institutions, even if only informal, to facilitate and promote interaction between governments in order to coordinate and to manage their activities. In this chapter we have examined a wide array of such institutions—from first ministers' conferences and the Council of the Federation to working groups of officials, with a variety of bodies, such as ministerial councils and regular meetings of premiers on a regional basis, in between. This intergovernmental machinery has its strengths, particularly at the level of ministerial councils, but also some weaknesses. Most notably, the body at the pinnacle of the system, the First Ministers' Conference, is considered by two of Canada's most highly regarded observers to be seriously deficient in its capacity to promote regular interaction among first ministers and to serve as a role model for the system as a whole: for Papillon and Simeon (2004) the FMC constitutes the 'weakest link'. Another general weakness affecting the system as a whole is the absence of decision rules for rendering decisions or resolving disputes, apart from default consensus or mutual veto. Furthermore, when decisions are reached, they are often clouded in ambiguity, allowing different parties to read into them what they will. On the other hand, as we will see in the next chapter, though ambiguity might be a weakness in some circumstances, in others it may be considered an important resource.

Chapter 7

The Management and Reform of Executive Federalism

'Managing the federation' and 'reforming the federation' are two expressions frequently used by federal politicians and public servants, as well as observers, though not always in the same breath. 'Managing the federation' implies the coordination of programs between and among governments as well as the 'steering' of the federation in a direction consistent with the aims of the government in question—especially the federal government, which clearly has an interest in guiding developments with respect to governance and the direction of the federation as a whole.

'Reforming the federation', by contrast, can have numerous meanings. It can mean improving the way the federation functions—with better coordination, less overlap and duplication, and greater efficiency, for example. It can also mean making the intergovernmental process more open and transparent; this would be consistent with the aim of reducing the 'democratic deficit', but could have the effect of reducing efficiency and hampering the kind of informal coordination that is often required for expeditious action. 'Reform' could also mean adopting new procedures, including clearer decision rules, to reduce government's risk of falling into the 'joint-decision-making trap' (Scharpf, 1988, 1997). Clearer decision rules would certainly help to break up the logjams around a number of contentious issues, but they would also reduce ambiguity—a commodity that, like 'trust ties' (Dupré, 1988), many consider one of the crucial lubricants that keep the federal machinery running.

In this chapter we begin by examining the management of the federation, starting with those agencies created specifically by governments to help manage their intergovernmental relations. We then turn to the prospects for reform, before concluding with a look at the tension between two competing needs: for flexibility and for certainty.

INTERGOVERNMENTAL AFFAIRS AGENCIES (IGAs)

In the era of what Dupré (1988) and Smiley (1987) referred to as the 'departmentalized' cabinet, relations between governments were handled through the personal interactions of first ministers or of ministers and senior officials. The key units for both the federal and the provincial orders of government tended to be the line departments or ministries, responsible for actual operations and services, rather than central agencies, and larger-than-life figures such as J.G. (Jimmy) Gardiner, long-time minister of Agriculture, or C.D. Howe, 'minister of everything' in both the King and St-Laurent cabinets, were often in charge. Intergovernmental issues, generally involving cost-shared programs, were typically handled within the confines of the federal and provincial departments concerned.

The 'departmentalized' cabinet was gradually displaced by the 'institutionalized' cabinet (Dunn, 1995; Dupré, 1988; Smiley, 1987) beginning in the 1960s. This transition involved a series of administrative reforms intended to establish a more integrated, whole-of-government approach right at the top, at the level of cabinet. Line departments and individual ministers continued to be important actors, but now direction and a horizontal corporate perspective were provided by cabinet (or cabinet committees), with ample support from central agencies. Individual departments and their ministers were obliged to look beyond their own needs and take into account the concerns of other departments and central agencies. All government operations were affected by the reforms, but the impact on intergovernmental programs and activities was especially significant because they were directly involved in some of the most salient political issues of the day, including public pensions and medicare—issues that had to be handled with particular care. Ottawa and a number of provincial governments created specialized central agencies to manage not only relations between governments but also internal ('intragovernmental') relations.

Quebec was the first to set up a Department of Federal–Provincial Relations, in 1961; it was reorganized and renamed the Department of Intergovernmental Affairs in 1967, when it also took on responsibility for international affairs. Ontario created a new Department of Treasury, Economics and Intergovernmental Affairs in the mid-1960s; then in 1978, when the constitutional debate became the dominant issue, the Intergovernmental Affairs portion was hived off and turned into a separate agency. The federal government created a Federal–Provincial Relations Office (FPRO) separate from the Privy Council Office (PCO) in 1975. By the end of that decade virtually all governments had some kind of specialized intergovernmental affairs agency in place. IGAs reached their apotheosis in the 1970s and 1980s, largely because of their crucial role in intragovernmental constitutional talks.

With the cooling of interest in constitutional change, however, the role and scope of IGAs were reduced. The FPRO was returned to PCO in 1995, and is now known as the Intergovernmental Relations Secretariat. There is still a separate minister of Intergovernmental Relations, however. In the Chrétien government, Stéphane Dion attained quite a high profile in that position, but it has become much less important under Stephen Harper, largely because the prime minister sees federal–provincial relations, especially with Quebec, as his personal domain. In some provinces the premier sometimes takes on the Intergovernmental Affairs portfolio and in others a separate minister assumes that function. In every case, however, the premier sets the tone and determines the substance of intergovernmental relations, just as the prime minister always dominates foreign policy even though there is a separate minister of Foreign Affairs.

IGAs are expected to promote a government-wide perspective on executive decisions and provide whatever coordination and support may be required to that end. In larger provinces, IGAs are also responsible for trade offices located abroad that serve the interests of the province; and they provide channels for communication with members of the province's academic and business communities who have a particular expertise or interest in the province's relations with Ottawa (Elton and McCormick, 1997). Still, there are variations in the ways different agencies perform their roles, and the manner in which they are organized. Some, like Alberta's, carry much more weight than others, having as part of their legal mandate the right to participate in all intergovernmental negotiations conducted by line departments. Other IGAs play more of an advisory role and less of a coordinating one.[1] These variations in part reflect the first minister's personal preferences and approach. They are also in good part functions of the prevailing conditions (economic, social, etc.) and political climate. If the general environment is uncertain or turbulent, there will be more emphasis on centralized control.

From the late 1970s through the early 1980s was an especially turbulent period; it was also the heyday of IGAs. At that time, when the constitution was the main item on the agenda, the kind of expertise most in demand within IGAs was that of constitutional lawyers and political scientists. When the constitution is the primary item, the main concern will be to protect and if possible extend the government's jurisdiction and link related issues to the government's broader objectives. Lawyers are well trained to pursue these kinds of objectives; they are also accustomed to working in adversarial situations. All this led Donald Smiley to observe that 'Intergovernmental affairs agencies appear to contribute to federal–provincial conflict rather than accommodation' (1980: 115).

In earlier times, Smiley noted, program officials in both federal and provincial line departments, when left to their own devices, were usually quite capable of reaching agreements on the basis of professional or technical criteria. The problem is that the absence of hierarchy between governments in a federal system demands flexibility and a willingness to compromise in order for the system to function—but compromise does not always come easily in the adversarial environment typical of governments and, especially, IGAs. To be sure, Smiley was writing at the height of the constitutional battles between Ottawa and the provinces, when the stakes were extremely high: at that time it may well have been difficult to envision how IGAs might operate in a context where the stakes were much lower. Today the role of the IGA is more akin to that of a facilitator, smoothing the path for other, more technically specialized departments or agencies. Overall, however, IGAs remain significant players.

THE NEW PUBLIC MANAGEMENT

The various forums, bodies, and agencies discussed in this and the previous chapter are by no means the only settings in which intergovernmental relations are conducted. Federal agencies such as Western Diversification and the Atlantic Canada Opportunities Agency (ACOA), based in their respective regions, have primary responsibility for negotiations with the provinces on matters such as economic cooperation agreements (as did their predecessors, such as the Department of Regional Economic Expansion).[2] As well, federal line departments such as Human Resources and Social Development (HRSD) are relatively decentralized; thus much of their interaction with provincial governments takes place in the regions. A large part of this interaction involves the ongoing management of intergovernmental agreements. But there are exceptions. In 1997–8, for example, when Ottawa and the provinces negotiated the Labour Market Development Agreements (LMDAs)—a series of parallel but bilateral agreements—much of the actual negotiating was conducted in the field by officials from Human Resources Development Canada (the predecessor of HRSD) (Bakvis, 2002). Federal regional councils, composed of all the senior federal officials based in each province (Juillet, 2000),[3] liaise regularly with their provincial counterparts, and though their activities tend to be limited to supporting joint conferences and the like, they nevertheless provide important communication links and can contribute to the fostering of 'trust ties' (Dupré, 1988).

In 1994 the Chrétien government launched a major initiative that it called Program Review (Aucoin and Savoie, 1998), aimed at cutting costs and streamlining operations. As part of this effort, a number of organizational reforms were introduced. Based on a set of principles known as the 'new public management', these reforms were supposed to improve flexibility and responsiveness in the public service by delegating responsibility for service delivery to specialized agencies operating with much greater autonomy than the traditional line departments had (Aucoin, 1995). New agencies such as the Canada Revenue Agency (CRA) and the Canadian Food Inspection Agency (CFIA)—which took over functions previously handled by Agriculture Canada, Health Canada, and Fisheries and Oceans, among other departments—operate within a legal framework that gives them greater flexibility in the areas of financial and human resource management and more latitude for negotiating with, or providing services to, other levels of government. For example, the CRA (previously Revenue Canada) struck an agreement with three of the four Atlantic provinces to administer a new 'harmonized sales tax' (HST) that combined their sales taxes with the GST (Mellon, 1997). (Conversely, in the case of Quebec the Quebec Revenue agency collects the GST on behalf of Ottawa.)

More recently, the federal government has been encouraging departments and agencies to improve their horizontal coordination and cooperation across departments in the development and management of new programs (Bakvis and Juillet, 2004). It is important to note that horizontal initiatives are not restricted to a single order of government. Arrangements may also be bilateral, involving both federal and provincial or territorial agencies, or even trilateral, involving agencies at the municipal level as well. Projects such as the Vancouver Downtown Eastside Agreement, the St Lawrence Action Plan, and the Network of Canada Business Centres all involve horizontal relationships extending across two or more levels of government (see Bourgault, 2002). Although arrangements like these are often described as recent innovations, there is in fact a long tradition of projects involving two or more governments that have been managed by jointly owned or run agencies, often in the form of Crown corporations. A number of these intergovernmental relationships are discussed further in Chapters 13 and 14.

CABINET, MINISTERS, PARTIES, AND OTHER CHANNELS

In addition to the various formal institutions and settings outlined above, the intergovernmental system includes some useful nooks and crannies in which informal—even furtive—meetings can take place. The kitchen in the Ottawa conference centre is perhaps the best-known example: it was there, in November 1981, that Jean Chrétien, Roy Romanow, and Roy McMurtry of the federal, Saskatchewan, and Ontario governments, respectively, hammered out the deal, eventually agreed to by nine of the ten provinces, that made the patriation of the constitution possible. Hotel washrooms have also featured in the resolution of intergovernmental differences. Finally, one should not ignore the role that political parties can play in intergovernmental relations.

It is customary for the federal cabinet to include one fairly senior minister for every province, with the possible exception of PEI. These 'political' or 'regional' ministers have a significant voice on all matters involving the federal party and government in their respective provinces, including matters that have nothing to do with their particular portfolios (Bakvis, 1991). They also serve as their provinces' representatives in cabinet and in relations with their colleagues: thus a minister of Transport in his or her regional capacity will also have considerable sway over the activities in their province of other departments, such as Fisheries or Industry. It is not uncommon for a federal and a provincial minister from the same province—even if they are from different political parties—to form an informal alliance under which federal money will flow to programs under provincial jurisdiction. This cross-jurisdictional activity can make life difficult for the officials who are supposed to manage the programs in question, but it is part and parcel of the intergovernmental environment. Thus even though political leaders preoccupied with enhancing their own visibility and jurisdiction will be inclined to take an adversarial stance vis-à-vis other levels of government, individual ministers will be under pressure to work cooperatively with their counterparts in the other order of government in order to promote the well-being of their local constituencies.

It is also worth noting that in the Westminster system cabinet government is seen as coterminous with party government: members of the political executive are recruited to cabinet through their political parties, and parties are the crucial links between electors and governments. Some argue that political parties also play a crucial role in connecting the constituent units of the federation—a view that is reflected in what Campbell Sharman (1994) has called a 'parties-based theory of federalism'. According to William Riker (1964) it is the extent and nature of the links between the national parties and their counterparts in the constituent units that determine the degree of centralization or decentralization in a federation. A federation with a symmetrical party system regionally and nationally, especially one with the same party in power at the national level and in most of the constituent units, is considered highly centralized. When Donald Smiley applied Riker's model to the Canadian federation, however, he concluded that Canada's party system was 'significantly more confederal than that of any other federation with which [he was] familiar' (1987: 117) and therefore played only a limited integrative role.

Indeed, some of the most notable rifts between Ottawa and specific provinces have occurred when the parties in power at the national and provincial levels shared the same name. In the 1930s and 1940s the Liberal government of Ontario under Mitchell Hepburn was distinctly at odds with the federal Liberal government under Mackenzie King. There was little love lost between Saskatchewan's Liberal Premier Ross Thatcher and Liberal Prime Minister Lester Pearson during the 1960s. The same can be said for the Liberal governments of Canada and Quebec in the 1970s and 1980s. In the 'free trade' election of 1988, the Liberal government of Quebec was much more closely aligned with Brian Mulroney's Progressive Conservative government than with the Liberal-led opposition. Except, perhaps, in the Atlantic region, most of the major provincial parties long ago severed their ties to their national counterparts, and even in Atlantic Canada the situation has changed since the creation of the new Conservative party in 2003. In Newfoundland, for example, there has been little love lost between Conservative Prime Minister Stephen Harper and Progressive Conservative Premier Danny Williams, who urged voters throughout the Atlantic region to vote against the Conservatives in the federal election of 2008.

In the 1980s David Smith, referring in part to the role played by regional ministers in cabinet, wrote approvingly of the national parties as the 'sinews of a healthy federalism' (Smith, 1985: 1). The 1993 election, however, saw a pronounced regionalization of the Canadian party system. With the rise of the Bloc Québécois and the Reform Party (and its successor, the Canadian Alliance) —both of which were essentially regional opposition parties—there was a sense that the party system had become dysfunctional, doing more to separate the components of the federation than to integrate them. The early years of the twenty-first century, however, saw a series of interesting developments: the creation of the new Conservative party out of Reform/Alliance and the remnants of the old Progressive Conservatives; the fact of minority government since 2004, first under the Liberals and then the Conservatives; and, finally, the Conservatives' success in winning 10 seats in Quebec in the 2006 and 2008 elections. These developments make it possible to see the role of parties in Canadian federalism in a somewhat less pessimistic light.

Bakvis and Tanguay (2008), in their analysis of federalism and the Canadian party system, note that in a minority situation the government and opposition parties will initially cooperate or collude to avoid a premature election. In this context, federal–provincial issues often become the subject of logrolling. Thus the NDP supported the budget of Martin's minority government (2004–6) on the condition of an increase in federal support for post-secondary education. Similarly, after some intricate bargaining and manoeuvring, all the party leaders supported the resolution proposed by the Harper minority government that 'the Québécois form a nation within a united Canada'. To be sure, this kind of inter-party bargaining on federal–provincial issues is quite different from the traditional bargaining or 'brokerage' that takes place *within* broad-based national parties. Whether it can be seen as a positive development is an open question. For one thing, this kind of bargaining—much like executive federalism—is very much elite-driven.

Nonetheless, it is one example of the many avenues available for the conduct of intergovernmental relations or issues directly germane to them. The fact that the shape and context of intergovernmental relations are constantly subject to change points to the fluidity of the intergovernmental process and its relative lack of institutionalization.

'TRUST TIES'

Smiley's suggestion that IGAs may do more to exacerbate than to mitigate conflict brings us to the question of what J. Stefan Dupré (1988), in one of the classic pieces on Canadian federalism, labelled the 'workability of executive federalism' and the factors that help promote more effective intergovernmental relations. It is worth noting that Dupré's definition of 'effectiveness' was fairly minimal. For him the important test was that the two sides be able to have a dialogue and perhaps reach some understanding about what needs to be done. The success or failure of an intergovernmental process should not be judged by the actual decisions resulting from it.

In his analysis Dupré distinguished between 'functional' and 'summit' issues. Issues of the first type—examples include the original Canada Assistance Plan (CAP) of the 1960s, social security, regional economic development, and labour market training—involve distinct policy areas and are best handled by specialists in those areas. Matters such as constitutional review and fiscal relations, by contrast, Dupré classified as summit issues—issues that require 'summitry' in the form of meetings among first ministers. Intergovernmental negotiations are most likely to be successful when they concern functional issues. But there is variation within each category, and much of this variation can be attributed to the presence or absence of 'trust ties'.

According to Dupré, trust ties are most easily generated between individuals from similar professional backgrounds. Thus even functional issues can be hard to negotiate if the two sides do not share a common outlook: in the case of labour market training agreements, for instance, there is bound to be tension if one side consists largely of economists and the other largely of educators. In the case of summit issues—specifically fiscal matters—Dupré noted that even though negotiations are not always successful, the chances of finding some common ground are relatively good. Because the Finance portfolio is so critical, the ministers appointed to it usually have a great deal of experience and a record of good sense; and because it is so complex, they tend to rely heavily on the advice of experts in the field. At the end of the day, therefore, federal and provincial ministers of Finance may not agree, but in most cases they will at least have established some common understanding. The latter example, according to Dupré, points to the extent to which intergovernmental relations is a product of relations *within* governments—that is, the *intra*governmental dimension. In his view, which generally confirms Smiley's, when functional or line departments are displaced by central agencies such as IGAs, the existing trust ties are likely to be compromised. When contemplating a shift in strategy, therefore, a government needs to consider the risk of undermining the goodwill that has been developed over time.

More generally, the *intra*governmental dimension draws attention to the fact that the internal organization of governments has a considerable bearing on the conduct of intergovernmental affairs. More is involved here than intergovernmental agencies themselves. What happens, for example, when Ottawa decides to offload its responsibility for a certain program onto provincial governments that are not set up in the same way as the federal government? At a minimum there will be delays as the provinces reorganize to handle their new responsibilities. The reverse can also be true. The federal government may wish to take over certain functions from the provinces (perhaps for reasons related to political credit and visibility) but then discover it lacks the necessary organizational capacity. In short, a mismatch in the organizational interface between the two orders of government can be highly problematic.

Finally, major shifts in government policy can seriously undermine trust ties. The most obvious example would probably be Ottawa's 1995 decision to cut its transfers to the provinces as part of its Program Review, which precipitated a

'general decline in trust levels' in all areas (Inwood et al., 2004: 269). The implications of Program Review for intergovernmental relations in the area of finance
were particularly significant. As Harvey Lazar (2005a) has noted, the cuts forced
the provinces to assume more of the responsibility for revenue generation. The
provinces are now much less dependent on Ottawa for funding than they were in
the past, and this general shift has meant a marked reduction in the interaction
between the federal and provincial Finance departments. Furthermore, because
every Finance department plays a guardian role within the government as a
whole—ensuring that other departments are allocated no more than is necessary
and do not overspend their budgets[4]—their relations with the latter are always
somewhat adversarial. That guardian role became more pronounced in the mid-
1990s, with predictable results for relations with other departments. Of course,
the more adversarial stance of the federal Finance department in particular has
also affected federal–provincial relations.

Thus Dupré's scenario, in which a common background in economics and a
shared language among Finance officials generated high levels of trust within and
between the federal and provincial Finance departments, may no longer apply.
Similarly, federal line departments looking to build or repair relations with their
provincial counterparts are more likely to see Finance agencies as obstacles than
as facilitators.

EXECUTIVE FEDERALISM UNDER CHALLENGE

There are two challenges that bear directly on executive federalism and the intergovernmental bodies associated with it. First are the demands from various
commentators and advocacy groups that executive federalism be made more
open and transparent; second is the absence of decision-making rules and the
implications of this absence for the making of public policy.

The notion of a 'democratic deficit' is increasingly invoked to argue that the
intergovernmental process should be opened up and made more transparent and
accountable. Some, such as Simeon and Nugent (2008; see also Simeon and
Cameron, 2002), even suggest that federalism, or at least Canadian-style federalism, is incompatible with democracy. Critics have pointed to the closed, secretive nature of much intergovernmental decision-making, as well as the apparent
lack of accountability. A disturbing example of the dark side of intergovernmental relations was the role played by the Canadian blood committee
(composed of federal and provincial officials) in the tainting of the blood supply
in the 1980s (Picard, 1995). Furthermore, one order of government will often use
federal–provincial relations as an excuse to escape accountability, arguing, for
example, that the reason some problem has not been addressed is that the other
order of government is responsible for it (Harrison, 1996).

On the other hand, federalism remains a vital bulwark of democracy in a territorially large and socially diverse country (Smith, 2004). Federal arrangements

were adopted in the American republic explicitly to prevent central tyranny by providing a system of checks and balances. Federal regimes typically protect minorities through the constitutional enshrinement of group and individual rights as well as the self-governing rights of constituent peoples and territorial units. So there is nothing inherently anti-democratic about federalism: quite the contrary.

Yet democracy can take a variety of forms, and these different forms invariably demand trade-offs between different democratic values, including those of federalism. For example, protection of minority rights invariably comes at the expense of simple majority rule. Furthermore, the close public scrutiny of negotiations that is required for an open and inclusive process tends to make effective collaboration difficult. For many citizens, efficient and timely delivery of services is a democratic value in itself (Simeon and Cameron, 2002).

Among the democratic values that have drawn the most attention is citizen participation, both through consultative processes and through actual participation in decision-making. The increased emphasis on this form of democracy reflects in part the fact that citizens today are better educated, less deferential, and much more demanding than they were in the past (Nevitte, 1996, 2002). The introduction of the Charter of Rights in 1982, in addition to constraining the powers of both orders of government, has encouraged the development of a more rights-oriented, participatory political culture. The process of constitutional patriation in itself served as a kind of awakening for numerous public interest groups, as well as minorities such as Aboriginal peoples. These groups played a significant role in forcing the first ministers to make whatever changes were necessary to ensure that the Charter and Aboriginal rights were included in the final package, running well-orchestrated campaigns and making effective use of the media. Perhaps even more critically, they mobilized public opinion to derail the Meech Lake ratification process, mainly with the objective of preserving the 1982 achievements. Then in 1992 pressure from these same groups helped to persuade the first ministers that a national referendum was essential to ensure popular support for the Charlottetown Accord—a referendum by definition representing the broadest possible form of citizen participation.

These developments led Kathy Brock (1995) to suggest that traditional executive federalism—13 or 14 white males at first ministers' conferences, for example—no longer had the legitimacy it enjoyed before the Meech Lake and Charlottetown conferences. Though she cautioned against premature predictions of the demise of executive federalism, she nonetheless suggested that the process had to become much more open and transparent, and argued that the opportunities afforded various citizen groups during the Charlottetown negotiations would make it difficult to return to a more closed, elitist process.

To be sure, Brock was writing about constitutional negotiations and did not necessarily mean to extend her argument to all other types of intergovernmental interaction. Yet it is striking that the openness of the Charlottetown process was largely absent in the latter half of the 1990s. During the negotiations leading up to the Social Union Framework Agreement, for example, there was no involvement, either direct or indirect, on the part of public interest groups, and not necessarily for want of trying. These groups were simply unable to gain any traction in the process.[5] And the problem was not simply that ministers and officials deliberately excluded them: public opinion was indifferent to their efforts. With the Chrétien government's more low-key approach to dealings with the provinces, and in particular Chrétien's wish to steer clear of constitutional matters and avoid first ministers' meetings unless absolutely necessary, executive federalism began to move in a new direction. It certainly did not revert to the way it had worked during the heyday of cooperative federalism in the 1950s: IGAs are still very much involved in the intergovernmental process, and outstanding issues such as health care attract considerable public interest and debate. Furthermore, the cuts to fiscal transfers resulting from Program Review caused considerable rancour among the general public. In other respects, however, the fact that intergovernmental relations during the Chrétien era were for the most part conducted away from public view attracted little controversy. Even Quebec's participation in SUFA, in the form of what Alain Noël (2001) called a 'Footnote', appeared to work remarkably smoothly. Although SUFA does refer to government's commitments to 'monitor and measure outcomes of its social programs and report regularly to its constituents on the performance of these programs' and to introduce 'effective mechanisms for Canadians to participate in developing social priorities and reviewing outcomes',[6] Simeon and Cameron (2002: 292) believe that SUFA's potential for enhancing democratic practices is 'pretty thin gruel'.

Executive federalism and federal–provincial tensions did attain a higher profile after Chrétien's departure. His immediate successor, Paul Martin became involved in very public discussions, followed by public concessions, over offshore resources and the clawback of equalization payments (see Chapter 9). The Harper government in its own way has also raised the profile and temperature of federal–provincial–territorial relations. It introduced substantial changes in the Equalization Program, including a resolution to the clawback and fiscal imbalance issues, which resulted in much public debate. And while it has been careful in its dealings with Quebec, the same cannot be said of its relations with Ontario. The federal minister of Finance, Jim Flaherty, has had a number of highly publicized spats with the Liberal premier of Ontario, Dalton McGuinty, and his cabinet ministers.

During the 2006 federal election campaign Conservative leader Harper made 'open federalism' a key part of his campaign platform. This approach, as Harper explains it, has more to do with the federal government respecting provincial jurisdictions, being less intrusive and seeking to elevate the tone of intergovernmental relations, than with making federalism more transparent.[7] In many ways the pattern of federal intergovernmental leadership under Harper is similar to that under Chrétien—not surprising, given that Harper's aversion to first ministers' meetings is perhaps even greater than Chrétien's. But the Harper government is also much more aloof, and the channels of communication are much more restricted than they were under Chrétien, leaving the provinces uncertain about where they stand vis-à-vis either Ottawa itself or the new programs affecting them that Ottawa has unilaterally announced. Part of this development can be explained by the Harper government's penchant for internal control and centralization, which leaves little room for individual federal ministers to play a role in intergovernmental relations. Ministers of Intergovernmental Relations in the Harper government, for example, have played a virtually invisible role on the intergovernmental stage.

Overall, the post-Chrétien period has seen intergovernmental relations take on a higher public profile, even in the absence of constitutional issues, with conflict spilling over into the media not just over health care—a perennial topic for public debate—but also over developments in the more arcane world of fiscal federalism generally, where citizens have had ample opportunity to observe a feisty Newfoundland premier, Danny Williams, take on both Paul Martin and Stephen Harper over the inclusion or exclusion of natural resource revenues in the equalization formula. Suddenly, it seemed, terms such as 'fiscal imbalance' and 'equalization clawback', long the preserve of economists and public finance specialists, had entered the public lexicon. The electoral victory of Danny Williams, premier of Newfoundland and Labrador, in October 2007, who ran on an explicit anti-Ottawa platform, suggests that government's success or failure in dealing with these issues can have significant consequences.

DEMOCRACY, FEDERALISM, AND REFORM

There appear to be two strategies or approaches for rendering the intergovern-mental process more democratic and transparent. The first is to open up the intergovernmental process itself, broadening participation by involving stake-holders and developing links with civil-society organizations. Julie Simmons (2004, 2005, 2008) has written extensively about a number of these develop-ments, mainly in connection with ministerial councils. One question that might be asked regarding this approach is how well the non-governmental participants represent the constituencies actually affected by the issues at hand. Another question is whether the public participation is anything more than a screen designed to deflect public scrutiny while the serious, hard-nosed negotiations continue to take place in private.

The other approach involves tackling the institutional underpinnings of execu-tive federalism—that is, the Westminster system, with its inherent tendency towards the concentration of power in the hands of an executive that uses party discipline and executive control of the machinery of government to maintain its dominance over the legislature. Under the rubric of 'legislative federalism' (Simeon and Nugent, 2008; Baier et al., 2005) it has been suggested that greater involvement of the legislatures at both the federal and provincial levels would help make the federal–provincial policy process more transparent. For example, proposed intergovernmental agreements might be required to undergo legislative scrutiny before they are formalized, legislative committees might be mandated to review intergovernmental affairs, and party discipline might be relaxed in order to give MPs greater freedom to examine and debate intergovernmental issues. Essentially, the argument is that tinkering with the institutions of executive federalism will have little impact unless some of the more fundamental aspects of parliamentary democracy are reformed first.

Baier et al. (2005) have argued that such reforms may have unintended consequences. First, reducing the concentration of power in the executive would reduce the capacity of first ministers to broker deals among themselves. It would also reduce the scope for elite accommodation—a longstanding feature of Canadian politics and of Canadian federalism in particular, which has played a crucial part in sustaining support for the idea of asymmetrical federalism and Quebec's unique position in confederation. Outside Quebec, recognition of Quebec's unique position has always been much stronger among elites than among ordinary citizens.

Second, newly empowered MPs might well try to use the federal spending power to play a more active and public role in areas under provincial jurisdiction, such as health care. Certainly they are less likely to observe jurisdictional niceties when pursuing issues that they believe are important to their constituents. Use of the spending power in the form of conditional transfers, for example, would likely increase tension not only with Quebec but with other provinces as well. On the other hand, a more democratic parliament, with greater legislative scrutiny and a more active role for MPs, could increase Ottawa's legitimacy. Instead of regarding the federal government as remote from their lives, citizens might begin to think of it as promoting their interests.

Minority government, which may well become more frequent at both the federal and the provincial level (note the results of the 2004, 2006, and 2008 federal elections), could also contribute to a greater role for MPs. According to Peter Russell (2008), the advantages—notably, greater democracy through greater involvement on the part of MPs—outweigh disadvantages such as more frequent elections, reduced stability, and less predictable legislative outcomes. Yet as we suggested in our discussion of the changing role of political parties, a minority parliament does not necessarily mean a larger role for MPs. This may have been true of the Liberal minority government led by Paul Martin, but under Stephen Harper there appears to be even more emphasis on party discipline, not only among the Conservatives but also on the opposition benches as party leaders focus on parliamentary manoeuvres and backroom negotiations. In order to control the fate of a minority government, party leaders need to have full control over their caucuses, which means less autonomy for MPs and parliamentary committees.

In brief, the prospects for reform of parliamentary institutions are far from certain. And if reforms should occur, it is not at all certain what the implications might be, either for intergovernmental relations specifically or for the stability of the Canadian federation more generally.

FLEXIBILITY VERSUS CERTAINTY

As we have seen, observers such as Lazar (2004) argue that ambiguity is essential to the Canadian confederation because of the flexibility it provides. Unfortunately, that ambiguity is a reflection of the absence of clear guidelines and decision rules—which means that by default the only meaningful decision-making rule left is unanimity. This situation has been described as contributing to the 'joint-decision-making trap' (Scharpf, 1988, 1989).

Two successful federal systems, Australia and the European Union, have developed weighted voting procedures to allow intergovernmental bodies to get around the unanimity obstacle. Other successful federations, such as Germany and Austria, provide for co-decision on national matters by having provincial delegates vote directly within their parliamentary upper houses. By contrast, Canadian federalism is characterized by low levels of institutionalization and a complete absence of explicit decision rules. Simeon and Papillon (2004) note that institutionalization is especially weak at the highest level, namely first ministers' conferences—a conclusion that leads them to characterize this body as the 'weakest link' in the Canadian intergovernmental system. The relatively new Council of the Federation, developed out of the longstanding Annual Premiers' Conference, does enjoy greater institutional support for its activities than first ministers' conferences do, and it meets on a more regular basis. Yet it too has limitations. It has not been able to overcome the tendency of its predecessor to serve as a platform for attacking the policies of the federal government. Nor has it managed to develop a set of rules or policies for dealing with interprovincial conflict.

There is more evidence of regularization and institutional support at the level of ministerial councils and officials' meetings. These bodies also allow for some participation on the part of non-governmental stakeholders, and they appear to have a greater capacity to generate trust ties. After studying a number of ministerial councils, however, Simmons found that

> policy co-ordination and consensus decision-making among governments do not require institutionalized intergovernmental forums for deliberation. It may even be the case that the lack of established supports, traditions, and procedures . . . created flexibility that encouraged rather than inhibited policy innovation (Simmons, 2004: 303).

This suggests that the absence of institutionalization is not necessarily a barrier to productive intergovernmental relations and that either institutionalization or lack of institutionalization can cut both ways.

Institutionalization is more advanced in the central agencies dedicated to the conduct of intergovernmental relations. Yet the IGAs' record of success in facilitating interaction is mixed. During the nearly two decades of constitutional negotiations in particular, they were often accused of increasing rather than mitigating conflict.

For Papillon and Simeon, the single most important intergovernmental body is the first ministers' conference or meeting, and the key to making it more effective lies in increasing its institutional character through the creation of a secretariat, the adoption of a regular meeting schedule, and so on. One thing we know is that increasing institutionalization would mean increasing certainty—and therefore reducing the ambiguity that gives the system the flexibility it needs. We also know that any attempt to put the FMC/FMM on a stronger institutional footing would require the cooperation of the first ministers, especially the prime minister.

So far Stephen Harper (like Jean Chrétien) has been decidedly wary of the intergovernmental process, not wishing to tie the hands of his government by subjecting its decisions to a bargaining process in which a successful outcome depends on reaching a consensus with the provincial and territorial first ministers. It is not inconceivable, however, that some future prime minister might be more amenable to institutional innovation. Either way, the point is that the office of the prime minister is so central, both within the federal government and within the intergovernmental system as a whole, that its occupant's influence is likely to be determinative. Whether the institutional innovations discussed here would have the desired effect remains open to debate.[8] But we can be sure intergovernmental relations will continue to be shaped by the personalities at the apex of the intergovernmental system: the first ministers. The FMC/FMM may well be the weakest link in the system, but for good or ill it remains by far the most important one.

SUMMARY

In this chapter we have emphasized the lack of formal mechanisms—rules, regular meetings, well-defined, widely accepted institutions—for intergovernmental activity in Canada. We have also noted some of the crucial means and conditions that do allow for interaction between and among intergovernmental participants, most notably 'trust ties'. Nevertheless, it is possible to identify a number of distinct patterns in Canada's intergovernmental relations. The most notable one is what Gibbins (1999) has described as '9-1-1' federalism, in which Ottawa breaks a stalemate in federal–provincial negotiations by negotiating with nine of the provinces—all of them *except* Quebec—and then, once a consensus has been reached with them, proceeds to negotiate bilaterally with Quebec; this was the pattern followed in the SUFA negotiations (though they included the territories as well as the provinces). In another common scenario, Ottawa will resolve an impasse by taking unilateral action. This approach appears to be especially characteristic of the Harper government, and has been most pronounced in the area of fiscal federalism. In a sense the Harper government seems to have reversed the usual pattern, reaching a quiet understanding with Quebec first and then tailoring its plan to meet the needs of the other provinces, a pattern that could be described as 1-1-9 rather than 9-1-1 federalism.

We will return to the tension between flexibility, rooted in ambiguity, and certainty in our concluding chapter. Here we will simply note that none of the patterns outlined above is terribly satisfactory from the perspective of sound public policy, if only because they all appear to be guided more by political calculation than by real needs in the social and economic realm. To the extent that these patterns, implicitly or explicitly, reflect Quebec's unique position in the federation, they continue the tradition of elite accommodation and are vulnerable to challenge by moves towards legislative federalism and democratization of the intergovernmental process. Furthermore, these approaches tend to be workable only when a serious crisis has been reached, which means that a whole array of intermediate issues that are important but fall short of constituting a crisis—issues such as the need for labour mobility standards, or for a national securities regulator—are left unresolved.

Chapter 8

Fiscal Relations: Basic Principles and Overview

Fiscal relations are an indispensable part of a federal system. In this chapter we examine three aspects of fiscal relations. First is their *function*—what they are intended to achieve—in theory and in practice. In all federations fiscal relations are a vital means of intergovernmental interaction; they provide for flexibility within an often rigid constitutional framework and for ongoing, pragmatic implementation of federation-wide objectives. Second is the specific *structure* of fiscal relations. In Canada this structure is relatively decentralized, reflecting the high value that the country places on provincial autonomy and equalization. Third is the way fiscal relations *change*. Fiscal relations are a subset of broader fiscal policy decisions, designed ultimately to fit into changing budgetary priorities and to reflect changing economic realities. They can also be intensely symbolic and political, representing broad political values and strong partisan positions.

All governments have expenditures and revenues. In federal systems of government, a number of factors determine who does what in terms of spending and taxing. These factors include the constitutional division of powers; the historical development of the relationship between the central government and the constituent units (in Canada, the provinces); the relative economic strength of the units, or of the country as a whole; and the values underpinning public finance (for example, the relative commitments to redistribution, equity, autonomy, or efficiency). The system of intergovernmental fiscal relations exists to smooth out a variety of vertical and horizontal imbalances, some temporary and some permanent. In so doing, they give practical effect to the *evolving* roles assigned to different governments in the system. In this respect they provide for frequent adaptation and ongoing flexibility.[1]

The structure of fiscal relations in Canada has three key components.[2] First is the constitutional division of powers. The fact that the federal and provincial orders of government have their own exclusive areas of jurisdiction does not prevent *de facto* overlap and interdependence. But it does give the provinces more independent regulatory and spending authority than is enjoyed by the constituent units in other federations (e.g., the states in the US or Australia, or the Länder in Germany). The federal government does have the power to spend on virtually anything, even on programs within provincial areas of jurisdiction, but only if that spending cannot be interpreted as an attempt to regulate in a field of provincial jurisdiction. The second component is the allocation of the power to collect revenue through taxation. Since the Canadian provinces have broad taxing power, the most important income and consumption tax fields are effectively shared between the two orders of government. Third, like all federal systems, Canada has a system of intergovernmental transfer programs to fill the gaps between the revenue-generating capacities and the expenditure responsibilities of the various governments, federal and provincial. The three largest transfer programs at present are the Canada Health Transfer (CHT), the Canada Social Transfer (CST), and the Equalization Program. The process by which governments agree (or disagree) on the structure of fiscal relations is highly contentious and political. Like executive federalism as a whole, however, decision-making is mostly informal, much of it is very technical and often done behind closed doors.

These components combine in real time to meet the needs of the day. Most fiscal arrangements are designed to last for a while—typically five years—but not forever. The fact is that they must change if they are to respond to changing economic and social conditions. This chapter summarizes several distinct phases of fiscal relations in Canada over the past sixty years. Four general patterns emerge. For most of the period since 1945 there has been a steady trend towards fiscal decentralization: in the war years both taxing and spending powers were concentrated at the federal level, but since then more and more activity has shifted to the provincial level. Another major trend, especially since the mid-1970s, has been a decrease in the conditions attached to fiscal transfers. Transfers expanded rapidly after the Second World War to meet the growing needs of social and other programs, but once those programs became mature the federal government relaxed the conditions that had been placed on most of the funds transferred. A third major trend, related to the first two trends, is a gradual change in the overall objectives that transfers have been expected to achieve, which in turn reflect changing political values; for example, a shift from equity to efficiency. Finally, there has been a continuing oscillation between fiscal arrangements jointly developed by the federal and provincial governments, and unilateral measures imposed by individual governments. All these trends have very real consequences for Canadians in terms of the money that stays in their pockets or is collected from them through taxation and spent on programs important to them. The most important fiscal federalism issues in Canada today are the subject of Chapter 9.

THE FUNCTIONS, PRINCIPLES, AND DYNAMICS OF FISCAL FEDERALISM

Fiscal relations are a key part of the operation of all federal systems—indeed, of any relationship among governments of any kind (Bird and Vaillancourt, 2006). They are in effect a family of relationships that work to ensure that all the governments within a given political community have the fiscal ability to match their legal autonomy and expenditure responsibilities. Whether the system is federal, as in Canada, or unitary, as in France, and whatever the levels involved—provincial–municipal, federal–provincial, federal–Aboriginal—the financial arrangements underpinning the relationship go a long way towards defining it. If one level of government has the money and another is always begging for it, cap in hand, no constitutional principle of independence or autonomy is going to change the practical fact of dependency.

Fiscal arrangements give practical effect to the distribution of power in a federal system. Formal constitutional provisions—such as sections 91 and 92 of the Constitution Act, 1867—would be irrelevant if revenues could not be collected and spent to support those functions. Moreover, fiscal relations are one of the most important means by which a federal constitution—especially one that is relatively old, as Canada's is—can remain flexible enough to adapt to changing conditions of governance and meet changing demands on the state. It was by adjusting their fiscal arrangements that governments were able to provide relief during the Great Depression, tax and spend as necessary in wartime, develop the post-war 'welfare state', and, more recently, balance their budgets and reduce their debts.

Fiscal relations also play a major role in the realization of the federation's overall objectives, especially those that reflect the values encompassed by the concepts of 'social union' and 'economic union' (discussed in detail in Chapters 10 and 11). The economic union requires efficiency in the movement of goods, services, capital, and labour throughout the federation. Common tax treatment and similar levels of public services contribute greatly to that efficiency. Harmonized fiscal policy also contributes to equity, by ensuring that similarly situated persons or corporations receive the same treatment. Since the social union seeks to achieve common social policy standards and entitlements (to varying degrees, depending on the policy), fiscal arrangements must be made to share wealth by redistributing revenue from richer individuals and regions to poorer ones. Efficiency is essential here too, to maximize the amount of wealth available for redistribution. Efficiency and equity are not the only important values in a federation, however, and a fiscal policy with these as its only goals would tend to uniformity and unity. Thus they must be traded off against federal values such as flexibility, diversity, autonomy, and accountability. To promote these latter values, fiscal arrangements also need to take into account three other objectives. The first is to ensure that the government that makes expenditures also raises the revenues to pay for them. The second is to ensure that local, regional, and national preferences in redistribution and equity are met. And the third is to ensure that governments have sufficient fiscal autonomy to make their own choices about public goods and service and levels of taxation. In effect, then, fiscal relations have to maintain a political balance between several competing values and objectives.[3]

'Balance' in the financial sense, not surprisingly, is another important part of fiscal relations. There are two types of fiscal balance in a federation: vertical and horizontal.[4] The term *vertical fiscal balance or imbalance* refers to the relative positions of the central government and the constituent units. In Canada this usually means the federal and provincial orders of government, but the same term can be applied to federal–territorial, provincial–local, federal–Aboriginal, and even federal–local relationships. A vertical fiscal gap between the central government and the constituent governments is a natural feature of all federations, simply because the central government's authority over the entire country allows it to tax mobile economic resources—wealth, profits, income, and consumption—wherever they occur. From an efficiency perspective, then, it makes sense that the central government has a greater fiscal capacity than the units, which usually have neither full legal taxing power nor the practical means to access national wealth in order to fund their expenditures. The result is a gap between federal revenues and provincial (state, etc.) expenditure needs (Lazar, St-Hilaire, and Tremblay, 2004). In every federation this gap is filled, at least in part, by cash transfers from the centre to the units. But this is not the only method available. A central government can also reallocate or transfer a larger share of taxes to the units, or even shift an entire tax field to them, permanently reducing part of its own superior fiscal capacity. Another way of closing the gap is simply to transfer the expenditure responsibility upwards, to the federal government. The Canadian federation has used all three of these methods over its history, but in general has relied on the cash transfer approach.

The term *horizontal fiscal balance or imbalance* refers to differences across the units: more specifically, in Canada's case, the differing fiscal capacities of the various provinces and territories to fund their own expenditure responsibilities. These imbalances arise primarily because of differences in economic activity and accrued wealth: in short, regional economic disparities. Virtually all federations find some way to even out horizontal imbalances, both for general equity reasons, to ensure a measure of fiscal equality across the country, and for constitutional purposes, to ensure that all the units are able to manage the responsibilities allocated to them. In some federations, such as Germany, rich provinces make direct payments to the poorer ones. More commonly, though, correction of horizontal imbalances is left to the federal government, which uses its fiscal capacity to redistribute wealth, most often through intergovernmental grants but also in some cases through transfers to persons: in Canada, for instance, payments made to individuals through the employment insurance program have the effect of redistributing wealth from the richer provinces to less prosperous ones. It's important to note that the federal government's ability to correct horizontal imbalances depends on the existence of the vertical gap—that is, the fact that the federal government is able to collect more revenue than it needs to fulfil its own responsibilities—since vertical transfers are the chief means of bridging the horizontal gaps. This means that the federal level would still need a superior revenue capacity even if provincial expenditure responsibility and revenue capacity were, on average, evenly matched (no vertical imbalance).

In sum, then, a system is said to be in balance when a government's revenue capacity matches its expenditure responsibilities. It is in imbalance when one government—almost always the central one—has an excess of revenue capacity over expenditure responsibility. And it is in imbalance when different constituent governments have widely differing fiscal capacities but are expected to deliver similar public services.

At this stage, readers familiar with the real world of government budgets and fiscal policy would probably say that the concept of revenue–expenditure balance outlined here is overly abstract. They would be right. Actual balance is very much in the eye of the beholder. What one person sees as excess revenue capacity another will see as a prudent budget surplus, and what looks like a revenue deficit to one observer may look like a preference for low taxes to another. Nonetheless, in most federations governments collectively try to overcome the worst effects of imbalance. And the magnitude of that task will change over time. How a given federation tries to achieve that balance (or to live with imbalance) says a lot, as well, about its underlying values as a political community.

Finally, to give life to the objectives and values just discussed, fiscal federalism requires certain more or less lasting structural components.[5] These include the legal powers to raise taxes and other revenues, to spend money, and to borrow money—powers that different federations will allocate to their various governments in different ways—and a set of mechanisms for sharing revenues and expenditure costs and otherwise transferring financial resources from one government to another. These features are often outlined in the federal constitution, in which case they can be formally changed only by constitutional amendment—a difficult task. This is not to say that the basic allocation of taxing and spending power is set in stone: change does take place informally, as modifications grow into political conventions, are incorporated into intergovernmental agreements and legislation, or gradually become accepted practice. Nevertheless, these processes do tend to take rather a long time, as even the smallest change in fiscal relations engenders a lot of debate. The basic allocation of taxing and spending power does change, but slowly.

Yet in other respects the stuff of fiscal relations is changing all the time. This is true in two senses. First, the revenues and expenditures of any government are in constant flux in response to economic growth or shrinkage, annual budgetary decisions, and international changes in interest rates, bond ratings, exchange rates and so on. These changes have immediate consequences for the effectiveness of specific intergovernmental arrangements to share revenues or costs. Thus fiscal arrangements often turn out to be more costly than planned, or insufficient to meet growing needs. Arrangements that have been especially well designed will anticipate external changes and automatically adjust to them. But, as we shall see, that situation is rare, despite the best efforts of policy planners.

The second sense in which change is a constant is that formal fiscal arrangements in most federal systems, including Canada, are designed only for the medium term—usually five years—in the knowledge that the changing conditions discussed above will sooner or later force adjustments. Many fiscal arrangements are based on some kind of formula that makes annual calculations about shared revenues or costs more or less automatic, providing yet more flexibility over time. Thus—in principle at least—fiscal arrangements like intergovernmental relations as a whole, are among the means by which a federation provides for a moderate degree of change and adaptation without constitutional reform. Even so, any particular incremental change can still give rise to enormous controversy. This has been especially true in the last decade.

THE STRUCTURE OF FISCAL RELATIONS IN CANADA

1. Constitutional Powers

Three aspects of Canada's constitutional allocation of powers play an important role in shaping fiscal relations within the federation. First, the fact that most fields of jurisdiction are exclusive to either the federal or the provincial order of government makes the two orders more independent of one another than they would be with a concurrent scheme of powers.

It also means that Ottawa has less scope than other federal governments to legislate specific conditions for programs to be delivered by the provinces (Watts, 2008). The requirement that fiscal arrangements respect the jurisdictional autonomy of the provinces—even if there is debate about what this requirement entails—is especially problematic because three of the major expenditure fields over which the provinces have jurisdiction are ones that have become central to advanced industrial societies over the past 60 years: health care, education, and social services/assistance.

The second aspect of the division of powers relevant to fiscal relations is the fact that both the federal and provincial governments have full access to the most important and most broadly based sources of tax revenue. Both can levy not only personal and corporate income taxes but also general sales or consumption taxes, as well as payroll taxes for specific purposes such as unemployment insurance, health care, and pensions. The capacity of the Canadian provinces to pay for their expenditure responsibilities from their own revenue sources is greater than that of their counterparts in most other federal systems. However, because key tax bases such as personal income and consumption of goods and services are shared, there is a risk that taxpayers will be subjected to conflicting demands and overwhelming tax burdens. Therefore the two orders of government must find ways to harmonize their taxes.

Finally there is the fact that the federal government's 'spending power', though recognized by the courts, is not spelled out in detail by the constitution. The spending power has been the means by which Ottawa has promoted a national (pan-Canadian) approach to social programs, including direct payments to individuals and to organizations for redistributive purposes. This practice has been controversial, however, particularly in Quebec, where there is strong support for the principle of strict provincial autonomy.

2. Revenue Sources and Tax Structure

As noted above, the federal government and the provinces share the most important and broad-based tax sources. The most important revenue types are:

- Personal income tax (PIT): levied by both the federal and provincial governments. The federal government collects the provincial tax together with its own except in Quebec, where there are parallel collection systems. Usually the provincial tax base is defined as a portion of the federal, but recently there has been some movement towards more independence in the definition of the tax base.[6] For example, Alberta uses a 'flat' rate for its income tax: the percentage charged does not rise as income rises.
- Corporate income tax (CIT): also levied by both governments, and also collected by the federal government for most provinces. Here too there has been some movement towards independent tax bases.
- Consumption or sales taxes: levied by Ottawa and all the provincial governments except Alberta. The federal government levies the Goods and Services Tax, which is harmonized with the provincial sales tax in Newfoundland and Labrador, Nova Scotia, and New Brunswick. In Quebec, where the provincial government collects the federal GST as well as its own provincial sales tax, the two taxes are determined on a nearly identical basis.
- Natural resource revenues in the form of mineral royalties, stumpage fees, and other specific taxes: a significant source of provincial-only taxes.
- Property taxes: levied by municipalities (under the authority of provincial law), although in some provinces revenue from property tax is directed to school boards on a province-wide basis.
- Payroll taxes: both the federal and provincial governments collect premiums from employers and employees for each person employed to pay for programs such as employment insurance, the Canada or Quebec Pension Plan, and, in some provinces, health care.
- Customs and excise duties: important tax sources at the time of Confederation, these are exclusively federal. The federal taxes on alcohol, tobacco, and gasoline are excise taxes.
- Gaming revenues: the provinces receive significant revenues from gaming (lotteries, casinos, horse racing, charitable bingos, video lotteries, etc.).

- Alcoholic beverages: Provinces get the lion's share of revenue from alcoholic beverages, partly through direct taxes on products, and partly through monopoly profits from provincial liquor corporations.

The overall trend for all revenue sources has been towards an increasingly large share for the provincial governments—in other words, fiscal decentralization.

Table 8.1 provides an overview of the main types and shares of taxes collected by the federal and combined provincial–local governments in Canada in 1997 and in 2005. It aggregates the tax and revenue types listed above into five main categories. In 1955, when Ottawa exercised strong central control over revenue generation, it levied approximately 70 per cent of all taxes. By the 1990s, however, its share had declined to only about 44 per cent, where it has remained ever since. The main reason for this decline was that provincial expenditure responsibilities (e.g., health care) were rising much more quickly than federal expenditure responsibilities (e.g., defence). In response to this trend, the federal government ceded considerable tax room on corporate and personal income to the provinces in the 1950s, 1960s, and 1970s. Since there are few constitutional prohibitions on provincial revenue-raising, taxes both big and small have proliferated at the provincial level.

Table 8.1   Federal and Provincial Own-source Revenues ($ millions)

	1997			2005		
	Federal	Prov.–local	Total	Federal	Prov.–local	Total
Income taxes	88,223	55,356	143,579	132,668	72,467	205,135
Consumption taxes	32,007	37,366	69,373	47,126	56,932	104,058
Payroll taxes	22,658	9,437	32,093	21,102	12,580	33,682
Property taxes	—	36,935	36,935	—	46,784	46,784
Other revenues	11,930	57,945	69,175	15,149	98,871	104,020
Total	154,818	197,039	351,855	216,045	277,634	493,679

SOURCE: Statistics Canada: Adapted from Treff and Perry (2005: Table A.1, p. A:2).

Note: Provincial includes territorial government.

In any federal system, tax decentralization has the potential to erode the fiscal, economic, and social integration that is one of the chief reasons for adopting a federal system in the first place. Explicit or implicit programs for fiscal equalization address one of the primary effects of decentralization of revenues: that is, horizontal fiscal imbalance, or inequity (Equalization is discussed below). Harmonization of taxes is also important—to ensure that similarly situated taxpayers are treated similarly, and to make it easier for capital, labour, goods, and services to move across the country. Among the most successful means of ensuring harmonization have been the Tax Collection Agreements (TCAs) by which the federal government agrees to collect taxes on behalf of any province or territory. TCAs are in place for federal PIT collection in all provinces and territories except Quebec, and for CIT for all except Ontario, Alberta, and Quebec. The federal government pays the collection costs, and in return the provinces accept a common definition of the tax base and a common approach to tax enforcement and allocation.

Harmonization through unified collection is less advanced for consumption taxes. Three of the Atlantic provinces (Newfoundland and Labrador, Nova Scotia, and New Brunswick) have agreed to a Harmonized Sales Tax, under which the provincial tax shares the same base as the GST and the federal government both collects the revenues and administers the tax. Quebec also has a harmonized federal–provincial GST, but it collects the tax on behalf of the federal government, not vice-versa. The other provinces continue to go their own way with separate provincial sales taxes, although the federal government remains committed to exploring further harmonization (Finance Canada, 2006: 50–1).

3. Intergovernmental Transfers

Canada—like other federal systems—uses intergovernmental fiscal transfers (sometimes referred to as 'grants') to reduce vertical and horizontal fiscal imbalances. Despite our relatively decentralized tax structure, in which the provinces get a fairly significant share of total revenues, a gap remains between the provinces' expenditure responsibilities and their ability to raise the revenues to fund them. There is also a wide disparity among the provinces in their potential to raise revenues. Table 8.2 provides an overview of the magnitude of these transfers for every fifth fiscal year from 1982–3 to 2007–8.

There are two basic types of transfer:

- Conditional transfers are payments made for specific purposes, usually introduced to induce provinces to participate in national social programs with similar entitlements across the country. The last major attempt to introduce a new social program in this way took place in 2004–6, when the Martin federal government negotiated with some provinces and territories to establish a national child care program. A similar venture, which actually came to fruition in 1994, was the program under which the federal government offers conditional transfers to the provinces for spending on municipal infrastructure. The Canada Health and Social Transfers (see below) are conditional, but loosely so.
- Unconditional transfers come with no expenditure strings attached, although there are specific formulae that determine which provinces get

Table 8.2   Major Federal Cash Transfers to Provinces and Territories, Selected Years: 1982–3 to 2007–8 ($ millions)

	1982–3	1987–8	1992–3	1997–8	2002–3	2007–8
Social program transfers	10,271	14,437	18,396	12,500	19,100	31,065
Equalization	4,865	6,605	7,784	9,738	8,859	12,925
Territorial Funding Formula	362	730	1,076	1,229	1,616	2,313
Total	15,498	21,772	27,256	23,467	29,575	46,303

SOURCES: For 1982–2003 to 2002–3: Finance Canada, 2006, Annex 3, Tables A3.1–A3.3; For 2007–8: Finance Canada, 2008.

Notes: Dollar amounts are nominal and reflect actual transfer amounts in the years indicated.

Social program transfers, 1982–3 to 1992–3, consist of the Established Programs Financing and the Canada Assistance Plan cash transfers; since 1997–8 they consist of the CHT/CST cash transfer.

what proportion of funds. Equalization is the most important of these programs.

There is a further important distinction between

- cash transfers: i.e., the payment of actual funds from the federal government to the provinces; and
- tax transfers: i.e., the ceding of tax room to the provinces in the form of a specific portion or points of personal or corporate income tax. The tax points have a nominal value when first ceded, but afterwards grow or shrink with the provincial tax base.

As we will see below, tax transfers are controversial in that once tax room has been ceded, it is hard to take back. Once a tax transfer has been established, the provinces tend to consider that money to be a part of their own-source revenue rather than an ongoing federal contribution, whereas the federal government will usually continue to count a tax transfer in its overall calculation of support to the provinces.

On the whole, there are probably fewer conditions attached to intergovernmental cash and tax transfers in Canada than in any other federal system. In fiscal year 2007–8 the three biggest programs, accounting for more than 95 per cent of all federal cash transfers, were the Equalization Program, the Canada Health Transfer (CHT), and the Canada Social Transfer (CST). The former is wholly unconditional, and although the CHT and CST include a few conditions (about meeting the five basic principles of medicare and ensuring that migrants from other provinces can qualify for welfare payments after a reasonable waiting period), they still leave considerable room for provincial interpretation, and the medicare conditions in particular are difficult to enforce.

Moreover, neither the CHT nor the CST is tied to the provinces' own expenditure programs. This is not the case in most other federal countries. Nor was it the case in Canada until the late 1970s. In the past, federal payments were conditional on matching provincial expenditure for specific purposes: thus if Ontario, for example, spent $100 million to build hospitals or universities, the federal government would match that expenditure with another $100 million. Elsewhere, such as in the United States, Australia, and Germany, most federal transfers still take the form of matching funds or are otherwise very specific as to purpose.

Equalization is by design the least conditional of the transfer programs. Its purpose is to ensure that all provinces have, at least in principle, the capacity to deliver comparable services at comparable rates of taxation. Introduced in 1957, with many minor adjustments since, the program tries to bring provinces with a fiscal capacity below the national average up to a national standard. Commitment to the principle of equalization, if not an actual formula, was incorporated into the constitution in 1982.[7] Equalization does not take funds from the richer provinces directly. Rather, the funds for this purpose come from the federal budget. Thus they are collected throughout the country, and individual taxpayers in the poorer provinces contribute, according to their income, as much as their counterparts in the richer provinces. Despite what some provincial political leaders imply, there are no direct transfers between provincial governments; equalization payments are made by the federal government, not the richer provinces as such; and provincial legislatures do not vote funds for these purposes. No funds are taken from wealthier provinces for the purpose of equalization.

From 1982 to 2007 the 'standard' used to determine entitlement to equalization payments was the average of the tax yields of five provinces—British Columbia, Saskatchewan, Manitoba, Ontario, and Quebec from more than thirty different revenue sources. With the most recent modifications the number of revenue groups was reduced to five and a ten-province standard was adopted. Against this standard each province's actual fiscal capacity is measured to determine the extent of its entitlement. In 2008 six of the ten provinces fell below the standard and therefore received equalization payments. The provinces not receiving equalization in 2008–9 were Ontario, Alberta, Saskatchewan, and British Columbia. In November 2008 the federal government announced that in fiscal year 2009–10 Ontario would receive equalization payments for the first time and, also for the first time, Newfoundland and Labrador would not be eligible.[8]

Most transfers to the territorial governments are based on what is known as the Territorial Funding Formula (TFF). The TFF is based on the special expenditure needs of the territories, rather than on revenue capacity alone. Although territorial governments also receive the CHT and CST, these funds are deducted from their TFF entitlements. In 2007–8 the three northern territories together received a total of $2.3 billion from the TFF (see Table 8.2).

4. The Process and Politics of Fiscal Relations

Intergovernmental relations on financial matters exhibit most of the main characteristics of executive federalism, as discussed in Chapters 6 and 7. The key discussions are restricted to governments, and are jealously guarded by cabinet ministers and their senior officials. Of course the subject matter of intergovern- mental fiscal relations is highly technical and necessarily complex. The apparent requirement within each government for secrecy in the preparation of budgets reinforces the usual tendency to treat the details of intergovernmental negotia- tion as confidential, not open to public scrutiny. Together, the complex nature of the issues under discussion and the lack of transparency make for a murky accountability that governments exploit to avoid accepting the blame for cutbacks in funding or program entitlements.

Intergovernmental relations involving fiscal issues are also highly bureaucratic and thus hierarchical. The structure is topped by the Federal–Provincial– Territorial conferences of Finance ministers, who usually meet twice a year at a time and with an agenda heavily determined by the federal chair (unlike other intergovernmental forums, these conferences do not include a provincial or terri- torial co-chair). Preparations for these meetings are made by deputy-ministers who report to the ministers and meet as the Continuing Committee of Officials, CCO. Several other committees report to the CCO; dealing with economic and fiscal data, fiscal arrangements, taxation, and the Canada and Quebec Pension Plans, they meet much more frequently but no less privately than their superiors.

First ministers also take part in fiscal relations, but there is no established decision-making structure or pattern of meetings. Instead, the first ministers become involved as political priorities dictate: examples include the meetings held in the 1970s to seek consensus on anti-inflation measures, the meeting after 1995 to determine how to restore funding to health care programs (this issue is discussed more fully in the next chapter), and the meeting scheduled in early 2009 to discuss the international economic crisis. In any case, routine interaction is left to the Finance ministers and their officials.

As with most other Canadian intergovernmental relations, the manner in which fiscal negotiations are conducted ranges across the spectrum from competitive to cooperative. It should come as no surprise that fiscal policy as a whole is only loosely coordinated. More often than not, decisions on fiscal arrangements are not the result of formal intergovernmental agreement, but rather reflect the final determination of the federal government alone. There will be extensive meetings in which government representatives will argue their positions and agree on some general approaches and principles, but the final decision is made by the federal government. Sometimes this occurs simply because the differing interests and positions of the provinces and territories make it impossible to reach a consensus, leaving Ottawa to dictate a solution. At other times the federal government will take decisions that are clearly contrary the wishes of the provinces. Indeed the provinces often resent what they deem to be 'unilateral' actions. In 1981, 1982, 1990, and 1995, for example, the federal government announced—with little or no advance notice—significant cuts to intergovernmental transfers for established social programs, essentially downloading the responsibility for budgetary restraint onto the provinces and territories.

Nonetheless, in some cases, political success depends on close federal–provincial agreement. A recent example is the series of health accords negotiated between 1998 and 2004, wherein each of the provincial and territorial governments agreed to very specific amounts and purposes for renewed health transfer payments. Finally, there are a few exceptional cases in which detailed rules require that any changes be formally agreed to according to a fixed voting formula; the most notable examples are the Canada and Quebec Pension Plans.[9]

Despite their technical nature, the secrecy in which they are made, and the ambiguity about who gets to decide fiscal matters and how that is done, fiscal arrangements remain at the heart both of federal–provincial relations and of the budget-making process in every government. Thus they are not immune to politics: in fact, they are among the most hotly contested political issues, reflecting real differences in ideology and regional interests. The lack of formal rules means that policy-makers are more open to external influences than they might otherwise be. Thus the federal cabinet may be swayed in a direction different from the one preferred by the provinces and territories: for example, by social policy interest groups pushing for stronger federal intervention in provincial spending programs. Finally, it bears repeating that intergovernmental fiscal issues always reflect the broader political and economic concerns of the day. These broader considerations can be best understood in their historical context, which brings us to the last part of this chapter.

CHANGING OBJECTIVES AND OUTCOMES, 1945–2005

In fiscal federalism, form follows function. The shape of programs reflects economic, social, and political priorities of the day. So the fiscal relations of 2008 are very different from those of 1945. But that is not the only reason why Canada's contemporary fiscal relations look the way they do. A contributing factor is what has come to be known as path dependency: governments become accustomed to certain patterns of taxation and expenditure, and various political interests (government departments, social interest groups, regional business communities, etc.) get attached to particular patterns in the design, flow, and magnitude of transfer payments and tax regimes. Thus, despite the occasional 'big bang', change usually takes longer than many would like, and we often have to settle for yesterday's solutions because there is no consensus on what to replace them with today.

The interplay between continuity and change can be seen in the following overview of the main phases in Canada's fiscal relations from 1945 to 2005, covering not only the main fiscal instruments but also the underlying objectives and values (the most recent years of the Harper government are discussed in Chapter 9).

- *1945–59: The era of strong central power.* In post-war Canada governments were concerned with preventing a return to the conditions of the Great Depression and to promote 'social reconstruction' through new social programs (the welfare state). Promoting national efficiency in industry and the labour force was another key objective. Having centralized revenue-raising during the war, the federal government gradually granted more tax room to the provinces while encouraging provincial spending on social programs such as health and education through conditional grant programs. A minimal equalization program began in 1957.

- *1960–76: Decentralization and the maturing of the welfare state.* As social programs (including comprehensive medicare, in place across Canada by 1970) continued to expand and mature, the provinces surpassed Ottawa in their shares of both national revenues and expenditures. Some federal transfer programs were consolidated in the Canada Assistance Plan (CAP) of 1966. The Equalization Program was broadened to include most forms of provincial revenue. Quebec was allowed special arrangements for greater tax room.

- *1976–82: Transition and delinking.* Economic decline and recession after the 1974 Arab oil embargo led the federal government to start delinking its transfer commitments from the actual growth of provincial spending. In 1976 the provinces agreed to Established Programs Financing (EPF), under which a single block transfer replaced several previous conditional transfers for health care and post-secondary education. The deal involved transfers of both cash and tax room. When the huge growth in Alberta's oil revenues in the late 1970s dramatically raised the national benchmark, changes to the equalization formula protected the federal government against the obligation to bring all the provinces up to the new standard. Yet intergovernmental transfers continued to grow relative to GDP. There were no more special deals for Quebec alone.

- *1982–95: A slow unravelling.* Federal transfers reached a high point in terms of their proportion of provincial revenues in 1982 and declined for several years thereafter (it would not start rising again until 1998). Starting in 1981, federal budgets announced a series of unilateral measures to limit transfer payments. In 1990 Ottawa put a limit on CAP funding for the richer provinces only, ultimately leading to controversy over whether all provinces should benefit equally from social program transfers.

Meanwhile the provinces were increasingly obliged to fund social programs from their own sources, with the result that the poorer provinces were already cutting back program entitlements and rationalizing services by the end of the 1980s.

- *1995–2005: The Big Bang and the gradual recovery.* The federal debt and deficit reached crisis proportions in 1994–5. In the 1995 budget Ottawa unilaterally cut its social transfers by roughly one-third, further reducing the federal contribution to growing provincial expenditure needs. In the process the EPF and CAP programs were consolidated into the single block program called the Canada Health and Social Transfer, then re-divided into the Canada Health Transfer and the Canada Social Transfer in 2004. The Equalization Program, however, was left relatively untouched. Recovery from the shock of the mid-1990s took roughly a decade, during which federal surpluses grew, new federal direct social programs were established, and the provinces—worried about unsustainable social program costs—mounted a successful campaign to restore the previous levels of federal funding to health care and put the issue of vertical fiscal imbalance on the national agenda.

What form will fiscal federalism take in the future? This is an important question not only for governments but for all Canadians, one that has featured prominently both in federal and provincial election campaigns, and in general discourse about Canadian politics and the federation over the past few years. The next chapter provides an overview of the contemporary issues in fiscal federalism, discussing the main options for change and the nature of the debate about fiscal relations in Canada today. How we deal with these challenges will be another test of the adaptabililty—and suitability—of Canadian federalism.

Chapter 9

Fiscal Relations: Current Issues

From the basic structure of Canadian fiscal federalism we now turn to specific issues. Never far from the surface, fiscal issues involving relations between the federal and provincial governments frequently erupt onto Canada's political landscape. In fact, the eruptions have been almost continuous since the early 1990s. Though less momentous and potentially destabilizing than constitutional politics, and often obscured by technical details, fiscal relations have often provoked passionate debates. This chapter examines key aspects of the major recent issues—debt control and deficit reduction, tax cuts, health care costs, equalization and oil revenues, the fiscal imbalance—with the goal of clarifying why they have been so contested and allowing readers to assess the merits of the arguments on both sides.

We begin with the events of the 1990s that set the context for the current debate—notably the 1995 federal budget and its consequences. The road back from the cutbacks and disruptions of that period has been long and full of turns that have occasioned a great deal of debate. The most frequent concern has been the vertical fiscal imbalance, but the search for solutions to that problem has been complicated by differing regional and ideological perspectives on matters such as the proper role of government in social programs (e.g., should public health care provision be more, or less, comprehensive than it is now?), the consequences of regional redistribution (e.g., do transfers perpetuate dependency in the poorer provinces?), and the balance of power in the federation (e.g., should provinces be able to tailor social entitlements to fit their needs, or should national standards prevail?).

We then turn to the two central programs through which Ottawa transfers funds to the provinces, the health and social transfer programs: how they were designed, how they have evolved, and whether they will be sufficient to meet future needs. Together the CHT and CST accounted for $33.1 billion in cash payments in 2008–9. For years, the most pressing concern was restoration of the funds that Ottawa cut from its health and social transfers in 1995. A 10-year plan to increase funding for health care was put in place in 2004, but finding additional money for other social policy areas, such as post-secondary education, child care, social assistance and income security, has been difficult.

Our third issue is the future of Canada's second largest transfer, the Equalization Program. Put into policy limbo in 2004, when the Martin government abandoned the program's longstanding funding formula, it was set on a new course in 2007 by the Harper government. Equalization cost $13.6 billion in 2008–9. It has not been affected by budget cuts, either in 1995 or subsequently, but recipient provinces have expressed concern that it does not meet their current expenditure needs and is not doing enough to ensure equity in fiscal capacity across the provinces. Oil and gas revenues in particular are creating a huge new fiscal disparity between the oil-producing provinces, especially Alberta, and the rest of Canada, which some think should be addressed through the Equalization Program.

We conclude with a brief look at the process through which decisions on inter-governmental fiscal issues are made and how it is being reformed to accommodate demands for greater public participation. Of particular concern is whether demands for greater accountability, transparency, and simplicity can be met without compromising other values central to Canadian fiscal federalism.

THE LEGACY OF 1995 AND THE DEBATE OVER FISCAL BALANCE

From the early 1990s, governments in Canada were preoccupied with the need for a more sustainable fiscal policy. Budgetary deficits had become chronic, and public debt was escalating. At the same time, tougher international competition and neo-liberal political trends sharply limited the scope for tax increases, and Canadian taxpayers in general were less confident than they had been that government would spend their money wisely. For the first time in many decades, a consensus emerged in favour of eliminating budget deficits and reducing public debt. Support for reducing public services was less strong, but in general Canadians were willing to accept tough measures.[1]

The Liberal government elected in 1993 faced a huge budgetary deficit and debt payments unprecedented in peacetime, based on deficits that had been accumulating ever since 1976. After its first year in office the Chrétien government was warned by the international financial community that its financial position was perilous. The turnaround effort that followed was to have a huge and continuing impact on fiscal federalism.

The budget plan announced by Finance Minister Paul Martin in February 1995 has become a milestone in Canadian politics. It reversed the growth of budgetary deficits, which had peaked at $42 billion in the previous fiscal year (1993–4), and laid the groundwork for a balanced budget that was eventually achieved in 1998. Based on the findings of a wide-ranging program review, federal spending was dramatically reduced: most programs experienced deep cuts and many were eliminated altogether. In addition, transfer payments to the provinces were sharply reduced, and the remaining programs (EPF and CAP) were combined to create a single Canada Health and Social Transfer (CHST). The Equalization Program, however, was not affected.

The first and most significant consequence of the fiscal policy introduced in 1995 was an improvement in Canada's overall fiscal position, which has contributed to stronger economic growth. Fiscal reform on the part of provincial governments has also played a part in that growth. But in the public imagination (and in the view of the international community) it was the federal government that set the course towards balanced budgets and reduced taxes.

A second major consequence was the cascading effect produced by the cuts to intergovernmental transfers. Forced to reduce their own spending, in many cases provincial and territorial governments offloaded some of their responsibilities onto local governments. At the same time there was a significant erosion of provincial trust in the overall fiscal system: could the provinces ever again trust Ottawa to keep its funding commitments? (The repercussions of this erosion of intergovernmental trust are a recurring theme throughout this book.)

Over the longer term it became apparent that, even as Ottawa's financial position was improving to the point that it began to produce surpluses, provincial expenditure responsibilities were continuing to grow. From the provinces' perspective, this seriously aggravated the vertical fiscal imbalance in the federation, leading to calls for more tax room, greatly increased cash transfers, and even a realignment of expenditure tasks. A fourth effect, especially prominent in the years leading to the Health Care Accord of 2004, was a renewed debate about the conditions that should be attached to federal funds, especially in the context of health care reform. Finally, the fact that the Equalization Program was left unscathed while social transfers were cut gave rise to questions about the value of regional redistribution. The provinces that did not receive equalization, notably Ontario and Alberta, found it unfair that this one program was kept intact while the transfers they received were being savaged. Although they did not question the basic principles and value of the Equalization Program, they called for removal of the redistributive elements in all other federal transfers, launching a campaign for equal per capita shares of CHST cash transfers.

Much of what Ottawa achieved was strongly endorsed both in Canada and abroad. In particular, successive federal governments made a point—both in 1995 and in the budgets that, at least until 2006, followed—of meeting their budgetary targets, through shrewd underestimating of revenues and overestimating of expenditures, and the creative use of budgetary reserves. In the process, confidence in the country's overall fiscal position was restored. This benefited the provinces in terms of reduced inflation and interest rates, but did little to improve their own difficult fiscal situations. In fact it made them much worse. For the provinces—notably New Brunswick, Alberta, Manitoba, and Saskatchewan—that had already balanced their budgets the federal cuts of 1995 made a tight fiscal situation even tighter, and for those that had yet to start, notably Ontario and Quebec, the process was both painful and long, lasting until 2000 (Gagné and Stein, 2006: 62–7; Finance Canada, 2006: 101–22). As late as 1999, net provincial debt continued to grow (Finance Canada, 2008: 225).

While the provincial premiers and their governments acknowledged the need for tough federal measures in 1995 and beyond, they all shared the view that the transfers they counted on were cut more deeply than any other federal program. Also, the sense of stability and predictability in federal funding of social programs, already weakened by a series of cuts and changes in the decade after 1982, took a huge hit in the 1995 budget. This led to a rare effort by the provinces and territories to establish a consensus position on fiscal federalism in the late 1990s.[2] It also prompted an effort to restore intergovernmental harmony that eventually led to the development of a new set of rules to discipline the exercise of the federal spending power, embodied in the Social Union Framework Agreement (see Chapter 10). However, the erosion of the old norms of intergovernmental relations made it hard to agree on the new rules and even harder to implement them. A decade after 1995, commentators noted that the damage to provincial trust in Ottawa was still evident (Inwood et al., 2005).

In sum, as the federal surplus grew, so too did provincial pressure for correction of the vertical fiscal imbalance. In fact, although the concept behind the term had been familiar in public finance and academic circles for decades, the term 'vertical fiscal imbalance' (VFI) itself did not enter the political discourse in Canada until 2002, when the Government of Quebec's Commission on Fiscal Imbalance detailed the nature of a VFI from both the Quebec and the broader provincial and territorial perspectives (Quebec, 2002). With the formation of the Council of the Federation in 2003, the issue of fiscal balance or imbalance (both vertical and horizontal) became a continuing part of the new institution's agenda and work-plan. Research was commissioned from independent bodies such as the Conference Board of Canada, and in May 2005 an advisory panel was established to provide an independent assessment of fiscal balance issues in time for a federal review expected in 2006. That panel, co-chaired by Robert Gagné and Janice Stein, released its report in March 2006.

The Gagné–Stein report found that for the previous decade the provinces had indeed had 'insufficient resources to accomplish the tasks for which they are constitutionally responsible', while the federal government had been 'running budgetary surpluses and . . . spending significantly in areas that the Constitution of Canada has assigned to the Provinces' (Gagné and Stein, 2006: 9). Furthermore, the panel predicted that the overall fiscal prospects of the provinces would worsen in future, particularly as a result of population aging and rising health care costs. Yet the federal budgetary surplus was projected to continue growing.

A variety of solutions to the VFI have been proposed, by the Gagné–Stein panel and others. They include transferring the entire tax proceeds of the GST to the provinces (Quebec, 2002); transferring more income tax points to the provinces (Quebec, 2002); significantly increasing the health care transfers (Romanow, 2002; Gagné and Stein, 2006); and increasing federal Equalization and TFF payments, even if that does not benefit all provinces (Senate, 2002; Gagné and Stein, 2006; O'Brien, 2006a, 2006b). Few experts argued for a wholesale realignment of federal and provincial spending responsibilities. Liberal governments from 1993 to 2006 used direct federal spending to make up the gaps in provincial funding adequacy—not a cooperative approach, but one that did address VFI to a degree. But the right-of-centre opposition parties (Reform, the Canadian Alliance, and their successor, the new Conservative party) had generally opposed such program realignment by stealth. And although the Harper government elected in January 2006 signalled a greater willingness to deal with the provinces' concerns about VFI, that did not mean that the provinces themselves were any closer to agreeing on what should be done.

The only unambiguous proponent of tax transfers was Alberta. Quebec supported tax transfers for some years but by 2005 seemed to prefer the idea of increasing Equalization payments as a way of reducing the VFI. Most of the other provinces were open to a combination of tax and cash solutions, but came around to Quebec's point of view. However, Ontario took a hard line against enhanced equalization, because it felt that this would divert to other provinces the funds required to correct a fiscal imbalance specific to Ontario.

Ontario's position is especially noteworthy because it is the largest province and has historically been seen as the principal beneficiary of the federal union in both economic and fiscal terms. Ontario governments have until recently tended to support federal fiscal policy and regional redistribution. Now it increasingly insists on a special case for Ontario alone (MacKinnon, 2005a, 2005b; Ontario, 2006; Canada, 2006c: 118–22). It claims that a chronic shortfall of at least $23 billion per year in federal funding is preventing the provincial government from dealing with major economic and social challenges. It attributes this shortfall to discriminatory treatment in areas such as employment insurance, labour market training, urban infrastructure, and immigration settlement. The fact that Ontario's analysis does not take into account the significant net economic benefit it receives as a member of the Canadian economic union (see Page, 2002) is not surprising; such benefits are difficult to translate into fiscal terms. For its part, the federal government counters that its fiscal position depends upon contributions from the taxpayers of the largest and wealthiest Canadian provinces, so that a wealthier province like Ontario must expect to receive less money per capita from the federal treasury than poorer provinces. Paradoxically and despite its relative wealth, Ontario will qualify for equalization payments in fiscal year 2009–10. In any case, what is at issue is balance, and the appropriate equilibrium is in the eye of the beholder.

Of course, provincial or territorial perspectives on their own do not determine how fiscal federalism works: it is the federal view that determines the outcome. And the federal perspective on the fiscal imbalance issue was for many years quite different from that of the provinces—especially under the Liberal prime ministers Jean Chrétien and Paul Martin. Their governments mounted arguments to counter most of the provincial positions.[3] For example, they maintained that the federal surpluses were not huge in relation to the deficits that had preceded them and the federal debt burden, which was roughly twice the size of all the provincial debts combined. Moreover, they argued, the provinces had plenty of access to revenues; some of their revenue sources (e.g., gaming) were growing rapidly; and Ottawa too faced spending pressures in areas such as security, the needs of on-reserve Aboriginal populations, and seniors' pensions.

Complicating the VFI issue is the wide range of provincial policy preferences and needs. What if the provinces have different expenditure needs and preferences? What if one province wants publicly funded day care and another doesn't? What if one province is prepared to impose a retail sales tax and another isn't? If one prefers better social programs over tax cuts, or vice versa? It is of course natural in a federation for provinces to differ on matters such as these. But the federal government argues that until a province makes at least an average effort to raise taxes, or to keep its expenditures within an average range of national standards, then it cannot claim imbalance.

A significant change in the federal approach to the VFI issues came with the change of government in 2006. The Conservative government acknowledged the existence of a vertical fiscal imbalance, as well as the unresolved issues on equalization. In its official documents the Harper government's position on VFI retains some elements of the orthodox federal response (see Finance Canada, 2006), but clearly there was a major political opening to resolve the issue by one means or another.

Stephen Harper had signalled his commitment to tackling the VFI in an important speech in Quebec City during the election campaign, in December 2005. In that speech and in subsequent statements (including the Speech from the Throne opening the new parliament after the January 2006 election, and the May 2006 budget documents), Harper made VFI a prominent part of his 'open federalism' approach, which included commitments to respect provincial jurisdiction and retreat from areas of provincial responsibility in which Ottawa had intruded, such as housing and university scholarships. Some have seen open federalism as a return to classical federalism, focusing on the Harper promise to restrict the use of the federal spending power to programs that have provincial consent. Moreover, on fiscal federalism as such—clearly seeking to distance the new government from its predecessor—the Conservatives promised in the 2006 budget new arrangements following five principles: improved accountability (to be achieved by clarifying roles and responsibilities); fiscal responsibility and budget transparency; predictable and stable long-term fiscal arrangements; a competitive and efficient economic union; and effective collaborative management of the federation.[4] They explicitly sought to restore stability and predictability to the formula-based Equalization and TFF programs and to avoid bilateralism and ad hoc arrangements. In return for a more decentralized and province-friendly fiscal policy, they asked that the provinces work towards tax harmonization and step up their efforts to improve the economic union (the latter issues are discussed in Chapter 11). The details of the fiscal arrangements finalized by the Harper government in its March 2007 budget are outlined later in this chapter.

While the changes in values and positions signalled by the Harper government are significant, it is important to emphasize the overall legacy of the 1995 budget earthquake and the effects of the long and often bitter debates over the vertical fiscal imbalance. By the late 1990s federal–provincial transfers for social programs were at their lowest point in 50 years. Just as significantly, the relative decline in those transfer programs meant that provincial governments were less dependent on federal transfers than at any point in the past half-century—and therefore less willing to let Ottawa define national social standards. In fact, according to the federal government, the provinces are less dependent on inter-governmental transfers than their counterparts in any other federation, and those transfers come with fewer conditions in Canada than anywhere else (Finance Canada, 2006). The current situation is well illustrated by the debate over health care funding, which leads us now to the CHT/CST.

TRANSFERS FOR SOCIAL PROGRAMS: THE EVOLUTION OF THE CHT/CST

The federal government created the Canada Health and Social Transfer in 1995 by combining two earlier transfer programs: the Established Programs Financing (EPF) for health and post-secondary education, and the Canada Assistance Plan (CAP) for welfare and social services. The purpose of this change was two-fold. First, Ottawa sought to complete the process, begun in the 1970s, of simplifying federal–provincial transfer programs and minimizing the conditions attached to them, in the process, decoupling federal financial commitments from actual program costs. Second, it needed to cut the level of transfer payments in general in order to meet its deficit reduction targets. Since, as we have seen, the Equalization Program was left more or less intact, the remaining programs took the brunt of the cuts. As a result, the public debate about the CHST was first and foremost about those cuts and, after 1998, restoration of the funding that had been taken away.

The CHST was not unconditional, but it was not fully conditional either. Rather, it was a hybrid that inherited two very general conditions from the old CAP and EPF programs. The first was that the provinces would impose no restrictions on the eligibility for welfare of new residents arriving from other provinces. The second was that the provincial health services would meet the five broad principles of the Canada Health Act.[5] As long as these conditions were met, the provinces could spend the money transferred from Ottawa as they saw fit. At a First Ministers Meeting in February 1999, where the federal government promised to begin restoring a portion of the funds cut in 1995, all provincial and territorial premiers undertook to spend any incremental CHST funds on health care. This was hardly a difficult decision politically, since provincial governments for a decade had made it their policy to increase health care funding while either holding post-secondary and welfare funding constant or cutting deeply in these areas.

In fact, funding for health care so dominated intergovernmental discussions that the federal government was eventually persuaded to separate it from other social spending. Thus in 2004 the CHST itself was restructured to create two new programs: the CHT and the CST. In the 12 years between 1995 and 2007, all the funding increases went to health, but at least the CST (which is not earmarked for any particular social program) has not suffered any further erosion. CST payments were expected to amount to $10.5 billion in 2008–9, and the Harper government's projections showed modest growth of 3 per cent per year for both the social and health transfer programs. Table 9.1 shows the details of the major transfer payments to each province and territory in fiscal year 2008–9.

Together, the CHST and its successors have been at the centre of three major controversies. The first issue was allocation—how much money each province would get. The second was the overall level of cash funding; discussions in this area usually focused on restoration of the funds cut in 1995. The third was the issue of conditions on federal funding, which were commonly defined as the issue of national standards for social programs. In this chapter we will deal primarily with the first two controversies, leaving the third for the discussion of the Social Union Framework Agreement in Chapter 10.

The CHT/CST inherited from the EPF and CAP a set of specific entitlements per province based on historic patterns of cost-sharing under the CAP and the value of the EPF tax points originally transferred to each province in 1976. For example, because Quebec and Newfoundland spent more per capita on social assistance and services than Ontario or New Brunswick, they received more in the form of matching funds under the CAP. Furthermore, as we noted in Chapter 8, in 1990 the federal government put a ceiling on its contribution to CAP for the three richest provinces. As a result, provincial per capita entitlements as determined by Ottawa for the inaugural year of the CHST, 1996–7, ranged from $825 for Alberta to $993 for Quebec to $1,018 for the Northwest Territories.

The four provinces with below-average entitlements—British Columbia, Alberta, Saskatchewan, and Ontario—began an immediate campaign for equal per capita shares. The federal government responded in its 1996 budget by announcing a plan to reduce the disparity by 10 per cent per year, so that it would be halved in five years. In the 1999 budget the rate of reduction was increased so that the disparity would be eliminated by 2001–2. Yet even in that year, when per capita CHST entitlements (including both cash and tax room components) were finally equal across all provinces, the actual cash payments

Table 9.1   Major Federal Cash Transfers to
             Provinces and Territories,
             Estimated Entitlements: 2008–9 ($ millions)

	CHT	CST	Equalization	TFF	Offshore accords	Total
Newfoundland and Labrador	359	160	158	—	742	1,418
Prince Edward Island	99	44	322	—	—	465
Nova Scotia	664	297	1,465	—	106	2,532
New Brunswick	533	238	1,584	—	—	2,354
Quebec	5,491	2,454	8,028	—	—	15,974
Ontario	8,576	4,102	—	—	—	12,678
Manitoba	846	378	2,063	—	—	3,287
Saskatchewan	804	342	—	—	—	1,146
Alberta	1,921	1,112	—	—	—	3,033
British Columbia	3,269	1,403	—	—	—	4,672
Nunavut	26	11	—	944	—	980
Northwest Territories	20	14	—	805	—	839
Yukon	23	10	—	564	—	597
All provinces and territories	22,629	10,565	13,620	2,313	848	49,975

SOURCE: Compiled from Government of Canada, Department of Finance website, tables on Major Transfers, updated to 29 April 2008 from <http://www.fin.gc.ca/FEDPROV/mtpe.html>, accessed 23 May 2008.

Note: Totals may not add up exactly because of rounding.

continued to vary because of the differences in the value of the tax point component inherited from the EPF.

The allocation issue thus became a politically charged, essentially zero-sum conundrum. In its earlier cuts to the CAP, Ottawa had tried to shield the poorer provinces, at least in part, from its program of fiscal restraint. One reason had been that among those provinces was Quebec, where the growing support for sovereignty in the early 1990s had made the federal government particularly reluctant to do anything that might be seen as detrimental to Quebec. After 1995, however, concern for unequal treatment ultimately trumped concern for redistribution and national unity: an illustration of changing values and shifting political weight in the federal system. The campaign for 'equal shares' drove a further wedge between the 'have' and 'have not' provinces. The battle was waged as much among the provinces as it was with the federal government. And it continued to resonate in the Harper government's budgets of 2007 and 2008, as we will see.

Nevertheless, the provinces and territories did find common ground on the issue of funding cuts. All charged that the federal government was unfairly offloading its deficit onto them. They claimed that cuts to transfer payments through the CHST between 1994–5 and 1998–9 amounted to 35 per cent, whereas federal programs in general were cut by only 7 per cent in the same period. As a result of this disproportionate degree of 'offloading', the provinces were forced to cut their funding to municipalities, universities and colleges, school boards, and hospitals.

The provinces' primary goal was to see federal cash payments restored to EPF/CAP levels, from the initial CHST allocation of $11.5 billion to $18.5 billion. This they achieved in September 2000, when the premiers secured Prime Minister Chrétien's agreement that the CHST would be increased to match the combined total of EPF/CAP funds in 1995 ($18.5 billion) and would reach $21 billion by 2005–6. Of the additional money, $2.2 billion was earmarked for 'early childhood development' initiatives, and the rest for health care. An additional federal grant of $2.3 billion over five years was also promised on the condition that it go to health information technology, medical equipment, and a transition fund for primary care reform. All the additional cash transfers to the provinces were to be distributed on an equal per capita basis.

Yet even this increase in funding for health care was not sufficient to meet the still burgeoning costs at the provincial level. Prime Minister Chrétien recognized this when, in 2001, he appointed former Saskatchewan Premier Roy Romanow to form a one-man commission of inquiry into the future of the health care system. Among other things, Romanow found that a publicly funded, single-tiered, universal health care system could not be sustained unless the funding gap between provincial expenditure requirements and federal support through the CHST was filled.[6] Estimating the then-current federal contribution to health care at 15 per cent of continuing provincial costs, Romanow recommended that the federal share should be increased to 25 per cent. The 2004 Health Care Accord reached by Prime Minister Martin with the provincial and territorial premiers established a framework for increasing the federal contribution over a period of 10 years by $41.2 billion in new investments, bringing the overall federal contribution on an annual basis by the end of the 10-year period to $30.5 billion.[7] Observers, including Romanow himself, have credited the agreement with ensuring both financial adequacy and stability to the intergovernmental financing of health care, and in the process, filling the 'Romanow gap'.[8]

Finally, in introducing the CHST the federal government invited the provinces to work with it to develop by mutual consent a set of shared principles and objectives that would underlie the operations of the new transfer. This commitment eventually led to the signing of the Social Union Framework Agreement in February 1999. But real progress was very slow, especially in health. Part of the problem was that the initial level of payments in the CHST, though obviously enough to make a difference, was not enough to give Ottawa the right to dictate to the provinces what they should do with their health care programs in particular. The federal government sought to re-impose conditions on its funding, in an effort both to preserve the principles of medicare and to promote specific federal priorities such as improvements to the primary care system (where people go first for treatment or advice, such as doctor's offices and emergency clinics), reduction of surgery wait times, and early childhood education. The more it pressed on these priorities, however, the more the provinces and territories insisted that federal funding match or be directly related to their actual costs.

Progress was made, eventually. In the 2000 agreement to restore CHST cash, all the provinces and territories, including Quebec, had agreed to a general statement of vision, a set of principles, and an action plan for health care reform; all except Quebec had also agreed to a plan for early childhood development. The 2004 agreement was much more substantial. It provided another set of broad principles, but went beyond that to set out an elaborate work plan on issues such as human resource planning, wait-time reduction, primary care reform, home care, a national pharmaceuticals strategy, and health promotion. More important, it required not only that governments report on their progress to a Canada Health Council, but that they report to citizens on an annual basis. The agreement finessed the issue of Quebec's reluctance to enter into joint social policy determination by including a side-deal on 'asymmetrical federalism' that allows Quebec additional flexibility in interpreting the specifics and timing of the intergovernmental commitments (Graefe, 2005).

In summary, much of the recent political debate regarding fiscal matters has revolved around social program transfers, including issues of allocation, adequacy, and conditions. Ultimately, however, the Chrétien and Martin governments put fiscal probity and healthier federal finances ahead of achieving cooperative national standards in social programs with the provinces. This is not to say that they provided no leadership with regard to creating new national social programs, but as often as not they did so through direct funding programs such as the gasoline tax rebate to municipalities (which local governments claimed would be used to improve social conditions in their communities), direct funding to students and universities for scholarships and research, and the National Child Benefit program. Some would say that all these programs were deliberately designed to avoid the complications associated with the more traditional intergovernmental finance mechanisms. However, most provinces view direct funding as a serious intrusion on provincial jurisdiction. The Conservative federal government under Stephen Harper has so far rejected such use of the federal spending power.

Otherwise the Conservatives have continued the broader commitment to longer-term, more stable and predictable transfers. As the next section will show, their enhanced commitment to the Equalization Program is in line with Quebec's view that Ottawa should deal with the VFI issue mainly through increased equalization payments (which also help to correct horizontal imbalances). The disadvantage of this approach is that the richer provinces have demanded, as a quid pro quo, a renewed emphasis on equal per capita shares in the remaining transfers (Courchene, 2007). Thus in their 2007 budget the Conservatives reworked the CST transfer to provide equal per capita shares across the provinces, stripping away some built-in equalizing features, and signalled their intention to do the same with the CHT when the current 10-year plan for health care funding expires in 2014–15. This marks a momentous shift in fiscal federalism, away from the concept of differential need and the principle of regional redistribution, towards the electoral clout and political opportunity offered by the richer and more populous provinces of Ontario, British Columbia, and Alberta.

EQUALIZATION: STILL THE GLUE THAT BINDS THE FEDERATION?

Equalization is the second largest intergovernmental transfer program in Canada, costing the federal government $13.6 billion in 2008–9. In that fiscal year it was distributed to all but four provinces (Ontario, Alberta, British Columbia, and Saskatchewan). The importance of the Equalization Program to its recipients varies widely. In 2006 equalization payments were projected to amount to 19 per cent of total revenues in the province of Newfoundland and Labrador; 25 per cent in Prince Edward Island; 22 per cent in Nova Scotia; 23 per cent in New Brunswick; 8.5 per cent in Quebec; 19 per cent in Manitoba; 1 per cent in Saskatchewan; and 1.5 per cent in British Columbia (Treff and Perry, 2005: Table 8.3). By 2008, largely because of increasing resource revenues, Saskatchewan and British Columbia were once again ineligible to receive equalization. In 2009 Newfoundland and Labrador will be in the same position, for the first time, while Ontario will be (just barely) eligible to receive payments, also for the first time.

The fact that the Equalization Program fared better than other federal programs in the 1990s was a reflection of the federal government's recognition that cutting equalization as well as transfer funds would amount to cutting payments to the poorer provinces even more deeply than to the rich, with the result that minimum national standards in public goods and services (loosely defined) would be even more seriously undermined. Thus the nominal budgetary allocation for equalization was never cut. Indeed, funding for the program was increased by 5 per cent in 1994. More important, however, was the fact that entitlements had not yet hit the ceiling built into the formula in 1982, according to which the overall year-to-year growth in entitlements was not to exceed the growth rate in the national economy. Together, tax cuts, outmigration in some provinces and a narrowing of provincial fiscal disparities kept entitlements below that level until the late 1990s. By 2000, however, the ceiling was becoming a serious problem, and the provinces put pressure on Finance Minister Paul Martin to lift it. After Martin became prime minister, in 2003, his government did just that. But other, more significant changes to equalization were in the works.

Throughout the 1990s, concerns about equalization had fallen into two categories. On the one hand, the richer provinces, together with some neo-liberal commentators and analysts, criticized the Equalization Program as too expensive (and therefore preventing Ottawa from reducing taxes to the degree that they believed it should), and as promoting fiscal dependency (and therefore preventing the recipient provinces from adjusting to economic realities).[9] They were supported in these views by a number of social policy analysts who questioned why regional redistribution should remain so relatively generous and why it was needed at all outside the Equalization Program (Banting, 1995; Milne, 1998). These arguments were influential. Many provisions aimed at regional redistribution were eliminated from intergovernmental transfer programs other than the formal Equalization Program, and there were major cuts in the regional redistribution features of other major federal funding programs such as (un)employment insurance. These changes gave rise to concern that cuts to the main Equalization Program would be next on the agenda.

A second set of concerns had to do with the overall design of the program from the perspective of the recipient provinces, which maintained that it did not work to fully equalize fiscal capacity; that it did not take into account differing expenditure needs; and that it discouraged resource development. Another problem was that the formula was overly complex and opaque. Such concerns led some to propose simpler and more transparently fair models to fulfil the constitutional commitment to equalization.

From 1982 until 2004 the equalization formula was based on a five-province standard (see Chapter 8). Excluded from this equation were Alberta (because of its volatile, often enormous, petroleum revenues) and the four Atlantic provinces (to counterbalance the exclusion of Albertans from the population total). Excluding Alberta got the federal government off the hook for bringing every province up to Alberta's oil-driven fiscal capacity. The problem was that in 2005 the five-province average worked out to only 92 per cent of the equalization that a full ten-province standard would have, even if petroleum revenues were excluded from the formula. The difference was an indication of Alberta's overall fiscal capacity, even without counting oil and gas revenues (O'Brien, 2006). Since 2000 and the renewed escalation of petroleum prices, Alberta in particular has enjoyed a huge increase in resource revenues, on top of its already enviable fiscal position. As a result, the overall fiscal capacity gap between Alberta and the other provinces has been widening, reversing what since the mid-1980s had been a trend towards convergence.

At the same time, Nova Scotia, Newfoundland and Labrador, and Saskatchewan have seen their equalization entitlements reduced as their own resource revenues have increased.[10] Their argument is akin to one that is often made in the case of welfare recipients: if taking a job would mean losing one dollar in welfare payments for every dollar they earn, where is the incentive to work? Of course this becomes a moot point if the job pays well enough, but the marginal effect is important for most people entering the job market. In the same way the marginal revenue effect is important to struggling provinces such as Nova Scotia and Newfoundland and Labrador. In July 2001, Ontario Premier Mike Harris took a lot of criticism for comparing those provinces to welfare recipients who win the lottery but still want their benefits. In fact, their offshore revenues had not yet amounted to much of a windfall. Yet under the equalization formula in place until 2004, individual provinces were penalized when their resource revenues were well above the average national tax yield for that resource category, even if in other respects their fiscal capacity remained low. Provinces in this situation could make little or no net gain, as for each dollar of new resource revenue they took in, they stood to lose as much as a dollar in equalization entitlement. Various side agreements and other provisions in the formula tried to limit this effect, but provinces such as Newfoundland and Labrador and Nova Scotia in particular found it hard to accept that there should be any 'clawback' when their overall per capita revenues still fell so far behind those of other provinces.

Another problem with the Equalization Program was that it did not take into account actual disparities in program needs or differing costs in meeting the same program needs. It concentrated only on revenue capacity, assuming that per-capita expenditure needs are the same. Yet clearly some provinces have significantly greater expenditure needs than others in key social program categories (disabled, sick elderly, university students, etc.). Also, the constitutional commitment to equity may not be fully satisfied without some compensation for these differences, since otherwise the levels of public services may not be 'reasonably comparable' across all provinces.[11] The Equalization Program did not account for these differences.

In summary, since the millennium there have been pressures both to refine and expand the Equalization Program, and to contain and reduce it. Two momentous steps were taken by the Martin government in 2004 and 2005 that served to focus the debate and ultimately move it forward. First was the announcement by Prime Minister Martin in October 2004, after consultation with the provinces, of a 'new framework for equalization and the territorial funding formula'. The new framework suspended altogether the formula for determining entitlements, and instead provided for moderate increases in transfers based on recent historical trends, with an annual escalator of 3.5 per cent. At the same time the federal government launched a review of equalization policy to be carried out by an expert panel chaired by a former senior official from Alberta, Al O'Brien. The second step came in February 2005, with the signing of the Offshore Petroleum Resources Accords: two 8-year agreements, one with Nova Scotia and one with Newfoundland and Labrador, that were intended to deal with their specific grievances in relation to resource revenues and the Equalization Program, and that built upon the original Atlantic Accord signed between the Government of Newfoundland and Labrador and the Government of Canada in 1985, and a similar agreement in 1986 with Nova Scotia.

Martin's new framework responded to concerns that the two programs (Equalization and TFF) were inadequate to meet provincial and territorial needs and that their formulas were overly complex and unfair. The new arrangements, though ad hoc and not structured by a formula, did provide for four years of stability and growth in the recipient provinces and territories. In the meantime the federal government would take soundings for a redesign of the two programs.[12] The renegotiation of the offshore accords with the two Atlantic provinces came in the context of the 2004 federal election campaign. Prime Minister Martin promised to deal with the long-standing concerns of the two provinces that, because of the equalization formula, they were not the principal beneficiaries of the offshore oil and gas resources, as it had been agreed in the 1980s that they should be. The bilateral agreements essentially arranged for significant off-set payments to be made separately out of federal revenues, to compensate for the 'clawed-back' equalization entitlements.[13]

Other provinces, notably Ontario and Quebec, criticized these bilateral arrangements as subverting the logic and purpose of the existing Equalization Program. As we noted above, the richest provinces, led by Ontario and Alberta, had waged a campaign after the 1995 budget to ensure that program transfers such as CHST would provide equal per capita funding for all the provinces. These provinces have also opposed any general measure to enhance the Equalization Program, which is essentially redistributive or even zero-sum in its effects. They perceived the bilateral agreements with the two Atlantic Provinces as entailing yet more redistribution outside the confines of the formal Equalization Program.

As the Martin era ended and the Harper Conservative era began, therefore, the issue of horizontal imbalance, or equalization, generated significant debate. In 2006 the provinces were at odds over what to do (Harding, 2006). Quebec, Manitoba, New Brunswick, and Prince Edward Island wished to see significant improvements in the program, and an emphasis on equalizing resource revenues. Saskatchewan, Nova Scotia, and Newfoundland and Labrador opposed the inclusion of any resource revenues if that would mean a significant reduction in their entitlements. Ontario and, less openly, Alberta opposed any enrichment of the program, while British Columbia seemed to be relatively neutral. What made it hard to find common ground was the unavoidable trade-off, with finite federal resources, between fixing the vertical imbalance and fixing the horizontal one. Common ground was achievable on health care in 2004, because all provinces and territories got nearly the same per capita share of an expanding fiscal pie.

Fortunately, and despite the lack of an interprovincial consensus, independent analysts seem to be coming together on a way forward. The two major independent panels noted above, one appointed by the provinces (Gagné–Stein), the other by the federal government (O'Brien), presented their reports in 2006, proposing ways to return the horizontal equity programs to a firmer foundation. Both reports called for a 10-province standard, one that includes Alberta. Gagné–Stein advocated that 100 per cent of resource revenues be included in the equalization formula, while O'Brien advocated 50 per cent. But both also acknowledged that the level of entitlements that such a new formula would generate could be more than the federal government could afford. They recommended scaling back the allocations accordingly, while still retaining what they hoped would be a more transparent and fairer determination of provincial entitlements. Another key difference between the two reports is that the federal expert panel (O'Brien) would impose a cap on equalization payments to any province whose per capita fiscal capacity is greater than that of a province not receiving equalization. This proposed equalization cap responds to concerns that the offshore resources agreement with Newfoundland and Labrador could soon move that province's per capita fiscal capacity, after equalization, ahead of Ontario's.

The March 2007 budget adopted most of the O'Brien report's recommendations. It placed both the Equalization and the Territorial Funding Formula programs back on the foundation of a long-term, transparent formula. By adopting the 10-province standard it provided for a significant increase in overall equalization entitlements (worth roughly $1 billion). It also simplified the estimates process, payment scheduling, and the representative tax system used to determine fiscal capacity.

If the federal government hoped to restore harmony with the new measures, however, it was disappointed, as three recipient provinces—Newfoundland and Labrador, Nova Scotia, and Saskatchewan—all bitterly denounced the new formula. All three provinces have rising non-renewable resource revenues from oil and gas, and all will lose ground as the new principles impose a more punitive approach. Two new measures, both recommended by the O'Brien report of 2006, place potential brakes on fiscal improvement in these provinces. The first includes 50 per cent of natural resource revenues in the formula for calculating fiscal capacity (which Saskatchewan claims Harper promised not to do); the second caps entitlements if they exceed the fiscal capacity of a non-recipient province (i.e., Ontario)—which could penalize Newfoundland and Labrador in particular. In addition, the new policy claims to respect the 2005 offshore accords by allowing Nova Scotia and Newfoundland and Labrador the option of either adopting the new formula or continuing with the pre-2007 status quo under the offshore agreements—but it does not allow them to do both. The two Atlantic provinces protested, telling the public that the Harper government had violated the spirit of the offshore accords—a charge that of course evokes broader constitutional principles, and values, including those of respecting the integrity of signed intergovernmental agreements, and interregional equity and justice. On the other hand, many observers outside the Atlantic region applauded the government for making the continuation of the accords so difficult as to discourage any future attempt at similar bilateral arrangements. As we have already noted, by late 2008 rising resource revenues had the effect of eliminating Newfoundland and Labrador from equalization entitlements, while qualifying Ontario for payments for the first time.

To conclude our discussion of equalization, it is worth noting that both the Gagné–Stein and the O'Brien reports essentially offered positive assessments of the program—as have most observers for the past 20 years. There is no such consensus of opinion on the vertical fiscal imbalance (Boadway, 2006). Both reports note that public support for the Equalization Program is relatively strong, and O'Brien in particular notes how effectively the program has worked to correct the horizontal fiscal imbalance:

> Without Equalization payments, the fiscal capacity of the least well-off province was between 58 and 68 per cent of the national average. With Equalization, the fiscal capacity of that province was raised to between 91 and almost 100 per cent of the national average (O'Brien, 2006a: 30).

These are important findings. They mean that despite its technical complexity and the often rancorous debate and ideological division that have surrounded the Equalization Program, it works. Canadian federal governments are likely to stick with the fiscal glue that has helped to hold the federation together for the past 60 years.

CONCLUSION

Fiscal federalism changes frequently—indeed, the arrangements for revenue-sharing within a federation are among the most important means it has for responding to changing economic, social, and political conditions. Exactly how Canada's fiscal relations will change in the next few years is impossible to predict. In late 2008, resource commodity prices fell dramatically, especially for oil, which will ultimately have an effect on federal and provincial revenues, as well as on transfers such as the Equalization Program. In the longer term, the effects of changes to global trade patterns and the value of the Canadian dollar, as well as broad social and environmental factors, are impossible to predict. There is no way of knowing how even one of these issues will affect fiscal policy in Canada, let alone how they will interact in the context of Canadian fiscal federalism. All we can say with any certainty is that much of the information on current programs and issues presented in this chapter will be out of date in a few years.

As for the process of fiscal federalism, the general trends towards more public participation, as well as greater accountability and transparency, in policy-making is beginning to make itself felt in the area of fiscal relations, if only sporadically. The most extensive and innovative exercise in public deliberation to date was probably the one conducted by the Canadian Policy Research Networks (CPRN) on behalf of the Romanow commission on health care. Nevertheless, two provincial commissions (Séguin in Quebec and Young in Newfoundland and Labrador) as well as various Senate and House of Commons committees have explicitly promoted public discussion of, and input into, fiscal policy options in recent years. In addition, both the Gagné–Stein and O'Brien panels consulted widely with specialists, and Gagné–Stein followed Romanow's example in engaging the CPRN to hold consultations across the country, encouraging members of the public to meet and discuss the values that should guide the sharing of public funds (Maxwell et al., 2007). This process revealed some significant differences between 'ordinary' citizens and governments on the subject of fiscal relations: citizens were much less concerned with issues of jurisdiction and autonomy and much more concerned with accountability and conditions. They were also clearly worried about mobility within the country and the future of pan-Canadian social program entitlements.

The impact of these and other soundings of public opinion do seem to have had some impact as part of a broader movement towards greater accountability, transparency, and simplicity. This is seen, for example, in the monitoring and reporting provisions in the 2004 Health Accord. Also, in many governments budgetary process is now also more open and consultative. But simplicity is not attainable—or even desirable—in fiscal federalism, where one size rarely fits all, and complex problems require complex solutions.

Meanwhile, fiscal federalism is no more or less collaborative a process than it has ever been. In the absence of more formal working rules for intergovernmental relations, Canadian governments are limited in their ability to solve 'collective action' problems—matters on which no one government has the authority to act, and the various governments concerned have no incentive to cooperate (Painter, 1991). Occasionally, when—as in the case of the 2004 Health Accord—there is a high level of policy convergence, good-faith negotiation can produce significant results. More often 'consensus' amounts to little more than platitudes about common goals and agreement on lowest-common-denominator action. On major issues, intergovernmental activity is, more often than not, still limited to the consultation stage: the final decisions continue to be left to individual governments' first ministers and cabinets.

The situation in early 2007, as the provinces and territories awaited the federal government's final decisions on its budget, illustrates the nature of this process. The provincial and territorial governments had not been able to agree on the details of a new equalization formula, how large the fund should be, or how it would be allocated. Even if they had, the federal Finance minister would not have felt bound to follow that blueprint, although it might have made his job easier. Ottawa's final decisions were communicated to the provinces in advance, before they were made public, but by then the budget was a *fait accompli*. Although the negative repercussions of the budget clearly tested the political skills of the premiers of Saskatchewan, Nova Scotia, and Newfoundland and Labrador, the federal government alone bore the brunt of the political consequences. The federal budget is not a joint initiative, so joint accountability is not a consideration. In this respect, accountability in the fiscal relations process takes the traditional form, in which individual governments are accountable to their legislatures.

In summary, fiscal federalism is highly political in that it lies at the heart of the most strategic choices that governments face. In the past few years we have seen major challenges to the overall framework of fiscal relations, and some momentous changes. Nonetheless, specific fiscal arrangements never last very long, in Canada or any other federation: they must always be adapted to deal with new economic and political realities. The ink may scarcely have dried on a hard-won agreement or a carefully tuned budget before some unforeseeable event makes it obsolete. Canada is no exception. In this chapter we have outlined the key issues as of 2008: debate about vertical and horizontal fiscal imbalance, the future of major social programs funded by the federal government but delivered by the provinces, and the effort to put the iconic Equalization Program on a new foundation. It is difficult to predict exactly where the next stresses on the system will emerge. Our aging population could well force major changes to funding for health care and other social programs. The current economic downturn could wreak havoc with revenues, while requiring increases in spending to stabilize the economy. And as proposals for fiscal solutions to the greenhouse gas problem (such as carbon taxes; see Chapter 12) arrive on the policy agenda, major intergovernmental discussions are likely to be required.

Chapter 10

The Social Union, SUFA, and Health Care

The concept of the 'social union' is relatively new in Canada. It is generally understood to encompass all the programs that make up our social safety net, beginning with publicly funded universal medical care but also including child care, social assistance, old-age support, and post-secondary education (though the latter is sometimes classified under the heading of the 'economic union' instead, because of its implications for labour markets and economic productivity).

The provincial governments have the most prominent role in the delivery of social programs, since they have the primary constitutional responsibility in that area. But the federal government, as we have seen, also plays a major role. Although Ottawa's main responsibility is to provide financial support, it also has jurisdiction over unemployment insurance, and it shares jurisdiction with the provinces over contributory pensions (Banting, 2008). At the same time, it is almost a political necessity for every federal government, regardless of partisan stripe, to play an active, visible role in maintaining and, when possible, enhancing the social safety net. The prominent role that the federal government has staked out for itself in this area of provincial jurisdiction has set the stage for innumerable conflicts over the years, especially in the field of health care.

The term 'social union' has connotations beyond social entitlements themselves, however. It also suggests the pan-Canadian nature of those entitlements, and the sense of a shared social purpose that most—though not all—governments in the federation seek to promote. In both senses, the social union is a relatively new feature of the federal system. In 1867 neither the state nor its citizens envisioned government as having a role to play in promoting the health and welfare of the society. The building blocks of the social safety net were not really put in place until after the Second World War, and the term 'social union' itself gained currency only in the early 1990s, at the time of the discussions leading to the Charlottetown Accord. For many years after 1945, the federal government took the lead in the creation and funding of the programs that would form the basis of the social union, sometimes working alone and sometimes in collaboration with the provinces. Then the severe budget cuts of the mid-1990s strained federal–provincial relations in this area, forcing governments and citizens alike to seek new ways to handle the social union. A central part of this effort was the Social Union Framework Agreement (SUFA) of 1999.

In this chapter we explore Canada's social union primarily through examination of that agreement: its contents, how it was negotiated, and its implications for the evolution of the social safety net. In the course of our discussion it will become clear that SUFA's impact has been limited. Few members of the general public would recognize the name SUFA, let alone know what the agreement entails. Nevertheless, in the mid- to late 1990s—a very difficult era for Canadian social programs—the SUFA negotiations underscored the importance that governments attached to social policy. And even if the overall SUFA framework has not become a major factor in intergovernmental relations, we would argue that some important elements of the agreement remain in effect, as evidenced in the way the Harper Conservative government has approached social policy and federalism since its election in 2006.

The social union encompasses a wide range of policy fields and an enormous variety of specific programs. Different policy fields tend to have their own approaches and internal logics (Boychuk, 2004; Esping-Anderson, 1990). Furthermore, different provinces have tended to design their social programs with different ends in mind. In the field of social assistance, for example, some provinces have tended to emphasize redistribution of wealth, while others have focused on incentives to encourage labour market participation (Boychuk, 1998). Nevertheless, most programs have evolved in the context of various federal cost-sharing programs. Since 1995, when the Canada Assistance Plan was folded into what was then called the Canada Health and Social Transfer (CHST), virtually all Ottawa's contributions for social programs have taken the form of block transfers with very few conditions or restrictions attached to them. Even now, however, intergovernmental relationships tend to vary from sector to sector within the broad area of social policy (Lazar, 2006). According to Lazar, interdependence is greater in some sectors than others, but most sectors are characterized by non-hierarchical relationships between governments.

The one exception has been health care. Although the Canada Health Transfer (CHT) is a block grant, under the Canada Health Act of 2004 it carries a number of restrictions—such as a ban on extra-billing for services deemed to be medically necessary—that help ensure universal access to the medical insurance program ('medicare'). Of all the programs delivered by governments in Canada, medicare is by far the most visible and the most important in terms not only of dollars spent but of political salience, practical impact, and overall resonance for

Canadians. Election surveys typically find that voters place health care at the top of the list of issues they consider most important: in 2006, for example, 41.4 per cent of respondents to the Canadian Election Survey identified health care as the most important issue, and in 2004 nearly 50 per cent did so.[1] In many respects health care constitutes a separate field from other social programs—a reality that was recognized when the Canada Health Transfer (CHT) was carved out of the Canada Health and Social Transfer (CHST) in 2004.

In short, heath care is a giant among Canada's social programs, and it has a giant's appetite for tax dollars. This appetite, as we shall see, has had, and will continue to have, serious consequences for the way the other components of the social union are handled and the support they receive. Finally, as a lesson in the negotiation of intergovernmental agreements, we will note how the SUFA process exemplified the approach to multilateral negotiations that Gibbins (1999) described as '9-1-1' federalism, which essentially defined the period from 1995 until the arrival of the Harper government in 2006.

THE SOCIAL UNION AND THE FEDERAL SPENDING POWER

Margaret Biggs (1996: 1) has described the social union as 'the web of rights and obligations between Canadian citizens and governments that give effect and meaning to our shared sense of social purpose and common citizenship'. Bob Rae, premier of Ontario in the period when the Charlottetown Accord was being negotiated, is often credited with popularizing the concept as a way of counter-balancing the emphasis on economic issues at that time. Since then, it seems that the term has most often been used to suggest something that, though it may not be completely defunct, is less robust than it once was. More specifically, there is a growing sense that the welfare state created after 1945, through intergovern-mental cooperation and federal spending, is under siege. We have outlined in previous chapters how the funding for Canada-wide social programs has been reduced. As a result of these reductions, many Canadians worry that the quality of the social programs to which they feel entitled may no longer be as consistent across Canada as it once was, and that individual provinces' emphasis on economic competitiveness is creating a 'race to the bottom' in social policy.

Thus policy thinkers, and some political leaders, have drawn on the concept of the social union in the course of rethinking how to achieve social rights and obli-gations without major federal funding and conditional programs. The social union debate, however, involves not only fiscal federalism but also constitutional issues, including—crucially—Quebec's status in the federation. The Constitution Act of 1867 foresaw a very limited role for the state in the lives of its citizens. It had nothing to say about most of the societal functions that governments today perform, and although, in assigning health, education, and social welfare to provincial jurisdiction, it recognized some governmental responsibility in these areas, its expectations were rudimentary. When the federal government began putting in place the foundations of the welfare state, in the middle decades of the twentieth century, its legislative power to take the necessary action was limited. In the cases of unemployment insurance (1940) and old-age pensions (1951, 1964) the constitution was amended to give the federal government the specific powers it needed. In other cases, however, Ottawa simply took advantage of its constitutional spending power (Watts, 1999b; Banting, 2008) to direct funding wherever it was needed, regardless of jurisdiction, either creating its own programs or sharing the costs of provincial programs. It did so for the very practical, and political, reason that a substantial majority of Canadians wanted it to do so.

Quebec has a long history of resisting federal programs, particularly those designed to bypass the provincial government and transfer money directly to non-governmental institutions (e.g., universities). Until the 1960s this resistance was motivated in part by the desire to preserve traditional Church-centred social values and more generally to preserve autonomy. With the Quiet Revolution, however, preserving Quebec's autonomy, language, and culture became the overriding concerns. Thus, with a few exceptions,[2] the Quebec government has sought to opt out of Canada-wide initiatives and use its share of federal funding to run parallel programs of its own design. Quebec's entitlement to federal funding has not been questioned—after all, Québécois pay federal taxes too. Questions have been raised, however, about the types of programs from which opting-out should be allowed: only from cost-shared programs, or also from directly delivered federal programs? Of course, Quebec has put forward a unique rationale for resisting the federal spending power, premised on its special identity. But other provincial governments have also had reason to question Ottawa's untrammelled use of the federal spending power to trench on provincial jurisdictions: notably, concern for their own autonomy and unease over their dependence on unstable federal funding. Given the open-ended nature of the spending power, and the absence of specific or even general rules to govern its use, it is not surprising that the provinces have long pressed for definitions and, above all, limitations. At the same time, there is concern that limiting federal spending would mean limiting the money available for social programs, especially in the smaller provinces.

From the late 1960s until the Charlottetown Accord of 1992, the issues of the spending power and social policy were never far from centre stage in the debate over constitutional reform. In 1969 Prime Minister Pierre Trudeau proposed constitutional amendments to regulate the use of the spending power that, if passed, would have legitimized use of the power while making it subject to provincial consent in some cases. The issue resurfaced in the 1978–81 negotiations, and in 1987 became the subject of a proposal in the Meech Lake Accord to add to the Constitution Act, 1867, a new section (106A) with the following wording:

The Government of Canada shall provide reasonable compensation to the government of a province that chooses not to participate in a national shared-cost program that is established by the Government of Canada after

the coming into force of this section in an area of exclusive provincial jurisdiction that is compatible with national objectives (Meech Lake Accord, 3
June 1987, Part 7).

After the demise of the Meech Lake Accord in 1990, a new effort to achieve
constitutional renewal began that eventually produced the Charlottetown Accord
of 1992. One reason for the controversy surrounding the Meech Lake agreement
had been the fear, especially among those outside Quebec, that the new section
106A would prevent the federal government from ever again making major
progress on national social programs.[3] Nonetheless, a watered-down version of
the same provision was included in the Charlottetown Accord: it limited the
principle of compensation to new, Canada-wide shared-cost programs and called
for an intergovernmental agreement or framework to govern the use of the
spending power more broadly. After the Charlottetown Accord in turn was
rejected, this time in a referendum, the idea of a constitutional amendment as
such was put on ice. However, the desire for new intergovernmental framework
revived after the landmark 1995 federal budget.

The consolidation of the EPF and the CAP into the CHST in the 1995 budget
reflected the federal government's priorities at the time: reducing the deficit,
paring back the welfare state, and withdrawing from heavily conditional funding
arrangements. By this time, therefore, the old debate over Ottawa's use of its
spending power in areas of provincial jurisdiction seemed largely irrelevant.
After a decade of federal cuts and unilateral changes to their funding programs,
the provinces were reeling, distrustful of the federal government, and determined
to pursue renewal of the social union on their own terms.

NEGOTIATING SUFA

The document formally entitled 'A Framework to Improve the Social Union for
Canadians' can be best understood—both in itself and as an illustration of the
way intergovernmental relations work in Canada—by examining the dynamics
of the negotiation process that produced it. There were essentially three parties
represented around the table: the provinces in general, the federal government,
and Quebec. In this section we will examine how these parties interacted to
produce a final agreement, and how the overall process illustrated the '9-1-1'
approach to federalism.

The General Provincial Position

The provincial and territorial governments took a leading role in the social union
debate from 1995 to 1999. The Annual Premiers Conference (APC), the predecessor of the Council of the Federation (COF) began as a low-key, informal
gathering, but by the 1980s it had become a major event. Between the annual

conferences, held each August, the chair (rotating each year among the provinces) would hold follow-up meetings by conference call, and senior officials also met frequently. Two key ministerial groups also met and provided input into APC meetings: the finance ministers and the Provincial–Territorial Council on Social Policy Renewal—a new group, created in 1995, that was to lead the work on social-union issues (Meekison, 2004).

The goal was not just to form a common front with respect to the federal government, but also to coordinate social policy and promote the social union through interprovincial cooperation. There is no evidence that the provinces intended to eliminate the need for federal–provincial interaction in pursuit of social-union goals, but the prevailing fiscal, political, and intellectual climate was such that they considered the federal government to be weak, unreliable, and therefore unable to exercise leadership. Key provinces—notably Ontario and Alberta, which at the time were both led by 'small-c' conservative governments— were determined to limit Ottawa's role in social policy more generally. They sought not only the restoration of the social-program funding that had been cut in the 1995 budget, but also permanent tax transfers, and a general decentraliza-tion of the social union framework.[4] Other provinces—notably Saskatchewan, Manitoba, New Brunswick, Nova Scotia, PEI, and Newfoundland and Labrador—were less interested in decentralization but no less desirous of achieving greater coherence in social policy.

In general, then, the provinces went into the SUFA negotiations with the following objectives:

- to secure restoration of CHST funding;
- to move towards the development of a joint decision-making process with the federal government;
- to arrange for joint interpretation and enforcement of social-policy objec-tives and standards (e.g., those in the Canada Health Act), with an independent dispute-resolution process; and
- to impose constraints on the federal spending power.

The Federal Position

The Chrétien government, having inherited the constitutional impasse of 1992, had no desire to pursue constitutional reform; it wanted to reform the federal system using pragmatic, non-constitutional means. This objective became even more urgent after the extremely close Quebec referendum on sovereignty in 1995. Ottawa's second objective was to maintain the leadership role in social policy matters that was an article of faith for the Liberal Party; this would be hard to achieve, given the damage done to social programs, and provincial trust, by the budget cuts of 1995. A third, more general objective was to reinvent the cumber-some federal government apparatus and reform the old top-down ways of artic-ulating and enforcing social-program standards.

From 1993 to 1998 the federal government had been inching its way towards a new rapprochement both with the provinces and with the social-policy community. It began by collaborating with the provinces in various policy fields, including municipal infrastructure, labour market development, internal trade, the national child benefit program, and pension-plan reform (Lazar, 2006). As the federal budgetary position improved, it once again became possible for Ottawa to contemplate new spending, including restoration of CHST cash. Overall, the Chrétien government began increasingly to differ in its position from that of Brian Mulroney's government, which had been less ambitious in social policy and more willing to settle with Quebec over its longstanding grievance on the spending power. Thus the federal government entered the SUFA negotiations with the following objectives:

- to retain flexibility in use of the spending power;
- to avoid getting trapped in new mechanisms for 'co-determination' (joint decision-making) with the provinces;
- to preserve and improve some Canada-wide standards for social programs;
- to enhance personal mobility rights in order to improve labour market efficiency;
- to encourage provincial cooperation by undoing some of the CHST cuts; and
- to pursue a transparent 'audit approach' to the social union.

The Quebec Position

Quebec's objectives differed fundamentally from those of the other provinces at all stages of the negotiation. Its starting position was that it would not join with the other provinces in a common, Canada-wide approach to social programs: from its point of view, a policy developed by the nine English-speaking provinces would be no better than a policy developed by the federal government. Therefore Quebec's goal was not to establish collective provincial leadership and improve interprovincial collaboration, but rather to maintain its autonomy in social programs.

Furthermore, the party in office at the time of the SUFA negotiations was the Parti Québécois, elected in 1994 and dedicated to taking Quebec out of the federation. Quebec has engaged in intergovernmental relations very selectively, determined to preserve its traditional view of the federal system and to cooperate with the other provinces only when there is no other choice (for example, when its share of federal funding is at stake).[5] Thus when the provinces and territories began meeting in the Council on Social Policy Renewal, Quebec attended only as an observer, not a participant.

In the middle of the process in the spring of 1998, Premier Lucien Bouchard decided that Quebec should become more involved. At the Annual Premiers' Conference that year in Saskatoon, Bouchard helped to draft an all-province position on federal social spending that was not far from Quebec's own traditional position. The new provincial consensus sought to place conditions on the federal spending power in areas of provincial jurisdiction and to allow provinces to opt out with full compensation in some circumstances. In return, Quebec seemed prepared to acquiesce to both the general thrust of the proposed framework, in favour of a pan-Canadian approach to social policy objectives, and the implication that the federal government had a legitimate role to play (Noël, 2001). Once this consensus had been reached, the negotiations with the federal government moved rapidly, leading to a final agreement six months later. Yet in the end the Quebec government chose not to sign on. The precise reasons behind this decision are open to debate, but clearly there were some concessions that Quebec was not prepared to make.

To summarize, Quebec went into the SUFA negotiations with just two main objectives:

- to defend its longstanding opposition to the use of the federal spending power in areas of provincial jurisdiction, together with its right to opt out with full financial compensation; and
- to see that the funds cut from the CHST in 1995 were restored.

In the end Quebec did not share the other provinces' interest in pursuing new joint programs with the federal government, or in developing new mechanisms for co-determination.

The negotiation of these three positions followed what has become a familiar pattern in Canadian intergovernmental relations. Some provincial and territorial governments had more in common with the federal Liberals than they did with other provincial governments; others may simply have seen it as being in their interest to side with Ottawa. In any event, once the federal government came to the negotiation table in earnest, it was able to play one province against another, undermining the common front. Quebec's position, by contrast, was grounded in a deeply held, principled theory of federalism, and it could afford politically to be outside the consensus. The other provinces were more pragmatic, but at the end of the day each of them needed to be seen as part of a pan-Canadian consensus. Alain Noël may have oversimplified slightly, but on the whole his description seems accurate:

> Governments from the smaller provinces wanted a strong central government; all except Quebec accepted, indeed demanded a pan-Canadian vision; Quebec was not trusted as an ally; and provincial politicians knew citizens favoured Ottawa on these questions (Noël, 2001: 18).

The negotiation process took place in two stages. First Ottawa reached an agreement with the nine provinces. Then it quietly negotiated with Quebec to see how that agreement might apply in its special circumstances; the understanding they reached was that even though Quebec was not a formal signatory to SUFA, it would still receive its share of the federal cash. It was the triangular relationship between Ottawa, Quebec, and the nine other provinces, and the two-stage negotiating process, that led Gibbins (1999) to coin the term '9-1-1 federalism'.

EXAMINING SUFA

Contents

SUFA has seven main sections. Some are better fleshed out than others, and, on the whole, the document is more of general guide than a detailed blueprint. The seven sections address (1) the basic principles and values of the social union; (2) personal mobility in social programs across Canada; (3) provisions to improve public accountability and transparency; (4) new rules for intergovernmental comity, or fair dealing; (5) specific recognition of the value of the federal spending power, but with rules for its use involving some provincial veto; (6) rules for dispute avoidance and resolution; and (7) provisions for review after three years. The main points in each section are as follows:

1. **Principles.** The purpose here was to establish from the start a firm sense of basic principles and common values underpinning the social union—values such as 'equality, respect for diversity, fairness, individual dignity and responsibility, and mutual aid'. Also included are the five principles of medicare incorporated in the Canada Health Act.

2. **Mobility within Canada.** A major innovation in Canadian intergovernmental arrangements, this section emphasizes that all Canadians must be free to pursue economic opportunities anywhere in the country. Therefore governments must eliminate 'any residency-based policies or practices' that might limit access to 'post-secondary education, training, health and social services, and social assistance'. The section also sets a deadline for compliance with the mobility provisions of the Agreement on Internal Trade (see Chapter 11), including 'mutual recognition of occupational qualifications'.

3. **Informing Canadians—Public Accountability and Transparency.** This section is also innovative and reflects Ottawa's determination to introduce 'new public management' principles such as performance measurement, citizen participation, and procedural transparency into intergovernmental relations. However, the commitments in this section are of a general nature, open to interpretation.

4. **Working in Partnership for Canadians.** This section deals with basic intergovernmental values and goes some way towards addressing

longstanding provincial grievances about federal unilateralism, though in rather general language. The federal government promises to give due notice and to consult the other governments on major changes to social policy or programs.

5. **The Federal Spending Power/Improving Social Programs for Canadians.** This section begins with a strong statement recognizing the value of the federal spending power. It then commits the federal government to consultation with the provinces one year prior to any significant funding changes in existing social transfers, and to obtaining majority provincial consent before introducing any new Canada-wide program for which other governments would provide some of the funding. This provision is a rare example of a co-decision rule in Canadian federalism. Any new program funding to the provinces must also abide by the accountability framework outlined in section 3. Provinces are permitted to opt out and receive compensation, but only if they already offer programs in a similar or related area. For new programs delivering funds directly to individuals and organizations, the federal government commits only to consultation, not co-decision.

6. **Dispute Avoidance and Resolution.** Responding to a key requirement of the provinces, this section also breaks new ground, outlining the basics of a process that includes joint fact-finding and the use of independent third parties. Among the issues to which this process would apply is the interpretation of medicare principles. Although the details for each sector are left to be worked out, this section too holds out the promise that some basic rules will be put in place.

7. **Review of SUFA.** After three years the agreement is to be reviewed, and opportunities are to be provided for the public to provide feedback.

The Health Care Side-Deal

At the same time that SUFA was signed, in February 1999, the first ministers agreed to changes concerning the CHST that made it easier for some provinces, notably Ontario and Alberta, to come on board. Specifically, the federal government agreed to increase funding for the CHST so long as all the new money went to health care,[6] and to accelerate the transition to equal per capita shares of the CHST for every province (see Chapter 9). Most observers agree that without this side deal SUFA would have ended up alongside the Victoria Charter of 1971, Meech Lake, and the Charlottetown Accord in the graveyard of failed federal–provincial agreements. For Ottawa it was important not only to have a continuing presence in the health care field, but also to ensure that the provinces (with the exception of Quebec) recognized its definition and specifications on what should constitute limitations on the federal spending power. And for the provinces—'haves' as well as 'have-nots'—the cash itself was all–important. In the light of this deal, it seems that health care funding was the dominant issue throughout the SUFA process, even though it was explicitly acknowledged only towards the end of the negotiations.

Implications

A few general comments on SUFA itself are in order, beginning with its value as an instrument of policy. Though the document's wording may seem complex to the average citizen-reader, for government technocrats and lawyers it is too vague and political. The bureaucrats who handled the negotiations worked with a much more technical, legalistic text, but were instructed by the political leaders to draft a more accessible version for the media and the public. In any case, inter-governmental agreements often rely heavily on generalities and ambiguity—partly to paper over differences and partly to provide some flexibility for the future. Also, like almost all Canadian intergovernmental agreements, the SUFA document is not legally binding: it is only as good as the commitment of the signatory governments. No citizen could take the document to court and seek redress for a government's failure to live up to its SUFA commitments. In this way the agreement is another example of the Canadian preference for ambiguity rather than rules in intergovernmental arrangements. Broad, non-specific commitments, without meaningful time-tables for implementation, are safe and comfortable because there is no penalty for not following through. As a policy instrument, therefore, SUFA has not been particularly useful.

On the other hand, the agreement can tell us a good deal about the state of Canadian federalism and intergovernmental relations in the late 1990s. In seeking to re-establish the comity required to make complex intergovernmental relations work, it suggests a desire—however short-lived—for a return to the cooperative federalism of the period from 1945 to the mid-1970s, when the commitments to common principles, joint planning, due notice, and consultation that SUFA put down in writing were all implicitly understood.

Those commitments appeared to suggest a renewed interest in cost-shared, joint social programs, but there has been little movement in that direction, as we will see in the next section below. In fact, the provincial-consent requirement in section 5 would seem to make such programs less likely, and at the time the federal government seemed to prefer its direct funding options.[7] Not long after signing SUFA, Ottawa announced a new Millennium Scholarship Foundation that would provide scholarships directly to university students (Bakvis, 2008). Though technically compliant, that program appeared to contravene the spirit of section 5. The fact that Quebec was not a party to the agreement is signifi-cant. Defenders of the traditional Quebec position on the spending power are still uneasy with SUFA's endorsement of the federal role and disturbed by the limited extent of SUFA's provisions to constrain its use. In particular, the financial compensation for not participating is narrowly defined, and Ottawa is not required to seek provincial consent at all for direct program spending in areas of exclusive provincial jurisdiction. It is no surprise that Premier Bouchard walked away from the agreement, even though he said publicly that Quebec agreed with the general principles of the social union. He also endorsed the 'side-deal' on the CHST.[8]

The Chrétien government stated that it would follow SUFA principles in relations with Quebec, even though the latter was not party to the agreement, and it kept its word, as did its short-lived successor under Paul Martin. The same has been true of the Harper Conservative government. At least one commentator has seen a 'de facto asymmetry' in this arrangement: Quebec's unique position, partly in and partly out of the social union, represents at least partial recognition of its special status—something it could not achieve through formal constitutional reform (Gibbins, 2001). Though many, including the federal NDP under Jack Layton, have applauded this arrangement, others believe it is detrimental to Canadian unity; some also argue that it is hardly in Quebec's interest to be subject to guidelines that it did not help to shape.

SUFA did take some important—if tentative—steps towards a new model of intergovernmental collaboration. In this model the federal government and the provinces and territories are supposed to be equal partners in policy formation and implementation. Yet most observers would concur that in the decade since the agreement was signed, its impact has been limited. It has been suggested that, just as the Chrétien Liberal government contravened the spirit of SUFA in creating the Millennium Scholarship Foundation, so did the Conservative government of Stephen Harper when, in 2006, it cancelled the federal–provincial child care agreements reached by the Martin government. It should be noted, however, that the Harper government did follow SUFA rules in giving a full year's notice and providing transition payments.

Practical impact aside, the agreement did include three innovative elements: (1) commitments to public accountability and transparency, which in theory should make it easier to sustain political support for joint efforts; (2) dispute-avoidance and resolution procedures; and (3) a formal co-decision rule requiring the consent of a majority of provinces before the federal government brings in any new Canada-wide intergovernmental transfer program. As we will note below, there is little evidence that these three commitments have been met in practice. Nonetheless, some progress has been made, and the fact that they exist in writing makes them important referents should governments once again decide that progress is needed in these areas.

SUFA IN PRACTICE: RELEVANT OR NOT?

Within three years of its signing, SUFA had become almost invisible. Governments did not do much to promote it to Canadians—but then such documents are rarely of interest to members of the public, apart from policy wonks and academics. At the same time, there is evidence that it has been used as a guide, at least by some elements within governments.

Two policy sectors illustrate how the agreement has been used. First, in the area of children's benefits (child care and early childhood education), Ottawa followed SUFA—at least for a while—in pursuing consultation with the provinces and territories in a series of meetings of the Federal–Provincial–Territorial Council on Social Policy Renewal. There was extensive consultation and participatory input from interest groups, including a joint national consultative exercise in 1999 that reflected commitments made in part 3 of the agreement. On the other hand, several provinces were leery of some of the national organizations involved, which they perceived to be too closely tied to the federal government. Governments also followed through to some degree on the commitment to more transparent reporting relationships (Phillips, 2001). On the content of policy initiatives, there was a lot of joint planning and objective setting, and a useful blending of direct federal and coordinated provincial programming.

The Harper government's abrupt cancellation of the bilateral child care agreements reached by the Martin government with all the provinces and territories demonstrates the fragile nature of virtually all intergovernmental agreements (Friendly and White, 2008): because they are essentially political, their durability depends on the political commitment of all parties concerned. The same is true of SUFA. Nevertheless, the fact that the Harper government followed the SUFA guidelines when it cancelled the child care agreements suggested that the agreement may have greater force than is generally acknowledged.

The other sector that has seen a lot of activity is health care—but in this case there has been much less collaboration. Here the transfer payments continue to be paramount. A significant step came in September 2000 when the federal government, in pre-election mode, agreed to restore full CHST funding, and to provide some supplementary money for specific health areas. In return all the provinces, including Quebec, agreed to a general statement of principles and an action plan on health care investment. Provisions for accountability and financial stability in these arrangements appear to follow the SUFA spirit—though SUFA is not mentioned in the public information explaining the agreement (likely out of sensitivity to Quebec). More fundamentally, governments continued to pursue separate tracks for health care reform: for example, both Saskatchewan and Alberta had their own commissions of inquiry under way before Ottawa appointed the Romanow Commission. At one point in 2000–1 the provinces pushed hard to put flesh on the bones of the SUFA dispute resolution provisions so that they could be applied to potential disputes concerning application of the medicare principles in the Canada Health Act. And at one stage, it appeared that Alberta would be invoking the dispute settlement mechanism on health care, but after some initial correspondence both Ottawa and Alberta dropped the issue (Maoni, 2008). The promised amplification of the mechanism never took place.

The largest deal ever on health care reform, at least in monetary terms, was negotiated in the course of two years and two first ministers' meetings, in 2003 and 2004, following the delivery in 2002 of both the Kirby report, *The Health of Canadians: The Federal Role* (Kirby, 2002) and the Romanow report, *Building on Values: The Future of Health Care in Canada* (Romanow, 2002). At the 2004 FMM, held during Paul Martin's tenure as prime minister, Ottawa committed itself to a 10-year plan to strengthen health care (Health Canada, 2004), which provided for increasing transfers, and a special fund, as well as a commitment, to reduce wait times in key areas such as cancer, heart disease, and joint replacements by 31 March 2007, while 'recognizing the different starting points, priorities, and strategies across jurisdictions' (Health Canada, 2004). The 10-year plan was accompanied by a separate communiqué explicitly recognizing Quebec's asymmetrical status. Reporting requirements in the 10-year plan are minimal: the provinces are simply required to report to their own residents on health system performance, and provinces need only 'seek advice from experts and health providers on the most appropriate indicators to measures of health system performance' (Health Canada, 2004).

Yet some progress has been made. Established as part of the 2003 Accord, the Canadian Health Council is funded by the federal government and tasked with preparing an annual report on health outcomes and the health status of Canadians. Alberta is not a member and Quebec has its own Council on Health and Well Being. Another arm's-length body is the Canadian Institute for Health Information (CIHI), a non-profit organization established in 1994 as a partnership among health care providers and governments, which now makes available information on subjects including wait lists, population health, and trends in the health care workforce. CIHI's board of directors consists mainly of senior public servants (often deputy ministers), from both the federal and provincial governments. In 2007 it released its first 'hospital standardized mortality ratio' study, naming specific hospitals, with the view to improving patient care by assessing mortality rates and their possible causes (CIHI, 2007).[9] Although there is virtually no reference to SUFA in any of CIHI's many publications, its activities—in particular its comparative studies on workforce trends and health care outcomes—in many ways represent the kind of reporting, not just to governments and health care providers, but also to the public, that the framers of SUFA may have had in mind.

CONCLUSION

Overall, the impact of SUFA has been limited. Indeed, some would argue that it has had no impact at all; that the only reasons it was accepted were that all the governments involved knew that the Canadian public was expecting something to come out of the long negotiations, and that the provinces needed health care money to flow more freely. Ottawa was extremely reluctant to accept any constraints on its spending power, and the limited provisions in SUFA were the most it would accept, while the provinces were reluctant to accept any kind of reporting requirement and in the end agreed only to report to their own legislatures, not to any external body. It appears that all governments were eager to distance themselves from the agreement once it had been signed and the health care cash was on its way. The review required after three years was conducted with little publicity and was cursory at best, consisting essentially of five focus groups across the country attended by former bureaucrats, academics, and representatives of civil-society organizations. Not long thereafter the Ministerial Council on Social Policy Renewal—the main coordinating body for SUFA at the political level—ceased meeting.

A good part of the problem can likely be attributed to governments' own reluctance to use SUFA for the purpose it was designed to serve: to facilitate intergovernmental coordination. Implementation of the agreement was left to individual sectors (health, social services, education), and the Ministerial Council on Social Policy Renewal does not appear to have made any attempt to ensure consistency across sectors. Compliance with the citizen-participation rule has also been uneven: nothing in the agreement could have forced Ontario's Harris Conservative government, for instance, to change its style with respect to public consultation and deliberation. Finally, and most important, there is the awkward position of Quebec, partly in and partly out of evolving arrangements in a way that is difficult to describe—though Gibbins's '9-1-1 federalism' captures its essence—let alone to formalize. At a minimum, Quebec's formal absence obliges the federal government to tread more warily than it might otherwise, undermining the quality of the social union as a whole. In a more general way, Quebec's non-participation means that SUFA can never become a truly national unifying symbol. And because of the agreement's overall ambiguity, it is difficult to use as a concrete guide to action.

In the last analysis, it may be that too much was expected of SUFA. As Tom McIntosh has noted, social policy development must take place at the ground level, and the shape of the social union will always depend much more on public opinion and the evolving fiscal policy framework than on any general intergovernmental agreement (McIntosh, 2002: 11). Harvey Lazar has observed that if SUFA were to become an effective instrument for promoting social policy it would likely increase the gulf between Quebec and the rest of the country; more modest success, then, would likely be safer for the federation in the long run (Lazar, 2000a). On a more optimistic note, it is worth keeping in mind that federal–provincial relations in the 1990s were in their most dismal state ever. If SUFA has helped in even a limited way to put the system back on a more cooperative and functional footing, that must be seen as a useful achievement.

Finally, 'social union' and 'SUFA' are not synonymous—particularly if by social union one means a shared sense of social purpose and a Canada-wide approach to social programs and entitlements. That understanding preceded SUFA and will probably long outlive it. Though references to SUFA and the 'social union' are relatively rare today, social programs still exist, and governments know that they cannot afford to abandon them entirely. In the 2008 federal budget plan (Finance Canada, 2008), terms such as 'social potential and security', 'social benefits', and 'social development' can all be seen as surrogates for 'social union'. The ongoing support for medicare and post-secondary education (through the Canada Student Loans program) outlined in the 2008 budget, among other programs, indicates that the basic elements of the Canadian social union are unlikely to disappear anytime soon.

Chapter 11

The Economic Union
and Economic Policy

Canada came into existence in 1867 as a federal community in good part to create a single new economy out of the old colonial economies. Yet regional economies continue to coexist both with the national economy and with a continental and global economy. The definition of what constitutes a particular economic space—regional, national, global—matters a lot in terms of the rules that apply and who gets to set them. At the same time, economic interests differ greatly within the society, depending on class, occupation, gender, urban–rural locale, and province or region. And since Canada is a federation of regions with sharply different economic conditions and interests, federal politics reflects those differences.

Governments rely on a variety of instruments to pursue economic policy in areas such as the money supply, taxation, spending, the regulation of trade (internal and international), contracts and property rights, labour standards, resources, transportation, energy, and communications. Policy outcomes reflect the nature of federal institutions, including the legal jurisdiction and fiscal powers of the two orders of government under the constitution and the way those powers have been exercised over time. Specific policies reflect both the governing instruments available and the way that jurisdiction is distributed across the different levels of government: thus the federal government is restricted in its ability to regulate the securities industry (for instance) because the provinces have primary jurisdiction in this area. Some areas of economic policy require the cooperation of federal and provincial governments, and economies can suffer if that cooperation is lacking.

Changes in economic conditions and economic thinking both have a major impact on the type of policies pursued. In the early years of confederation, the Canadian economy was still developing: the vast lands of the Canadian west had barely begun to be opened up; resources were just beginning to be exploited systematically; and the track was still being laid for the transcontinental railway that would be completed in 1885. The policy requirements of a developing agricultural or resource economy differ considerably from those of a manufacturing or diverse urban economy. As well, policies can and do change in response to economic boom and bust conditions, changes in the nature and intensity of trade (who we trade with, and the importance of trade to the economy overall), and the terms of trade (e.g., are wheat prices high or low?). Also, it matters where the attention of policy-makers is directed. Is it on macroeconomic indicators such as growth, inflation, unemployment, or productivity? Or is it on microeconomic factors such as comparative advantage of specific sectors (forest products or automobiles), training of the labour force, technological innovation, or promoting sustainable development and reducing pollution?

The interests of the society and the state tend to crystallize into broader ideological positions on economic policy. The largest and most deceptively simple issue in this ideological context is the role of government intervention in the economy. Should government actively intervene in the marketplace to pursue objectives such as equality of opportunity, full employment, acceptable living standards, or environmental quality? Or should government stay on the sidelines and intervene only to secure personal safety, protect property rights, and provide essential public goods and services? There have been enormous differences of view on this issue over the course of Canadian history. The ideological consensus of the day might be in favour of inflation control, a made-in-Canada oil price, free trade with the United States, or reducing regional disparities. Regardless of the goal, if there is a jurisdictional division of authority over the subject matter and a regional difference of interest in the policy outcome, federal–provincial politics will play a part in determining how this goal will be pursued, or even whether it will be pursued at all. In the Canadian federation these differences play themselves out in intergovernmental arenas on a regular basis.

This chapter outlines four of the most important concerns of economic policy-making in the current federal system: maintenance of the economic union; management of the national economy as a whole; regional equity; and the challenges of remaining competitive in the era of globalization and transnational economic integration.

THE ECONOMIC UNION

One of the primary goals of the act of confederation in 1867 was to create a larger market than was available in the three existing colonies (the United Province of Canada, Nova Scotia, and New Brunswick) and lay the groundwork for its expan-

sion, with the addition of new provinces and territories, into a genuinely continental economy extending from the Atlantic to the Pacific. In this sense
economic union represents a form of economic and political integration:
creating a whole out of a set of parts. Political institutions are created to establish
free economic space and to regulate the activity within that space (Trebilcock,
1987). Both before and after Confederation, Canada's economy was integrated
within that of the British Empire. Yet since 1921 we have had more trade and
investment with the United States than with Britain, and since the 1980s in
particular our economy has become increasingly integrated with the American
and global economies.

As a form of integration, economic union assumes the creation of a single new
political community. New political institutions shape the boundaries of
economic activity. Some of the means used to this end are 'negative', such as legal
constraints against intervention in the marketplace; others are 'positive', such as
the pursuit of unified or harmonized regulation and the creation of joint public
works or other public goods and services that help sustain the new, larger
economy (Tinbergen, 1965; Scharpf, 1996). In the process, economic unions (or
'common markets', as they are sometimes called) create significant benefits for
the community:

1.   *market integration*: the expanded economic space realizes economies of
     scale and specialization over time;
2.   *increased bargaining power*: a larger economic unit exercises greater influ-
     ence or market power in relation to external countries and markets;
3.   *sharing of costs*: spreading costs over a larger population enhances the
     ability to undertake defence expenditures and large developmental projects
     and other public goods; and
4.   *pooling and sharing of risks*: federation as an insurance scheme, particularly
     in the context of regional economic diversity (Economic Council of
     Canada, 1991: 31–3).

All federal constitutions provide for an economic union, with varying degrees
of precision. Arguably the most powerful constitutional provisions are those that
prohibit barriers to free trade within the union. In 1867 the former colonies
turned over the right to impose tariffs to the newly created federal parliament.
According to section 121 of the Constitution Act [1867], 'All articles of the
Growth, Produce, or Manufacture of any one of the Provinces shall . . . be
admitted free into each of the other Provinces': that is, no tariffs can be imposed
on goods moving from one province to another. Historically, this provision has
been narrowly interpreted as applying only to discriminatory taxes, and only on
goods. But economic union is about more than the elimination of tariffs on
goods; it is also about the free movement of services, labour, and capital. Over the
years various provincial governments, and even the federal government, have
found ways to hamper the free flow of all three of those items. Although

Canadians did acquire the explicit right to move and to take up a livelihood in any part of the country in 1982, under the Charter of Rights and Freedoms (section 6), the lack of a broader constitutional guarantee (such as the 'commerce' clause in the US constitution) has been of concern for some decades. The 1867 constitution also granted the federal parliament control over key factors affecting 'positive integration', such as jurisdiction over trade and commerce (the courts later ruled that this power covered only international and interprovincial trade, not intra-provincial trade), the raising and borrowing of money, banking, bankruptcy, patents, and interprovincial works (what we would now call infrastructure) such as railways, canals, and telegraph installations. These jurisdictional powers ensured that the federal government controlled all the chief levers of economic power deemed necessary in the nineteenth century to build a national economy. Meanwhile the provinces retained considerable legal jurisdiction over other important economic matters, such as the ownership and management of Crown land and other natural resources, civil law (including labour law), and the sale of securities. They also had control of social services such as health, education, and welfare. In the nineteenth century, however, the latter were not the major public concerns through which provinces today exercise so much economic and fiscal clout; rather, they were provided mainly by private organizations such as churches, and the provinces' responsibility for them amounted mainly to regulating those organizations.

In 1867 and for many years thereafter, creating the Canadian economic union called for a lot more than constitutional provisions: it also required bold and visionary action. The Fathers of Confederation foresaw a transcontinental economy held together by a band of steel. Building that economy took some fifty years of western expansion and consolidation activity on the part of the new Dominion (federal) government, following an economic strategy that entailed the acquisition of the Hudson's Bay Company's lands, agricultural settlement and industrial growth facilitated by massive immigration, the construction of a transcontinental railway, and the imposition of high external tariffs for the protection of domestic manufacturers. This basic strategy was embodied in Prime Minister John A. Macdonald's 'National Policy', announced in 1878, which remained more or less in place until the Second World War (Eden and Molot, 1993).

Thus the economic union created a new pattern of economic activity. The east–west economy came to be characterized by a distinctly regionalized division of labour, which in turn generated or perpetuated significant disparities in wealth and population densities (Mackintosh, 1939; Shearer, 1985). While all provinces participated in the country's staples-based export economy (fish, fur, timber, paper, grain, and minerals demanded by markets in the US and overseas), the long-term goal was to develop a more advanced manufacturing economy. The three Maritime provinces initially did well in the new national economy, benefiting from significant new industrialization. But as the centres of both population and economic life moved westward, manufacturing became concentrated in central Canada, especially southern Ontario and Quebec. Meanwhile the territories and provinces west of Ontario remained in essence an economic colony of the east, exploited by the railways and banks controlled in Montreal and Toronto, but receiving few of the benefits of the protected manufacturing economy.

By the 1930s a variety of regional and ideological protest movements had emerged in response to these economic developments, demanding a reorientation of federal economic policy and compensation for the effects of past policies.[1] The federal government responded with the series of key policies put in place between 1945 and 1975, including national income security programs such as the old age pension and unemployment insurance, fiscal equalization, and shared-cost social programs (see Chapters 8, 9, and 10). Meanwhile the provinces began to build their own economic development strategies around the ownership and management of natural resources and other regional advantages. Some of these provincial strategies reinforced the national economic design, but just as many sought to thwart it (Simeon and Robinson, 1990; Brown and Leslie, 1994).

By the 1970s the management and sustainability of the Canadian economic union was becoming an important political issue in its own right. As we noted above, economic policy depends on which economy is being considered—regional, national, or global. What is good for one is not always good for the other, and governments in Canada have competed fiercely to control economic outcomes. The provinces eventually employed the legal, fiscal, and political power at their disposal to resist a movement towards national economic integration that they saw as contrary to their more local interests. In response to their calls for 'regional equity', over the decades many policies and programs were put in place by federal and provincial governments alike to mitigate the free-market effects of the Canadian economic union. By the 1970s, however, the business community, economists, and other observers were expressing concern that, as a result of all these interventions, the economic union was becoming too fragmented, and that its benefits could be lost, at a considerable cost to overall economic welfare.

This conflict received particular attention in the work of the Royal Commission on the Economic Union and Development Prospects for Canada (Macdonald Commission; Canada, 1985). The Commission found a wide variety of internal barriers to trade, including agricultural supply management policies restricting the quantities of poultry, eggs, and dairy products that could be shipped from one province to another; discriminatory government purchasing policies that favoured local manufacturers or suppliers of goods and services; barriers to free movement of labour in the form of occupational qualifications and provincial regulation of professions; regionally differentiated federal unemployment policy; regulated railway freight rates that discriminated across regions; differing provincial labour laws; and many federal and provincial industrial and primary sector subsidies that were considered to distort trade. Tellingly, the Commission found that many of these barriers were as much the fault of the federal government as they were of the provinces (agricultural supply boards, for example, were jointly created).

All these policies had (and some continue to have) important economic and social rationales behind them. The issue is not the merits of such policies but rather their cumulative effect on the economic union. The cost of the barriers to the Canadian economy has been disputed, but the most reliable estimates in the 1980s put it at approximately 1 per cent of annual GDP—not a huge amount, but not an insignificant one either (Trebilcock et al., 1983). The most worrisome factor seemed to be the dynamic effect of increasing recourse to government intervention at cross purposes to the overall growth of the national economy, which gave rise to concern that trade within Canada would become no freer than trade among separate countries. These were serious concerns in a period of freer international trade and a growing movement for an independent Quebec. For the federal government, and increasingly for many of the provinces, tackling internal trade barriers became a strategic necessity with respect to both national unity and national competitiveness in the face of global economic integration.

Identifying the problem is one thing, however; finding a solution that does not upset the balance of power within the federation is another. In the episodic constitutional negotiations from the 1960s to 1992, new rules to strengthen the Canadian economic union were prominent on the agenda. Yet, except for the movement of labour provision in section 6 of the Charter of Rights, none of the measures proposed met with success, largely because the provinces feared that they would either increase Ottawa's power over the economy or restrict their ability to intervene in their own economies as they saw fit. It would take the dominance of free trade politics and the pressure of international negotiations (discussed later in this chapter) to make significant headway towards reform.

MACROECONOMIC MANAGEMENT

Macroeconomic policy concerns the economy as a whole: usually the national economy but sometimes the regional. Its objectives are large-scale: ensuring overall growth and stability with respect to booms and busts, controlling the rate of inflation, and promoting employment. By contrast, microeconomic policy focuses on specific sectors and industries, companies and households.

Particularly since the Second World War, it has generally been thought that governments have a basic responsibility to stabilize the economy, that is, to even out the booms and busts of the business cycle. Thus stabilization policy is important, even if the prevailing ideology favours market-driven solutions to problems. The main instruments are fiscal and monetary policies. Fiscal policy involves government expenditure and taxation; monetary policy involves interest rates and the money supply. In the post-war period, fiscal policy was associated with what is known as Keynesianism—using government expenditures as a way of countering the effects of a slowing economy and, conversely, raising taxes, or cutting spending, when the economy shows signs of overheating. Proposed by the British economist John Maynard Keynes, Keynesianism was particularly popular during the critical rebuilding phase after 1945, when citizens and policy-makers were anxious to avoid any repetition of the Great Depression. Keynesianism is also associated with the creation of the post-war welfare state: it assumes both a capacity and an appetite for major government intervention in the economic lives of citizens.

For the nearly three decades during which Keynesian thinking held sway, macroeconomic policy gave rise to considerable tension in the federal system. In essence, the federal government—especially the economists in the department of Finance—became convinced of the need for centrally controlled macroeconomic management along Keynesian lines. This required well-coordinated fiscal and monetary policy, but the relative independence of the Bank of Canada, and the fact that fiscal policy (taxation and spending) was shared with the provinces, made coordination difficult to achieve. During the war, Ottawa had effectively centralized fiscal control through tax rental agreements with the provinces, but after 1945 it had to gradually relinquish some of that control in the face of polit-ically powerful provincial demands. Still, the perceived need for the strong central control required by Keynesian management strengthened Ottawa's hand.

The relative importance of Keynesian ideas, their effectiveness, and the extent to which Canada actually put them into practice are all open to debate (Campbell, 1987). What can be said is that in the 1970s—an era of rising energy prices and stagflation (inflation combined with absence of economic growth)—the influence of Keynesianism began to wane and other economic philosophies gained ascendance, particularly those of Milton Friedman and what is variously known as neoconservatism or supply-side economics. These ideas really came into their own with the election of Margaret Thatcher in the UK in 1979 and Ronald Reagan in the US in 1980. The key component in neoconservative, supply-side economics is monetary policy. Thus a neoconservative government will respond to a rise in inflation by raising interest rates and/or tightening the money supply, and when economic stimulation is needed it will cut both government expenditures and taxes. The effectiveness of supply side economics has also been extensively debated. Nevertheless, these ideas took hold in many countries, including Canada, in the 1980s. Thus Canadian economic policy in the late 1980s and early 1990s relied heavily on high interest rates to tame infla-tion. Indeed, in the late 1980s, the Bank of Canada pursued what amounted to a 'zero inflation' target.

Under section 91 of the Constitution Act, 1867, jurisdiction over money and banking lies with the federal government, which means that Ottawa has effective control over monetary policy. The situation is different with fiscal policy, however, as we have seen. Both levels of government have the right to collect most types of taxes, although Ottawa's fiscal capacity is greater. This is not neces-sarily the case on the expenditure side. Some of the largest areas of government expenditure are health care, education, social welfare, and infrastructure, all of which are primarily if not entirely under provincial jurisdiction. Thus both levels of government have at least some capacity to make macroeconomic policy, although the federal government has the more powerful toolkit.

The issue of which government controls the levers of macroeconomic management is further complicated by the difficulty of developing a single national policy that deals effectively with the needs of all the regions in Canada. One can legitimately ask: is it really possible to have a single, effective macroeconomic policy? With different sectoral strengths, terms of trade, and levels of development across the regions, growth cycles and inflation pressures differ. It is virtually impossible that a single monetary policy, for example, with a single national set of inflation targets, a single exchange rate, and a single interest rate, will ever match the optimal requirements for any specific region. Suppose, for instance, that inflation builds up in a high-growth area such as southern Ontario or Alberta, while prices remain flat in low-growth regions: higher interest rates would curb inflation in the hot regions, but would further chill activity in the regions where growth is already low. Using fiscal policy gives the federal government somewhat more leeway for regional flexibility, especially on the spending side, but can still work against the macroeconomic objectives of one or more regions. For instance, if the federal government cuts its spending to curb inflationary growth, in the process it could dampen sustainable growth in a province or region attempting to catch up.

There is also considerable room for provincial macroeconomic policies to work at cross purposes with those of the federal government. This is precisely what happened in Ontario between 1985 and 1995, when the province's Liberal and NDP governments were increasing their spending in direct contradiction of the federal effort to bring incipient inflation under control. The federal minister of Finance and the governor of the Bank of Canada complained vehemently that Ontario was undermining the effectiveness of their policies. On the provincial side, it naturally helps to be a sizeable 'have' province. A small 'have-not' province would not have the capacity to launch a counter-cyclical strategy, and the national impact of such activity would be negligible in any event. This notwithstanding, Ottawa's reluctance to turn over additional tax room to the provinces— for financing health care, for example—can be explained at least in part by concern that some provinces might use the tax room for counter-cyclical objectives inconsistent with the objectives that Ottawa has deemed appropriate for the country as a whole.

In brief, federal and provincial governments have clear incentives to work cooperatively when it comes to stabilization and other macroeconomic policies. Ways of bringing the provinces into the deliberations of the Bank of Canada and the federal department of Finance, and improving coordination over fiscal policy in particular, have been discussed for years. The Continuing Committee of Officials on Fiscal and Economic Matters, which provides for the flow of information between the two orders of government, remains the only body that has attained any kind of quasi-formal standing; and its powers are decidedly limited.

Suggestions that the provinces could play a role in nominating or even appointing members to the Board of Governors of the Bank of Canada have not been followed up.[2] However, the federal government has put in place a more extensive pre-budget consultation process, and the Bank of Canada also consults more widely with the business and other communities, including provincial ministers of Finance, than it did in the past. Ottawa's moves in the direction of greater transparency and wider consultation may not have been intended specifically to increase provincial participation, but they have perhaps reduced the pressure to institute more formal federal–provincial mechanisms.

By late 2007 the macroeconomic policy area was comparatively calm, largely because economic growth had been strong and relatively balanced across the regions over the past decade. Unemployment was at a 30-year low and consumer confidence was high (Cross, 2007). The Conservative government had inherited a substantial surplus from its Liberal predecessor, some of which it used to reduce the fiscal gap with the provinces. There were no signs that the Harper government was inclined to adopt a Keynesian-style macro policy or to centralize fiscal policy; but neither was it much inclined to share its governance of monetary policy. Nor were any of the provinces inclined to run deficits to prime their own economies. A year later, however, the worldwide turmoil in financial markets and the threat of recession forced all governments—federal and provincial—to begin running deficits, regardless of the promises that the federal government, for example, had made in the lead-up to the 2008 October election. The federal government's inherited surplus had pretty well disappeared by late 2008.

As the inevitable downturn approaches, it is not hard to imagine a scenario that could entail a revival of federal–provincial conflict over macroeconomic policy. Inflationary pressures, largely fuelled by an overheating resource economy in western Canada and by international oil and food prices, put upward pressure on interest rates in 2007–8. There was concern as well that provincial governments such as Alberta's were spending too much or encouraging too much investment in the energy sector and not saving their energy revenue windfall. Meanwhile, buoyant resource prices had pushed up the Canadian dollar, creating problems for Canadian exporters.

The downturn in the US economy especially has major implications for Canada. The collapsing housing market, weakening consumer demand, and tightening credit are all having an impact in Canada, particularly in sectors that depend on exports to the US (lumber and autos, for instance). How federal macro policy responds to these challenges, or to any potential external shock—a major climate event, a worldwide flu epidemic, a collapse of Asian markets, trade disruptions resulting from terrorism—cannot be predicted: what we do know is that the effects will be felt differently across the country, making a coherent federal response difficult. Nonetheless, the provinces will likely leave most macroeconomic decisions to the federal government. Where provincial attention is more likely to focus is on regional growth and development—that is, microeconomic concerns.

NATIONAL VERSUS REGIONAL ECONOMIC DEVELOPMENT

Canada's economy has always been the product of both natural and human-made forces. As a political community Canadians have been engaged in economic development activities from the beginning. Even in the current era of free markets and laissez-faire industrial policy, no government in Canada—or anywhere else—can afford to leave economic prosperity entirely to chance or the vagaries of the market. Structural or microeconomic policy is all about shaping the economy in ways that reflect the specific market conditions and needs of individual industries and sectors. To this end governments use various instruments such as regulation, information, taxation, spending, and even Crown corporations (i.e., government ownership and management) to encourage certain kinds of economic activity at the micro level. The fact that the levers of micro policy are shared among the various governments, federal and provincial, means that there is considerable potential for competition both among provinces and between the provinces and the federal government. There has been a long history of both conflict and cooperation in this area.

As we noted in our discussion of the economic union, in the nineteenth century a national economy would not have succeeded without a strategic approach on the part of the new 'Dominion' government. Yet the very efficiency of this new economy—combined some claim, with a bias in favour of central Canada as the location for more advanced economic activity—over time created pressures not only for both redistributive justice, which eventually took the form of fiscal transfers such as equalization and Canada-wide social programs, but for allocative justice. Over time, governments came to recognize that they needed to pay attention to the allocation of economic activities across the country.

There are essentially two perspectives on the best way to design an economic allocation policy. One perspective, taken mainly by those in the federal government, the national media, major business and labour organizations and key provinces such as Ontario, favours ensuring that structural policy is optimal at the national level and then seeing what needs to be done for those regions that lag behind. The other perspective, taken by all the provinces and territories with the occasional exception of Ontario, as well as many regionally based industrial and labour interests, focuses from the outset on the optimal structural policy for a particular provincial or regional economy and assumes that the national economy will be strong so long as all the regional economies are strong. Both can lead to viable economic strategies. However, the region-centred strategy depends more on federal cooperation and provincial economic levers than the national one does.

Within these two approaches to economic allocation policy, the ideological emphasis on markets versus government intervention has varied over time. Just as macroeconomic policy between 1940 and 1975 was dominated by interventionist thinking along Keynesian lines, so too was microeconomic policy. It was considered the state's role to take strategic control over the structure of the economy, favouring one sector over the other and promoting technological sovereignty. Canada's attempts to pursue such a strategy, however, have been affected both by federalism and by our North American setting. North America has been much less willing than Europe and Japan (not to mention countries with centrally planned economies, such as the Soviet Union) to accept centrally directed bureaucratic decision-making about industrial structure. Indeed, the Americans in particular have promoted a strong alternative in the form of international liberalism combined with considerable domestic laissez-faire (Dyson, 1980; Hall and Soskice, 2001). This strategy has had adherents in Canada as well. In the brief sketch that follows we outline the interaction of national and regional perspectives in an era when interventionist industrial strategies were assumed to be most effective, that is, up to the mid-1980s. In the following section we deal with the effects of the free trade era on these competing strategies.

Examples of federal programs designed primarily to promote a national economy are not hard to find. They essentially encompass all of federal trade policy in the century between the 1870s and 1970s, military procurement programs during and after the two world wars, public development and ownership of railways and airlines, railway freight rate structures that promoted internal trade in finished goods from central Canada to the west and east, and oil and gas pipeline construction and regulation. Examples of provincial programs designed to promote the regional economy are also legion. They include the development of hydroelectric and other sources for electricity supply, first by Ontario and later by all provinces, including Quebec (where the public takeover of private hydro firms in the 1960s was one of the central events of the Quiet Revolution). All provincial and territorial governments have used their jurisdiction over natural resources, primarily energy, forests, and minerals, to promote specific industries, and many have used Crown corporations to develop the telephone and telecommunications industries.

Somewhat rarer are examples of federal policies that had the effect of promoting the development of only one region or the other, such as the partnership between the federal Atomic Energy Corporation and Ontario Hydro for nuclear power; the 1965 Autopact agreement with the US that did so much for the Ontario automobile sector; and various projects to promote the development of petroleum resources off the Atlantic coast. More common are federal subsidy or other programs that are available for economic opportunities in all provinces, but that in practice serve to reinforce existing regional strengths such as the pharmaceutical and aerospace sectors in Quebec, the informatics and computer industry in Ontario, or—in the case of employment insurance—the fisheries sector on the east coast.

The potential for conflict between the various national and regional strategies has been significant. As we outlined in Chapter 1, a certain amount of competition is perceived to be one of the advantages of federalism. And of course economic theory points out the value of competition within markets for goods, services, labour—even ideas. Competing provinces can learn from one another about what works best in terms of economic policy. Competition for investment and markets among private sector actors in regional economies makes the latter more productive. And competition between governments (for votes, one presumes) to attract investment can result in better economic policies all around. Such competition is often benign. But if public spending or tax breaks are designed merely to attract industry away from another jurisdiction without actually increasing net economic activity, this beggar-thy-neighbour or negative-sum approach can be destructive (Brown, 2002b).

More fundamentally, sharply competing economic strategies can generate significant political conflict. The energy conflicts of the 1970s and 1980s are a case in point. As David Milne wrote in his 1986 book *Tug of War*, not only did Canada face 'incredible gyrations in supply and pricing in the world oil and gas market', but these dynamics 'ricocheted back onto the federal structure itself', in a volatile mix of east-versus-west regional politics, centralist versus provincialist constitutional visions, and free-market versus interventionist economic policy (Milne, 1986: ch. 3). In a period of rising international petroleum prices, the oil-producing provinces, especially Alberta, looked to foreign capital to diversify and develop their economies, while the Trudeau government in Ottawa looked to its National Energy Program to restore federal control over a strategic sector, promoting a made-in-Canada oil price and increased Canadian ownership. Seldom have the two perspectives on allocation of economic activity clashed so dramatically.

Finally, a more generic form of structural policy area characterized by strong federal–provincial interaction is regional economic development policy: in effect, a set of interventions intended to improve economic conditions in specific areas perceived to be lagging behind other regions. The issue of regional dispar-ities came to the fore in the late 1950s and became a major issue in the 1960s and 1970s. Prime Minister Trudeau recognized the issue as a threat to national unity when he was elected in 1968, and his government established the Department of Regional Economic Expansion (DREE) a year later. More than a decade later, in 1982, the Trudeau government and the provinces agreed to enshrine in the constitution a commitment to the promotion of equal opportunities and the furthering of economic development to reduce disparities in opportunities for all Canadians.[3]

This policy field has been controversial and problematic, however. There is little consensus among policy analysts about what really works or what mix of government policies and programs will genuinely reduce regional disparities and foster economic development. Another concern is the lack of consistency in federal and provincial efforts that results when politicians and bureaucrats become too impatient and insist on changing the programs and agencies deliv-ering regional development before they have a chance to work. As well, regional development has perhaps been seeking to accomplish too much. As the leading student of the field, Donald Savoie, put it, 'In trying to be all things to all regions, Canadian regional development has . . . lost its way' (Savoie, 1995: 386). The more cynical might say that regional development policy is whatever a government deems it to be—which means that it can serve a variety of purposes, some of them only tenuously linked to economic development.

Both levels of government have been active in this field since at least the early 1960s, with some efforts, such as the Agricultural and Rural Development Act (ARDA) in western Canada, going back to the 1930s (Careless, 1977). At times federal and provincial governments have worked closely with each other; at other times the federal government in particular has felt the need to work on its own, keeping provincial governments at a distance. Indeed, there appears to be a distinct pattern: the two levels of government, most frequently at the level of officials, develop good working relations (this was certainly true in the early 1960s); then elements within the federal government, feeling frustrated or wishing to impart greater clarity to the field, decide either to consolidate or to take on direct responsibility for certain activities previously handled by provincial governments. Thus in 1969 Ottawa brought together a number of its development programs into a new single agency, the DREE. Using an approach focused on selected 'growth pole' areas in Atlantic Canada, DREE officials frequently bypassed provincial agencies in favour of dealing directly with municipalities, business associations, and companies.

By the early 1970s, however, unhappiness among provincial governments and many federal politicians led them to take quite a different tack. DREE was decentralized and mandated to work closely with the provinces in negotiating General Development Agreements (GDAs), under which Ottawa would provide the bulk of the funding for programs delivered primarily by provincial agencies. Predictably, by the early 1980s the federal government in particular was once again frustrated. The lack of visibility and political credit for Ottawa's spending on provincially delivered development programs was one reason cited; another was the lack of opportunity for federal politicians (especially ministers) to influence program direction and content, which was handled by a relatively cohesive community of regionally based DREE and provincial officials (Savoie, 1981). Thus DREE was abolished in 1982 and federal line departments took over the responsibilities, and funding, of various former DREE programs.

Five years later the federal government felt the need to once again have a distinct presence in the regional development area. Hence a new set of agencies was created—including the Atlantic Canada Opportunities Agency (ACOA) and Western Economic Diversification, through which Ottawa, while making funding available for 'cooperation' agreements with the provinces, retained responsibility for delivering funding programs directly to businesses. In recent years, regional development programs have received less attention, and much less funding support than other programs. Nonetheless, agencies such as ACOA remain an important part of the nexus between federal and provincial governments in the area of economic policy, and more generally in the area of providing the federal government with a profile and a capacity for gathering information about regional issues and sensitivities.

GLOBALIZATION, FREE TRADE, AND COMPETITIVENESS

In Canada, the globalization of business activities accelerated after the recession of 1980–1. Thereafter we see greatly increased international trade and foreign direct investment, the development of a worldwide chain of goods and services providers, and the rise of global capital markets—all facilitated by advances in technology such as personal computers, the Internet, and wireless communications. Economic globalization both fuelled and was fuelled by international liberalization, initially through the auspices of the General Agreement on Tariffs and Trade (GATT), established in 1947, then in Canada's case with the Canada–US Free Trade Agreement (FTA) of 1989, the North American Free Trade Agreement (NAFTA) of 1994, and the World Trade Organization Agreements of 1995. The move towards bilateral free trade with the US was a particularly bold and controversial step that changed fundamentally the context for economic policy-making in Canada.

Although the Mulroney Conservatives were ideologically predisposed to free trade as part of the neoconservative package that also included deregulation, deficit reduction, and privatization, pursuit of a comprehensive agreement with the US had not been part of their election platform when they were elected in September 1984.[4] By 1985, however, an impressive intellectual and policy consensus had emerged in favour of a comprehensive agreement, led by the influential Macdonald Royal Commission appointed by the previous Trudeau government and supported by the leadership of the Canadian business community as well as by several provincial governments. They advocated free trade for two major reasons: to achieve more secure access to American markets, which after the recession of 1980–1 was moving in an increasingly protectionist direction, and as a strategy to increase the global competitiveness of Canadian industry.

The decision to enter into negotiations marked the end of the road for the old National Policy, with its emphasis on a protected Canadian market and the east–west economic union. In this respect, Quebec's shift in the early 1980s from promoting Canadian protection to embracing freer trade was pivotal. Quebec, at the time under the somewhat inscrutable leadership of Liberal premier Robert Bourassa, was likely hoping to develop stronger international trade linkages and at the same time become less dependent on domestic trade. Quebec was joined by Alberta, Saskatchewan, British Columbia, New Brunswick, and Newfoundland in strong support for liberalization. Ontario and PEI were mainly opposed, while Manitoba and Nova Scotia remained ambivalent (Brown, 1991). Nonetheless, all the provinces, including those on balance opposed to the FTA, had come to the conclusion that the interventionist economic strategies of the Trudeau government (NEP, the Foreign Investment Review Agency, etc.) were not working (Brown, 1993).

In fact, the federal government actively sought the support of the provinces for the bilateral negotiations. Canada's trade negotiators wanted a comprehensive agreement (a 'big deal') and recognized that many of the trade measures on the table were under provincial jurisdiction. Politically, Mulroney was committed to collaborative federalism and believed the controversial policy required broad regional support. This virtually ensured that, even if the provinces would not have a place at the actual bargaining table with US and Canadian negotiators, at least they would be consulted extensively. Mulroney met with the premiers 14 times during the 18-month negotiation period, and provincial ministers and senior officials met with the federal negotiating team once a month or more. The provinces did not have the opportunity to 'ratify' the agreement as such, but the fact that eight of them ultimately supported the FTA gave the federal government considerable political cover.

In constitutional terms, the FTA (and later the NAFTA and the WTO Agreements) had the potential to upset the federal–provincial balance and spark a major court test of the distribution of powers. Some argued that the federal parliament should be able to implement any trade agreement in its entirety, using a broad interpretation of the 'trade and commerce' power in the Constitution Act, 1867, to impose it on the provinces. Others argued that the courts would rule, as they had in 1937 in the Labour Conventions case,[5] that the watertight compartments argument still held and that the federal parliament could not legally enforce the terms of a trade agreement in matters under provincial jurisdiction (Richards, 1991; Whyte, 1990). In the end the actual FTA did not impinge on provincial jurisdiction to the extent that some had feared, because so many of the provisions were prospective (that is, covering only new policy in the future). Still, the full extent of the effect of the FTA and subsequently the NAFTA and WTO agreements remains a subject of academic controversy (Brown, 2002b; Robinson, 2003). Federal legislation implementing the FTA and NAFTA passed without a constitutional challenge, perhaps because it required so few actual changes in provincial measures. It is also likely that provinces such as Ontario preferred not to challenge federal authority in the courts and risk losing a major jurisdictional battle.

Analysts will continue to disagree on the legal consequences of trade liberalization, and whether its 'neutering' effect is greatest for the federal or the provincial order of government. After all, a free trade agreement like the FTA or the NAFTA is in effect a form of economic constitution that prohibits the signatory governments from intervening in their economies in a wide swath of policy areas in order to achieve the negative integration mentioned earlier in this chapter. Yet political debate has not dwelt extensively on this matter, but rather on the general effects of trade liberalization as part of the neoconservative approach to fiscal and social policy.

In the meantime, free trade became Canada's industrial strategy. Together, the FTA and NAFTA have made it very difficult to impose discriminatory or differential pricing on resources, including oil and gas. They have partly liberalized government procurement markets, some agriculture markets, and some services. In addition, they prohibit direct export subsidies and allow our trading partners to penalize us if we provide subsidies specific to a single industry. However, the

WTO agreements do permit generally available government assistance to industry, such as for research and development and for firms in underdeveloped regions.

Free trade has also affected Canada's internal trade. Concerns about the fragmentation of the Canadian economic union mounted during the 1970s and early 1980s—concerns that became more urgent with the intensification of integration and liberalization. Since so many aspects of the Canadian economy were being integrated into the continental and global markets, especially its goods-producing sectors, the institutional integration of the FTA and NAFTA set the rules for our national market as well. Neither the federal nor the provincial governments could prevent their new trading partners from identifying policies that were already considered barriers to trade within Canada as barriers to international trade as well. Thus we came to the ironic fact that much of the heavy lifting required to reform the economic union was achieved not through domestic constitutional amendment or intergovernmental agreement, but through international trade treaties (see Table 11.1).

The process offered a fascinating example of a two-level game in the domestic politics of trade liberalization (cf. Putnam, 1988). Working through international agreements made it easier for the Canadian provinces to agree on the removal of barriers because regional rivalries could be subsumed in a larger pool of potential gains and concessions. The freer the trade became across international borders, the freer it would become within Canada. After all, in political terms it seemed unsustainable that trade could be freer for Ontario with Michigan than with Manitoba. Even with its barriers, the Canadian economic union was much wider and deeper than the North American union, particularly with respect to labour and services. But this had not stopped most Canadian businesses from promoting further opening of markets within Canada as a way of improving their international competitiveness.

Thus the Canadian governments negotiated their own domestic free trade agreement, called the Agreement on Internal Trade (AIT), in 1995. The scope and time frame of the AIT were heavily influenced by the international agreements (Doern and MacDonald, 1999). Its 18 chapters are remarkably similar to the 20-odd chapters of the FTA and NAFTA, and many of the general principles and even the jargon and logic of the detailed provisions—and their loopholes—were borrowed from the GATT, the FTA, NAFTA, and the draft WTO agreements. The result was a unique hybrid between an international trade agreement and a domestic intergovernmental agreement.

The AIT does have major limitations as a tool for the resolution of intergovernmental trade disputes, however. It is not constitutionally entrenched, and there are no legal remedies if it is breached. It has a weak administrative structure, and the federal and provincial ministers who form its governing body operate by consensus only. For good or ill, the AIT relies heavily on negative integration—reducing barriers by imposing new rules applicable to all governments—rather than centralized regulatory power to extend the scope of national integration (Brown, 2002b). And to some extent, just as in international trade policy, trade

Table 11.1   International Agreements and Reform of the
Canadian Economic Union, 1989–95:
Selected Outcomes/Measures Affecting Internal
Trade in Canada

Instrument	Selected Measures
FTA (1989)	Freer trade in wine and spirits
	Non-discrimination in trade by monopolies
	No performance requirements on investors
	National treatment for service regulation
NAFTA (1994)	Non-discriminatory government procurement
	Freer trade in financial services
	More liberalization of investment
	Side deals on labour standards, environment
WTO Agreements (1995)	'Tariffication' (use of tariffs) in place of agricultural quotas
	Agreement on subsidies
Agreement on Internal Trade (1995)	Non-discriminatory government procurement
	Free trade in alcoholic beverages including beer
	Non-discriminatory monopoly practices
	Code of Conduct on Incentives used by federal and provincial governments
	Access to common carriers (e.g., telecoms)
	Voluntary mutual recognition of occupational standards

liberalization works best when there is continuous negotiation to remove new barriers to trade and to expand the scope and depth of integration. The parties to the AIT have made some progress towards improving the overall rules for internal trade, although many observers have found the pace of change too slow (Knox, 1998, 2001; MacDonald, 2002). More progress has been made at the regional level; examples of regional commitments include economic integration initiatives in the Atlantic provinces since the early 1990s, the Ontario–Quebec labour mobility agreement of 2006, and the extensive Trade, Investment and Labour Mobility Agreement (TILMA) reached in 2006 between Alberta and British Columbia.[6]

Finally, the Harper federal government, first elected in January 2006, has made strengthening the Canadian economic union a policy priority. The Speech from the Throne of October 2007 referred to 'the federal government's rightful leadership' in this context, and Ottawa has made it clear to the provinces that it intends to exercise that leadership as a sort of quid pro quo for taking a more decentralized approach to fiscal relations (dealing with the vertical fiscal imbalance) and to social programs (restricting the use of federal spending power) (Kent, 2008).

The specific priorities for reform of the economic union fall into three categories. First is a commitment to work with the provinces on a variety of improvements and extensions to the AIT, including an endorsement and encouragement of the bilateral approach building on the Alberta–BC TILMA. Second is a commitment to extend tax collection and general tax harmonization agreements; an agreement reached with Ontario on corporate income tax in 2006 was a promising first step in this direction. Third is the initiative led by Finance Minister Jim Flaherty to achieve greater integration of regulation of the Canadian securities market; in the spring of 2008 new federal legislation was proposed to create a single new federal regulator.[7] All these initiatives are still works in progress, and there is no indication that the Conservatives will get any farther than their predecessors did in the previous decade. Ultimately, much may depend on whether the federal government is able to link agreement on these matters to the success of other initiatives more important to the provinces.

To summarize, the dynamics of economic development in the Canadian federal system are significantly different today from what they were 20 years ago. International trade is freer, the Canadian economy is much more dependent on trade, and our governments have taken seriously their obligations under various trade agreements to limit their intervention in the marketplace. The free trade context has forced all governments in Canada to focus on the concept of overall economic competitiveness. Canadian manufacturers of goods—whether fridges, shoes, aircraft, or computer software—must compete directly with firms from around the world in both domestic and international markets. The competition in other sectors is more indirect. Private service sectors, for example, such as banking, retail and consulting, and public services, have less direct competition at home, but still need access to capital and technology, and ultimately cannot survive without the kind of productivity gains made in manufacturing (Porter, 1990).

This is not to say that governments are no longer spending to promote economic development. However, the programs are less trade-distorting than they were in the past and more concentrated on building on general advantages by improving training, education, and infrastructure, and establishing a more competitive tax and regulatory framework. Policy is also increasingly focused at the local level and on softer factors such as the environment, social and cultural amenities, community tolerance and cohesion, and overall quality of life. Another dominant idea in economic development circles is the importance of 'networks' bringing together private firms big and small with universities and other research establishments and governments to promote denser economic activity. Such networks work best in urban clusters, but with strong strategic support they can also contribute to rural development (Haddow, 2008; Krugman, 1999). The intergovernmental challenge is to achieve broad-based horizontal coordination across federal, provincial, and local government agencies, drawing on a wide array of social and economic policies and programs, to overcome obstacles in a specific sub-region or urban area (e.g., northeast New Brunswick or Greater Toronto).

The increasing focus on urban issues reflects a realization that cities are major drivers in the national and global economies. In the game of competitive cities, federalism still matters in Canada and in other federations because provincial governments are the most important shapers of urban destiny (Sancton, 2008; compare Courchene, 2005). Provincial spending on economic development declined markedly in the mid-1990s, not because of free trade restrictions but because of fiscal cutbacks. That spending rebounded over the past decade as federal and provincial budgetary situations improved. However, the four richer and larger provinces (Alberta, British Columbia, Ontario, and Quebec) now have a much greater capacity to fund urban and rural development than do the six smaller and generally poorer provinces and the three northern territories. Federal programs alleviate some but clearly not all of this growing disparity (Brown, 2006; Haddow, 2008).

CONCLUSION

This chapter has emphasized the fundamental importance of economic issues to the federal system. The creation of a single new economy was one of the original goals of Confederation. The national economy integrates the regional economies but the latter continue to exist, just as Canada's national economy continues to exist despite its increasing integration with the US and global economies. The Canadian economic union is a major achievement, but its relatively weak constitutional status means that it requires continuous attention by the federal and provincial governments. In political terms, the location of economic activity and the level of its development are never neutral issues. The federal and provincial orders of government each have considerable powers to shape the national and regional economies with a variety of macroeconomic and microeconomic policy tools. Their often competing goals for economic development can generate sharp conflict.

Certainly the introduction of free trade between Canada and the US presented a major challenge for intergovernmental relations, threatening to upset the constitutional balance in the system and forcing governments to tame many of their development policies. Yet the federal system has proven remarkably adaptable to these new economic conditions, and has done so in a relatively cooperative fashion without provoking a constitutional crisis. If, as a result of the emerging international economic recession in 2008–9, governments turn more frequently to intervention in the economy than they have in the past 20 years, there will likely be increased intergovernmental friction. Still, a return to the deep-seated conflict over the economy of the 1970s seems improbable. Another challenge—one that is becoming increasingly urgent and has profound implications for economic policy as well as intergovernmental relations—is the subject of the next chapter, on the environmental union. The environmental challenge will almost certainly transform how we approach economic development in the future. Like free trade, it has the potential to upset the federal–provincial balance, mainly because the provinces, left to their own devices, have not been able to agree on an effective regulatory regime. In this case, however—unlike that of free trade—federal leadership has been weak, ambiguous, and inconsistent, and intergovernmental relations have not yet been very effective.

Chapter 12

The Environmental Union

The concept of the environmental union, like its social and economic counterparts, suggests a shared sense of purpose and a Canada-wide approach.[1] At the same time environmental issues pose some of the most difficult, and most interesting, challenges the Canadian federation has faced, raising questions about constitutional jurisdiction and the effectiveness of our institutions. Climate change—specifically global warming and the international effort to reduce 'greenhouse' emissions—is a major political issue, with serious implications for both regional and national interests.

The Canadian federation occupies one of the largest land masses on earth. Bordering on three oceans, it encompasses enormous ecological diversity and abundant natural resources. At home and abroad, the image of Canadians as stewards of a vast, untouched northern wilderness has been central to the national identity. The economic value of forests and minerals is obvious, but the basic natural elements—earth, water, air—are priceless, for they underlie all value in any society. Until relatively recently, the quality of these elements was generally taken for granted, but today their economic value is increasingly recognized. Resource allocation and development decisions must take into account the costs of potential environmental degradation, and activities that damage the environment by depleting non-renewable resources, reducing biodiversity, or producing dangerous substances such as greenhouse gases must be restrained. Meanwhile, economic tools and mechanisms (e.g., carbon taxes, emission trading systems) are becoming increasingly important as policy instruments for managing the environmental union.

The Canadians most affected by major shifts in environmental quality—including climate change, resource depletion, and agricultural or industrial incursion on traditional ways of life—are those living closest to the land: residents of farming, coastal, resource, and remote northern communities. Those who live in more urban settings—64 per cent of Canadians—are even more likely to be exposed to some industrial pollutants. But urban dwellers in general tend to be more removed than their rural counterparts from direct trade-offs between development and environmental protection. Among politicians as well as the public, overall awareness of environmental issues has grown tremendously since the 1970s. Perceptions of urgency vary, of course, depending on current events. A major toxic spill, a flood, a health emergency, or a local anti-development campaign will spark a rise in concern, while a sudden economic downturn or a rapid increase in energy prices will easily push environmental issues into the background (Bakvis and Nevitte, 1992). But despite short-term fluctuations, public concern has continued to rise over time (Harrison, 1996).

A significant challenge for policy-makers in this relatively new area is the fact that air, water, and much of the land are public goods from which everyone benefits, and for which no one pays. A policy designed to control the effluents from pulp and paper mills, for example, benefits all Canadians, but the costs must be borne by the pulp and paper industry. Some of these costs can be passed on to the consumers of paper products, but in a highly competitive global market, paper producers see strict pollution control as a disadvantage—especially if their competitors in other provinces or countries are not subject to similar controls. In this way a relatively local problem can become intergovernmental and even international. In the past, Canadian governments have chosen to subsidize the adoption of new, less-polluting technological processes for pulp and paper production. But will that always be the best (or most politically feasible) use of scarce public funds? In any case, what one so often sees in environmental politics is a trumping of the interests of those for whom policy costs are concentrated (polluting industries or developers) over those for whom policy benefits are diffuse (the general public) (Harrison, 1996; cf. Olson, 1971).

In virtually all countries, environmental policy has been a continuing struggle. It pits vested economic and industry interests against local citizens (e.g., those opposed to the development of a new quarry in the neighbourhood) and nationally and internationally organized advocacy groups demanding stronger environmental regulation (e.g., Greenpeace or the World Wildlife Fund). It creates struggles within governments as well as between them as policy-makers weigh real environmental risks against the costs of industrial or social adjustment. Governments must also judge the breadth and depth of public opinion on environmental issues. How much are individuals willing to sacrifice when faced with sharp rises in gas prices, high costs for recycling, or restrictions on their use of land? The challenges multiply for transboundary problems such as greenhouse gases, which involve both domestic and foreign policy interests. The latter are not always the same, and negotiating simultaneously with domestic interests and international players presents a major challenge for the national government, even in a unitary state (see Putnam, 1988). All these complications are magnified in a federation such as Canada.

FEDERALISM AND THE ENVIRONMENT IN CANADA

The fact that Canada is constitutionally and politically a federal state has important implications for the way we deal with environmental issues. Federalism is about both sharing power and preserving autonomy—sometimes local and sometimes national. Many federal theorists see federalism as promoting liberal and democratic values by setting up competitive governments capable of satisfying diverse needs and preferences. In this context environmental concerns can be simultaneously local, regional, national, and international in scope. People in different communities may value the environment differently, or be willing to make different kinds of economic and social trade-offs to preserve environmental quality. In federations, local and provincial or state governments normally have the power to make decisions on more localized environmental matters such as land use, water treatment, waste disposal, and forest management, while the national or federal government makes decisions about environmental issues that are national in scope or that cross provincial boundaries, such as air or water pollutants, or the manufacture, sale, and transportation of toxic substances. In all federations, policies and programs developed by the national (central) government are frequently implemented and delivered by the provincial and local governments.

Interactions between governments on environmental matters take three main forms: cooperative, competitive, and concurrent. Cooperation is obviously required for the many environmental issues that cross jurisdictional boundaries. Routine cooperation is for the most part very effective, but has some important limitations.[2] Competition may seem an odd term in this context; it refers to situations in which governments—federal, provincial and territorial, local, Aboriginal—operate on their own, following their own inclinations, with or without the approval of other governments. This happens in many environmental policy areas. A particular province may be aggressive or passive, pass lax or tough regulations; the federal government may take strong action on clearly federal matters and impose national policies on provinces, or may choose to do nothing at all. Analysts distinguish between direct interjurisdictional competition (two jurisdictions, each seeking to attract more industry, provide more protection for citizens, or preserve more environment than the other) and policy emulation across jurisdictions (looking at what others have done and trying to do the same, if not better). If the competition is to offer the most industry-friendly, minimal environmental regime, those jurisdictions are said to be in a 'race to the bottom'; if it is to offer the most stringent environmental protection, they are said to be in a 'race to the top' (Harrison, 2006a; Olewiler, 2006). Finally, 'concurrency' refers to the constitutional principle of an explicitly shared power. In most federations the authority to legislate on environmental issues is considered to be concurrent, although the federal legislation will usually prevail in the event of conflict. This enables federal governments to pass general, framework law on matters such as national standards for emissions or regulatory processes, while leaving considerable scope for provincial or local governments to fill in the details according to their particular regional interests and values.

Canada's unique blend of cooperation, competition, and concurrency is largely a reflection of its size and geographic diversity. Because the federation encompasses several different ecological zones, regional climates, and major watersheds, some environmental problems are confined to one region alone, or have differing effects across regions. And since economic activities and levels of development differ across the country, the issues of concern vary accordingly: environmental problems associated with urban sprawl do not affect all provinces to the same degree, and environmental issues related to oil and gas production are of particular concern in Alberta and the other petroleum-producing provinces. All the provinces and territories are still trying to encourage industrial development, so they will not want environmental policy to impose undue costs on potential investors. On the other hand, environmentally friendly development and a high level of environmental quality are becoming increasingly important for attracting investment and human capital.

Other environmental issues are also regionally concentrated. Depletion of fish stocks, for instance, has severely affected some coastal communities, especially in the Atlantic region. Acid rain was really an issue—though a very serious one—only in eastern Canada, whereas soil salination is a concern confined to the Prairies. Finally, even though the effects of global warming are not confined to the far north, they are perhaps more pronounced there than anywhere else. A second factor that has significant implications for environmental policy is the constitutional division of powers (Winfield and Macdonald, 2008; Valiante, 2002). Environmental issues as they came to be defined in the late twentieth century were not a consideration in the mid-nineteenth century, and so the Constitution Act, 1867, makes no mention of them. Gradually, however, a jurisdictional approach to the environment has emerged through legislation and judicial review. As is common in all federations, aspects of the environment are the concern of all levels of governments. Provincial governments have responsibility for local matters and most issues with respect to the land, its use, and development, as well as the ownership and management of most natural resources (fisheries being a major exception). Therefore the provinces have assumed jurisdiction for most local environmental issues or matters that can be contained within their boundaries. Much of this provincial power is then delegated to the local governments that take responsibility for the water supply, the regulation of land use, and waste disposal. Meanwhile, the federal government has assumed jurisdiction over environmental issues that are more than local in scope, that cross provincial or international boundaries, that are especially costly or technically difficult to handle, or that have major implications for the national economy or national security.

The federal government's constitutional powers are not as strong in Canada as they are in other federations because the distribution of powers is mainly exclusive rather than concurrent, as is common elsewhere. The decision to spell out the provincial powers was deliberate, intended specifically to confine federal power. Nonetheless, the courts have been gradually expanding federal power and it is possible that one day the federal parliament will be able to legislate in a broader range of areas. Today the bulk of Ottawa's legal authority consists in its jurisdiction over trade and commerce, coastal fisheries, and criminal law, along with the 'peace, order, and good government' clause. In fact, environmental protection was at the centre of the *Crown Zellerbach* case, in which the Supreme Court of Canada ruled that Ottawa could use its POGG power to act in a matter that the provinces concerned were unable to tackle, even though it fell under provincial jurisdiction.[3] In 1997, the Supreme Court ruled (in the *R. v. Hydro-Québec* case) that federal legislation, specifically the Canadian Environmental Protection Act (CEPA) could be upheld using the criminal law power of the federal parliament.[4]

Legal jurisdiction is especially important in the environmental field because so many of the proposed solutions to environmental problems involve regulation. Governments seek to regulate the way private individuals and companies use the environment because on their own these private actors would not bear the costs of such a public good. But no government holds all the legal resources, and it is often unclear, especially for new and emerging issues, which one has the final authority. In many federations this problem is solved by constitutional concurrency. The federal legislatures of countries such as Germany, the United States, Mexico, Brazil, and Australia pass general regulatory laws, specifying standards, but leave the implementation and enforcement to the provincial and local governments. Although Canada's constitution does not provide for such formal concurrency, *de facto* concurrency is quite common in environmental matters. Finally, governments may seek to fine-tune the constitutional division of labour, as was done recently in Switzerland (Watts, 2008: ch. 5). In most federations, however, problems of ambiguity and overlap are still most commonly addressed by way of intergovernmental negotiation.

COOPERATION AND COMPETITION

Intergovernmental cooperation is no more the rule in the environmental union than it is in any other aspect of the Canadian federation. Governments often act unilaterally when the matter in question is sufficiently clear-cut or localized—a clean-up of a specific site, for example, or an environmental impact assessment of a minor project. In other cases, however, they act unilaterally because other governments will not cooperate with them, or because they need to take action that fully meets the needs of their electorate, and is not compromised by the interests of other governments. Competitive policy-making can amount to an incredibly rich experiment in what works and what does not, especially in a federation with multiple jurisdictions making decisions that affect millions of people. In the US, where 50 individual states have been making their own environmental policy choices, the overall effect has been a moderate 'race to the top' led by California, which has tended to set the standard for vehicle emissions (Rabe, 2004: ch. 1). This kind of interjurisdictional competition occurs on the international scale as well—between the US and Canada, for instance, or among the member countries of the European Union.

Canada too has seen interjurisdictional competition on the environmental front in recent years. In 2007 Quebec introduced a narrowly-based tax on carbon fuels; in June 2008 Quebec signed a pact with Ontario to establish an inter-provincial cap-and-trade system by January 2010;[5] and a month later British Columbia became the first jurisdiction in North America to implement a broad-based carbon tax—despite opposition from Ottawa. A recent study of environ-mental policies and indicators in six provinces found that intergovernmental competition on the environment has not amounted to the 'race to the bottom' that some might have feared. Governments have not been competing to reduce pollution controls, for instance, in order to attract industry. The general trend has been more positive: in the late 1980s, for example, some provinces set out on their own to raise the standards for dioxin emissions in the pulp and paper industry. These standards were superseded in 1992 by new, less stringent, national standards for dioxin emissions (Olewiler, 2006: 138–40). However, the recent steps taken by Quebec, Ontario, and BC on carbon emissions suggest that a new 'race to the top' may be getting underway.

Responding to environmental problems of national, international, or even global scope would logically seem to be the business of the federal government alone. Unilateral federal action is called for when an environmental problem requires a single, unambiguous, and consistent regulatory regime of a kind that would be very difficult for the provinces to agree on. The federal parliament already has partial jurisdiction over large areas of the environmental policy field, including fish habitat and trans-boundary air pollutants. And the Supreme Court's rulings in the *Crown Zellerbach* and *Hydro-Québec* cases suggest that the POGG and criminal law powers in the Constitution Act, 1867, could justify new federal regulatory powers in certain cases. Environmental advocacy groups have been calling for strong unilateral action ever since the 1960s (Boardman, 1992). But even key milestones of federal environmental legislation—the Canada Water Act, 1970; amendments to the Fisheries Act, 1970; the Clean Air Act, 1971; the Canadian Environmental Protection Act, 1992; and the Canadian Environmental Assessment Act, 1992—were usually the product of extensive intergovernmental consultations.

The alternative to competition or unilateral action is cooperation of some kind. Two or more neighbouring governments will cooperate to deal with a specific regional issue, or to take a particularly regional approach to a national or international issue. In the long lead-up to the Canada–US Air Quality Agreement of 1991, for example, governments on both sides of the border cooperated extensively, especially in the 'downstream' region represented by the Conference of New England Governors and Eastern Canadian Premiers. Similarly, Quebec, British Columbia, Manitoba, Ontario, and Quebec are currently collaborating with seven US states on a project called the Western Climate Initiative, aimed at setting regional goals for reducing greenhouse gas emissions (GGEs) and establishing a regional cap-and-trade system.[6] The federal government and one or more provinces will occasionally come together in a bilateral or regional forum to hold a joint environmental assessment (e.g., the Great Whale hydro project; the Hibernia oilfield project). For larger, more complex efforts, however, the most important forums are still the multilateral Federal–Provincial–Territorial conferences of ministers and the subsidiary meetings of senior officials and experts.

Kathryn Harrison, a leading scholar in the field, has suggested that one reason the federal government is willing 'to relinquish the lead role to the provinces' and embrace intergovernmental cooperation is in order 'to avoid electoral blame'— in effect, to pass the buck (Harrison, 1996: 20). In any case, Ottawa is averse to trampling on provincial jurisdiction lest it provoke regional discontent, and to pick a fight with Quebec could be damaging to national unity. Unilateral action would also require strong public support, and Canadians' record on that score has not been consistent. Finally, leadership is costly: for Ottawa to develop and enforce a new set of environmental standards would entail major bureaucratic and technical investment, potentially duplicating provincial efforts. With a few exceptions, such investments have been considered more than Ottawa could afford, especially in the fiscal crisis years of the 1990s.

For all these reasons the more common approach has been for the federal government to work with the provinces and territories on environmental problems. If a regulatory standard or process is required, it is not 'federal' but 'national'—jointly created either by all the governments or by a few of them through bilateral or regional arrangements. This collaborative approach has produced a long series of agreements, and the intergovernmental machinery devoted to it is well established. The problem—by no means confined to environmental policy—is that Canadian intergovernmental institutions do not deal well with issues requiring uniform, consistent regulatory results. The main intergovernmental body, the Canadian Council of Ministers of the Environment (CCME), brings together hundreds of officials in committees and task forces, and conducts extensive consultations with the environmental NGO community. When the product of all those efforts goes to the ministers for final approval, however, the decision is made on the basis of consensus bargaining alone. Typically no votes are taken; governments can refuse to take part; and agreements cannot be enforced in law. Thus the CCME and similar processes tend to produce lowest-common-denominator outcomes (Fafard, 2000).

Intergovernmental processes can take years to complete, and even then the results are often weak and unsubstantial. The Canadian Environmental Protection Act—broad federal legislation first introduced in 1988—underwent four years of negotiations before Ottawa felt it had sufficient consensus to pass through parliament. The big four provinces—British Columbia, Alberta, Ontario, and Quebec—opposed the original bill vigorously and relented only after the legislation was changed to allow for the recognition of 'equivalent' provincial measures to stand for potential new federal regulations in some cases. Negotiations over the Canada-Wide Agreement on Environmental Harmonization took five years, from 1993 to 1998; and it took three years, from 1997 to 2000, to produce an anodyne and ultimately ineffective agreement on a 'national action plan' to deal with greenhouse gas emissions.

One way of dealing with the limitations of the cooperative machinery is by reducing the need for cooperation in the first place. Thus governments try to fine-tune their respective responsibilities to avoid overlap. In this approach, termed 'rationalization' (Harrison, 2002: 125–7), the governments involved negotiate new national standards for environmental regulation, and then decide definitively which government will be responsible for implementing and enforcing the regulations. This approach offers the same certainty as unified federal action, but allows the governments to choose the style of implementation they prefer: more decentralized and flexible, or more uniform and centralized. Rationalization has always been an option in Canadian intergovernmental relations. It has been used much more extensively in the environment and other fields since the 1995 federal budget cuts forced Ottawa to abandon a strong federal implementation and enforcement presence.[7] The best example is the Environmental Harmonization agreement of 1998, which set in train a variety of processes, overseen by the CCME, to review environmental problems. The key outcome has been a series of new Canada-wide standards negotiated in separate sub-agreements. Although most of them call for flexible provincial implementation, they can be amended only with the unanimous consent of the parties, any one of which can withdraw on six months' notice. These sub-agreements place 'a strong emphasis on "one-window" delivery of environmental protection services by a single order of government' (Winfield and Macdonald, 2008). Examples include sub-agreements on environmental assessment, for specific sets of pollutants such as mercury, dioxins, and furans, and the clean-up of contaminated sites. In some cases the federal Department of the Environment takes the lead in implementation (e.g., monitoring major air pollutants).

Nevertheless, the Harmonization Accords have been likened to a series of 'joint decision traps', relying too much on consensus and producing lowest-common-denominator results (Fafard, 2000). Standards are being set and enforced, but according to observers—in particular environmental NGOs—they tend to be weaker than might be expected if only one jurisdiction were involved. Provincial governments with strong economic interests in resisting higher standards have generally been successful in doing so (Winfield and Macdonald,

2008: 281–4). On the other hand, the threat of unilateral federal action seems to have produced a more stringent Canada-wide standard in some cases (Harrison, 2002: 134–9).

Individual federal administrations (e.g., Chrétien, Martin, Harper) will favour different modes of interaction, some choosing mostly cooperation, some mostly competition.[8] However, no federal government in recent decades has shown much determination to take strong centralized action on the environment. The Harper government, with its apparently decentralist 'open' approach to federalism, has not broken with this pattern.

THE CASE OF CLIMATE CHANGE POLICY

Many of the factors addressed so far in this chapter—the difficulties of accepting environmental costs, the interaction between the economy and the environment, regional and jurisdictional differences over environment policy, and the mechanisms and dynamics of intergovernmental and international relations—come together in the climate change file. Although other environmental issues also have international dimensions, climate change is likely to become the classic example of the challenges posed by multilevel governance. For Canada the issue has two external dimensions: as a major foreign policy matter with significant multilateral implications that must be handled through the United Nations, and as a major bilateral and continental issue with the United States. Domestically, therefore, addressing the issue means negotiating a variety of difficult federal–provincial issues, including treaty ratification and implementation, national and regional competitiveness, and adjustment to a carbon-reduced economy, in addition to the challenges of reaching intergovernmental consensus where required.

The need to reduce greenhouse gas production has been on the international agenda since at least 1992, when the Rio de Janeiro 'Earth Summit' produced the United Nations Framework Convention on Climate Change. The commitments made at that time to stabilize greenhouse gas emissions (GGEs) were largely voluntary. Five years later, the international consensus had firmed up to the point that an international meeting in Kyoto, Japan, set binding targets for reductions in GGEs, applicable to all industrialized countries. When Canada signed the Kyoto Protocol, it agreed that by 2010 it would reduce its GGEs to a level 6 per cent below its output in 1990.

The Kyoto agreement could not take effect, however, until it had been ratified by a sufficient number of countries. Although the US had signed the agreement, in March 2001, it announced that it would not seek ratification in the Senate. The Canadian government did ratify, in December 2002, and the accord finally took effect in 2005. In the meantime, the federal, provincial, and territorial governments all sought to implement the Kyoto commitments. But shortly after its election in January 2006, the Harper Conservative government announced that the Kyoto targets were not realistic and that Canada would not be able to honour its commitments after all. Since then it has been seeking a new international consensus on what it sees as a more realistic approach, with binding commitments not only from all industrialized countries but also from the developing world, which had been left out of Kyoto, in particular large emitting countries such as China, India, and Brazil. The government has signalled its intention to regulate emissions by Canadian industry, implementing these if possible through equivalency agreements with the provinces (Environment Canada, 2007; Prime Minister's Office, 2007), but in setting its targets for emissions it has taken an approach similar to that promoted by the US government, based on industry intensity.[9]

During the decade and a half between the Rio summit and Ottawa's latest position statement, climate change issues were dealt with extensively through domestic intergovernmental relations. Under the joint auspices of the CCME and the Council of Ministers of Energy, intergovernmental coordinating committees worked on a national action plan, released in 1995. According to Winfield and Macdonald (2008), this plan amounted to little more than seeking voluntary reductions of emissions and promising a variety of incentive programs to conserve energy. Meetings intensified in the lead-up to the international meetings in Kyoto, and the provinces agreed with the Chrétien government on the modest target of reducing emissions to the 1990 level by 2010. However, the prime minister unilaterally deepened Canada's commitment not once but twice, breaking ranks with the provinces (although Quebec did support tougher targets), first to 3 per cent below the 1990 level, then to 6 per cent below it (Harrison, 2007). While Chrétien was apparently moving to maximize Canada's influence in bridging the gap at Kyoto between the EU and other industrialized countries, his actions soured the intergovernmental mood in Canada. Back home, meeting privately with the other first ministers in January 1998, he was forced to admit that he had no plan for achieving the Kyoto targets, and that he would consult with them further before ratifying the protocol, if indeed Canada were to ratify it at all (Simpson et al., 2007: 61).

In any case, the Chrétien government continued to be committed to a joint implementation strategy to deal with the climate change issues. After the Kyoto meeting, the intergovernmental process was stepped up considerably with the addition of a well-staffed federal secretariat and extensive involvement of nongovernmental 'stakeholders' at 16 separate 'tables' to discuss more specific matters such as vehicle emissions, electricity production, and emission trading. Over a period of three years, this process eventually produced a 'National Implementation Strategy and Business Plan', signed by all the parties except Ontario and released in October 2000. The plan laid out broad principles, spending commitments, and voluntary undertakings, but established no specific provincial or sectoral targets for achieving the Kyoto commitments, nor any binding regulatory process for reducing emissions. In the words of one prominent account, it was 'a roadmap to nowhere' (Simpson et al., 2007: 63).

Once the US had signalled its intention to withdraw from Kyoto, the Alberta government announced its opposition to Canadian ratification and withdrew from the intergovernmental process. Since 2002 the federal government has gone forward on its own to ratify the agreement, announce industry GGE reduction targets, and begin regulating those targets. By 2008, however, after two changes of government (and three minority parliaments), it is clear that Canada cannot possibly meet its Kyoto targets, and the debate has already moved to 'post-Kyoto' strategies. In the meantime, the provinces—like the states in the US—have taken the initiative in pursuing a variety of measures on their own.

In all this one fact has always been clear: on-the-ground implementation of international commitments on GGE reductions requires the participation of all levels of government. Every government itself is responsible for a certain amount of carbon and other emissions through its own administrative operations. The provinces have major control over natural resources and their management, as well as most major electricity producers, while local governments can influence land use and urban development, transportation use, and other consumer behaviour. All governments have at their disposal important fiscal and regulatory instruments that they can use to induce emission reductions in the society and economy at large. A major court decision in the 1930s established that the federal government has clear jurisdiction over the negotiation and ratification of international treaties, but that it cannot implement them in areas of provincial jurisdiction.[10] The provinces clearly have the right to regulate GGEs in the industry sectors within their jurisdiction; but could the federal parliament pass a Canada-wide scheme? Some refer to recent Supreme Court judgments in support of their view that federal legislation such as the Canadian Environmental Protection Act could be used to regulate GGEs.[11] It seems that both the Martin and Harper governments have contemplated this option (Marshall, 2007). Yet for all the reasons noted above (national unity constraints, regional differences, and a commitment to act collaboratively rather than unilaterally)—and also, perhaps, because it remains unclear how far federal legislation could go before it provoked a constitutional challenge—Ottawa has chosen thus far not to pursue that route (although the Martin government of 2003–6 came close).

In any event, the jurisdictional problem is secondary to the economic and political challenges of deciding what to do, how far to go, and how fast. Should Canada accept the United Nations' view on the causes and effects of global warming? Should it take a bold approach along the lines of Kyoto? Oppose Kyoto as overly damaging to the economy? Or—in light of the integration of our economy with that of the US—simply follow the American lead? What should Canada's share of emission reductions be? Some think that Canada ought to be given some leeway as a world energy producer, while others think we are morally obligated to lead the way because, on a per capita basis, we are among the world's top GGE producers. The answers to those questions have been partly ideological, pitting the green movement against business, and in Canada have revealed some significant differences between the Conservative party and its centre-left opponents—the Liberals, NDP, Bloc Québécois, and Green party. The current Conservative party has roots in both the Progressive Conservatives, who when last in power under Mulroney had a reasonable record on environmental issues, and the western-based Reform and Alliance parties. However, most of its electoral strength comes from the latter, which were hostile to the climate change agenda and highly suspicious of proposals for a carbon tax as harking back to the disastrous National Energy Program of 1980. The Harper government, elected in 2006 with a preponderance of seats in western Canada, initially reflected the Reform–Alliance position, but has had to deal with a resurgence of public opinion in favour of tougher measures to reduce GGEs. While still committed to an intensity-based emissions policy, and focused now on what are basically post-Kyoto international negotiations, the Harper government seems—in mid-2008—to be inching towards a tougher approach. All three of the current federal opposition parties have been proposing the adoption of what the Conservatives (and the Liberals when in power under Chrétien and Martin) have thus far avoided: binding national measures in the form of either a carbon tax or a cap-and-trade system. Liberal leader Stéphane Dion proposed an ambitious plan for a carbon tax in June 2008, but it died when the Harper Conservatives were re-elected in October 2008.

As for the provinces, a recent Suzuki Foundation report describes them as 'all over the map' (Marshall, 2006), reflecting various combinations of regional interests and ideological values. In terms of direct interests, the differential impact of GGE production is stark. The main sources of GGEs in Canada are transportation, electricity generation using fossil fuels, oil and gas production, residential and commercial fuel consumption, industrial production, and agriculture. Whereas fossil fuels are used for transportation across Canada, oil and gas production, along with electricity generation from carbon sources (oil, coal, natural gas) are regionally concentrated. By 2004 Alberta's oil and gas industry, especially the oil sands projects, had made the province the largest producer of GGEs in Canada. Ontario, with the largest population, greatest urban density, and significant industrial production, was the second-largest emitter, and Saskatchewan, also a significant oil and gas producer, with a big agricultural sector, had the highest per capita emissions. Provinces that rely on water power for most of their electricity and industrial production, such as Quebec and Manitoba, are much less emissions-intensive (Simpson et al., 2007: 23–6).

The provincial governments' positions on climate change in general have reflected the intensity of their emissions. Alberta, Ontario, and Saskatchewan have been slow to get on board the Kyoto bandwagon, while Manitoba and Quebec had less to lose and embraced the Kyoto agenda early on. Provinces that are major hydrocarbon producers—chiefly Alberta but also Saskatchewan and Newfoundland and Labrador—have been anxious lest GGE reductions put a halt to the burgeoning of their economies. In Ontario, where stricter emissions controls would have serious implications for the auto industry and the costs of reducing coal-fired electricity production would be high, the neoconservative Mike Harris government (1995–2002) was skeptical about global warming in general and hostile to the Kyoto process. Even the Liberal government of Dalton McGuinty has been cautious; details on the cap-and-trade proposal mentioned earlier are still sketchy, and implementation won't happen until 2010. Other provinces such as Nova Scotia and Prince Edward Island depend heavily on fossil fuels for electricity generation. And all provinces worry about their general economic competitiveness if the regulation of carbon and other emissions in Canada is substantially more stringent than it is in the United States.

Still, we have already seen how some provincial and state governments have taken it on themselves to fill what they have apparently perceived as a policy vacuum in their respective federal capitals. Many observers believe that carbon taxes and cap-and-trade regimes are the most effective policy instruments for deep and long-term reductions in carbon emissions (Simpson et al., 2007). And even the provinces with the most to lose from carbon tax or regulatory regimes are putting major efforts into alternative approaches based on new technologies. Both Alberta and Saskatchewan, for instance, have ambitious plans to use carbon capture and storage to substantially reduce their emissions.

These varied provincial initiatives are pointing the way ahead for their own jurisdictions. This is appropriate, since policy responses to climate change must be tailored to local and regional conditions. This much competitive federalism can deliver. However, it may not be enough—nationally or globally—if the sum of provincial efforts does not add up to a national response at least as significant as Canada's share of the global problem. In any case, a piecemeal, province-by-province approach is unlikely to be either consistent or comprehensive. There is also a real risk that a patchwork of schemes would fracture the Canadian market-place in ways that would make it significantly more difficult to operate competitively. If the US government succeeds in establishing a comprehensive regulatory approach before Canada does, that could quickly become the position that Canadian governments are forced to adopt as their own (Mason, 2008).

It is possible that the Canadian intergovernmental process—spurred on by the competitive processes just outlined—could achieve more substantive results in the future. Unilateral federal action is also possible, likely after consultation with the provinces and territories. Like free trade in the 1980s and 1990s, the climate change issue may ultimately be finessed without a major federal–provincial showdown, especially if public opinion is driving all governments to act more substantively and more quickly. Certainly the jurisdictional issues will be easier to resolve if there is a stronger political consensus in the country as a whole. In the meantime Canada's environmental union remains very much contested terrain.

SUMMARY

This chapter has offered a brief sketch of the issues and dynamics involved in an important, relatively new area for intergovernmental relations in Canada. As with so much of public policy, the truth is in the details, and those are beyond the scope of this book. The environment is of increasing concern to Canadians, and is an important part of our identity. It is not yet clear, however, that Canadians agree on either the standards of environmental quality they want to see enforced or the social and economic trade-offs they are willing to make to deal with major environmental problems.

Federalism only adds to the difficulty of addressing environmental concerns, since different regional interests must be accommodated and multiple levels of government share responsibility for dealing with various types of environmental issues. The environment is, in *de facto* terms, a concurrent, overlapping responsibility among our governments. The challenge therefore is for those governments to get their act together. However, underlying the constitutional and regional factors are the same competing values of federalism that we have seen elsewhere in this book. Our institutions privilege local and provincial autonomy and decentralized responses to many issues. In many cases this is appropriate. At the same time, Canadians expect fairness, equality, and consistency on matters that are Canada-wide in scope. Intergovernmental mechanisms for addressing environmental issues are well established, but—as usual with executive federalism—their effectiveness is limited by the length of time it takes to reach agreement and by the fact that outcomes are frequently diluted and compromised. A fascinating by-product of the difficulty of developing an adequate national policy is what we have been calling competitive federalism, in which the federal, provincial, and territorial governments simply go ahead with their own solutions. This can have the effect of encouraging—or shaming—other jurisdictions into following suit. But competitive, piecemeal policy is no substitute for comprehensive, binding, and consistent policy. Canadian federalism makes the latter very difficult to achieve.

The climate change file illustrates all these points. It offers many examples of the challenges posed by multilevel governance: from the rules hammered out in the United Nations International Convention on Climate Change and the Kyoto protocol, right down to the policies adopted by the local municipality to cut back on greenhouse gas emissions. In the context of foreign policy, it tests the federal government's authority to enter into and ratify treaties, and underlines its apparent inability to implement such treaties in areas of provincial responsibility. The fact that there is still no substantial consensus on climate change, let alone enforceable regulation, more than 15 years after the Rio summit makes it hard not to suspect that Canadian executives of the various governments have simply been hiding behind their ineffective intergovernmental machinery and blaming each other for their failure to act. Even so, it would be unfair to lay all the blame at the feet of federalism. Climate change has been a deeply contested issue in Canada, as it is in most parts of the world. Very substantial economic, social, and political interests and values are at stake. Reaching a strong national consensus on what to do in this area is bound to take time. In the absence of a stronger consensus, it is all the more difficult for governments to sort out the practical details of how best to proceed among the various legal responsibilities and political mandates. Thus governments are responding to their own needs with a mixture of partly coordinated and partly competing efforts. It may not be pretty, but it is the Canadian way.

Chapter 13

Local Government and Federalism

Much of our discussion so far has concentrated on the relationship between the two orders of government that formed the original confederation compact: the provinces and what was then called the Dominion, now known as the federal government of Canada. From time to time we also have made reference to the territorial governments. For many purposes, however, the territories can be considered equivalent to the provinces, particularly since the Charlottetown process of 1992, when they became full participants in first ministers' meetings and annual premiers' conferences. Two very different types that we have not yet discussed are the subjects of this chapter and the next: local and Aboriginal governments.

'Local government' is a broad category, including not just municipalities of all types—from villages and rural districts to towns, cities, counties, and (sub-provincial) regions—but a wide variety of local and regional agencies responsible for services such as education (school boards), policing (regional police services), health care, and regional planning. Municipal governments in Canada are directly elected, and so, in most cases, are the special-purpose agencies. The latter cover defined territories that are sometimes the same as the municipalities with which they are associated, and sometimes encompass a number of municipal units.

Local governments exercise an impressive array of executive and legislative powers, including the powers to levy taxes, regulate businesses, and determine land use for construction and development purposes. It could even be argued that their impact on the daily lives of Canadians is at least as great as that of the provincial governments. Yet local government is not constitutionally recognized as an order of government. Nor do local governments have anything like the legal and financial autonomy that the federal and provincial governments enjoy. In fact, any or all of a local government's powers can easily be taken away by the provincial government, which has constitutional jurisdiction over it. In this era of increasing 'glocalization'—simultaneous emphasis on the global and the local, and the links between them—interdependence, and multilevel governance, it seems especially important to look at the place of local government in Canadian federalism.

CITIES AND LOCAL GOVERNMENT[1]

Canada is a heavily urbanized country, with over 68 per cent of the population living in cities.[2] The government closest to those people, the one in charge of the infrastructure of everyday life, is the city government, and local government remains one of the primary sites for participation in democratic self-government. Economically, too, cities play an increasingly important role. In the past the focus was usually on the overall performance of the national economy, and the crucial factor determining a country's success was thought to be the policy of the national government. Today, however, it is recognized that national competitiveness is only a reflection of the success of local economies—which themselves depend on responsive, efficient local governments to provide the public goods and services they need. Finally, a common expression in the social justice and environmental movements—'Think globally, act locally'—points to the recognition that local, decentralized action can often be more effective than standardized policy developed at the centre. In any case, policy interdependence places a greater burden on all governments in a federal system to act more harmoniously, to manage conflict better, and to cooperate more effectively when required.

Yet Canada's federal system consists of two entirely separate intergovernmental relationships that only rarely intersect. The relationship between our federal and provincial orders of government is one of equals, in principle if not always in practice. But there is no such equality in the relationship between the province and the local level. In fact, Canada's provinces are essentially unitary systems. Under the Constitution Act, 1867, local governments are created by provincial governments, they exist at their pleasure, and the provinces have the power to intervene in local affairs as they wish. A province could even decide to dissolve a local government—though to do so would be to risk voters' wrath. In Germany local government is recognized as a third order of government and concurrent legislative powers give the federal government the authority to act in local matters. The latter is also true of the US. In Canada, by contrast, exclusive provincial jurisdiction means that the only way for Ottawa to play an active role in local affairs is by using the federal spending power to allocate funds to individuals and organizations at the local level. Moreover, in Canada the network of intergovernmental relations does not normally extend to local government. Canada as a whole may be one of the most decentralized federal systems in the world, but within each province the centralization of power is almost complete.

Still, local government is a vital part of the democratic system. Local government came to Canada, as it did to the United States, from the English municipal tradition of counties and towns. Under the French regime and in the early days of British rule, local governments were essentially instruments of the colonial authorities (Graham et al., 1998). Local democracy took hold only in the nineteenth century, with the gradual emergence of local elected councils. The settled agricultural lands of the eastern colonies (except Newfoundland) were divided into administrative units called counties, within which were rural municipalities and towns, but cities—beginning with Saint John, New Brunswick, which was granted a royal charter in 1785—became corporate entities with a measure of decision-making autonomy, provided their by-laws did not conflict with colonial law. In 1867 the BNA Act assigned municipal government and local special-purpose bodies (school and hospital authorities, etc.) to the jurisdiction of the provincial legislatures, but otherwise made no reference to local government; nor did its successor, the Constitution Act, 1982.

When it comes to local government, then, the provinces are essentially unitary states. Provincial legislatures do occasionally reform the functions, fiscal relations, and boundaries of municipalities, though they would rarely abolish them altogether (Corry, 1947). Has the time come to change this arrangement? Questions along these lines have been raised repeatedly since the 1960s, and in recent years a number of specific reforms have been proposed. For example, under the rubric of a 'new deal' for cities, it has been suggested that provinces could grant cities greater legislative autonomy through 'city charters': 'separate provincial acts [establishing] asymmetrical and more empowering relationships between cities and provinces' (Good, 2007: 4). One example is the 'Greater Toronto Area Charter' proposed by local elites in 2001, under which the greater Toronto area would become a full partner with the federal and provincial governments; would be fully entitled to participate in intergovernmental discussions over matters such as transfer payments; and would assume responsibility for matters including housing, health care, and immigrant and refugee settlement (Good, 2007: 7).

Both the Toronto City Charter proposal and the concept of city charters generally have been endorsed and promoted by the Federation of Canadian Municipalities. Interest in these ideas has grown significantly since the 1990s, when provinces such as Ontario, Quebec, and Nova Scotia undertook large-scale municipal amalgamation projects and what were euphemistically called 'service exchanges', in which municipalities were relieved of some responsibilities but then were assigned new ones. Among the consequences of these changes was the mobilization of citizens as well as civic leaders in protest against them. As Kristin Good notes, 'the amalgamation of Toronto . . . created a powerful new political unit that could serve as a platform for local leaders and more effectively challenge provincial power' (Good, 2007: 6). Interest in these ideas continues to grow, especially as the need for infrastructure renewal becomes increasingly urgent.

WHAT LOCAL GOVERNMENT DOES, AND HOW

What local governments actually do differs somewhat across the provinces. The core functions are the same everywhere: garbage, roads, water, sewers, land use planning and control. But in other areas there are significant differences. In British Columbia, for instance, the province is directly responsible for public transit, while in Ontario the province ceased all contributions to the operating budgets of public transit systems in 1998, although some provincial funding was restored in 2001. In large cities in western and central Canada, policing is provided directly by the municipality, while across much of rural Canada it is provided either by the Royal Canadian Mounted Police or by other police forces under direct contract from the province. In Manitoba and Ontario, municipalities deliver social assistance and other social services directly and pay for a portion of those services. Elsewhere this is a direct provincial responsibility. School boards have greater or lesser autonomy in one province or the other, and are funded to varying degrees by municipal property tax revenues. Overall, though, the breadth and scope of municipal governments and special-purpose local bodies of all kinds (police commissions, planning councils, watershed boards, school boards, health authorities, etc.) are similar. Provincial differences are somewhat greater with respect to rural municipalities. In Ontario, for instance, governance arrangements vary depending on community size and history; there are a few 'single-tier' municipalities, and in most cases services for several small 'lower-tier' municipalities are provided by a larger 'upper-tier' entity called a county, region, or district. British Columbia has no counties and instead is divided into roughly thirty 'regional districts', each of which encompasses multiple city, town, or village governments, while Manitoba has chosen a single-tier approach.

Canada has gone through two waves of municipal mergers, amalgamations, and 'rationalization' of functions. The first wave, in the 1950s and 1960s, resulted in the annexation by the core city municipalities of large stretches of suburban and rural land for anticipated development, and the creation of new regional, multi-purpose municipalities such as the Urban Community of Montreal, Metropolitan Toronto, Ottawa–Carleton, and the 'uni-city' of Winnipeg. The second wave, which hit eastern Canada in the late 1990s, saw the creation of more rationalized, single-tier city structures through amalgamation of the sort imposed on Halifax, Montreal, and Toronto. The latter proved to be highly controversial. In Quebec, for example, the PQ government forced the amalgamation of the Montreal, Quebec City, and Hull–Gatineau urban regions, shortly after it released a White Paper on the topic (Hamel and Rousseau, 2006). The Quebec Liberal party took advantage of popular discontent with this top-down move in the 2003 election, promising the affected municipalities that, if elected, it would give them the opportunity to retrieve a good part of their lost autonomy through a local referendum process. The Liberals won and kept their word. On the Island of Montreal, former suburban municipalities held de-merger referenda and 15 of them successfully regained much—but not all—of the autonomy they had lost, leaving citizens uncertain about which government was responsible for what (Hamel and Rousseau, 2006: 155).

Amalgamation in Ontario was more permanent but no less controversial. A number of municipalities that stood to be swallowed up resisted, launching campaigns for the hearts and minds of local citizens. Among the rationales put forward by the Ontario and Nova Scotia governments to justify amalgamation were direct cost savings from economies of scale and consolidated services and the need to create a single administrative and political platform in order for an urban entity 'to be able to compete in the world marketplace' (quoted in Sancton, 2002: 269).[3] At the time, critics questioned the promise of cost savings, noting that the integration of different collective agreements and service standards under conditions of amalgamation generally led to increases in wages and service expectations, thereby pushing up costs. It has indeed been found that costs have gone up rather than down.[4] Of the risk that urban areas would be unable to compete in the global economy without amalgamation, Andrew Sancton, citing findings from the American literature, has argued that

municipalities are *not* critical to launching explosive cycles of regional growth, but they are crucial in managing growth. . . . If municipalities are able to do well the things that municipalities have traditionally done, their cities will be more competitive over a longer period of time (Sancton, 2002: 267–8).

Generally, Canadian local government has enjoyed a worldwide reputation for effective and efficient local infrastructure and services. In a period when many American cities were experiencing urban decay and unplanned sprawl, Canadian cities were recognized as being better run and more livable—'cities that work'. The quality of both the infrastructure and the services—and therefore their value in terms of economic competitiveness—has been put in question in the past decade, however, as a result of painful adjustments to the entire Canadian public sector. Local governments are now increasingly preoccupied with economic development issues. Yet few of them have the policy levers they need to renew their economies, let alone rebuild their infrastructure—certainly not without the cooperation, and financial support, of the provincial and federal governments. Justified or not, a perception has arisen in Montreal, Vancouver, and especially Toronto that the provincial governments ignore them politically and are too preoccupied with the problems of smaller cities, towns, and rural areas to attend to their needs (Berridge, 2002; FCM, 2005; Sancton, 2008).

PROVINCIAL–LOCAL RELATIONS

The basic structure of the relationship between provincial and municipal governments has changed little in more than 150 years. The legal relationship in all provinces is modelled on legislation adopted by the United Province of Canada in 1849. Under the Baldwin Act (and its successor, the Municipal Act, as well as the corresponding legislation in other provinces), all local government powers were specifically delegated. The legislation typically assigns more power and responsibility for services and infrastructure to the larger cities (Graham et al., 1998), but it is not a general grant of power and it constrains municipalities as much as it empowers them in legislative and fiscal terms.

In recent years four provinces—Alberta, British Columbia, Newfoundland and Labrador, and Ontario—have begun to reform their basic legal relationship with local governments, creating more room for local decision-making. Alberta's Municipal Government Act provides for the most comprehensive reform (Graham et al., 1998; FCM, 2001): it defines local functions more broadly; grants municipalities powers as 'natural persons' (i.e., enjoying full status under corporate law); streamlines the number of additional statutes that govern local government; provides for inter-municipal dispute resolution; permits municipalities to carry a deficit, within defined limits; allows for some expanded tax room in areas such as entertainment, retail sales and gasoline taxes; and in general restricts provincial intervention to matters of declared 'provincial interest'. Similarly in British Columbia, a provincial law called the 'Community Charter', passed in 2003, established a set of principles for municipal–provincial relations, an accountability regime, and a number of broadly defined powers, including provisions for concurrency. Significantly, provisions in the BC Charter require extensive public consultation and local referenda in the event of any proposed amalgamation or merger of municipalities. It also provides for a dispute settlement mechanism should conflicts arise between municipalities or between municipalities and the provincial government. BC and Alberta are the only two provinces where municipal–provincial relations are referred to as 'intergovernmental'.

Recent legislation in Newfoundland and Labrador goes a step further, recognizing each of the province's eight cities as an autonomous order of government. It provides a general grant of power covering 15 spheres, subject only to general provincial standards covering environment, protection of persons and property, and building codes, and undertakes not to amend the legislation without consulting the city or cities affected.

It may be only a matter of time before most of the other Canadian provinces adopt legislation similar to that described above. In the meantime, day-to-day relations between provincial and local governments are defined largely by the political environment in the province, and by the provincial fiscal and expenditure decision-making process. Local government powers, even where they are expanding, remain limited and must be exercised with sensitivity to the overall provincial regulatory stance, whether it is pro-development, pro-environment, devoted to comprehensive planning, or open to local flexibility and manipulation. By the same token, local expenditures and revenue patterns are highly dependent on provincially determined policy, including transfer payments.

Apart from the formal legislated relations between provinces and municipalities, direct political relations are also important. Every province has a federation or association of municipalities. These bodies provide formal avenues for representation and lobbying, principally to the minister and department of Municipal Affairs, but often also to the premier, minister of Finance, or cabinet as a whole. The Federation of Canadian Municipalities plays a similar role at the federal level. Both the federal and provincial organizations play important roles in providing policy advice and technical support to individual municipalities, especially the smaller ones.

Less structured political connections are formed through the direct relationships that develop between individual mayors or councils and provincial ministers and officials. All the larger cities rely as much or more on their own lobbying efforts as they do on their membership in provincial associations. Partisan connections are also important for some local politicians, even though at the local level political parties are weak or non-existent. Political coalitions thrive in some cities (e.g., Montreal's Civic Party) but in most places there is no party structure at all, let alone any formal linkage with federal or provincial parties. For the most part, then, local politicians and bureaucrats are free to pursue non-partisan relations with all governments and parties. On the other hand, the virtual absence of political mobilization at the municipal level may mean that local and urban issues are insufficiently debated or considered in a systematic way in the political community at large (for discussion see Graham et al., 1998).

Finances are key to the provincial–local relationship. Local government finances in relation to overall public financial arrangements in Canada are noteworthy. In 2006 Canadian expenditures on local government (broadly defined) totalled 7.4 per cent of GDP, and 28 per cent of total provincial spending. The per capita spending varies enormously, from $320 in Prince Edward Island to $1,650 in Ontario. These differences reflect varying urban size, service costs, and the fact that municipalities deliver a narrower range of services in some provinces, especially the Atlantic provinces (Kitchen, 2000). What local government spends its money on changes only marginally from year to year: the three largest categories are transportation, protection of persons and property, and environment. Two important trends in the past two decades have been an overall reduction in debt charges, and increased spending on social services. In the latter case, however, the increase is due not to any absolute growth in spending on social services but rather to the shifting of some responsibilities from the province to the local level.

On the revenue side the past decade has witnessed a dramatic increase in dependence on 'own-source' revenues (as opposed to transfer payments from the province), particularly for general local government, that is, municipalities.

Own-source municipal revenues increased from 77.1 per cent in 1988 to 84.6 per cent in 1998 and 82.8 per cent in 2005; these increases were reflected in significant increases in property taxes (both rates and yields) and user fees. Transfer payments to municipal governments accounted for only 15.4 per cent of their revenues in 1998, principally in the form of conditional grants from the provincial governments (although there is also a trend to 'block' grants with fewer conditions attached). However, transfer payments to the local government sector as a whole—i.e., municipalities and other local governments combined—take up a larger share of total revenues, at 38.8 per cent, and underscore the increasing dependence on provincial transfers of school boards in particular.[5]

In keeping with the trend to greater reliance on own-source revenues, municipal governments have seen modest increases in their ability to levy taxes. Examples of municipal taxes (some in place for many years now) include hotel occupancy taxes (Vancouver), business occupancy taxes (Winnipeg), gasoline and other fuel taxes (Vancouver, Victoria, Montreal, and Calgary). In addition, Manitoba practises a form of revenue sharing, transferring a fixed share of provincial personal income tax (2 percentage points) and corporate income tax (1 percentage point) to municipalities in the form of unconditional grants (FCM, 2001). Finally, two significant long-term funding arrangements from the federal government have recently been put in place. First, in 2004 Ottawa began rebating to municipalities all of the funds the latter paid on the GST for purchases of goods and services, at an estimated cost of $7 billion over 10 years. Second, in 2005 the federal government began sharing with the municipalities, through agreement with the provinces, a portion of the federal excise tax on gasoline (five cents per litre, or one-half of the federal tax). Money from this Gas Tax Fund is paid to municipalities through the provinces on a per capita basis, and is to be used for environmentally sustainable infrastructure.

Throughout the 1990s the trend in provincial–municipal finance across Canada had been towards a clearer allocation of expenditure responsibilities in line with local revenue bases, and a reduced reliance on provincial transfers. To manage the increased responsibilities resulting from what they see as provincial 'offloading', local governments have been—and still are—forced to reduce costs (either by improving delivery efficiency or by cutting service levels), and in some cases to raise local property tax rates. Where the fiscal problems were most severe, in eastern Canada, they contributed to the wave of municipal mergers set in motion by provincial governments convinced that 'rationalization' would lead to long-term cost savings. Still, chronic fiscal problems at the local level in Canada have in turn led to important policy trends. First is the trend towards public–private partnerships as a means of delivering services both more economically and more effectively, especially in the not-for-profit sector (Graham et al., 1998). Second is a preoccupation with expanding the local tax base through a variety of economic development efforts. Third is a tendency to neglect longer-term investment and maintenance in infrastructure, both provincial and local, until problems—economic, social, environmental—become critical. The important new contributions from the federal government of the past few years aside, the overall fiscal situation of municipal government has not changed. Municipalities remain heavily dependent on property taxes. It remains to be seen whether a new age of carbon taxes and other environmentally-oriented levies is about to begin; if it does, these policy instruments may require a rethinking of the fiscal tools at the disposal of the city governments in particular.

THE FEDERAL ROLE

By now it should be clear that the primary relationship for local governments is with the provincial governments that have created them, and that often dominate them in fiscal and regulatory terms. Yet local governments would welcome a larger role for the federal government, both as a counterbalance to provincial dominance and to provide a national focus for urban and local government issues with more than local impact. Whether the federal government has sufficient political interest to sustain such a policy focus remains to be seen. Over the years, Ottawa has at times shown strong interest in the urban agenda, only to backtrack when the provinces have resisted. The most notable example was the short-lived Ministry of State for Urban Affairs (MSUA), which Ottawa created in 1971 and disbanded in 1978 in the face of provincial opposition and criticism from federal line departments that resented the MSUA's efforts to persuade them to take a more active interest in urban matters.

The constitutional division of powers ensures that the federal government has no direct influence on local government. But federal operations such as airports, railways, and defence establishments have a real effect on local communities. So do federal spending programs in areas such as health, post-secondary education, job training, housing, and community, regional, and industrial development. Yet in most cases the federal government treads softly where municipal and other local government authorities are involved, and it has more than once been warned off by provincial governments. Quebec even has special legislation that prevents municipalities from accepting money directly from the federal government.

Nonetheless, members of the federal parliament take a keen interest in local issues. Individual MPs are often frustrated by the constitutional constraints on their activity with respect to their constituencies, and in a competitive political environment they may seek to outflank provincial governments (especially those with different political ideology) in appealing directly to voters on matters of local interest. For MPs in particular, the political interest in local issues—urban or rural—is all about their own democratic legitimacy and relevance. MPs gain visibility and credit in their constituencies when they are able to persuade the federal government to invest in local infrastructure projects, especially when the MPs themselves announce and help to shape the program.

Furthermore, the federal government has historically played an important role in local and urban issues.[6] With strong direct advocacy from Canadian municipalities during the Great Depression, Ottawa provided direct funding to local governments for public works. And after the Second World War it provided support for local initiatives such as agricultural and regional development, sewage treatment works, and make-work projects. The most important and sustained effort, extending from the 1940s to the late 1970s, was the Central Mortgage and Housing Corporation (CMHC), which played a crucial role in developing housing standards, funding public housing, and promoting community planning (Artibise, 2001). Many of these programs were delivered through intergovernmental agreements with the provinces, allowing funds to pass through to local authorities. In addition, from 1971 to 1978 the Ministry of State for Urban Affairs had a mandate to coordinate various federal economic and social programs important to urban development.

Canadian governments are less closely connected today, particularly in welfare-state programs. Fiscal and program decentralization in general has led to a reduced role for the federal government. Since 1980 federal involvement in local government programs has declined in terms of both money and intensity. Its direct involvement is now confined to a few significant issues and programs: economic development in specific urban areas, usually the product of tri-level agreements; national tri-level infrastructure programs; funding for certain housing programs aimed at easing the homelessness crisis in larger urban centres (but much reduced from the more general federal housing programs of the past); transportation coordination; some redevelopment of port lands; and the recent GST rebate and Gas Tax Fund.

Paul Martin's brief term as prime minister, from December 2003 to February 2006, represented the high-water mark in terms of recent federal interest and involvement in urban and local affairs (Sancton, 2008: 321–5). Martin himself shared the growing intellectual interest in what Neil Bradford (2004) has called the 'new localism'. Emphasizing the importance of local, place-specific factors in both economic prosperity and social health, advocates of the new localism call for collaborative governance (by the public and private sector) at the local level, and argue that upper-level governments should enable local solutions, not impose them. They also stress the need to scale down or even redesign regional or province-wide social policies with neighbourhood dynamics in mind. The new policy focus on urban dynamics has drawn attention to the inadequacy of infrastructure investment, the need to address urban-specific social issues such as immigrant settlement, and the extent to which the fiscal system has starved city governments. Politically, however, the Martin government could not ignore rural and small-town municipalities. Thus it was always careful to present its policy agenda as one for both cities *and* communities. Its most significant contributions were a renewed commitment to the infrastructure program (a further $7 billion in 2004), and the new fiscal arrangements noted above, such as the Gas Tax Fund. All of these arrangements benefit small municipalities as much as they do the large cities. The Harper government's approach to local government is not hugely different from that of its predecessor, but it is arguably more focused, and less ambitious in terms of social policy. As well, in keeping with their 'open federalism' approach, the Conservatives seem to be taking more care not to tread on provincial jurisdiction in pursuing local issues. It has thus far maintained the key financial support programs. In 2007 it announced $33 billion in funding over seven years through its *Building Canada: Modern Infrastructure for a Strong Canada* program, although a good portion of that funding had been announced previously as part of earlier programs.[7] As well, the Infrastructure Canada secretariat responsible for administering this program, created in 2002 and first housed within the Treasury Board Secretariat, subsequently became a department within a restructured (and renamed) 'Transport, Infrastructure and Communities' portfolio of the Government of Canada.[8] For the first time since the demise of the Ministry of State for Urban Affairs in the 1970s, the federal government has a distinct profile in the urban field.

At the same time, there has been a subtle shift in emphasis since the election of 2006, reflecting the fact that the Conservatives' main base of electoral support is suburban rather than urban (as it was for the Liberals) (Sancton, 2008). For example, the Conservatives appear to be more willing than the Liberals were to allow federal funds to be spent on roads—a more pressing issue for suburban and rural voters than for city dwellers. They are also pursuing their (sub)urban agenda on a more political level, approaching the mayors of big cities, for example, directly rather than working through bureaucratic channels. Under the previous Liberal government a fairly close network of links and interactions had developed between city bureaucrats and their colleagues in federal departments such as Transport Canada, Infrastructure Canada, and Human Resources and Development Canada, as well as the urban policy group in the Privy Council Office established in 2002. According to Loleen Berdahl (2006), the federal government's main regional development agency in the west, Western Economic Diversification, was particularly important as a point of contact for municipal officials under the Liberals. The Harper government, with its penchant for centralizing policy initiatives, has put more emphasis on direct contact at the political level within municipalities, particularly in areas such as Vancouver and the lower mainland, possibly because urban and suburban areas in Ontario and BC offer attractive opportunities to make electoral gains. During the 2008 federal election campaign, a number of Conservative candidates running in suburban ridings emphasized how those communities would benefit if they elected a representative on the government side of the house—someone who could improve their access to federal funding for bridges and roads.

One of the most important links between the federal government and municipalities is the Federation of Canadian Municipalities (FCM). Although it describes itself as a lobby group working on behalf of more than 3,700 municipalities, in many ways this organization serves as a bridge between municipalities and the federal government. With its headquarters in Ottawa and a staff of more than 120, it actually has a much more substantial presence than the Council of the Federation. It also has a solid connection with the federal government, largely because it manages and delivers a good deal of international development work for the latter, much of it involving urban development and local government issues. In fact the FCM is Canada's primary source of expertise in this field. Even though it is not clear exactly how this international development expertise helps the FCM in promoting its domestic agenda, the organization has been remarkably successful in highlighting the infrastructure needs of Canadian municipalities. In 2006, for example, when the ongoing debate on the fiscal imbalance was at its peak, the FCM released its own statement on the issue in a document entitled *Building Prosperity from the Ground Up: Restoring Municipal Fiscal Balance* (FCM, 2006), which stressed the fact that inadequate funding was starving the municipalities more than it was the provinces. It seems likely that the FCM's efforts in Ottawa had something to do with the federal government's increased commitment to infrastructure programs and the launch of the Gas Tax Fund.

According to Stevenson and Gilbert (2005: 541), the FCM's success can be credited both to effective leadership, both internally and externally, and to a strategy of avoiding the 'high politics' of constitutional issues—an area that the FCM emphasized in the 1970s and 1980s—in favour of the 'low politics' of practical issues important to citizens, such as improved infrastructure.The Big Cities Mayors Caucus within the FCM has been particularly effective in helping the organization cater to its diverse members and manage tensions between them. If tri-level relations among municipalities, provinces, and the federal government are now becoming more of a reality, the FCM can take a good portion of the credit; it has also become an integral part of this tri-cornered relationship.

ASSESSING THE INTERGOVERNMENTAL SYSTEM

Intergovernmental issues related to municipalities can be classified in three groups. Some are primarily local: the widespread movement to regional coordinating bodies and multi-purpose bodies; the increasing recourse to public–private partnerships; and the turmoil in large urban areas, especially in eastern Canada, over boundary and governance issues in the context of municipal amalgamation. Others are primarily *provincial–local*. These include reductions in provincial transfer payments and the offloading of program responsibilities; and the movement in some provinces to reform municipal legislation to reduce the regulatory burden, increase fiscal flexibility, and provide for a broader definition of municipal spheres of jurisdiction. Finally there are some issues that are truly tri-level: *federal–provincial–local*. Three issues in particular are worth noting: the renewal of local infrastructure through cooperative cost-shared, tri-level agreements such as the *Building Canada* program; the federal government's withdrawal from almost all housing programs (the exception was a program targeting homelessness, renewed just before the 2008 election); and the federal government's responsibility for Aboriginal peoples, which—as we shall see in the next chapter—involves it in complex Aboriginal–municipal–provincial negotiations.

The intergovernmental system through which the above issues and others are debated, managed, and resolved (or not) is divided into two sub-systems that only rarely intersect. One is the federal–provincial system, which thrives on informality and a competitive ethos that encourages each government to pursue its own interests, and offers the governments concerned a broad range of choice as to when, how, and under what conditions they will pursue cooperative solutions.

The other sub-system is the provincial–local one. In this system the municipalities have less formal status than even the smallest province in the first sub-system, because their position is not entrenched in the federal constitution. The provinces are the units that together make up the federation, but municipalities have no such essential role in relation to the province. In principle, then, a province might feel no more obliged to negotiate with its municipalities than it would with any given interest group. If formal processes for joint decision-making are inadequate in the federal–provincial system, they are non-existent in the provincial–local one. This is not to say that negotiations do not take place: they do, especially when major reforms are proposed. From day to day, however, the relationship appears to be more one of patron-client. As we have noted, some provinces are now moving to give local governments more autonomy. In the meantime, the fact that Ontario, Nova Scotia, and Quebec were able to force municipalities to amalgamate illustrates the fundamental inequality of the relationship. The competitive ethos that we have described in the context of federal–provincial and inter-provincial relations is alive and well in inter-municipal relations too. Cooperation through joint bodies, agreements, and various communication mechanisms does resolve many overlapping issues. Unlike the federal government in its relations with the provinces, however, most provincial governments have both the legal power and the political will to impose 'take-it-or leave-it' cooperation on municipalities when inter-municipal devices fail.

We have noted that the federal–provincial and provincial–municipal–rarely intersect. If all three levels of government are to be involved, the negotiations typically take place in two stages—first federal–provincial, then provincial–municipal. Even in the Canada Infrastructure Program, the nature and extent of municipal involvement in the identification and management of projects varied by province. Each provincial government essentially determined the municipal role (Andrew and Morrison, 1995). The chief exceptions to this pattern have come in specific urban settings involving one province only, such as the Winnipeg Core Initiative or the Halifax gateway transportation planning initiative (Bakvis, 1991; Graham et al., 1998). These tri-level arrangements often use innovative mechanisms such as jointly owned and controlled Crown corporations to manage the projects in question.

Despite the grand schemes of some in the municipal sector, especially those in the big city governments, major reform in this area seems unlikely. To integrate federal–provincial with provincial–municipal relations in a sort of super tri-level relationship is likely more than the system could bear. A tri-level relationship could be unwieldy at best and might only magnify the existing weaknesses of executive federalism, such as its dependence on consensus decision-making.

Regional diversity is another reason for avoiding multilateral tri-level relations: local problems need local solutions tailored to fit the regional context. On the other hand, limiting the federal role in local matters is not conducive to the national definition and mobilization of consent for broader public policy object-ives. For Ottawa to deal with individual cities on a one-by-one basis could lead to regional antagonisms and injustices.

In conclusion, the need for Canadian governments to pursue tri-level coordin-ation is likely to increase. A fully integrated tri-level system will not be required, but our governments will have to find new ways to achieve that coordination. Plenty of room exists for Ottawa to develop a renewed federal vision on urban issues, if it is prepared to work sensitively with the provinces and flexibly in each urban area with the relevant local governments.

CONCLUSION

Constitutionally, municipalities are creatures of the provinces. Yet many analysts have argued that multilevel governance—from global to local, as well as every level in between—is where the future lies. Is there an argument to be made that, regardless of their legal status, local governments have a role to play in the inter-governmental scheme of things?

Certainly there have been tri-level arrangements in which local governments have collaborated with the provincial and federal orders of government on joint initiatives, or arrangements that cross international boundaries. However, these projects have tended to be one-of-a-kind, involving a single province or cross-border relationship, and focusing on a particular place or issue, such as Vancouver's downtown east side, or border security between BC and Washington state. The provinces usually determine the extent to which municipalities partici-pate, and the centralized, top-down nature of our Westminster parliamentary system means that they tend to keep municipalities on a relatively short leash. So far, then, it is not possible to say that local governments have proven their ability to function as equals with the senior orders of government.

This is not to say that the municipal governments should not be given more autonomy, however, including autonomy in raising revenues. Large urban conglomerates are essential for fostering national well-being and economic growth, and municipal governments can play an important role in creating the environmental conditions that will favour such growth. Those conditions include not only good quality infrastructure but also a general climate, made up of less tangible factors related to culture and diversity, that Richard Florida (2004) has associated with the rise of the 'creative class'. It remains with the provinces, however, to decide whether to give municipalities more room for manoeuvre—as BC, Alberta, and Newfoundland and Labrador have done. Constitutionally, the federal government can exercise only indirect influence; it is not in a position either to grant additional tax sources to cities or to change their constitutional status. In examining the argument that municipalities should be seen as major players in the intergovernmental game, we noted the basic logistical problem of trying to integrate federal–provincial with provincial–municipal relations into a sort of super tri-level relationship. Such a move is likely more than the system can bear, we argue. On the other hand, organizations such as the Federation of Canadian Municipalities have been effective in giving voice to municipalities on critical issues such as the need for rebuilding infrastructure and linking municipalities to Ottawa. And one consequence of the spate of municipal amalgamations over the past decade—unintended, to be sure—was the development of larger platforms for the political leaders of Canada's largest cities. Use of those platforms in mobilizing public opinion can be seen as another element in the dynamic interplay between municipalities, provinces, and the federal government.

Finally, the rush of federal–provincial–municipal programs introduced late in the Chrétien period and pushed to the forefront during Paul Martin's brief tenure as prime minister has left a legacy in the form of a new web of tri-level relationships, including institutional support for these relationships. The allocation of funding from Ottawa to the municipalities under the Municipal Rural Infrastructure Fund (MRIF) and the Gas Tax Fund is managed by 'Oversight Committees', one for each province. In the case of the GTF, the oversight committees are currently composed of the federal minister of Transport, Infrastructure and Communities and his counterpart at the provincial level, the senior officials at the federal and provincial level and, critically, the provincial municipal association in each province. According to Michael Buda (2008: 37), these committees 'provided provincial and territorial municipal associations with, in most cases, their first entry into federal–provincial relations, . . . [allowing] them to build capacity and a network in this area'. Although the Conservative government has been more cautious than its Liberal predecessors in pursuing the urban and communities' agenda, it has nonetheless continued to work with the oversight committees in implementing and managing the GTF. Those committees may well serve a template for federal–provincial–municipal activities and interactions in the future.

Chapter 14

Aboriginal Governments and Federalism

Aboriginal government is a challenging topic for a book on Canadian federalism. The subject matter is complex and perceptions of the issues are fundamentally contested among political actors and scholars alike. Yet Aboriginal governments, policy, and politics are increasingly salient issues for Canadians. Here we confine ourselves to an overview of the most significant trends affecting the federal system as a whole, the emerging characteristics of Aboriginal government as a third order, and the nature of intergovernmental relations with that third order.

Since the early 1970s, Aboriginal nationalism has joined Quebec nationalism as a significant challenge to the Canadian federation. The existence in Canada of political communities with separate or co-existing national identities has led many Canadians to think of their country as not merely a bilingual, multicultural union of provinces, but a special kind of entity that Kymlicka (2003) calls 'multi-national'. Indeed, some Aboriginal people reject Canadian sovereignty and seek something amounting to independent status. Many Aboriginal nations and communities claim collective ownership over land and other natural resources as an unsurrendered Aboriginal right, challenging the control and ownership of the Canadian state, both federal and provincial. Many Aboriginal organizations have condemned the failure of Canadian political institutions to provide for Aboriginal representation within them. Meanwhile, Aboriginal people continue to face racism—some would say neocolonialism—in the broader Canadian society.

In response to these challenges many different solutions have been proposed. These include restoration of Aboriginal nations as sovereign states, recognition of Aboriginal government as a third order within the federation, development of what has been called treaty federalism or confederalism, an Aboriginal house of parliament, separate Aboriginal electoral districts, and even a First Nations province. The structures and practices of Canadian federalism, however, present some significant obstacles to Aboriginal aspirations of self-determination and decolonization.

Aboriginal peoples did not take part in the negotiation of the Confederation deal and were not consulted on its terms. Rather, the Canadian state took over, without any explicit Aboriginal consent, the role of the British Crown, including the fiduciary obligations towards Aboriginal peoples first set out in the Royal Proclamation of 1763 (RCAP, 1992: 10–19). The only reference to Aboriginal matters in the entire Constitution Act, 1867, came in section 91(24), which awarded jurisdiction over 'Indians, and lands reserved for Indians' to the federal parliament.[1] Accordingly, the federal parliament continued the effort, begun under the government of the United Province of Canada (1840–67), to settle the Aboriginal population on reserves under the terms of the Indian Act, 1860, and its successor statutes.

A further obstacle to Aboriginal aspirations is the fact that the Constitution Act, 1867, distributed all law-making powers between the two orders of government, federal and provincial. Thus part of the problem today is to create a space for Aboriginal self-government within the dual monopoly of power established by the federal constitution.

Just as the provincial legislatures continue to hold authority over the local governments under their constitutional jurisdiction, so the federal parliament continues to have jurisdiction over the band governments established under the Indian Act of 1876. For many years the band-and-council governance of reserves was almost completely hollow; administrators with the Department of Indian Affairs made all the key decisions. Since the 1960s, Indian Affairs has withdrawn from day-to-day administration on reserves, but the strictures of the Indian Act, along with the broader bureaucratic and accountability procedures of the federal government, continue to constrain band leaders. The governance power that band councils exercise is not fully theirs, but is merely delegated to them by the Act. And rather than being general in scope it is severely limited to local matters. The federal minister of Indian Affairs has wide powers to disallow or override band actions, set aside elections, and suspend financial management. Although band governments have a range of options for the specifics of their financial relationship with the federal government (involving more or less autonomy), they have no options with respect to the basic legal status of the band council established in the Act. The band members hold band property—both land and most housing—communally, are exempt from many federal and provincial taxes, and pay no municipal property tax. Bands' own-source revenues come from the sale of natural resources, leasing of land and buildings, and direct profits from band enterprises. Still, for most bands these sources provide no more than 10 per cent of the total annual budget; the rest of their funding comes from annual transfers negotiated with the Department of Indian and Northern Affairs (RCAP, 1996: vol. 1, ch. 9; Abele et al., 2005). There are more than 600 bands currently registered under the Indian Act, with a median size of fewer than 1,000 persons. The relatively small size of each band limits its financial and administrative capacity; thus there is concern that First Nations governments, as they now generally prefer to be called, are simply too small to serve as the basis for broader innovation in Aboriginal self-government.

Because Aboriginal peoples were not considered partners in the creation of the federation, no provision was made for them, either formally or by convention, to have representation in its central intrastate institutions—in parliament, in cabinet, or in any other government post. Indeed, the treatment of many Aboriginal peoples assumed one of two difficult choices: a separate existence as registered 'status Indians' on reserves and outside Canadian citizenship (at least until the Diefenbaker Bill of Rights of 1960), or as 'non-status Indians', living off-reserve and undistinguished from other Canadians. Therefore there is a historic legacy of division between the status and non-status Indian population.

The two other groups that, with Indians, are classified as Aboriginal peoples are the Inuit and the Métis. Formerly known to outsiders as Eskimos, the Inuit—Inuktitut for 'the people'—are indigenous to the territory north of the tree line, in the Northwest Territories, Nunavut, northern Quebec, and Labrador. Their language and culture differ significantly from those of their First Nations neighbours. The Métis are descendents of the intermarriage of Aboriginal people and Europeans, beginning in the fur trade era. Although there are Métis people in eastern Canada, the Métis Nation is centred in the west, where a unique Métis society, culture, and economy were well established by the time of Confederation. Today the Métis Nation is pursuing a number of Aboriginal rights, mainly relating to traditional resource use. Neither the Inuit nor the Métis have ever been part of the Indian Act regime, but they were recognized as Aboriginal peoples in the Constitution Act, 1982.

Since Aboriginal governments were recognized by the Canadian state only in the form of band councils, they did not have the standing or the political clout to be included in the evolving executive federalism of the twentieth century. Worse, Aboriginal peoples became 'victims of the competitive nature of Canadian federalism' (Papillon, 2008: 296). The federal and provincial governments have alternately claimed jurisdiction over Aboriginal persons or rejected responsibility for them as it suited their interests. This has been especially true for the growing numbers of Aboriginal people living in cities, who in 2006 made up 54 per cent of the Aboriginal population in Canada, and for the Métis, who have often fallen between the jurisdictional cracks, ignored by both the established orders of government.

For these reasons Aboriginal peoples have been largely alienated from federalism and the Canadian state in general. From the late 1970s onwards, the question of whether and under what terms Aboriginal peoples should fit into the federal system has been a significant constitutional and political issue. The importance of this issue is much greater than mere numbers might suggest (Murphy, 2005: 22). According to the 2006 Census, the 1.2 million Aboriginal

Canadians make up only 4 per cent of the total Canadian population. However, the Aboriginal population is growing six times faster than the non-Aboriginal population. It is much younger than the Canadian average, with 48 per cent under the age of 24, compared with just 31 per cent for the non-Aboriginal population (Statistics Canada, 2008). And the social and economic conditions in which many Aboriginal people live—both in Aboriginal communities and in cities—are far below Canadian norms. Incomes and employment rates are far below average, while rates of financial dependence are far above. Infant mortality rates, life expectancy, and disease prevalence (including addictions) are also much worse in Aboriginal communities. These are the bare facts that give Aboriginal issues their moral and political urgency.[2]

FROM COLONIALISM TO ABORIGINAL NATIONALISM

Political relations between the European settlers and Aboriginal peoples under the French and British empires, though troubled, were on a more equitable footing than they would be after 1867. According to contemporary observers and current scholars alike, the early French and British treaties (those before 1763) described essentially confederal arrangements, in which Aboriginal peoples retained a large degree of autonomy and continued to govern themselves (RCAP, 1992: 11–19). The Royal Proclamation of 1763, covering most of what is now eastern Canada, confirmed the right of Aboriginal people to their traditional lands, which by law could be ceded only through formal treaty negotiations with the Crown.

Even so, by Confederation, the room for nation-to-nation relationships had shrunk considerably as a result of European settlement, the division of British North America into provinces and territories under settler control, and the much reduced importance of the military and economic partnership that had been the basis of the more equitable early relationship. Eleven new treaties (the 'numbered' treaties) were signed between 1871 and 1921 with Aboriginal nations west of the Great Lakes, but the Aboriginal–state relationship became increasingly colonial. Under the Indian Act regime in particular, lands for exclusive Aboriginal use were reduced to small, often isolated reserves, and policies were specifically designed to hasten assimilation by suppressing Aboriginal languages, cultures, and traditional forms of governance.

Canadian citizenship was extended to all Aboriginal persons in 1960, and in 1969 the Trudeau government issued a White Paper proposing an end to the special relationship of Aboriginal peoples with the Canadian state. The White Paper outlined plans for the abolition of the Indian Act regime, an equitable end to the historic treaties entered into with Aboriginal nations, and the final extinguishment of all special Aboriginal rights. Arguing that 'the road of different status has led to a blind alley of deprivation and frustration' it sought full equality and undifferentiated citizenship for persons of Aboriginal descent, so that Aboriginal peoples would be treated constitutionally no differently from any other

Canadians (Cairns, 2000: 51–2). Ironically, it was this plan that sparked a powerful movement for Aboriginal rights. Led by treaty-based First Nations in the west, Aboriginal political organizations successfully resisted the proposed changes. They galvanized Aboriginal peoples around national and local strategies to restore their cultures, their rights to Aboriginal title, and their rights under the various, near-dormant treaties, and to replace the Indian Act regime with constitutionally protected self-government. In the process they found allies in progressive political parties and other movements, in the media and academic community, and in an international movement of decolonized indigenous peoples.

Major victories came with the Supreme Court's judgments in the *Calder* (1973) and *Baker Lake* (1980) cases,[3] which established the legal grounds for recognition of Aboriginal title and claims to compensation for lands seized without due consent. An even more important milestone was the recognition and affirmation of 'existing Aboriginal and treaty rights' in section 35 of the Constitution Act, 1982. Just as the Charter of Rights and Freedoms has empowered rights-oriented citizens and interest groups in Canada as a whole to litigate their interests with the state, so it has empowered Aboriginal people to use the courts to define and defend their rights in the Constitution. As Martin Papillon has put it, the Supreme Court has 'effectively created a legal space, albeit a limited one, for Aboriginal peoples to assert their presence in the political landscape of the Canadian federation' (2008: 298). Major cases such as *Guerin, Sioui, Sparrow, Delgamuukw,* and *Marshall*[4] have established rights to land, resource sharing, and aspects of governance and Aboriginal culture. Other cases have not been successful, however, and the courts—especially the Supreme Court of Canada—have come under increasing scrutiny and criticism for their generally expansive interpretation of Aboriginal rights; the controversy in this area is clearly reminiscent of the one surrounding judicial activism and the role of the courts in connection with the Charter.[5]

Other consequences flowing from the 1982 constitution included the prospect in section 35(3) that new treaties based on land claim agreements could also gain constitutional protection—a vitally important provision given that huge expanses of traditional Aboriginal territory, including Labrador, most of the Yukon and Northwest Territories, and practically all of British Columbia, had never been subject to treaties and title to the land had not been formally ceded to the Crown. This has set in train a series of negotiations, some concluded but many still ongoing, for new land settlements and treaties. (Current treaty negotiations are discussed below.) A second consequence of the new constitution was a series of conferences held in 1983–7 in which the federal and provincial governments met with representatives of the Aboriginal peoples to discuss constitutional matters affecting them, in particular to clarify their rights under section 35. Those discussions resulted in constitutional amendments to section 35, establishing that treaty rights would include existing and future land claims agreements, that Aboriginal and treaty rights were guaranteed equally to 'male and female persons', and that the federal and provincial governments would consult with Aboriginal representatives before amending sections 25 and 35 of the Constitution Act (dealing with Aboriginal rights).[6] Although the process was disappointing to Aboriginal peoples in that significant differences remained on the meaning and implementation of a right to self-government (Hawkes, 1989), it did give Aboriginal leaders a national forum, as well as valuable experience in finding consensus among their very diverse communities.

The limitations of Aboriginal political and legal power became painfully clear in 1987, when—a few weeks after rejecting Aboriginal demands for extensive definition and clarification of their self-government rights—the same federal and provincial governments, meeting at Meech Lake, unanimously agreed to Quebec's conditions for re-entering the constitutional fold. In the long march between Meech Lake in 1987 and the Charlottetown Accord of 1992, which included the famous Mohawk stand-off at Oka in the summer of 1990, Aboriginal peoples played a prominent role. First they helped to block the ratification of Meech; then they played a central role in the negotiation of the Charlottetown agreement, which would have formally established the inherent right of self-government and recognized Aboriginal governments as one of three orders of government in Canada (CICS, 1992). The Charlottetown Accord was rejected by voters, including many Aboriginal people, in the national referendum of October 1992 (Turpel, 1993: 141–4). Nevertheless, the experience made it abundantly clear that most Aboriginal people consider themselves constituent parts of the Canadian federation, and that fundamental change to the constitution cannot take place without their participation.

THE RCAP MODEL AND ITS CRITICS

The opening for major reform of the federal constitution to accommodate and embrace Aboriginal peoples closed in 1992 with no prospect of a return in the foreseeable future. The 'post-constitutional' era has been marked by continuing contestation over the meaning of Aboriginal self-determination and the appropriate model for Aboriginal governance and relations within the federal and intergovernmental system. Even so, we have witnessed a series of political developments that would have seemed impossible two decades ago, which amount to substantial, if at times frustratingly slow, progress towards Aboriginal self-determination and national renewal.

An important part of that progress was the report of the Royal Commission on Aboriginal Peoples (RCAP). Prime Minister Brian Mulroney established the Royal Commission in early 1991, following an undertaking to do so as part of the negotiated end to the armed stand-off in Oka in September 1990. Consisting of three Aboriginal and three non-Aboriginal members, the commission conducted extensive public hearings and other consultations as well as an impressive research program. The key difference this time was that the RCAP sought to be as much an inquiry *of* Aboriginal peoples as it was a commission *on* them. Though time-consuming—the final report was not released until the fall of 1996—and expensive, costing over $50 million, the RCAP produced the most comprehensive review in Canadian history of the constitutional, legal, political, economic, social, and cultural issues affecting Aboriginal Canadians. The final report and recommendations addressed matters at the heart of the federal system, and have essentially become the benchmarks against which subsequent government actions and policy options have been measured.

The RCAP focused primarily on restoration of Aboriginal nationhood and self-determination, finding that only by returning to some approximation of the original 60 to 80 tribal groups ('nations' in the RCAP terminology) in what is now Canada, based on traditional territories and cultures, could the artificial legal divisions and inequalities among Aboriginal peoples be overcome. A nation-to-nation relationship would encompass existing and new treaties, but would require a transition from the 600-plus small, independent band governments to larger, more administratively feasible units. It could encompass participation in governance by nation members living away from the core land base, for example in cities. Such a relationship, in the RCAP view, would also provide for Aboriginal people outside the Indian Act system, especially those living in cities, to exercise Aboriginal rights, including the right to self-government. It envisaged a third order of government negotiating new agreements with the federal, provincial, and territorial governments to deal with jurisdictional powers, financial transfers, and access to land and other resources (RCAP, 1996: vol. 2). In addition to the nation-based territorial model, the report noted two other governance models: the public government model now operating in Nunavut, where Aboriginal persons make up such a large proportion of the population as to be guaranteed significant power, and a 'community of interest' model, a non-territorial form of government for Aboriginal persons living in cities or in a single province, but not governing the traditional land base. In sum, the RCAP vision built on the rights entrenched in the Constitution Act, 1982, and is close to what was proposed in the Charlottetown Accord: a model of Aboriginal self-determination and self-government embedded in the federal system. Among its other key recommendations were a new treaty process, a lands and treaties tribunal, new principles-based financial arrangements, and a new royal proclamation to signal the beginning of a new relationship.

Not all Aboriginal people have accepted the basic RCAP paradigm, however. Existing band chiefs and councils, with all their vested interests in reserve communities, have been wary of any plan to eliminate their power base, even if a new model might ultimately provide their communities with more power. Even more critical have been those who argue for greater separation from the Canadian state than the RCAP recommended, in what would essentially be internationally sovereign enclaves surrounded by Canadian territory (see Alfred, 1999). Other critics have called for a more unambiguous emphasis on treaties: under 'treaty federalism', each Aboriginal nation would have its own treaty with the federal government and exist outside the federation as such (see Henderson, 1994; Ladner, 2003; Tully, 2000; for discussion Papillon, 2008: 296–8). For other

Aboriginal critics, what counts is not so much the model of Aboriginal government that is adopted, but that Aboriginal rights, particularly over lands and resources, be recognized and protected.

Concern over the RCAP and other models of Aboriginal self-determination has been even greater outside the Aboriginal community. Thomas Flanagan, a Calgary political scientist with close ties to the Harper Conservatives, has staked out what is probably the most comprehensive critique of Aboriginal rights and self-government aspirations in his book *First Nations, Second Thoughts* (Flanagan, 2000). He claims there is widespread unease with the notions of Aboriginal nationality and a multinational Canada. He also outlines concerns about the political, economic, and administrative feasibility of constitutionally protected Aboriginal governments with extensive powers akin to those of provinces, though he would support Aboriginal government on a municipal scale. In his view, the best way for Aboriginal societies to make progress would be by emphasizing individual rights—for example, individual ownership of property on reserves that is now held communally. Somewhat more sympathetic to the Aboriginal cause but also concerned about how far Aboriginal national self-determination should be pursued is Alan Cairns. In his book *Citizens Plus* he argues that the RCAP model would create a kind of parallel citizenship, and that the emphasis would be better placed on Aboriginal people's participation in a common, shared Canadian citizenship. He also worries that Aboriginal communities that are set too far apart from the Canadian polity will lose their claim to the financial and other resources their people need to improve their lives (Cairns, 2000).

Responses to the RCAP from the federal, provincial, and territorial governments have been piecemeal. It is not unusual for royal commission reports to be more or less ignored on their release but to provide a long-term blueprint for change. This seems to be the case with the RCAP. Some key aspects of the Commission's recommendations, including policies relating to cultural reconciliation, symbolic recognition, and urban issues, have been taken up by various federal and provincial governments. Moreover, many of the RCAP recommendations were couched in comprehensive, Canada-wide terms. By the time they were released in 1996, four years after the defeat of the Charlottetown Accord, there was no longer a national-scale constitutional reform process able to deal with them. The federal government under Jean Chrétien shied away from large-scale constitutional solutions, preferring to focus on more modest reforms, although these included formal recognition of the inherent right of self-government as one of the 'existing' Aboriginal rights affirmed in section 35 of the Constitution Act, 1982.[7] The key problem, however, continues to be the interpretation of that inherent right. According to Peter Russell,

the [Federal] government's understanding of what the inherent right means is quite different from Aboriginal understandings of that concept. For Aboriginal Peoples . . . self-government and self-determination have to do with the responsibility they have from their creator for looking after their societies and the lands, waters and creatures that sustain them. Authority of this kind may be denied by others but it cannot be taken away or granted to them by other governments or authorities. The federal government's approach, however, continued to be one of devolving powers to Aboriginal Peoples rather than making room for Aboriginal Peoples to recover control over their own societies according to their own evolving traditions (Russell, 2004: 257).

One of the most concrete initiatives undertaken during the Chrétien years was a proposal for a new First Nations Governance Act, to replace the Indian Act. By stressing transparency and accountability, this legislation would have likely made for more effective band governments and improved the administrative relationship between those governments and the federal Department of Indian Affairs and Northern Development (DIAND). But it was no substitute for genuine negotiation of the broader inherent right of self-government and thus did not have the support of the First Nations leaders.

EMERGING MODELS OF ABORIGINAL GOVERNANCE AND INTERGOVERNMENTAL RELATIONS

More than a decade after the release of the Royal Commission report, some key governance structures remain unchanged, while some new ones are emerging. The Indian Act and the 600 small band councils are still in place. Neither non-status nor registered Indians living off-reserve benefit from self-government. And Métis claims to land, resources, and self-government have been only minimally realized, proceeding for the most part through the courts.

As Michael Murphy concludes, the literature on Aboriginal issues has tended to focus on abstract legal and normative theories rather than what actually works on the ground (Murphy, 2005: 8). Yet what is happening on the ground is in fact impressive. Four key developments are worth noting here.

First, significant progress has been made in settling comprehensive land claims and establishing self-governing arrangements in the northern territories, as well as in Labrador. In none of these areas has the Indian Act applied. Land claims agreements have been concluded with the Inuit and Innu peoples of Labrador, the Council of Yukon Indians (CYI), and the Tlicho people in the western part of the Northwest Territories. In the Inuit-dominated eastern part of the old Northwest Territories, a claims settlement reached in 1993 with the Inuit led to the division of the territory and the creation of the Nunavut public government in 1999. Covering a quarter of Canada's land mass, the new territory stands as a major milestone in self-determination for the Inuit, who constitute roughly 85 per cent of its population.

In Yukon, where Aboriginal peoples make up about 20 per cent of the population, the federal and territorial governments reached a comprehensive umbrella agreement with the CYI on a framework for self-government in 1993. Negotiations with the 16 individual First Nations on community self-government agreements are underway, of which several have now been completed. In the Northwest Territories, where Inuvialuit, First Nations, and Métis peoples constitute about 50 per cent of the population, negotiations are proceeding on two tracks: one to settle land and resources claims (essentially a new treaty process) and self-government agreements with the specific Aboriginal peoples and the other to devolve powers from the federal government to the territory, as well as further devolution within the territory. The negotiations are complex and seem frustratingly slow, but the stakes could not be higher for the Aboriginal peoples concerned, given their growing populations and the fact that the Territories are in the early stages of what could be a major resource and economic development boom.

Second, there is the British Columbia Treaty process, in which some 40 First Nations are negotiating with the provincial and federal governments on treaties specifying land use, resource sharing, and governmental jurisdiction. The landmark achievement here is the Nisga'a agreement, ratified in 1999, which established local and regional government by the Nisga'a people over a defined territory in northern British Columbia, with participation by members of the community resident in urban locations in the province. The agreement is truly federal in that it specifies in significant detail the sharing of jurisdictional authority between the federal parliament, the province of British Columbia, and the Nisga'a government. In cases of conflict, the federal or provincial law is to prevail in most instances, but there are some circumstances in which the Nisga'a law takes precedence (Russell, 2004: 260–1). The Nisga'a deal has been criticized by non-Aboriginal people as overly cumbersome and ceding too much jurisdiction to the Nisga'a, and by Aboriginal people as conceding too many Aboriginal rights (and too much land), but it is now entrenched and protected under the constitution.

Third, a host of innovative arrangements have been negotiated by First Nations, either individually or in groups, with federal and provincial governments to assume control over various aspects of community life. This is a ground-up approach focusing on regional and local solutions. Examples include the 1997 agreement under which the Mi'kmaq in Nova Scotia have gained what amounts to shared jurisdiction over primary and secondary education in the province (a model now being extended to other provinces); resource co-management agreements and on-going negotiations in most provinces and territories, covering wildlife and fisheries as well as forest and mineral resources; and partnership contracts between governments (federal, provincial, and municipal) and dozens of urban Aboriginal organizations for the conception, planning, and provision of public services to meet the specific needs of Aboriginal people living in cities. In addition, it is worth noting that, despite the restrictions of the Indian Act, considerable progress has been made towards devolution of program and financial responsibilities to Aboriginal people.[8] Examples include options for levying property taxes, multi-year financial arrangements to provide flexibility in program funding, and the establishment of urban reserves.

Fourth is the continuing effort to develop national-level responses to Aboriginal demands through negotiation with national Aboriginal organizations such as the Assembly of First Nations (AFN) and the Congress of Aboriginal Peoples. The primary variable here is of course the overall policy approach of the federal government in power, but the nature of Aboriginal leadership is also important. Since 1992 the government with the most ambitious agenda for reforming the federal–Aboriginal relationship has been that of Paul Martin in 2003–6 (Abele, Lapointe, and Prince, 2005). Following the failure of the Chrétien government's attempt to replace the Indian Act, the Martin government focused on symbolic acts of recognition and respect for Aboriginal peoples, while improving basic programs to cover essential services such as health, water, and housing in Aboriginal communities. The culmination of this effort came in November 2005 with the signing of the Kelowna Accord, in which national Aboriginal organizations, the provinces and territories, and the federal government reached agreement on a plan to increase program funding to Aboriginal communities by $5 billion over ten years (CICS, 2005). Martin's key ally in this more pragmatic effort was AFN Grand Chief Phil Fontaine.

The Conservative government of Stephen Harper chose not to honour Martin's Kelowna agreement. Instead it proceeded with a controversial plan to compensate former students of the residential school system and present a formal apology in the House of Commons. It also worked with the AFN to draft new legislation, passed by parliament in 2008, that will expedite the settlement of specific land claims. However, the Harper government clearly does not place the same priority on Aboriginal issues that the Martin government did. One reason is likely neoconservative opposition to expensive programs and complex governance arrangements; another may be indifference, if not hostility, to some Aboriginal aspirations on the part of the Conservatives' electoral base. Still, even this government has not abandoned the ongoing negotiations for new treaties and self-government agreements outlined above, and of course it retains its legal and constitutional obligations, clearly outlined by the courts, to uphold and respect Aboriginal and treaty rights.

Meanwhile, Aboriginal governments and organizations continue their diverse and often innovative efforts not only with the federal, provincial, and territorial governments but also with municipalities and a wide variety of business, labour, and other civil-society organizations across a wide range of policy fields, including education, policing, health care, social services, economic development, and land and other resource management. Aboriginal organizations are on the ground across the country delivering essential services to their people. The resulting multilevel governance is a major contribution to the ongoing evolution of the federal system (Papillon, 2008: 303–6). Except in the very largest of Canada's cities, this multilevel governance is arguably much more advanced on matters concerning Aboriginal people than it is on municipal affairs. And though some aspects of Aboriginal governance are still highly dependent on the 'senior levels' of government, especially in financial terms, the cohesiveness and collective values of Aboriginal communities provide advantages in intergovernmental relations that even the largest Canadian city governments are unlikely ever to possess.

In conclusion, the Aboriginal governance revolution—if that is not too bold a word—has forced us to change our perceptions of the Canadian federation. We are living with a new reality of diverse self-rule and shared-rule arrangements that reflect an increasingly broad, if still contested, recognition and accommodation of Aboriginal nationalism. Aboriginal governance and intergovernmental relations remain works in progress. There is as yet no overarching constitutional framework into which every Aboriginal people and aspect of Aboriginal rights can be placed. Yet major legal, political, and administrative changes are underway, along with a slow but steady process of cultural, social, and economic renewal in Aboriginal communities. In the meantime, social and economic challenges continue to mount. The persistence of poverty, underdevelopment, and abuse in many Aboriginal communities is unacceptable in a society as wealthy and developed as Canada as a whole. Progress in bridging the gap between these two realities is painfully slow, but much has been achieved since 1969. The hope and expectation of the Aboriginal peoples, and of many other Canadians, is that achieving greater self-determination will play an even bigger role in bridging the gap in the years to come.

Conclusion: Ambivalent Federalism

THE DEEP PATHWAYS OF CANADIAN FEDERALISM

Many years ago the constitutional scholar J.A. Corry is said to have advised a student that 'A neat and tidy mind is a crippling disability when studying federalism' (quoted in Burgess, 2007: 2). The complexity and nuance of Canadian federalism are certainly daunting. Yet mastering the details is essential for a deeper understanding. As in any complex political and social system, the full truth is in the minutiae. But understanding is also to be found in looking at big pictures and identifying the broad forces driving the federation and its evolution. Thus far we have focused on the specifics of the Canadian federal system and the relations between its constituent governments. Now, in our concluding chapter, we turn to a summary of the key characteristics of Canadian federalism, a portrait that can emerge more clearly now that the detail has been laid out.

Our grasp of why the federal system operates the way it does and what drives its structures and dynamics is based on three foundational concepts in the political science of complex government systems: federal society, its ideology and values, and the nature of the specific regime, including its institutions and operating norms. While the overall system can be seen as the product of interaction between state and society, we believe that institutions are embedded in a specific society and nurtured by a specific political culture (ideology and values), both of which are also federal (cf. Cairns, 1986). Canadian federalism is ambivalent in both its goals and its character, and its foundational premises remain contested, primarily because the federal components of the society and political culture are often at odds with the existing institutions and their operating norms.

And as much as these institutions reflect their social and cultural context, they occupy deeply grooved pathways—reinforced after 140 years of operation.

For prominent scholars of federalism, such as W.S. Livingston, a federal society both gives rise to and sustains a federal system of government (Livingston, 1971; cf. Smith, 2004). The underlying society is 'federal', in his view, where there exists diversity that is more than just territorial and where that diversity in itself leads to federal governance. Federalism is thus a political theory of power-sharing for diverse or multiple societies, adopted historically by numerous separate societies that have come together to form a single new political community. The process of union, and the ongoing process of integration that follows, may create a less federal society over time; this has arguably been the case in Australia and Germany. Certainly in Canada the original federal society of French and English linguistic communities, Catholic and Protestant religious communities, and pre-existing colonial units guaranteed that a federal form of union would be adopted in the 1860s for the British North American colonies, rather than the unitary state on the British model that some preferred. Here, however, despite the development of strong integrative forces, we have not seen a lessening of the federal aspect of our society. In English-speaking Canada, including the poly-ethnic immigrant communities that have integrated into it, economic and social mobility and the development of common values and symbols, including the Charter of Rights, have created a vibrant pan-Canadian nationalism. On the other hand, we have an equally vibrant Quebec nationalism, well established in the Canadian psyche since the 1960s, which for much of the past 40 years has posed a serious threat to the sustainability of the federal regime. Less well established but also significant is Aboriginal nationalism, which has its own separatist tendencies, and is certainly capable of resisting absorption into a pan-Canadian political consciousness.

Two other fundamental realities of our federal society are the territorial diversity of the original provinces and the ecological, economic, and cultural differences that are inevitable in a country as vast as Canada. These regional identities remain highly potent, as anyone who has lived in or even visited Calgary, Halifax, or Iqaluit can attest. Still, the regional landscape is changing with intensifying urban development and the westward movement of population and economic clout. An increasingly globalized economy integrated in a North American context also complicates the picture. North–south integration with the United States weakens one of the original rationales for the union—a point not lost on Quebec sovereignists. But there is no discernible lessening of the desire for a separate political community (or communities) north of the US: quite the contrary. In any case, as in 1867, the underlying society in Canada remains resolutely federal in the Livingston sense; the only difference is that the cleavages have changed to some degree.

The second component of Canadian federalism is federal ideology and its underlying basis in the specific political values of the federal society. In the original confederation bargain there were in fact several competing federal ideologies at work, which continue to be reflected in the constitutional regime. Each has its own ideas about the nature of the federal union and the purposes to which it should be put. Many of the founding Fathers of Confederation sought a strong central government that would have a more or less imperial relationship with the provinces, and emphasized the components' common British allegiance and heritage. They assumed that the new union would integrate the diverse colonies over time, reducing regional differences and transcending linguistic and religious differences. Another view of the union, centred in Quebec, envisioned a pact of two nations, in which federal government was not simply a way station to national unity, but a permanent form of power-sharing that preserved minority rights and sectional self-government. Later this view broadened into a view of the federation as a pact among regions or provinces, without the connotation of a special role for Quebec that the two-nations theory entails. The advocates of each of these three ideological perspectives would find comfort in various provisions of the constitution and the ways in which they have been interpreted by judicial review. On many issues, however, the constitution remains ambivalent or silent (Simeon and Robinson, 1990: ch. 3; Whyte, 1987; Gibbins, 1999).

The very act of compromise—a common feature in the founding and sustaining of all federations—reflects another value in federal ideology (Riker, 1964). Federal bargains among competing interests, and the striving for an equitable balance in the institutional design and operation of a federation, are expressions of this spirit. The emphasis on balance between linguistic interests, between federal and provincial powers, and between richer and poorer regions, has been present from the beginning. It is seen in the rhetoric of George-Étienne Cartier's 'new political nationality', in the legal theory of the Judicial Committee of the Privy Council (and later the Supreme Court of Canada), and in the work of more contemporary federal theorists and scholars.[1]

Nonetheless, in general political discourse in Canada, federalism is often restrained rather than bold, and implied rather than explicit. Of course, in the original political debates and election campaigns over union in the 1860s, political factions identified themselves as either for union or against it, and later, when Newfoundland was considering union with Canada in 1947–8, Smallwood's 'confederates' successfully combined a social brand of liberalism with federal values. In recent years, however, it is mainly in Quebec and in the context of significant support for a post-federal future for Quebec (variously known as sovereignty, sovereignty-association, confederalism, or separation) that 'federalists'—defined as those who support a continued federal union with Canada—become a major defining force in politics. Few people in Alberta, Ontario, or Nova Scotia would feel any need to call themselves federalists. In that sense, almost all Canadians outside Quebec would be federalist, but would give their federal ideology meaning through greater or lesser support for regional or provincial autonomy, for regional equity, for federal balance between the federal and provincial governments, and for pan-Canadian values, among other concepts.

Federal ideology in Canada gets blended with and subordinated to other ideological movements affecting broad or narrow segments of the society. These include conservatism, liberalism, socialism, and variants of nationalism. Social democrats and social liberals tend to promote a view of federalism that empha-sizes pan-Canadian standards and social entitlements, as well as strong support of individual and collective rights, particularly as expressed in broad interpreta-tions of the 1982 Charter of Right and Freedoms. At the same time they recog-nize the value of federalism in providing multiple sites for progressive politics; a frequent example is the pioneering of medicare in Saskatchewan in the 1960s. Economic liberals and conservatives would tend to support a more decentralized vision of federalism and its operation, emphasizing the 'classical' interpretation based on the division of powers and provincial autonomy over social programs, with somewhat less emphasis on regional sharing. As liberals they would also support the Charter, but not perhaps in its broadest interpretations. Neoconservatives and others have been inspired by economic theorists of the public choice school who stress the importance of federalism for preserving liberty and enhancing democratic participation. Their emphasis is on competi-tive federalism: reduced overlap among jurisdictions, less collusive cooperation (that is, fewer deals behind closed doors among governments), and more diverse policy outcomes. Finally, nationalists too find federal ideology useful, as long as it serves national goals. In Quebec even federalist parties must put Québécois national perspectives first. Aboriginal nationalists will similarly embrace feder-alism where it suits their interests—for instance, in the concept of treaty federalism. Canadian nationalists are more conflicted. Few would want a non-federal future for Canada, and all are realistic enough to recognize that Canada is not governable in the absence of federalism. There is a simple, patriotic support for the federal union, but often without a deep understanding of what the actual operation of the federation means for national goals (according to a *Globe and Mail* poll, few Canadians know that the provinces own their natural resources, let alone support the idea) (*Globe and Mail*, 26 Jan. 2008).

One more characteristic of Canada's political culture is important to under-score. This is the changing nature of democratic norms and political beliefs in citizens' rights and capacity to judge for themselves about political matters. In recent decades we have witnessed a significant decline in deference to authority among Canadians, a trend that is consistent with decreasing trust in government and a general decline in citizens' sense of their ability to change government policies (Nevitte, 1996, 2002). This has had major consequences for the practice of elite accommodation that has made possible so many of both the initial and the sustaining compromises in the history of the federation. Most analysts would cite this change in the political culture as a major factor in the failure of the Meech Lake and Charlottetown accords, placing significant limits on what polit-ical leaders can achieve without mass support. These limits, though not unique to Canada, certainly present a challenge to the politics of federal integration in a diverse and divided society. They make it especially important that federal ideology be articulated in such a way that ordinary citizens can understand and act on it.

The actual federal regime is the third element in our summary sketch of Canadian federalism. Students of Canadian politics have had drilled into them the three main features of the overall Canadian regime: parliament, federalism, and the Charter. In terms of the daily operation of our federation, the combination of a federal constitution with Westminster parliamentary traditions is by far the most prominent institutional feature, not only in the actual rules but also in the conventional norms that drive the regime. Canada was the first parliamentary federation in history, and one characteristic it shares with all the others that followed (Australia, Germany, India, and Malaysia, among others) is the dominance of the executive in intergovernmental relationships—a dominance exemplified by 'executive federalism' discussed at some length in this book. Executive dominance—arising from the fusion of the executive and legislative branches in the form of government cabinets drawn from and responsible to the legislature—remains a fact of life for government in Canada at both the federal and the provincial level. Executive federalism is a by-product of that fact.

The second major regime feature is the distribution of powers. Canada is unique in that its constitution sets out two long lists of exclusive federal and provincial legislative powers. Most federations rely much more on concurrent or shared powers. Over time, depending on the public mood and policy necessity, Canadian governments have cooperated extensively in ways that suggest a more concurrent spirit (for example, in the creation of national social programs, or in the negotiation and implementation of free trade agreements). But the presence in our federal society of strong social forces working against integration— Quebec nationalism, various movements for greater regional autonomy—acts as a natural brake on cooperation and collaboration to a degree unknown in federations such as Germany, Australia, or even the United States. These social forces have been supported by the courts' interpretation of the division of powers, especially in the first 75 years. Time and again they emphasized the 'watertight compartments' of legislative jurisdiction, or at the least the need to retain federal–provincial balance in awarding jurisdiction in case of disputes. The result has been a federal system that continues to put a much greater emphasis on the autonomy of constituent units than do most other federations, where concurrent or federal framework legislation serves as a significant constraint on the actions of states or provinces.

Third, the relatively decentralized nature of fiscal federalism in Canada—for instance, the provinces' ownership of their natural resources, and the fact that federal–provincial transfers are largely unconditional—reinforces the legal capacity of the provinces to act on their own, often in competition with one another. Although the enormous differences in fiscal capacity between the smaller provinces and a powerhouse such as Alberta means that horizontal imbalance is significant, the vertical fiscal gap between the federal government and the provinces as a whole is nonetheless the smallest among the federations.

The Equalization Program not only illustrates the federation's explicit commitment to horizontal equity but also sustains provincial autonomy.

Finally, our electoral and party institutions also play a role in maintaining the federal system. The single-member plurality electoral system has a tendency to produce majority governments,[2] especially at the provincial level, reinforcing the separate political bases of the federal and provincial party systems. Moreover, the party system in Canada is only weakly integrated (Bakvis and Tanguay, 2008). A Conservative premier such as Danny Williams in Newfoundland and Labrador does not always need the help of the federal Conservative party to get elected. And a federal Conservative government cannot rely on his support either, as the 2008 federal election showed.[3] Each first minister must rely on his or her own electorate. These features reinforce the Canadian tendency towards competitive federalism.

The mantra of provincial autonomy is especially strong in Quebec, which alone resisted the development of the federal welfare state back in the 1950s. The ideology of provincial autonomy is of course rooted in the fact that only Quebec has a French-speaking majority, with a mission to promote and protect its unique society in the North American context. But there also is a strong minority instinct that leads Quebecers to fear that their preferences will be overshadowed by those of 'English Canada'—although the latter has never been as monolithic as many Quebecers assume. Together, Quebec's insistence on autonomy and its fear of persecution as a minority in the Canadian whole have had profound consequences for the federal regime. Not only does Quebec review especially carefully any cooperation proposal coming from Ottawa and the other provinces, and often seek some form of asymmetry in policy or administration, but it also resists any changes to the rules of the federation that might put it in a position to be outnumbered or to lose the autonomy achieved in the original confederation settlement. The effect of Quebec's continuing ideological position is to reinforce the general tendency to competitive and decentralized outcomes. There is no clearer example of this regime feature than the case of the Council of the Federation. As we saw in Chapter 6, the Liberal government of Jean Charest strongly promoted the creation of this new body (achieved in 2003) as a way of increasing the provinces' capacity to reach agreement among themselves. Yet the operating rules of the Council only reinforce the essential autonomy of each member, and do nothing to facilitate substantive outcomes. None of the provinces at the table in 2003 objected. The consequences of this regime feature for Canada's ability to deal with future challenges are taken up later in this conclusion.

First, however, it is worth noting that the current disinclination of the federal partners, and Canadians more generally, to commit to a more cooperative federation, one less wedded to the autonomy of federal and provincial governments, is unlikely to change any time soon. Peter Russell, in his book *Constitutional Odyssey* (2004), probably puts it best. He observes that even in the heyday of efforts at formal constitutional change, from the 1960s to 1992, Canadians failed to express popular support for a new constitutional regime in either a national referendum or a federal election. As significant as the achievements in the 1982 Constitution Act are, Russell contends that since 1867 constitutional change in Canada has generally been much more organic than revolutionary. Moreover, Russell suggests that the window of opportunity for significant formal constitutional change effectively closed with the failure of the referendum on the Charlottetown Accord. In his view, Canadians are tired of repeated attempts to amend the constitution and are wary of the instability engendered by constitutional politics.

If Russell's assessment is correct, one would have to be pessimistic about our future ability to provide for meaningful provincial or regional representation in the Senate, for instance, or permit constitutional recognition of local government, or put Aboriginal self-government on a stronger constitutional footing, or improve the capacity for intergovernmental decision-making, or give more formal recognition to Quebec's national identity. On the other hand, the relatively successful record of organic adaptation through the institutions of executive federalism, judicial review, and fiscal federalism provide grounds for a more optimistic assessment. These processes have contributed significantly to the staying power of the federal regime and remain full of potential.

CONTINUITY AND CHANGE: INTERGOVERNMENTAL OUTCOMES SINCE 1970

We now move from the pathways of federalism to the traffic that has flowed along them. Here we deal with the specific policy outcomes and operations of intergovernmental relations, variables that are dependent on the society, ideology, and institutions of federalism. In several chapters of this book we have examined the interactions and relationships between governments and society. We focused on what can be considered its primary features: the institutional and constitutional frameworks that make up the intergovernmental system; the political leaders and government officials who work the system and animate it; the main economic, social, and political issues that provide grist for the intergovernmental mill; and the major challenges facing the system now and in the future.

What have we learned? At a macro level it appears that the system has changed little since the early 1970s. This was the time when Richard Simeon, in his landmark *Federal–Provincial Diplomacy*, first highlighted the federal–provincial arena as the main crucible for Canadian policy-making. Arguing that federal–provincial diplomacy constituted the modus operandi of Canadian federalism, at least with respect to major policy issues, Simeon drew attention to the people representing the federal and provincial governments, the relations and relationships between them, and the arenas in which they operated. More than 35 years later, the basic institutional framework, the actors, and the strategies that these actors have used in pursuing their interests have remained largely the same.

The first ministers' conference remains at the pinnacle of the intergovernmental system, even if it is used much less today than it once was, while the first ministers themselves remain the primary actors, using the many levers available to them to ensure that they control their government's agenda. Ministers and ministerial councils also remain important, as do the officials of both orders of government as they race from one meeting or teleconference to another, laying the groundwork for another meeting of elected officials, patching up tattered relations after a failed meeting, or, better yet, working out the details of implementation or preparing for a new intergovernmental agreement. As was the case in the 1960s and early 1970s—essentially the era described by Simeon—nongovernmental actors continue to try and gain entry to intergovernmental sessions, with varying degrees of success.

To a lesser extent the same can be said of the public policy issues driving the system. In the 1960s and early 1970s fiscal federalism and social policy were among the main items on the intergovernmental agenda, along with the constitution. The last issue is currently much less prominent. Since the failure of Charlottetown, three prime ministers (four if one includes the brief tenure of Kim Campbell) have declined to reopen the constitutional file, though elements of the constitutional debate still surface occasionally—at the time of the debate around the Clarity Act, for instance, or in proposals to reform or abolish the Senate. But the other two issue domains—social policy, centred on health care, and fiscal federalism—continue to dominate intergovernmental discussion. As we noted above, debate over Quebec's ongoing assertion of its unique identity continues to shape virtually all issues entering the federal–provincial arena. Finally, it is perhaps not a coincidence that from 2004 to 2009 (and counting) we have once again been in an era of minority government at the federal level, as was the case in the 1960s and early 1970s. In brief, to quote Yogi Berra, it's 'déjà vu all over again', despite the sometimes dramatic events of the past three decades.

Those events include two referenda over Quebec sovereignty, the second of which in 1995 failed by only the slimmest of margins; two bitter battles over energy policy in the 1970s and early 1980s between Ottawa and the west (more specifically Alberta); constitutional patriation and the adoption of a Charter of Rights and Freedoms; and two major efforts at constitutional amendment aimed primarily at securing Quebec's position but also secondarily the position of Aboriginal people in the constitution, including a nation-wide referendum that went down to defeat. The same period saw a dramatic transformation of the party system, with the Progressive Conservatives dropping from a governing majority party to just two seats, the rise of the Bloc Québécois in Quebec and Reform in the West, and the Liberals governing with a majority that was anchored almost exclusively in Ontario. This highly regionalized party system, coupled with the Quebec referendum in 1995, suggested that the Canadian federation was on the cusp of the perfect storm; only a 'No' vote in the Quebec referendum prevented the federation from sliding into what could well have been the final end game. By 2004 the Canadian Alliance (previously the Reform party) succeeded in merging with the remnants of the old Progressive Conservative party to create a new Conservative party, which formed a minority government after the 2006 election. Most remarkably, this new, non-traditional, party, originating in the west and seen as the expression of western Canadians' desire to exert far more influence over Ottawa policy-making, has come to look very much like the party of John A. Macdonald and Georges-Étienne Cartier in its mission as an institution of federal integration. As so many times before, Quebec became the lynchpin of the new Conservatives' strategy to become the governing party, one that has been at work not only in the 2006 and 2008 election campaigns, but throughout their time in government. The parliamentary resolution affirming that 'the Québécois form a nation within a united Canada', the decision to give Quebec direct representation on international bodies such as UNESCO, the enrichment of the Equalization Program in response to Quebec's complaints about the supposed fiscal imbalance—all these measures have been part of the same strategy.

Program Review in the mid-1990s and the election of a distinctly right-of-centre government in Ontario, followed by provincially initiated discussions on the state of the Canadian social union, appeared to herald a dramatic transformation of the social safety net that had been brokered and put in place in the 1960s (Banting, 2008). Ottawa, in creating the Canada Health and Social Transfer, at the same time cut overall transfers to the provinces. In return, the provinces were tacitly given more leeway in areas such as social assistance (previously funded under the Canada Assistance Plan) and the environment, but not in health care, where Ottawa retained a keen interest in maintaining its self-proclaimed role as the guardian of medicare. The Social Union Framework Agreement of 1999 promised a new era of collaborative federalism, progress in areas such as mobility rights, transparency, and limits on the federal spending power, despite the fact that Quebec was not a signatory to the agreement. A decade later, SUFA is but a historical memory with no practical effect, while many of the original cuts in transfers to the provinces have been restored.

The Free Trade Agreement with the US of 1989, followed by the North American Free Trade Agreement of 1994, appeared to both proponents and critics to signal a new era of north–south trade flows (Courchene and Telmer, 1998; Hale, 2004); the erosion of Ottawa's sovereignty; the rise of new political and economic linkages in the form of alliances between cities, provinces, and states in various combinations; and new forms of multilevel governance. Yet while municipalities have become more active and cohesive, and Ottawa has been paying more attention to cities and local communities, the primary focus remains on the federal–provincial relationship. Battles between the federal and provincial governments still dominate the intergovernmental agenda. Canadian municipalities, in part working though the Federation of Canadian Municipalities, were successful in raising the profile of municipalities and drawing attention to their enormous infrastructure needs. Yet both Ottawa and the provinces have been very careful in managing the fledging federal–local relationship. Indeed, the Harper government, under the rubric of 'open federalism', has signalled that it prefers working through the provinces and respecting provincial jurisdiction, although in the lead-up to the 2008 election it was not above highlighting the availability of federal infrastructure money to municipalities as part of its pitch to suburban voters.

The 1990s also saw what has been perhaps the single most important challenge to executive federalism so far. Throughout the 1970s and 1980s, executive federalism had been under attack by citizen groups and academics, foremost among them Donald Smiley (1979). This may reflect the general decline in deference to political authority mentioned earlier. In brief, even though the Charlottetown Accord went down to defeat in 1992, the process used to craft it arguably marked a definitive change in the broad political culture. That process involved extensive public consultations, inclusion of Aboriginal leaders directly in high-level negotiations, and, of course, the use of a referendum. 'The End of Executive Federalism?' (Brock, 1995) is the title of an often cited article, which suggested that the executives of the 14 federal–provincial and territorial governments could not go back to their old pattern of negotiating behind closed doors and excluding legitimate actors such as First Nations. Yet this is exactly what happened with the AIT and SUFA negotiations. Aboriginal leaders were excluded, and the many public interest groups that had played an active role in Charlottetown were kept at a safe distance. The spirit of Charlottetown appeared to revive briefly in 2005, when Aboriginal people, the provinces, and the federal government all reached agreement on the Kelowna Accord. But that agreement was quickly rejected by the incoming Harper government. More than three years and one federal election later, there is no reason to expect it will be resuscitated. To be sure, the frequency of first ministers' meetings has been reduced, particularly under Prime Ministers Chrétien and Harper (less so under Martin) and a full-fledged first ministers' conference has become an extremely rare event. But ministerial councils and meetings of senior and middle-ranking officials are as frequent as ever, likely even more so. Indeed, new technologies have promoted increasingly easy communication by e-mail and telephone among the officials laying the ground work for sessions between elected officials.

This summary of the traffic in the pathways of federalism shows that, despite considerable societal and economic changes over the past half-century, both the basic nineteenth-century constitutional framework and the mechanics and practices of twentieth-century executive federalism remain intact. Despite all the tumult and drama, the Canadian federal system appears to be remarkably stable. How well equipped is it to deal with twenty-first century challenges?

CHALLENGES AHEAD

What are those challenges likely to be? Many would cite globalization and an increasing emphasis on north–south trade. The lack of a single securities regulator, the continuing presence of interprovincial barriers to trade, the absence of a coherent labour market strategy, and our lagging productivity growth rate all appear to suggest that Canada could be performing much better. Yet for more than a decade Canada has been near the top of OECD and G8 countries with respect to unemployment, deficit reduction, and overall economic performance. Canada, especially under the FTA and NAFTA, has developed what some might see as an unhealthy dependence on US markets, but even here matters have been improving with the international boom in commodity markets: over the past decade, more of our exports have been going to non-US destinations. The instability of global financial markets in late 2008, and the threat of widespread economic recession, will likely affect Canada's competitiveness as well. Thus the international economic environment will continue to be challenging, but there is no evidence that federalism will be an impediment to the management of the Canadian economy or that Canada's performance will decline in relation to that of other countries. On the contrary, Chapter 11 outlined how the federation managed to achieve a reasonable degree of intergovernmental consensus on major changes in Canada's international trade regime without upsetting the federal balance. Similarly, there is no evidence that regional blocs of provinces or cities, with or without allies south of the border, are problematic (Canada, 2006). The cap-and-trade agreement on carbon emissions announced by several Canadian provinces and US states in 2008 suggests that cross-border alliances can serve to encourage innovation and action.

Executive federalism as we have described it above remains largely unchanged and reflects the strong tendency to decentralization and competition embedded in our federal political culture. However, underpinning executive federalism is the dominance inherent in the executive in the Westminster parliamentary model. Reducing that dominance in the parliamentary context will mean the executive's dominance in intergovernmental relations will also be reduced, or so the argument goes. In recent years such a reduction has often been advocated. Within a model that has been called 'legislative federalism', legislatures could take a more active interest in intergovernmental affairs, with parliamentary reforms at both the federal and provincial levels, including but not restricted to reducing the scope of party discipline or empowering of legislative committees. Review of intergovernmental agreements by parliamentary committees and advocacy groups, as well as the use of these committees as entrees into the system, could affect intergovernmental dynamics, although the consequences might be unpredictable. Baier et al. (2005) as well as Simeon and Nugent (2008) have argued that more direct involvement of MPs or MLAs in scrutinizing the intergovernmental process might well undermine some of the norms of elite accommodation that are still so evident in forums such as the Council of the Federation. Those traditional norms, it should be stressed, led the COF to endorse Quebec's unique position in confederation—an endorsement that, although it fell short of constitutional recognition, was nonetheless a significant development. In other respects, newly empowered MPs of all parties, in responding to what they see as the concerns of Canadians, may feel the need to press for use of the federal spending power in areas under provincial jurisdiction simply in the belief that Ottawa ought to be directly involved in resolving pressing social issues. To the extent that they actually succeed in seeing the spending power deployed more generally, this could exacerbate existing jurisdictional disputes with provincial governments or trigger new ones.

Responding to the needs and demands of Aboriginal peoples will be another continuing challenge. We have seen clear progress on these issues, both in Aboriginal societies and institutions and in their relations with the Canadian state, including the intergovernmental system. However, problems will continue to grow with the Aboriginal population. The greater visibility of the problems will lead governments to address the issues in more substantial ways, which could lead to more comprehensive institutional reform.

Yet it is difficult to foresee a resolution of Aboriginal constitutional concerns, especially if Quebec's ambivalent position in the federation is not addressed. Quebecers' support for major regime change in the form of secession (or sovereignty) has reached new lows in recent years and its major proponent, the Parti Québécois, does not favour another referendum, at least for now. But support for some sort of change in the relationship between Quebec and Canada remains strong. Only a small minority of Quebecers support the status quo. Yet to address Quebec's constitutional issues without also addressing those of Aboriginal peoples would seem to take us back to Meech Lake, while addressing both sets of issues at the same time would take us back to Charlottetown. No one wants to return to either Meech Lake or Charlottetown anytime soon. How, and under what political circumstances, one could foresee a return to comprehensive constitutional negotiations remains as unclear now as it was in 1992—underscoring Peter Russell's observation that since 1992 the federation has essentially reverted to its more standard pattern of organic, incremental evolution.

The ambivalent and paradoxical position of Quebec brings us to the final item on our list of the fundamental challenges facing the Canadian federation. This is the absence of effective mechanisms, institutions, and decision rules governing the resolution of even relatively mundane matters. The years since the failure of Charlottetown have seen the creation of the AIT and the COF, both designed to deal with major issues affecting relations between governments: internal trade in the case of the AIT and national as well as interprovincial issues in the case of the COF. Both of these bodies stopped short of adopting meaningful rules for achieving co-decision on substantive issues, and the AIT's dispute resolution mechanism has been criticized as weak-hearted (Brown, 2006). Papillon and Simeon (2004) have suggested that one of the main reasons the FMC constitutes the 'weakest link' in the intergovernmental system is its lack of meaningful decision rules.

The working rules of our intergovernmental system reflect the strong political culture of competition and arm's-length autonomy among governments. With few exceptions—notably the constitutional amending formula (section 38, Constitution Act, 1982) and the rules governing changes to the Canada

Pension Plan—agreement in Canadian intergovernmental relations is achieved by consensus alone. Typically, decisions that will produce substantial and binding outcomes require unanimity. Thus even the smallest participant has veto power. Otherwise, reaching a consensus means accepting the kind of watered-down general principles and anodyne language typical of international diplomacy. Three reforms already adopted in other federations or quasi-federations might be helpful in Canada. First, intergovernmental bodies could increase their decision-making capacity by adopting a 'qualified majority' rule. Because this model requires more than a simple majority of votes for a decision to pass but stops short of demanding unanimity, it speeds up the decision-making process. At the same time, because it allows for as many votes to be taken as necessary to achieve agreements binding on all parties, it gives decision-makers a chance to get more deeply into the substance of the matter at hand. Second, intergovernmental councils could increase the institutional support available to them by establishing more bodies (secretariats, for instance) capable of undertaking independent research. Third, greater frequency and regularity in scheduling, and clearer provisions for agenda-setting, would not only permit all governments involved to agree in advance on what is to be discussed at annual or semi-annual conferences, but would allow for more thorough preparation. All these features are found in the Council of Ministers of the European Union, and the intergovernmental system in Australia (Brown, 2002; Scharpf, 1999; Painter, 1998).

On the other hand, ambiguity remains an important element in governing the Canadian federation. In the past, the cloaking of intergovernmental agreements in ambiguity has allowed the various actors to read into such agreements their particular objectives and understandings and to reach a consensus of sorts. In a diverse and binational federation such as Canada, 'institutionalized ambivalence' (Tuohy, 1992) can go a long way towards preserving harmony and stability. To repeat Harvey Lazar's observation: ambiguity 'was the mid-wife of Canada's birth [and] remains central to the Canadian politics of today' (Lazar, 2004: 4). Many of the intergovernmental success stories noted above involved the judicious application of ambiguity. Similarly, Gagnon and Erk (2002: 324) note that 'when important differences between the constituent nations of a federal partnership exist, ambiguity can be a potential source of longevity for the federal arrangements.' But they also stress that ambiguity must be supported by an underlying trust among the federal partners.

The benefits of ambiguity notwithstanding, greater precision and transparency in some of the ground rules governing the operation of the federation may still be beneficial in an era where citizens are more sophisticated and less deferential. They might also help to forestall increasing centralization of the system, if only because in the face of stalemate the federal government is often the only government that can fill the resulting power vacuum. The Clarity Act of 2000 showed how helpful it can be to establish some basic rules and understandings. In recognizing the legitimacy of a province's attempt to secede from the federation—

following the expression of the people's consent through a referendum on a clear question—and by specifying the mutual obligations of both parties, the Clarity Act has largely succeeded in lowering the temperature of the sovereignty debate. It has also allowed the debate to shift focus to the question of clearer recognition of Quebec's position within the Canadian federation.

The most powerful actors in the federal system—the federal government and the largest provinces—have the most to gain from continued ambiguity and loose working rules in intergovernmental relations, since these give them the flexibility they need to either take a strong public stance or fudge the issues, as it suits them. According to the theory of competitive federalism, power in a federal system is best kept divided and at arm's length, and governments should not be encouraged to rely too much on cooperation. Certainly formal requirements for joint decision-making can lead to political gridlock, as has been the case in the past in Germany and the European Union (Scharpf, 1988; 2006). Yet in light of our own regionalized political culture and strong provincial autonomy, we would argue that Canada may suffer from too much competition rather than too little. There are cases where jurisdiction cannot easily be divided, and governments must cooperate. In fact, some of the most difficult challenges facing our system in the future are likely to come in situations where multilevel governance is unavoidable. In such cases—when public health services must be coordinated to deal with an epidemic, for instance, or a plan established to reduce our carbon footprint, or a strategy developed for negotiating with the US on softwood lumber—failure to achieve timely and substantive multilevel governance will be costly.

If political consensus across the country is sufficiently strong, intergovernmental agreement does usually follow, as happened with respect to health care funding between 1998 and 2004. But what about issues such as greenhouse gas emissions, where the interests and possibly the values of Canadians seem deeply divided? The record of achievement on this issue has so far been weak. In such cases ambivalence leads in the short run to mutual veto and in the longer run to a vacuum that can be filled only by the federal government, which could well argue that the courts should award it permanent jurisdiction in that area. More effective rules for genuine federal–provincial and interprovincial co-decision could limit institutional ambiguity and the freedom of movement of each government, while forestalling central dominance of the system. Changing the rules to allow more effective joint decision-making would be difficult, but the changes could be incremental and need not involve constitutional amendment. Reaching basic agreement on such rules is likely the most critical challenge facing the Canadian federation over the coming decades.

Meeting that challenge will not be easy, but there is a lot to be optimistic about. As hard as it may be to make the federal system work, and however strongly its underlying values and premises may be contested, it is nonetheless the political system that makes Canadian unity possible. It is the platform on which millions of Canadians get on with their productive lives, building one of the world's largest and most dynamic economies and achieving a level of human development that ranks regularly in the top ten of the United Nations index. Most Canadians take for granted or ignore the complexities of federalism and the continuing negotiations that are necessary to maintain our union. Their support for federalism, where it exists at all, is often shot through with ambivalence. But few would deny the ultimate success of Canada as a whole. In our view, this success is due in no small measure to our federal arrangement.

Notes

INTRODUCTION

1. There are two exceptions. The constitutional amending formula specifies the so-called 7/50 rule—7 provinces encompassing 50 per cent of the population—for certain areas (further enhanced through federal legislation in 1996 to accommodate Quebec and the West), and unanimity in other areas (Smith 2002a; Heard and Swartz, 1997). A similar rule applies for the Canada and Quebec Pension Plan agreements (see Banting, 1994).
2. See <http://www.australia2020.gov.au/>.
3. On the importance of elite accommodation in divided societies, see Lijphart (1977, 1999). Lijphart and others note that elite accommodation generally involves acceptance of principles of non-majoritarian decision-making so that typically minorities have a good chance to exercise a veto over matters of importance to them and dominant groupings in turn respect the idea that more than a simple majority is required for the passage of significant measures.

CHAPTER 1: UNDERSTANDING FEDERALISM AND INTERGOVERNMENTAL RELATIONS

1. In this book we will generally use the term 'order of government' rather than 'level of government', to emphasize the independent and autonomous nature of governments in a federal system. 'Level' implies a hierarchical relationship that may be apt in some respects but is generally not characteristic.
2. The metaphor comes from Lord Atkin's reasoning in the *Labour Conventions Reference*, A.C. 327 (1937).
3. Donald Smiley (1987) is generally credited with coining the term.
4. Elite accommodation is a key component in what is called 'consociational democracy' a non-majoritarian mechanism for arriving at decisions in democratic political systems. See Arend Lijphart (1977).
5. This definition draws on the work of Brown (2002a), Marks and Hooghe (2001), and Peters and Pierre (2002a).

CHAPTER 2: THE ECONOMIC, SOCIAL, AND INSTITUTIONAL BASES OF CANADIAN FEDERALISM

1. The Canadian north also includes the Arctic Islands, jurisdiction over which was transferred to Canada in 1880 (Abele, 1987).
2. See Michael Bliss (2000). Jennifer Smith (2002b) has written a critical commentary on this perspective, arguing that it is overblown with respect to political culture and dependency in the Atlantic Provinces.

3. In 1890 the Manitoba government abolished support for denominational schools, whose status had been protected under the Manitoba Act of 1870, which provided for the protection of the new province's largely French-speaking Roman Catholic minority. The same act contained a provision that allowed Ottawa to intervene with remedial legislation in the event that the rights of either Catholics or Protestants were not respected by the provincial government. The province's abolition of denominational schools and the use of French in the courts and the legislature was seen as a major affront to the rights of French-Canadians outside Manitoba and resulted in a nation-wide political controversy. Although the federal Conservative government presented remedial legislation to Parliament in 1896, it was never passed and the government itself was defeated that same year. The subsequent Liberal government under Laurier brokered a compromise with Manitoba, under which limited support was provided for French-language instruction and religious education within the public school system.

4. For a fuller discussion of the different conceptions of nation and nationality in the context of larger states and federations see Gagnon and Iacovino (2007), Kymlicka (1995), Taylor (1993), Tully (1995), and Webber (1994).

5. Bakvis and Tanguay (2008: 112).

6. That is, those willing to say 'Yes' to the survey question, 'If a referendum were held tomorrow, how would you vote?' Note that the question asked by polling firms typically referred to 'sovereignty association', reflecting the wording used in the 1980 referendum question. In 2006 the Leger (2008) polling firm changed its question, dropping the word 'association'. For a detailed exploration of sovereignty and its attitudinal correlates see Blais and Nadeau (1992).

7. See also Gagnon and Garcea (1988).

8. Trudeau was particularly troubled by the idea of treaties between different segments of a society. His liberal vision demanded a much more uniform citizenship. See Cairns (2000).

CHAPTER 3: INTERGOVERNMENTAL RELATIONS AND THE POLICY PROCESS: A FRAMEWORK

1. For representative examples of the recent literature in this area see Nye (2004) and Nye and Keohane (2002).

2. The classic piece on the importance of the *intra*governmental dimension is J.S. Dupré (1988).

3. On issues and agenda-setting generally see Kingdon (1984); on Canadian applications and critiques of this literature see Howlett (1997, 1998) and Soroka (2002).

4. This behaviour is often described as 'garbage-can decision-making'. See Atkinson and Powers (1987).

5. The term 'spending power' has a legal and constitutional meaning (i.e., Ottawa has the power to spend, but not manage, in areas not under its jurisdiction). This power is discussed further in Chapter 4, on the constitutional framework.

6. For some representative examples, see Ostrom (1973) and Sproule-Jones (1975, 1993).
7. Among others we may note C.B. Macpherson (1962), Pratt and Richards (1979), Garth Stevenson (1979), Simeon and Robinson (1990), James Bickerton (1990), and Janine Brodie (1990).
8. See Young and Everitt (2005) for an analysis of advocacy groups from a Canadian perspective.
9. See Julie Simmons (2005). For an analysis of various policy networks in Canada see the contributions to Coleman and Skogstad (1990).
10. Representative works include Considine (2005), Fischer and Forester (1993), Forester (1993), Gillroy (1997), and Houghton (2008).
11. See Pal (2005), ch. 3, and Howlett and Ramesh (2003), ch. 5.

CHAPTER 4: THE CONSTITUTION AND CONSTITUTIONAL CHANGE

1. A point established in *Liquidators of the Maritime Bank v. Receiver General of New Brunswick* [1893], A.C. 487.
2. See Table 3.1 in Chapter 3, which shows, among other things, the proportion of provincial revenues derived from federal transfers.

CHAPTER 5: JUDICIAL REVIEW AND DISPUTE RESOLUTION

1. In *A.G. Ontario v. A.G. Canada (the Local Prohibition Case)*, A.C. 348 (1896), the JCPC ruled that 'the exercise of legislative power by the parliament of Canada, in regard to all manners not enumerated in sect. 91, ought to be strictly confined to such matters as are unquestionably of Canadian interest and importance, and ought not to trench upon provincial legislation with respect to any of the classes of subjects enumerated in sect. 92.' Determining what qualifies as a matter of 'Canadian interest and importance' continues to occupy the Court. The effect of the last part of the quotation above makes POGG a third compartment. There is a prior claim to section 92—legislation must first be found to not fit a section 92 heading before it can qualify for POGG justification.
2. The New Deal package was originally referred to the Supreme Court of Canada in November 1935 by an ambivalent Mackenzie King, who had replaced Bennett as prime minister that October. The package of cases included the *Labour Conventions Reference*, A.C. 327 (1937), the *Employment and Social Insurance Reference*, A.C. 355 (1937), and the *National Products Marketing Act Reference*, A.C. 377 (1937). Five of the eight legislated reform measures presented to the JCPC were rejected as *ultra vires* the federal government.
3. By the end of the five years that the 'cap on CAP' existed, federal funding for CAP programs in Ontario had dropped from 50 to 29 per cent. See Allan M. Maslove, 'The Canada Health and Social Transfer: Forcing Issues', in Gene Swimmer, ed., *How Ottawa Spends 1996–97: Life under the Knife* (Ottawa: Carleton University Press, 1996), 288.

CHAPTER 6: EXECUTIVE FEDERALISM: SITES AND SETTINGS, COUNCILS AND CONFERENCES

1. The terms 'prime minister' and 'premier' mean the same thing in their institutional origins. In the early years of the Canadian regime they were interchangeable, but conventional usage eventually settled on 'prime minister' for the federal head of government and 'premier' for the heads of provincial governments and, after the late 1970s, the government leaders of the territories. In Quebec and the French language generally the premier is called the 'premier ministre'. The generic term 'first minister' has been used since the 1970s.

2. See <http://www.scics.gc.ca/serv_e.html> on how CICS sees its role.

3. <http://www.coag.gov.au/index.htm>.

4. For a history of the First Ministers' Conference see CICS (2004).

5. To this end, the Ontario government commissioned Queen's University economist Thomas Courchene to write a detailed working paper on this subject (Courchene, 1996).

6. This involved Nova Scotia's 'Campaign for Fairness'. See <http://www.gov.ns.ca/fairness/>. These developments are examined in greater detail in Chapters 8 and 9.

7. For a review of the history and the various proposals related to the Council of the Federation see Meekison (2003).

8. For a discussion of the promise, and the limitations, of the Council of the Federation shortly after it was launched see the series of papers commissioned by the Institute of Intergovernmental Relations at <http://www.queensu.ca/iigr/working/archive/FedFR.html>.

9. <http://www.scics.gc.ca/menu_e.html>.

10. Meetings of Finance ministers and officials are not listed because they are not serviced by the CICS. Instead they are handled directly by the federal Department of Finance.

11. The official title of this ministerial council was the 'Federal–Provincial–Territorial Council on Social Policy Renewal'.

12. For detailed analysis of ministerial councils see Julie Simmons (2003, 2005, 2008).

13. See Simmons (2005) for a superb analysis of different ministerial councils and associated networks.

14. Struck by the federal government, the Deutsch Commission was composed of a single commissioner, J.J. Deutsch—an economist, the principal of Queen's University, and previously a senior official in Ottawa.

15. See Tomblin (1995) for a more detailed discussion of the origins and development of the Council of Maritime Premiers.

16. <http://www.cmp.ca/cap-pub-en.htm>. This agreement was struck under the rubric of a special 'Conference of Atlantic Premiers'.

17. See, for example, Western Premiers' Conference press release of June 6, 2002: <http://www.scics.gc.ca/cinfo02/850086008_e.html>.

CHAPTER 7: THE MANAGEMENT AND REFORM OF EXECUTIVE FEDERALISM

1. All IGAs have at least four components: basic objectives; a legal mandate; an organizational structure; and political and financial resources. Variations in these components can make for significant differences in the weight that different IGAs carry vis-à-vis line departments and other agencies. The most powerful agencies, which we might term coordinating agencies, monitor and analyze the policies of other governments and often assist program specialists from line departments in negotiating agreements. They have the right to participate in all intergovernmental negotiations, and as part of their legal mandate are required to co-sign all agreements. Because their responsibilities are significant, they often have considerable resources, such as their own social and economic policy groups, which may include specialists in various key areas. Quebec, Alberta, and Newfoundland have all used this model from time to time. These provinces have also been among the most zealous in pursuing their intergovernmental objectives. Other IGAs follow what might be called the cabinet secretariat model: these play more of a coordinating role, reviewing all cabinet memoranda to ensure that all the relevant ministers and departments have been consulted. Although they are likely to have specialized expertise, they can also provide general policy advice and under some circumstances may offer alternative perspectives to those of line departments. Typically, they will not have a legal mandate, but because they are able to review all cabinet memoranda, they can nonetheless be very effective. BC, PEI, and New Brunswick are among the provinces that have relied on this model. A third model can be called the advisory secretariat. IGAs of this type typically report to cabinet and may offer advice, but are not part of the cabinet's regular support apparatus. They also advise line departments and are in a position to offer alternative perspectives. Neither cabinet nor line departments are required to heed their advice, however. Thus their influence depends almost entirely on their relationship with cabinet. See Pollard (1986).
2. See Savoie (1981, 1992).
3. <http://www.tbs-sct.gc.ca/frc-cfr/menu_e.html>.
4. For an analysis of this guardian role and how it has evolved in recent years see David Good (2007, esp. 73–4).
5. For example, Maude Barlow, representing one of the more prominent public interest groups, the 'Council of Canadians', complained bitterly over the 'profoundly undemocratic' process. See Graham Fraser (1999).
6. <http://socialunion.gc.ca/news/020499_e.html>.
7. See the contributions to Banting et al. (2007).
8. For a range of perspectives see papers in the *Special Series of Working Papers on the Council of the Federation*, available online at the Institute of Intergovernmental Relations and the Institute of Research on Public Policy, 2003: <http://www.queensu.ca/iigr/working/archive/2003.html>, accessed May 2008.

CHAPTER 8: FISCAL RELATIONS: BASIC PRINCIPLES AND OVERVIEW

1. Fiscal federalism theory predicts strong similarities in the nature of intergovernmental fiscal relationships in federations around the world. These similarities have been confirmed by comparative studies. For classic literature and recent updates see Musgrave (1959), Oates (1972), Bird (1986), and Ter-Minassian (1997).

2. For a comprehensive historical and structural study of Canadian fiscal federalism to about 1990 see Boadway and Hobson (1993).

3. There is an enormous literature on competing values in Canadian fiscal federalism—a literature that in itself reflects those tensions. For overviews see Boadway and Hobson (1993) and Lazar (2000b). In addition, two recent public reports provide excellent overviews of competing values: see Gagné and Stein (2006) and O'Brien (2006a, 2006b).

4. Our analysis here is informed by Lazar, St-Hilaire, and Tremblay (2004) and Boadway (2005); see also Courchene (2004a), Dion (2004), and Gagné and Stein (2006).

5. Economists specializing in public finance take a keen interest in fiscal federalism, seeking to determine what specific combination of taxing and spending responsibilities is optimal from the perspective of important economic principles such as efficiency, utility, and welfare. Should the federal government be responsible for collecting all taxes on mobile factors such as personal or corporate income? Should the federal government be primarily responsible for redistribution? Should the fiscal capacity of all governments in a federation be the same? Should revenue capacity match expenditure responsibility? These are questions that have engaged theorists and empirical researchers for decades. See references cited in note 1 above; also Breton and Scott (1978).

6. For more detail on tax harmonization and tax collection agreements see Brown, (2001).

7. The text of section 36(2) reads as follows: 'Parliament and the government of Canada are committed to the principle of making equalization payments to ensure that provincial governments have sufficient revenues to provide reasonably comparable levels of public services at reasonably comparable levels of taxation.' For a discussion of the history and effect of section 36 see Brown (2007).

8. See 'Canada's Finance Ministers Meet to Discuss Global Financial Crisis', Toronto, 3 November 2008; News Release, Department of Finance, Government of Canada, online at <http://www.fin.gc.ca/news08>, accessed 24 November 2008.

9. For a thorough review of executive federalism in the finance area see Leslie, Neumann, and Robinson (2004).

CHAPTER 9: FISCAL RELATIONS: CURRENT ISSUES

1. The issues of debt reduction and balanced budgeting are contested politically, but we stand by our assessment that the majority of the Canadian public supported strong fiscal medicine in the 1990s. For various perspectives on the 1995 budget and changing political and public opinion perspectives on fiscal policy in the 1990s, see Courchene and Watson (1997) and MacKinnon (2003).

2. See, for example, the joint position paper prepared for the 1998 Annual Premiers Conference, Provincial–Territorial Finance Ministers, *Redesigning Fiscal Federalism*.

3. For the classic pre-2006 position, see Department of Finance website 'The Fiscal Balance in Canada: The Facts' 2002 at <http://www.fin.gc.ca/toce/2002/fbcfacts2_ e.html>, accessed in June 2002; for a more enduring version of the argument see Dion, 2005.

4. For discussion of the various options open to the Harper government and an analysis of its potential approach to fiscal relations, see *Policy Options* 27, 7 (September 2006). On 'open federalism' see Banting et al. (2006) and Fox (2007).

5. The five principles of medicare incorporated in the Canada Health Act are universality, comprehensiveness, accessibility, portability, and public administration. The act also prohibits extra billing and user fees for hospital and medical care services, and authorizes the use of financial penalties to enforce these prohibitions. The provinces continue to endorse these principles, although there is some pressure within and outside governments to re-interpret them.

6. It should be noted that not everyone agreed with the general diagnosis and prescription outlined by the Romanow report. The Senate of Canada committee chaired by Michael Kirby recommended greater market competition and the injection of private capital (Kirby, 2002).

7. For the 2004 accord see the Health Canada website: <http://www.hc-sc.gc.ca/hcs-sss/delivery-prestation/fptcollab/2004-fmm-rpm/index_e.html>, accessed 18 Jan. 2007.

8. For Romanow's view see Brian Laghi and Simon Tuck, 'The Prognosis is Good', *Globe and Mail*, 17 Sept. 2004.

9. See for example Courchene (1995) and Boessenkool (1996). A broad survey of views in the literature and a comprehensive bibliography are available in O'Brien (2006).

10. The case for Newfoundland and Labrador was made in the report of the Royal Commission on Renewing and Strengthening Our Place in Canada (see Government of Newfoundland and Labrador, 2003); Nova Scotia made its case in a 'Campaign for Fairness'. See <http://www.gov.ns.ca/fairness/>, accessed 18 Jan. 2007. For the position of the Government of Nova Scotia as of May 2008 see Department of Finance website: <http://www.gov.ns.ca/finance/en/home/budget/equalization.aspx>, accessed 24 May 2008; Saskatchewan's case was made by Courchene (2004b).

11. See the text of section 36(2) of the Constitution Act, 1982, in note 7, Chapter 8 above.

12. The text of the October 2004 release can be found at <http://www.fin.gc.ca/toce/2004/eq_tff-e.html>, accessed 22 May 2008.

13. See <http://www.fin.gc.ca/activty/offshore.html>, accessed 22 May 2008.

CHAPTER 10: THE SOCIAL UNION, SUFA, AND HEALTH CARE

1. Respondents were asked to choose which of five issues was most important to them in the election. For 2006 the breakdown was as follows: health care (41.4%), taxes (11.6), social welfare (11.0), corruption in government (27.8), and the environment (6.9) (total N=4,057). For 2004: health care (49.7%), taxes (13.3), social welfare (9.2),

corruption in government (22.6), and the environment (4.4) (total N=4,323). These figures are based on data from pre-election interviews. For details on the two Canadian Election Surveys, see <http://www.ces-eec.umontreal.ca/ces.htm>.

2. For example, Quebec generally embraced the federal proposals for medicare funding in 1970.

3. Richard Simeon (1990) points out that defenders of Meech argued that the new provision would, in fact, strengthen the federal spending power by constitutionally recognizing it, and notes that many observers thought the critiques were unfounded and overblown.

4. This position was best articulated in a paper by Thomas Courchene (1996) commissioned by the government of Ontario. Courchene argued that, ultimately, the provinces should establish a process in which they would collectively develop and enforce national standards and create new national social programs themselves, without the involvement of the federal government.

5. It is mainly in social policy fields that Quebec appears to be disengaged; it takes a more active role in economic and fiscal policy.

6. The federal government agreed to an increase of $2 billion for a total of $14.5 billion for 1999–2001 and a further $0.5 billion to 2003–4. For discussion of these points, see Hobson and St-Hilaire (2000).

7. For examples of policy dealing with children, see Friendly and White (2008).

8. Quebec also participated fully in the first ministers' consensus announced in September 2000 for the further restoration of the CHST funding and to place general conditions on where the new funding would go. However, no mention is made of SUFA in the official statement.

9. See <http://secure.cihi.ca/cihiweb/dispPage.jsp?cw_page=AR_1789_E&cw_topic=1789>.

CHAPTER 11: THE ECONOMIC UNION AND ECONOMIC POLICY

1. Among these were labour and farmer parties and movements from the 1890s; the Progressive movement and party in the west after 1919; the nonpartisan Maritime Rights Movement of the 1920s; the social democratic CCF formed in 1933; and the more right wing populist parties of Social Credit (Alberta) and Bloc Populaire (Quebec) formed in the 1930s.

2. Such suggestions were made by the Macdonald Royal Commission in 1985, and later as part of the 'Canada Round' of constitutional negotiations in 1990–1. See Coleman (1991).

3. See section 36(1) Constitution Act, 1982. For a discussion of the history and effects of section 36 see Brown (2007).

4. The term neoconservatism is used in North America to denote pro-market ideology. In Europe and elsewhere the term 'neoliberal' is used, which captures the essence of the ideological roots more fully, but the two terms can be employed interchangeably.

5. *A.G. Canada v. A.G. Ontario (Labour Conventions Reference)* (1937) A.C. 326.

6. Details on the ongoing progress and mechanism of the AIT are available on the website of the Internal Trade Agreement at <http://www.ait-aci.ca/index_en.htm> (accessed July 2007). For links to bilateral or regional agreements endorsed by the AIT, see link to 'trade enhancement agreements' at <http://www.ait-aci.ca/index_en/progress.htm> (accessed July 2007).

7. On securities regulation integration see the consultation discussion paper released by the Minister's Expert Panel on Securities Regulation at <http://www.expertpanel.ca/eng/documents/public-consultation-paper.php>, accessed 28 May 2008.

CHAPTER 12: THE ENVIRONMENTAL UNION

1. See the contributions to Fafard and Harrison (2000).

2. We are using 'cooperative' and 'cooperation' rather than 'collaborative' and 'collaboration' in this context because the latter terms relate specifically to the concept of collaborative federalism while the former are more inclusive and refer to more than just governments.

3. The case citation is *R. v. Crown Zellerbach*, [1988] 1 S.C.R. 401. For comment see Lucas (1989: 174–7).

4. *R. v. Hydro-Québec*, [1997] 3 S.C.R. 213. For discussion see Baier (2002: 26–7).

5. Under a 'cap-and-trade' system, government sets an overall limit, or cap, on total emissions, but allows polluters to trade emission credits among themselves.

6. <http://www.westernclimateinitiative.org/>, accessed 1 November 2008.

7. Rationalization is often discussed as an example of the New Public Management. See Aucoin (1995) and, specifically on the environment, Doern (2002), Harrison (2002), and Winfield and Macdonald (2008).

8. For a concise review of various federal governments' approaches to the environment from 1972 to 1995, see Harrison (1996). For the Chrétien era, see VanNijnatten and MacDonald (2003). On the climate change file in particular, see Simpson et al. (2007).

9. Emission targets based on industry intensity aim to reduce the amount of emissions per unit of production, but do not aim to reduce emissions overall.

10. See the discussion of the Labour Conventions case in Chapter 11.

11. See the citations in notes 3 and 4 above.

CHAPTER 13: LOCAL GOVERNMENT AND FEDERALISM

1. Part of the analysis for this part of the chapter is drawn from research conducted for the Government of Ontario in 2000, and published in a different form in Brown (2003b).

2. In 2006 Statistics Canada identified 33 census metropolitan areas as 'cities', with populations ranging from 116,570 (Peterborough, ON) to 5,113,149 (Toronto). See <http://www12.statcan.ca/english/census06/data/popdwell/Table.cfm?T=205&SR=1&S=3&O=D&RPP=33>, accessed 29 Oct. 2008.

3. The governments continue to hold these views despite skepticism in academic and other quarters about the claim that amalgamation saves money. See Downing and Williams (1998), Lightbody (1998), Vojnovic (1998), and Sancton (2002).

4. For example, James McDavid (2002: 538), in his study of police services in the new Halifax Regional Municipality following amalgamation, found that the process resulted in 'higher costs (in real dollar terms), lower number of sworn officers, lower service levels, no real change in crime rates, and higher work loads for sworn officers'. For further views see Downing and Williams (1998), Lightbody (1998), Vojnovic (1998), and Sancton (2000).

5. See McMillan (2006).

6. For a useful study on federal–local mechanisms of cooperation, see Stoney and Graham (2008). The study is part of a comprehensive research program on public policy in Canadian municipalities, focusing on the federal role. For information see <http://www.ppm-ppm.ca/>.

7. See Canada (2007). The $33 billion includes the Gas Tax Fund and $4 billion of sun-setting expenditures from previously announced funds, such as the Canada Strategic Infrastructure Fund.

8. <http://www.tc.gc.ca/aboutus/Abouttic.htm>, accessed 23 Oct. 2008.

CHAPTER 14: ABORIGINAL GOVERNMENTS AND FEDERALISM

1. In legal terms, 'Indian' refers to a specific group of Aboriginal peoples defined by the Indian Act; 'status Indians' are registered with the federal government and are entitled to a number of rights and benefits that are not available to 'non-status Indians'. The two other groups officially recognized in section 35(2) of the Constitution Act, 1982, as Aboriginal peoples are the Inuit and Métis. Most of the people formerly called Indian now use either their specific national names (Cree, Nisga'a, Mi'kmaq, etc.) or the more general term 'First Nations'.

2. The Assembly of First Nations has brought together a variety of statistical indicators, drawn for the most part from federal government reports. See <http://www.afn.ca/article.asp?id=764>, accessed 1 June 2008.

3. *Calder et al. v. Attorney-General of British Columbia* [1973] S.C.R. 313 (S.C.C.); *Hamlet of Baker Lake et al. v. Minister of Indian Affairs and Northern Development* (1980)107 D.L.R. (3d) 513 (F.C.T.D.).

4. *Guerin v. The Queen* (1985) 13 D.L.R. (4th) 321 (S.C.C.); *Sioui v. Attorney General for Quebec* (1987) C.N.L.R. (4th) 118 (Q.C.A.); *Regina v. Sparrow* (1987) 36 D.L.R. (4th) 246 (B.C.C.A.); *Delgamuukw v. The Queen* (1997) 3 S.C.R. 1010; *Regina v. Marshall* (1999) 3 S.C.R. 456 (S.C.C.).

5. For varying views on the role of the courts see Macklem (2001), Cairns (2000), Flanagan (2000), and Murphy (2001).

6. Subsections 35 (3), 35(4) and 35.1 were added to the Constitution Act, 1982, by the Constitutional Amendment Proclamation, 1983.

7. See Indian and Northern Affairs, 1995 and 1997.

8. For a succinct review of the various funding arrangements for Aboriginal governments in Canada in place in the year 2000, see Prince and Abele (2000).

CONCLUSION: AMBIVALENT FEDERALISM

1. See for example Trudeau (1968), Lederman (1975), and LaSelva (1996).
2. The tendency is not ironclad. The last three federal elections (2004, 2006, and 2008) have produced minority governments, and in recent years at least five Canadian provinces have elected minorities as well, but majority government is still the rule.
3. 'PM dismissive of Nfld., Premier says' *Globe and Mail* 15 Jan. 2008: A4. During the 2008 election Williams ran what he called an 'ABC' ('Anyone But Conservative') campaign, urging voters throughout the Atlantic provinces to reject Conservative candidates. No Conservatives were elected in Newfoundland and Labrador.

Court Cases

Attorney General of Canada v. Attorney General of Alberta (1916 Insurance Reference), 1 A.C. 589 (1916).

Attorney General of Nova Scotia v. Attorney General of Canada, S.C.R. 31 (1951).

Attorney General of Ontario v. Attorney General of Canada (the Local Prohibition Case), A.C. 348 (1896).

Attorney General of Ontario v. Canada Temperance Federation, A.C. 193 (1946).

Citizens Insurance Co. v. Parsons, 7 A.C. 96 (1881).

Employment and Social Insurance Reference, A.C. 355 (1937).

Fort Frances Pulp & Power Co. v. Manitoba Free Press, A.C. 695 (1923).

General Motors of Canada Ltd. v. City National Leasing, 1 S.C.R. 641 (1989).

In Re: Board of Commerce Act, 1 A.C. 191 (1922).

In Re: Regulation and Control of Radio Communication in Canada, A.C. 304 (1932).

Johannesson v. West St. Paul, S.C.R. 292 (1952).

Labour Conventions Reference, A.C. 327 (1937).

Liquidators of the Maritime Bank v. Receiver General of New Brunswick, A.C. 487 (1893).

Munro v. National Capital Commission, S.C.R. 663 (1966).

National Products Marketing Act Reference, A.C. 377 (1937).

P.E.I. Potato Marketing Board v. H.B. Willis, 2 S.C.R. 392 (1952).

Pronto Uranium Mines, Ltd. v. O.L.R.B., 5 D.L.R. (2nd) 342 (1956).

Reference Re: Anti-Inflation Act, 2 S.C.R. 373 (1976).

Reference Re: Canada Assistance Plan (B.C.), 83 D.L.R.(4th) 297 (1991).

Reference Re: Firearms Act (Canada), 164 D.L.R. (4th) 513 (1998).

Reference Re: The Secession of Quebec, 161 D.L.R. (4th) 385 (1998).

Re: Offshore Mineral Rights of B.C., S.C.R. 792 (1967).

Re: Regulation and Control of Aeronautics in Canada, A.C. (1932).

Russell v. the Queen, 7 A.C. 829 (1882).

R. v. Crown Zellerbach Canada Ltd., 1 S.C.R. 401 (1988).

R. v. Hydro-Québec, 151 D.L.R. (4th) 95 (1997).

Toronto Electric Commissioners v. Snider, A.C. 396 (1925).

References

Abele, F. 1987. 'Canadian Contradictions: Forty Years of Northern Political Development'. *Arctic* 40, 4: 310–20.

———, R. Lapointe, and M. Prince. 2005. 'Symbolism, Surfacing, Succession and Substance: Martin's Aboriginal Policy Style'. In G.B. Doern, ed. *How Ottawa Spends, 2005–06: Managing the Minority*. Montreal: McGill–Queen's University Press.

———, and M. Prince. 2002. 'Alternative Futures: Aboriginal Peoples and Canadian Federalism'. In Bakvis and Skogstad, eds (2002).

Alfred, T. 1999. *Peace, Power and Righteousness: An Indigenous Manifesto*. Toronto: Oxford University Press.

Andrew, C., and J. Morrison. 1995. 'Canada Infrastructure Works: Between Picks and Shovels and the Information Highway'. In S.D. Phillips, ed. *How Ottawa Spends 1995–95: Mid-Life Crises*. Ottawa: Carleton University Press.

Artibise, A., and E.D. Lee. 2000. 'Multiple Realities: The Role of the US Federal Government in Revitalizing American Cities'. Presentation by the Public Policy Research Centre, University of Missouri, St Louis.

Atkinson, M.M., and R.A. Powers. 1987. 'Inside the Industrial Policy Garbage Can: Selective Subsidies to Business in Canada'. *Canadian Public Policy* 13: 208–17.

Aubin, B. 2005. 'Polls May Show Separatism Rising'. *Maclean's*. May 9.

Aucoin, P. 1995. *The New Public Management: Canada in Comparative Perspective*. Montreal: Institute for Research on Public Policy.

———, and D.J. Savoie, eds. 1998. *Managing Strategic Change: Learning from Program Review*. Ottawa: Canadian Centre for Management Development.

Australia. 'Australia 2020 Summit Report: Initial Summit Report'. Canberra: Department of Prime Minister and Cabinet, 2008.

Bache, I., and M. Flinders. 2004. *Multi-Level Governance*. Oxford: Oxford University Press.

Baier, G. 1998. 'Tempering Peace, Order and Good Government: Provincial Inability and Canadian Federalism'. *National Journal of Constitutional Law* 9, 3: 277–306.

———. 2002. 'Judicial Review and Canadian Federalism'. In Bakvis and Skogstad, eds (2002).

———. 2005. 'The EU's Constitutional Treaty: Federalism and Intergovernmental Relations, Lessons from Canada'. *Regional and Federal Studies* 15, 2: 205–23.

———. 2006. *Courts and Federalism: Judicial Doctrine in the United States, Australia and Canada*. Vancouver: University of British Columbia Press.

———. 2008. 'The Courts, the Division of Powers and Dispute Resolution'. In Bakvis and Skogstad, eds (2008).

———, H. Bakvis, and D.M. Brown. 2005. 'Executive Federalism, the Democratic Deficit, and Parliamentary Reform'. In G.B. Doern, ed. *How Ottawa Spends, 2005–06: Managing the Minority*. Montreal: McGill–Queen's University Press.

————, and P. Groarke. 2003. 'Arbitrating a Fiction: The Nova Scotia/Newfoundland and Labrador Boundary Dispute and Canadian Federalism'. *Canadian Public Administration* 46, 3: 315–38.

Bakvis, H. 1991. *Regional Ministers: Power and Influence in the Canadian Cabinet*. Toronto: University of Toronto Press.

————. 1996. 'Federalism, New Public Management, and Labour Market Development'. In P. Fafard and D.M. Brown, eds. *Canada: The State of the Federation 1996*. Kingston: Institute of Intergovernmental Relations, Queen's University.

————. 2000. 'Rebuilding Policy Capacity in the Era of the Fiscal Dividend'. *Governance* 13, 1: 71–103.

————. 2002. 'Checkerboard Federalism? Labour Market Development Policy in Canada'. In Bakvis and Skogstad, eds (2002).

————. 2008. 'The Knowledge Economy and Post-Secondary Education: Federalism in Search of a Metaphor'. In Bakvis and Skogstad, eds (2008).

————, and L. Juillet. 2004. *The Horizontal Challenge: Line Departments, Central Agencies and Leadership*. Ottawa: Canada School of Public Service.

————, and N. Nevitte. 1992. 'The Greening of the Canadian Electorate: Environmentalism, Ideology and Partisanship'. In R. Boardman, ed. *Canadian Environmental Policy: Ecosystems, Politics and Process*. Toronto: Oxford University Press.

————, and G. Skogstad, eds. 2002. *Canadian Federalism: Performance, Effectiveness and Legitimacy*. Toronto: Oxford University Press.

————, and ————, eds. 2008. *Canadian Federalism: Performance, Effectiveness and Legitimacy*. 2nd edn. Toronto: Oxford University Press.

————, and A.B. Tanguay. 2008. 'Federalism, Political Parties and the Burden of National Unity: Still Making Federalism Do the Heavy Lifting?' In Bakvis and Skogstad, eds (2008).

Banting, K.G. 1987. *The Welfare State and Canadian Federalism*. 2nd edn. Kingston and Montreal: McGill–Queen's University Press.

————. 1994. 'The Decision Rules: Federalism and Pension Reform'. In D. Conklin, et al., eds. *Pensions Today and Tomorrow: Background Studies*. Toronto: Ontario Economic Council.

————. 1995. 'Who 'R Us?'. In T. Courchene and T. Wilson, eds. *The 1995 Federal Budget: Retrospect and Prospect*. Kingston: John Deutsch Institute for the Study of Economic Policy, Queen's University.

————. 1997. 'The Past Speaks to the Future: Lessons from the Post-War Social Union'. In Lazar, ed. (1997).

————. 2008. 'The Three Federalisms: Social Policy and Intergovernmental Decision-Making'. In Bakvis and Skogstad, eds (2008).

————, R. Gibbins, P.M. Leslie, A. Noël, R. Simeon, and R. Young, eds. 2006. *Open Federalism: Interpretations, Significance*. Kingston: Institute of Intergovernmental Relations, Queen's University.

Bentley, A.F. 1967. *The Process of Government*. Cambridge, MA: Belknap Press.

Berridge, J. 2002. 'Cities in the New Canada'. Toronto: TD Forum on Canada's Standard of Living.

Bickerton, J. 1990. *Nova Scotia, Ottawa, and the Politics of Regional Development*. Toronto: University of Toronto Press.

Biggs, M. 1996. 'Building Blocks for Canada's New Social Union'. Ottawa: Canadian Policy Research Networks.

Bird, R.M. 1986. *Federal Finance in Comparative Perspective*. Toronto: Canadian Tax Foundation.

———, and F. Vaillancourt, eds. 2006. *Perspectives on Fiscal Federalism*. Washington, DC: World Bank Institute.

Black, E.R. 1975. *Divided Loyalties: Canadian Concepts of Federalism*. Montreal: McGill–Queen's University Press.

Blais, A., and R. Nadeau. 1992. 'To Be or Not to Be Sovereignist: Quebeckers' Perennial Dilemma'. *Canadian Public Policy* 18, 1: 89–103.

Bliss, M. 2000. 'The Fault Lines Deepen'. *Globe and Mail*. May 2.

Boadway, R. 2005. 'The Vertical Fiscal Gap: Conceptions and Misconceptions'. In H. Lazar, ed. (2005).

———. 2006. 'Two Panels on Two Balances'. *Policy Options* 27, 7: 40–5.

———, and P. Hobson. 1993. *Intergovernmental Fiscal Relations in Canada*. Toronto: Canadian Tax Foundation.

Boardman, R., ed. 1992. *Canadian Environmental Policy: Ecosystems, Politics and Process*. Toronto: Oxford University Press.

Boessenkool, K. 1996. *The Illusion of Equality: Provincial Distribution of the Canada Health and Social Transfer*. Toronto: C.D. Howe Institute.

Bourgault, J., ed. 2002. *Horizontalité Et Gestion Publique*. Québec: Les Presses De l'université Laval.

Boychuk, G.W. 1998. *Patchworks of Purpose: The Development of Provincial Social Assistance Regimes in Canada*. Montreal: McGill–Queen's University Press.

———. 2004. *The Canadian Social Model: The Logics of Policy Development*. Ottawa: Canadian Policy Research Networks.

Bradford, N. 1998. *Commissioning Ideas: Canadian National Policy Innovation in Comparative Perspective*. Toronto: Oxford University Press.

———. 2002. *Why Cities Matter: Policy Research Perspectives for Canada*. PRN Discussion Paper No. F/23. Ottawa: Canadian Policy Research Networks.

———. 2004. 'How Ottawa Spends: Managing the Minority'. In G.B. Doern, ed. *How Ottawa Spends: Managing the Minority*. Montreal: McGill–Queen's University Press.

Breton, A. 1985. 'Supplementary Statement'. *Report of the Royal Commission on the Economic Union and Development Prospects for Canada*. Ottawa: Supply and Services Canada.

———, and A. Scott. 1978. *The Economic Constitution of Federal States*. Toronto: University of Toronto Press.

Brock, K. 1995. 'The End of Executive Federalism?'. In F. Rocher and M. Smith, eds. *New Trends in Canadian Federalism*. Peterborough: Broadview Press.

Brodie, J.M. 1990. *The Political Economy of Canadian Regionalism.* Toronto: Harcourt Brace Jovanovich.

Brown, D.M. 1991. 'The Evolving Role of the Provinces in Canadian Trade Policy'. In D.M. Brown and M. Smith, eds. *Canadian Federalism: Meeting Global Economic Challenges?* Kingston: Institute of Intergovernmental Relations, Queen's University and Institute for Research on Public Policy.

———. 1993. 'The Evolving Role of the Provinces in Canada–United States Trade Relations'. In D.M. Brown and E. Fry, eds. *States and Provinces in the International Economy.* Berkeley: Institute of Governmental Studies Press, University of California.

———, ed. 2001. *Tax Competition and the Fiscal Union: Proceedings of a Symposium at Queen's University, June 2000.* Working Paper Series. Kingston: Institute of Intergovernmental Relations, Queen's University.

———. 2002a. 'Fiscal Federalism: The New Equilibrium between Equity and Efficiency'. In Bakvis and Skogstad, eds (2002).

———. 2002b. *Market Rules: Economic Union Reform and Intergovernmental Policy-Making in Australia and Canada.* Montreal: McGill–Queen's University Press.

———. 2003a. 'Getting Things Done in the Federation: Do We Need New Rules for an Old Game?'. Kingston: Institute of Intergovernmental Relations, Queen's University.

———. 2003b. 'The Role of Federal (Central) Governments in Local Affairs'. In N. Glavatskaya, ed. *Analysis of Revenues and Expenses of Local Budgets.* Moscow: Consortium for Economic Policy Research and Advice.

———. 2006. 'Still in the Game: Efforts to Tame Economic Development Competition in Canada'. In Harrison, ed. (2006b).

———. 2007. 'Integration, Equity and Section 36'. *Supreme Court Law Review 37 S.C.L.R. (2d).*

———, and P.M. Leslie. 1994. 'Economic Integration and Equality in Federations'. In A. Mullins and C. Saunders, eds. *Economic Union in Federal Systems.* Sydney: The Federation Press.

Burgess, M.D. 2007. 'Success and Failure in Federation: Comparative Perspectives'. In *The Federal Idea: A Conference in Honour of Ronald L. Watts.* Kingston: Institute of Intergovernmental Relations, Queen's University.

Bzdera, A. 1993. 'Comparative Analysis of Federal High Courts: A Political Theory of Judicial Review'. *Canadian Journal of Political Science* 26, 1: 3–29.

Cairns, A.C. 1971. 'The Judicial Committee and Its Critics'. *Canadian Journal of Political Science* 4, 3: 301–45.

———. 1977. 'The Governments and Societies of Canadian Federalism'. *Canadian Journal of Political Science* 10, 4: 695–725.

———. 1986. 'The Embedded State: State–Society Relations in Canada'. In K. Banting, ed. *State and Society: Canada in Comparative Perspective.* Toronto: University of Toronto Press.

———. 1992. *Charter Versus Federalism: The Dilemmas of Constitutional Reform.* Kingston: McGill–Queen's University Press.

———. 2000. *Citizens Plus: Aboriginal Peoples and the Canadian State.* Vancouver: University of British Columbia Press.

Cameron, D.R. 1978. 'The Expansion of the Public Economy: A Comparative Analysis'. *American Political Science Review* 72, 4: 1243–61.

———. 1986. 'The Growth of Government Spending: The Canadian Experience in Comparative Perspective'. In K. Banting, ed. *State and Society: Canada in Comparative Perspective*. Toronto: University of Toronto Press.

Cameron, K., and G. White. 1995. *Northern Governments in Transition: Political and Constitutional Development in the Yukon, Nunavut and the Western Northwest Territories*. Montreal: Institute for Research on Public Policy.

Campbell, R. 1987. *Grand Illusions: The Politics of the Keynesian Experience in Canada, 1945–75*. Peterborough: Broadview Press.

———. 1995. 'Federalism and Economic Policy'. In F. Rocher and M. Smith, eds. *New Trends in Canadian Federalism*. Peterborough: Broadview Press.

Canada. 1985. 'Report of the Royal Commission on the Economic Union and Development Prospects for Canada.' Ottawa: Ministry of Supply and Services.

———. 2006. 'The Emergence of Cross-Border Regions between Canada and the United States, Roundtable Synthesis Report'. Ottawa: Policy Research Initiative.

———. 2007. *Building Canada: Modern Infrastructure for a Strong Canada*. Ottawa: Transport, Infrastructure and Communities.

Careless, A. 1977. *Initiative and Response: The Adaptation of Canadian Federalism to Regional Economic Development*. Montreal: McGill–Queen's University Press.

Choudry, S., and R. Howse. 2000. 'Constitutional Theory and the Quebec Secession Reference'. *Canadian Journal of Law and Jurisprudence* 13, 2: 143–69.

CICS. 1992. *First Ministers Meeting on the Constitution, Consensus Report on the Constitution, Final Text, Charlottetown, 28 August 1992*. Ottawa: Canadian Intergovernmental Conference Secretariat.

———. 2005. *Strengthening Relationships and Closing the Gap, November 24–25, Kelowna, B.C.* Ottawa: Canadian Intergovernmental Conference Secretariat.

CIHI. 2007. 'HSMR: A New Approach for Measuring Hospital Mortality Trends in Canada'. Ottawa: Canadian Institute for Health Information.

Clarkson, S., and C. McCall. 1990. *Trudeau and Our Times*. Vol. 1. *The Magnificent Obsession*. Toronto: McClelland and Stewart.

Coleman, W.D. 1991. 'Monetary Policy, Accountability and Legitimacy'. *Canadian Journal of Political Science* 24, 4: 711–34.

———, and G. Skogstad, eds. 1990. *Policy Communities and Public Policy in Canada: A Structural Approach*. Toronto: Copp Clark Pitman.

Considine, M. 2005. *Making Public Policy: Authority, Organization and Values*. Cambridge, UK: Polity Press.

Cook, R. 1972. *French-Canadian Nationalism*. Toronto: Macmillan of Canada.

Corry, J.A. 1947. *Democratic Government and Politics*. Toronto: University of Toronto Press.

Council of the Federation. 2004. *Council of the Federation: Internal Trade Workplan*. Ottawa: Council of the Federation.

Courchene, T.J. 1995a. 'Glocalization: The Regional/International Interface'. *Canadian Journal of Regional Science* 18, 1: 1–20.

————. 1995b. 'Redistributing Money and Power: A Guide to the Canada Health and Social Transfer'. *Observation* 39. Toronto: C.D. Howe Institute.

————. 1996. *Access: A Convention on the Canadian Economic and Social Systems*. Toronto: Government of Ontario.

————. 2004a. 'Hourglass Federalism: How the Feds Got the Provinces to Run out of Money in a Decade of Liberal Budgets'. *Policy Options* 24, 4: 12–17.

————. 2004b. 'Confiscatory Equalization: The Intriguing Case of Saskatchewan's Vanishing Energy Revenues'. *Choices* 10, 2: Montreal: Institute for Research on Public Policy.

————. 2005. 'Citistates and the State of Cities: Political Economy and Fiscal-Federalism Dimensions'. Montreal: Institute for Research on Public Policy.

————, and C. Telmer. 1998. *From Heartland to North American Region State: The Social, Fiscal and Federal Evolution of Ontario*. Toronto: Centre for Public Management, University of Toronto.

————, and T. Wilson, eds. 2007. *The 1997 Federal Budget: Retrospect and Prospect*. Kingston: John Deutsch Institute for the Study of Economic Policy, Queen's University.

Cross, P. 2007. 'Year End Review: Westward Ho!'. *Canadian Economic Observer* 20, 4. Catalogue no. 11-010-XIB.

Cutler, F. 2004. 'Government Responsibility and Electoral Accountability in Federations'. *Publius* 34, 2: 19–38.

Dahl, R.A. 1967. *Pluralist Democracy in the United States: Conflict and Consent*. Chicago: Rand McNally.

Diamond, M. 1961. 'The Federalist's View of Federalism'. In G.C.S. Benson, ed. *Essays in Federalism*. Claremont, CA: Claremont Men's College.

————. 1973. 'The Ends of Federalism', *Publius* 3, 2: 129–52.

Dicey, A.V. 1959. *Introduction to the Study of the Law of the Constitution*. 10th edn. E.C.S., ed. Wade. London: Macmillan.

Dion, S. 2002. 'Fiscal Balance in Canada'. *Sharing the Wealth: Choices for the Federation (The CRIC Papers)*. Montreal: Centre for Research and Information on Canada: 33–7.

————. 2004. 'Fiscal Balance in Canada'. In H. Lazar, ed. *Canadian Fiscal Arrangements: What Works, What Might Work Better*. Kingston: Institute of Intergovernmental Relations, Queen's University.

Doern, G.B. 2002. 'Environment Canada as a Networked Institution'. In R. Boardman and D. VanNijnatten, eds. *Canadian Environmental Policy: Context and Cases*. 2nd edn. Toronto: Oxford University Press.

————, and M. MacDonald. 1999. *Free-Trade Federalism: Negotiating the Canadian Agreement on Internal Trade*. Toronto: University of Toronto Press.

————, and G. Toner. 1985. *The Politics of Energy: The Development and Implementation of the NEP*. Toronto: Methuen.

Downing, T.J., and R.J. Williams. 1998. 'Provincial Agendas, Local Responses: The "Common Sense" Restructuring of Ontario's Municipal Governments'. *Canadian Public Administration* 41, 2: 210–38.

Dunn, C. 1995. *The Institutionalized Cabinet: Governing the Western Provinces.* Montreal: McGill–Queen's University Press.

Dupré, J.S. 1988. 'Reflections on the Workability of Executive Federalism'. In R. Olling and M. Westmacott, eds. *Perspectives on Canadian Federalism.* Scarborough: Prentice Hall.

————, D.M. Cameron, G.H. McKechnie, and T.B. Rotenberg. 1973. *Federalism and Policy Development: The Case of Adult Occupational Training in Ontario.* Toronto: University of Toronto Press.

Dyson, K. 1980. *The State Tradition in Western Europe.* New York: Oxford University Press.

Economic Council of Canada. 1991. 'A Joint Venture'. Ottawa: Ministry of Supply and Services.

Eden, L., and M.A. Molot. 1993. 'Canada's National Policies: Reflections on 125 Years'. *Canadian Public Policy* 19, 3: 232–51.

Elazar, D.J. 1962. *The American Partnership.* Chicago: University of Chicago Press.

Elton, D., and P. McCormick. 1997. 'The Alberta Case: Intergovernmental Relations'. In J. Bourgault, M. Demers, and C. Williams, eds. *Public Administration and Public Management: Experiences in Canada.* Ste Foy: Institute of Public Administration of Canada.

Environment Canada. 2007. *Turning the Corner: An Action Plan to Reduce Greenhouse Gases and Air Pollution (News Release).* Ottawa: Environment Canada.

Esping-Anderson, G. 1990. *The Three Worlds of Welfare Capitalism.* Princeton, NJ: Princeton University Press.

Fafard, P. 2000. 'Groups, Governments and the Environment: Some Evidence from the Harmonization Initiative'. In Fafard and K. Harrison, eds (2000).

————, and K. Harrison, eds. 2000. *Managing the Environmental Union: Intergovernmental Relations and Environmental Policy in Canada.* Kingston: Institute of Intergovernmental Relations, Queen's University.

Federation of Canadian Municipalities, 2000. *Annual Report, 1999–2000.* Ottawa: Federation of Canadian Municipalities.

————. 2001. Early Warning: *Will Canadian Cities Compete? A Comparative Overview of Municipal Government in Canada, the United States and Europe.* Ottawa: Federation of Canadian Municipalities.

————. 2005. *Cities: Partners in National Prosperity.* Ottawa: Federation of Canadian Municipalities, Big Cities Mayors Caucus.

————. 2006. *Building Prosperity from the Ground Up: Restoring Municipal Fiscal Balance.* Ottawa: Federation of Canadian Municipalities.

Finance Canada. 2006. *Restoring Fiscal Balance in Canada* (Budget 2006). Ottawa: Department of Finance.

————. 2007. *Restoring Fiscal Balance for a Stronger Federation* (Budget 2007). Ottawa: Department of Finance.

————. 2008. *The Budget Plan 2008: Responsible Leadership for Uncertain Times.* Ottawa: Department of Finance.

Fischer, F., and J. Forester, eds. 1993. *The Argumentative Turn in Policy Analysis and Planning.* Durham, NC: Duke University Press.

Flanagan, T. 1998. *Game Theory and Canadian Politics*. Toronto: University of Toronto Press.

———. 2000. *First Nations? Second Thoughts*. Montreal: McGill–Queen's University Press.

Florida, R. 2004. *Cities and the Creative Class*. New York: Routledge.

Forester, J. 1993. *Critical Theory, Public Policy, and Planning Practice: Toward a Critical Pragmatism*. Albany, NY: SUNY Press.

Fox, G. 2007. 'Harper's Open Federalism: From the Fiscal Imbalance to "Effective Collaborative Management" of the Federation'. *Policy Options* 28, 3: 44–7.

Fraser, G. 1999. 'Social-Union Discussions Called "Reform by Stealth"'. *Globe and Mail*. January 21.

Friendly, M., and L. White. 2008. 'From Multilateralism to Bilateralism to Unilateralism in Three Short Years: Child Care in Canadian Federalism'. In Bakvis and Skogstad, eds (2008).

Gagné, R., and J. Stein. 2006. *Reconciling the Irreconcilable: Addressing Canada's Fiscal Imbalance: Report of the Advisory Panel on Fiscal Imbalance*. Ottawa: Council of the Federation.

Gagnon, A.-G., and J. Erk. 2002. 'Legitimacy, Effectiveness, and Federalism: On the Benefits of Ambiguity'. In Bakvis and Skogstad, eds (2002).

———, and J. Garceau. 1988. 'Quebec and the Pursuit of Special Status'. In R. Olling and M. Westmacott, eds. *Perspectives on Canadian Federalism*. Scarborough: Prentice Hall.

———, and R. Iacovino. 2007. *Federalism, Citizenship, and Quebec*. Toronto: University of Toronto Press.

Galloway, G. 2007. 'Calvert Threatens to Take Ottawa to Court; Saskatchewan Opens Second Front in Revenue Dispute'. *Globe and Mail*. June 14.

———, and C. Alphonso. 2007. 'I'll See You in Court, PM Tells Atlantic Premiers; Defiant Harper Says Atlantic Accord Hasn't Been Broken and Challenges Newfoundland and Nova Scotia to Legal Fight'. *Globe and Mail*. June 12.

Gibbins, R. 1999. 'Taking Stock: Canadian Federalism and Its Constitutional Framework'. In L. Pal, ed. *How Ottawa Spends, 1999–2000*. Toronto: Oxford University Press.

———. 2001. 'Shifting Sands: Exploring the Political Foundations of SUFA'. *Policy Matters* 2, 3: 1–20.

Gillroy, J.M. 1997. 'Postmodernism, Efficiency, and Comprehensive Policy Argument in Public Administration: A Tool for the Practice of Administrative Decision Making'. *American Behavioral Scientist* 41, 1: 163–90.

Good, K. 2007. 'Urban Regime-Building as a Strategy of Intergovernmental Reform: The Case of Toronto's Role in Immigrant Settlement'. Paper presented at the Canadian Political Science Annual Meeting, Saskatoon, SK.

Government of Newfoundland and Labrador. 2003. *Main Report of the Royal Commission on Our Place in Canada [Young Report]*. St John's: Government of Newfoundland and Labrador.

———. 2008. *Budget Address, 2008*. St John's: Department of Finance.

Graefe, P. 2005. 'The Scope and Limits of Asymmetry in Recent Social Policy Agreements'. *Asymmetry Series*. Kingston: Institute for Intergovernmental Relations, Queen's University.

Graham, K., S. Phillips, and A. Maslove. 1998. *Urban Governance in Canada*. Toronto: Harcourt.

Grodzins, M. 1966. *The American System*. Chicago: Rand McNally & Company.

Hale, G.H. 2004. 'Canadian Federalism and the Challenge of North American Integration'. *Canadian Public Administration* 47, 4: 497–524.

Hall, P., and D. Soskice, eds. 2001. *Varieties of Capitalism*. Oxford: Oxford University Press.

Hamel, P., and J. Rousseau. 2006. 'Revisiting Municipal Reforms in Quebec and the New Responsibilities of Local Actors in a Globalizing World'. In R. Young and C. Leuprecht, eds. *Canada: The State of the Federation, 2004: Municipal–Federal Relations in Canada*. Kingston: Institute of Intergovernmental Relations, Queen's University.

Harding, K. 2006. 'Premier's Bid for Unity Turns to Acrimony: No Deal Achieved on Equalization Plan'. *Globe and Mail*. 6 June.

Harper, S. *Senate Reform*. 2006. Available at <http://www.pm.gc.ca/eng/media.asp?id=1306>.

Harrison, K. 1996. *Passing the Buck: Federalism and Canadian Environmental Policy*. Vancouver: University of British Columbia Press.

———. 2002. 'Federal–Provincial Relations and the Environment: Unilateralism, Collaboration and Rationalization'. In D. VanNijnatten and R. Boardman, eds. *Canadian Environmental Policy: Context and Cases*. 2nd edn. Toronto: Oxford University Press.

———. 2006a. 'Provincial Interdependence: Concepts and Theories'. In Harrison, ed. (2006b).

———, ed. 2006b. *Racing to the Bottom? Provincial Interdependence in the Canadian Federation*. Vancouver: University of British Columbia Press.

———. 2007. 'The Road Not Taken: Climate Change Policy in Canada and the United States'. *Global Environmental Politics* 7, 4: 92–117.

Hawkes, D.C. 1989. *Aboriginal Peoples and Constitutional Reform: What Have We Learned?*, *Aboriginal Peoples and Constitutional Reform*. Kingston: Institute of Intergovernmental Relations, Queen's University.

Health Canada. 2004. *10-Year Plan to Strengthen Health Care*. Ottawa: Health Canada.

Heard, A. 1991. *Canadian Constitutional Conventions: The Marriage of Law and Politics*. Toronto: Oxford University Press.

———, and T. Swartz. 1997. 'The Regional Veto Formula and Its Effects on Canada's Constitutional Amendment Process'. *Canadian Journal of Political Science* 30, 2: 339–56.

Henderson, J.Y. 1994. 'Empowering Treaty Federalism'. *Saskatchewan Law Review* 58: 241–329.

Hicks, S.R.C. 2004. *Explaining Postmodernism: Skepticism and Socialism from Rousseau to Foucault*. Phoenix, AZ: Scholargy.

Hobson, P., and F. St-Hilaire. 2000. 'The Evolution of Federal–Provincial Fiscal Arrangements: Putting Humpty Together Again'. In H. Lazar, ed. (2000c).

Hofferbert, R. 1974. *The Study of Public Policy*. Indianapolis: Bobbs–Merrill.

Hogg, P. 1979. 'Is the Supreme Court of Canada Biased in Constitutional Cases?'. *Canadian Bar Review* 57, 4: 721–39.

————. 2002. *Constitutional Law of Canada*. 5th student edn. Scarborough: Thomson Carswell.

————. 2005. *Constitutional Law of Canada*. Student edn. Scarborough: Thomson Carswell.

Hooghe, L., and G. Marks. 2001. *Multi-Level Governance and European Integration*. London: Rowan and Littlefield.

Houghton, D.P. 2008. 'Positivism 'Vs' Postmodernism: Does Epistemology Make a Difference?'. *International Politics* 45, 2: 115–28.

Howlett, M. 1997. 'Issue-Attention Cycles and Punctuated Equilibrium Models Re-Considered'. *Canadian Journal of Political Science* 30, 1: 5–29.

————. 1998. 'Predictable and Unpredictable Policy Windows: Institutional and Exogenous Correlates of Canadian Federal Agenda-Setting'. *Canadian Journal of Political Science* 31, 3: 495–524.

————, and M. Ramesh. 2003. *Studying Public Policy: Policy Cycles and Policy Subsystems*. Toronto: Oxford University Press.

Hueglin, T. 1999. *Early Modern Concepts for a Late Modern World: Althusius on Community and Federalism*. Waterloo, ON: Wilfrid Laurier University Press.

————. 2003. 'Federalism at the Crossroads: Old Meanings, New Significance'. *Canadian Journal of Political Science* 36, 2: 275–94.

Hurley, J.R. 1996. *Amending Canada's Constitution: History, Processes, Problems and Prospects*. Ottawa: Government of Canada.

Indian and Northern Affairs Canada. 1995. *Aboriginal Self-Government: The Government of Canada's Approach to the Implementation of the Inherent Right and the Negotiation of Aboriginal Self-Government*. Ottawa: INAC, Public Works and Government Services.

————. 1997. *Gathering Strength: Canada's Aboriginal Action Plan*. Ottawa: INAC, Public Works and Government Services.

Inwood, G.C., C. Johns, and P. O'Reilly. 2004. 'Intergovernmental Officials in Canada'. In J.P. Meekison, H. Telford, and H. Lazar, eds. *Canada: The State of the Federation 2002*. Kingston: McGill–Queen's University Press.

James, P. 1993. 'Energy Politics in Canada, 1980–1981: Threat Power in a Sequential Game'. *Canadian Journal of Political Science* 26, 1: 31–59.

Juillet, L. 2000. *The Federal Regional Councils and Horizontal Governance*. Ottawa: Treasury Board Secretariat.

Katzenstein, P.J. 1985. *Small States in World Markets: Industrial Policy in Europe*. Ithaca, NY: Cornell University Press.

Kelly, J.B. 2001. 'Reconciling Rights and Federalism During Review of the Charter of Rights and Freedoms: The Supreme Court of Canada and the Centralization Thesis, 1982 to 1999'. *Canadian Journal of Political Science* 34: 321–55.

————. 2008. 'The Courts, the Charter, and Federalism'. In Bakvis and Skogstad, eds (2008).

————, and M. Murphy. 2005. 'Shaping the Constitutional Dialogue on Federalism: The Canadian Supreme Court as Meta-Political Actor'. *Publius* 35, 2: 217–43.

Kent, T. 2008. 'The Harper Peril for Canadian Federalism'. *Policy Options*, Feb. 2008: 12–16.

Keohane, R.O., and J.S. Nye. 2001. *Power and Interdependence*. New York: Longman.

Kingdon, J.W. 1984. *Agendas, Alternatives, and Public Policies*. New York: Harper Collins.

Kirby, M. 2002. *The Health of Canadians: The Federal Role: Final Report*. Ottawa: Senate of Canada.

Kitchen, H. 2000. 'Provinces, Municipalities, Universities, Schools and Hospitals: Recent Trends and Funding Issues'. In H. Lazar, ed. (2000c).

Knox, R. 1998. 'Economic Integration in Canada through the Agreement on Internal Trade'. In H. Lazar, ed. (1997).

Krugman, P. 1999. *The Spatial Economy: Cities, Regions and International Trade*. Cambridge, MA: MIT Press.

Kwavnick, D., ed. 1973. *The Tremblay Report: Report of the Royal Commission of Inquiry on Constitutional Problems*. Toronto: McClelland and Stewart.

Kymlicka, W. 1995. *Multicultural Citizenship: A Liberal Theory of Minority Rights*. Oxford: Oxford University Press.

————. 1998. *Finding Our Way: Rethinking Ethnocultural Relations in Canada*. Toronto: Oxford University Press.

————. 2003. 'Citizenship, Communities and Identity in Canada'. In J. Bickerton and A. Gagnon, eds. *Canadian Politics*. 3rd edn. Peterborough: Broadview Press.

Ladner, K. 2003. 'Treaty Federalism: An Indigenous Vision of Canadian Federalism'. In F. Rocher and M. Smith, eds. *New Trends in Canadian Federalism*. 2nd edn. Peterborough: Broadview Press.

Laforest, G. 1995. *Trudeau and the End of a Canadian Dream*. Montreal: McGill–Queen's University Press.

LaSelva, S.V. 1996. *The Moral Foundations of Canadian Federalism: Paradoxes, Achievements and Tragedies of Nationhood*. Montreal: McGill–Queen's University Press.

Laski, H.J. 1939. 'The Obsolescence of Federalism'. *New Republic*: 367–9.

Laskin, B. 1947. 'Peace, Order and Good Government Re-Examined'. *Canadian Bar Review* 25, 10: 1054–87.

———— 1951. 'The Supreme Court of Canada: A Final Court of Appeal of and for Canadians'. *Canadian Bar Review* 29, 10: 1038–79.

Lazar, H., ed. 1997. *Canada: The State of the Federation 1997: Non-Constitutional Renewal*. Kingston: Institute of Intergovernmental Relations, Queen's University.

————. 2000a. *The Social Union Framework Agreement: Lost Opportunity or New Beginning?*. Kingston: Institute of Intergovernmental Relations, Queen's University.

————. 2000b. 'In Search of a New Mission Statement for Canadian Fiscal Federalism'. In Lazar, ed. (2000c).

————, ed. 2000c. *Canada: The State of the Federation 1999–2000: Toward a New Mission Statement for Canadian Fiscal Federalism*. Kingston: Institute of Intergovernmental Relations, Queen's University.

————. 2003. *Managing Interdependencies in the Canadian Federation: Lessons from the Social Union Framework Agreement*. Kingston: Institute of Intergovernmental Relations, Queen's University.

————. 2004. *Canadian Social Union: Reality and Myth*. Kingston: Institute of Intergovernmental Relations, Queen's University.

————. 2005a. 'Trust in Intergovernmental Fiscal Relations'. In Lazar, ed. (2005).

————, ed. 2005b. *Canadian Fiscal Arrangements: What Works, What Might Work Better*. Kingston: Institute of Intergovernmental Relations, Queen's University.

————. 2006. 'The Intergovernmental Dimensions of the Social Union: A Sectoral Analysis'. *Canadian Public Administration* 49, 1: 23–45.

————, and F. St-Hilaire, eds. 2004. *Money, Politics and Health Care: Reconstructing the Federal–Provincial Partnership*. Montreal: Institute for Research on Public Policy and Institute of Intergovernmental Relations, Queen's University.

————, ————, and J.-F. Tremblay. 2004. 'Vertical Fiscal Imbalance: Myth or Reality?' In Lazar and St-Hilaire, eds (2004).

Lederman, W.R. 1975. 'Unity and Diversity in Canadian Federalism: Ideas and Methods of Moderation'. *Canadian Bar Review* 53: 597–620.

Leger Marketing. 2008. 'Referendum Voting Intentions in Quebec'. Montreal: Leger Marketing.

Leslie, P., R. Neumann, and R. Robinson. 2004. 'Managing Canadian Fiscal Federalism'. In J.P. Meekison, H. Telford, and H. Lazar, eds. *Canada: The State of the Federation, 2002: Reconsidering the Institutions of Canadian Federalism*. Kingston: Institute of Intergovernmental Relations, Queen's University.

Lightbody, J. 1998. 'Council Multiplicity and the Cost of Governance in Canadian Metropolitan Areas'. *Canadian Journal of Urban Research* 7, 1: 27–46.

Lijphart, A. 1977. *Democracy in Plural Societies: A Comparative Exploration*. New Haven, CT: Yale University Press.

————. 1999. *Patterns of Democracy: Government Forms and Performance in Thirty-Six Countries*. New Haven, CT: Yale University Press.

Lindquist, E.A. 1999. 'Efficiency, Reliability, or Innovation? Managing Overlap and Interdependence in Canada's Federal System of Governance'. In R.A. Young, ed. *Stretching the Federation: The Art of the State in Canada*. Kingston: Institute of Intergovernmental Relations, Queen's University.

Livingston, W.S. 1952. 'A Note on the Nature of Federalism'. *Political Science Quarterly* 67, 1: 81–95.

————. 1956. *Federalism and Constitutional Change*. Oxford: Clarendon Press.

Lowi, T. 1979. *The End of Liberalism: The Second Republic of the United States*. 2nd edn. New York: Norton.

Lucas, A. 1989. 'The New Environmental Law'. In R.L. Watts and D.M. Brown, eds. *Canada: The State of the Federation, 1989*. Kingston: Institute of Intergovernmental Relations, Queen's University.

McCarthy, S. 2002. 'Premiers Derail Klein Plan: Nunavut Leader Warns Colleagues of Lasting Damage from Climate Change'. *Globe and Mail*. August 3.

McDavid, J.C. 2002. 'The Impacts of Amalgamation on Police Services in the Halifax Regional Municipality'. *Canadian Public Administration* 45, 4: 538–65.

MacDonald, M. 2002. 'The Agreement on Internal Trade: Trade-Offs for Economic Union and Federalism'. In Bakvis and Skogstad, eds (2002).

McIntosh, T. 2002. 'As Time Goes By: Building on SUFA's Commitments'. In T. McIntosh, ed. *Building the Social Union: Perspectives, Directions and Challenges*. Regina: Saskatchewan Institute of Public Policy.

MacKinnon, D. 2005a. 'Fairness in Confederation: Fiscal Imbalance: Driving Ontario to "Have-Not" Status'. Toronto: Ontario Chamber of Commerce.

———. 2005b. 'Fairness in Confederation: Fiscal Imbalance: A Roadmap to Recovery'. Toronto: Ontario Chamber of Commerce.

MacKinnon, J. 2003. *Minding the Public Purse: The Fiscal Crisis, Political Trade-Offs and Canada's Future*. Montreal: McGill–Queen's University Press.

Mackintosh, W.A. 1939. *The Economic Background of Dominion–Provincial Relations*. Toronto: Macmillan.

Macklem, P. 2001. *Indigenous Difference and the Constitution of Canada*. Toronto: University of Toronto Press.

McMillan, M.L. 2006. 'Municipal Relations with the Federal and Provincial Governments: A Fiscal Perspective'. In R. Young and C. Leuprecht, eds. *Canada: The State of the Federation, 2004: Municipal–Federal–Provincial Relations in Canada*. Kingston: Institute of Intergovernmental Relations, Queen's University.

Macpherson, C.B. 1962. *Democracy in Alberta: Social Credit and the Party System*. Toronto: University of Toronto Press.

McRae, K.D., ed. 1974. *Consociational Democracy: Political Accommodation in Segmented Societies*. Toronto: McClelland and Stewart.

McRoberts, K. 2003. 'Conceiving Diversity: Dualism, Multiculturalism, and Multinationalism'. In F. Rocher and M. Smith, eds. *New Trends in Canadian Federalism*. 2nd edn. Peterborough: Broadview Press.

Maioni, A. 2008. 'Health Care'. In Bakvis and Skogstad, eds (2008).

Mallory, J.R. 1954. *Social Credit and the Federal Power in Canada*. Toronto: University of Toronto Press.

Marshall, D. 2006. *All over the Map 2006: Status Report on Provincial Climate Change Plans*. Vancouver: David Suzuki Foundation.

———. 2007. *Briefing Note: Picking up the Slack: The Provinces' Potential to Act on Climate Change*. Vancouver: David Suzuki Foundation.

Maslove, A.M. 1996. 'The Canada Health and Social Transfer: Forcing Issues'. In G. Swimmer, ed. *How Ottawa Spends 1996–97: Life under the Knife*. Ottawa: Carleton University Press.

Mason, G. 2008. 'Plans to Curb Greenhouse-Gas Emissions Blowing Off in All Directions'. *Globe and Mail*. June 5.

Maxwell, J., P. McKinnon, and J. Watling. 2007. 'Taking Fiscal Federalism to the People'. *Policy Options*. March: 35–8.

Meekison, J.P. 2003. 'Council of the Federation: An Idea Whose Time Has Come'. Kingston: Institute of Intergovernmental Relations, Queen's University.

———. 2004. 'The Annual Premiers' Conference: Forging a Common Front'. In J.P. Meekison, H. Telford, and H. Lazar, eds. *Canada: The State of the Federation, 2002: Reconsidering the Institutions of Canadian Federalism*. Kingston: Institute of Intergovernmental Relations, Queen's University.

Mellon, H. 1997. 'Blending the GST with Provincial Sales Taxes'. In M. Westmacott and H. Mellon, eds. *Challenges to Canadian Federalism*. Scarborough: Prentice Hall.

Milne, D. 1986. *Tug of War: Ottawa and the Provinces under Trudeau and Mulroney*. Toronto: J. Lorimer.

———. 1998. 'Equalization and the Politics of Restraint'. In B.A. Hobson, ed. *Equalization: Its Contribution to Canada's Economic and Fiscal Progress*. Kingston: John Deutsch Institute for the Study of Economic Policy, Queen's University.

Ministry of Supply and Services. 1985. *Report of the Royal Commission on the Economic Union and Development Prospects for Canada*. Ottawa: Royal Commission on the Economic Union and Development Prospects for Canada [Donald Macdonald, chair], Ministry of Supply and Services.

———. 1991. *A Joint Venture*. Ottawa: Economic Council of Canada, Ministry of Supply and Services.

———. 1992. *Partners in Confederation: Aboriginal Peoples, Self-Government and the Constitution. Royal Commission on Aboriginal Peoples, Department of Supply and Services*. Ottawa: Ministry of Supply and Services Canada.

Monahan, P. 1987. *Politics and the Constitution: The Charter, Federalism and the Supreme Court of Canada*. Toronto: Carswell.

Morton, F.L. 1995. 'The Effect of the Charter of Rights on Canadian Federalism'. *Publius* 25, 3: 173-88.

Murphy, M. 2001. 'Culture and the Courts: A New Direction for Canada's Jurisprudence on Aboriginal Rights?'. *Canadian Journal of Political Science* 34, 1: 109–29.

———. 2005. 'Relational Self-Determination and Federal Reform'. In M. Murphy, ed. *Canada: The State of the Federation 2003: Reconfiguring Aboriginal–State Relations*. Kingston: Institute of Intergovernmental Relations, Queen's University.

Musgrave, R.A. 1969. *Fiscal Systems*. New Haven, CT: Yale University Press.

Naylor, C.D. 1986. *Private Practice, Public Payment: Canadian Medicine and the Politics of Health Insurance, 1911–1966*. Montreal: McGill–Queen's University Press.

Nevitte, N. 1996. *The Decline of Deference: Canadian Value Change in Cross-National Perspective*. Peterborough: Broadview Press.

———, ed. 2002. *Value Change and Governance in Canada*. Toronto: University of Toronto Press.

Noël, A. 2001. 'Power and Purpose in Intergovernmental Relations'. *Policy Matters* 2: 1–26.

———. 2002. 'Without Quebec: Collaborative Federalism with a Footnote?'. In T. McIntosh, ed. *Building the Social Union: Perspectives, Directions and Challenges*. Regina: Canadian Plains Research Centre.

———, F. St-Hilaire, and S. Fortin. 2003. 'Learning from the SUFA Experience'. In A. Noël, F. St-Hilaire, and S. Fortin, eds. *Forging the Canadian Social Union: SUFA and Beyond*. Montreal: Institute for Research on Public Policy.

Nye, J.S. 2004. *Soft Power: The Means to Success in World Politics*. New York: Public Affairs Press.

Oates, W.E. 1972. *Fiscal Federalism*. New York: Harcourt Brace Jovanovitch.

O'Brien, A. 2006. 'Achieving a National Purpose: Improving Territorial Formula Financing and Strengthening Canada's Territories'. Ottawa: Department of Finance, Expert Panel on Equalization and Territorial Formula Financing.

Olewiler, N. 2006. 'Environmental Policy in Canada: Harmonized at the Bottom?' In Harrison, ed. (2006b).

Olson, M. 1971. *The Logic of Collective Action: Public Goods and the Theory of Groups.* Cambridge, MA: Harvard University Press.

Ontario. 2006. *Strong Ontario: Seeking Fairness for Canadians Living in Ontario.* Toronto: Intergovernmental Affairs.

Ostrom, E. 1990. *Governing the Commons.* Cambridge: Cambridge University Press.

Ostrom, V. 1973. 'Can Federalism Make a Difference?' *Publius* 3: 197–238.

Page, M. 2002. 'Provincial Trade Patterns'. Ottawa: Statistics Canada: Agriculture Division.

Painter, M. 1991. 'Intergovernmental Relations: An Institutional Analysis'. *Canadian Journal of Political Science* 24: 269–88.

———. 1998. *Collaborative Federalism: Economic Reform in Australia in the 1990s.* Cambridge: Cambridge University Press.

Pal, L.A. 2006. *Beyond Policy Analysis: Public Issue Management in Turbulent Times.* 3rd edn. Scarborough: Thomson Nelson.

Papillon, M. 2008. 'Canadian Federalism and the Emerging Mosaic of Aboriginal Multilevel Governance'. In Bakvis and Skogstad, eds (2008).

———, and R. Simeon. 2004. 'The Weakest Link? First Ministers' Conferences in Canadian Intergovernmental Relations'. In J.P. Meekison, H. Telford, and H. Lazar, eds. *Canada: The State of the Federation, 2002: Reconsidering the Institutions of Canadian Federalism.* Kingston: Institute of Intergovernmental Relations, Queen's University.

Peters, B.G., and J.A. Hoornbeek. 2005. 'The Problem of Policy Problems'. In P. Eliadis, M.M. Hill, and M. Howlett, eds. *Designing Government: From Instruments to Governance.* Montreal: McGill–Queen's University Press.

———, and J. Pierre. 2005. 'Swings and Roundabouts? Multilevel Governance as a Source of and Constraint on Policy Capacity'. In M. Painter and J. Pierre, eds. *Challenges to State Policy Capacity: Global Trends and Comparative Perspectives.* Houndmills: Palgrave Macmillan.

Peters, S. 1996. *Exploring Canadian Values. A Synthesis Report.* Ottawa: Canadian Policy Research Networks.

Phillips, S.D. 2001. 'SUFA and Citizen Engagement: Fake or Genuine Masterpiece'. *Policy Matters* 7, 2: 1–36. Montreal: Institute for Research on Public Policy.

Picard, A. 1995. *The Gift of Death: Confronting Canada's Tainted-Blood Tragedy.* Toronto: Harper Collins.

Pierson, P. 1995. 'Fragmented Welfare States: Federal Institutions and the Development of Social Policy'. *Governance* 8, 4: 449–78.

Porter, M. 1990. *The Competitive Advantage of Nations.* London: Macmillan.

Prime Minister's Office. 2007. *Prime Minister Stephen Harper Calls for International Consensus on Climate Change (News Release).* Ottawa: Prime Minister's Office.

Prince, M., and F. Abele. 2000. 'Funding an Aboriginal Order of Government in Canada: Recent Developments in Self-Government and Fiscal Relations'. In H. Lazar, ed. (2000c).

Pross, A.P. 1992. *Group Politics and Public Policy*. Toronto: Oxford Univesity Press.

Putnam, R. 1988. 'Diplomacy and Domestic Politics: The Logic of Two-Level Games'. *International Organization* 42, 3: 427–60.

Quebec. 2002. *A New Division of Canada's Fiscal Resources*. Report of the Commission on Fiscal Imbalance [Seguin Report]. Quebec: Government of Quebec.

Rabe, B.G. 2004. *Statehouse and Greenhouse: The Merging Politics of American Climate Change Policy*. Washington, DC: Brookings Institution Press.

Rhodes, R.A.W. 1996. 'The New Governance: Governing without Government'. *Political Studies* 44, 4: 652–67.

Richards, J.G., and L. Pratt. 1979. *Prairie Capitalism: Power and Influence in the New West*. Toronto: McClelland and Stewart.

Richards, R.G. 1991. 'The Canadian Constitution and International Economic Relations'. In D.M. Brown and M. Smith, eds. *Canadian Federalism: Meeting Global Economic Challenges?* Kingston: Institute of Intergovernmental Relations, Queen's University.

Riker, W.H. 1964. *Federalism: Origin, Operation, Significance*. Boston: Little, Brown.

———. 1969. 'Six Books in Search of a Subject or Does Federalism Exist and Does It Matter?'. *Comparative Politics* 2, 1: 135–46.

Robinson, I. 2003. 'Neo-Liberal Trade Policy and Canadian Federalism Revisited'. In F. Rocher and M. Smith, eds. *New Trends in Canadian Federalism*. 2nd edn. Peterborough: Broadview Press.

Rogowski, R. 1974. *Rational Legitimacy: A Theory of Political Support*. Princeton, N.J.: Princeton University Press.

Romanow, R. 2002. *Building on Values: The Future of Health Care in Canada*. Ottawa: Commission on the Future of Health Care in Canada.

Royal Commission on Aboriginal Peoples. 1992. 'Partners in Confederation: Aboriginal Peoples, Self-Government and the Constitution'. Ottawa: Department of Supply and Services.

———. 1996. *Final Report*. 6 vols. Ottawa: Public Works and Government Services Canada.

Russell, P.H. 1977. 'The Anti-Inflation Case: The Anatomy of a Constitutional Decision'. *Canadian Public Administration* 20, 4: 632–65.

———. 1983. 'The Political Purposes of the Canadian Charter of Rights and Freedoms'. *Canadian Bar Review* 61, 1: 30–54.

———. 1985. 'The Supreme Court and Federal Provincial Relations: The Political Use of Legal Resources'. *Canadian Public Policy* 11, 2: 161–70.

———. 2004. *Constitutional Odyssey: Can Canadians Become a Sovereign People?* 3rd edn. Toronto: University of Toronto Press.

———. 2008. *Two Cheers for Minority Government: The Evolution of Canadian Parliamentary Democracy*. Toronto: Emond Montgomery.

Sancton, A. 2000. *Merger Mania: The Assault on Local Government*. Montreal: McGill–Queen's University Press.

———. 2008. 'The Urban Agenda'. In Bakvis and Skogstad, eds (2008).

Savoie, D.J. 1981. *Federal–Provincial Collaboration: The Canada–New Brunswick General Development Agreement*. Montreal: McGill–Queen's University Press.

———. 1992. *Regional Economic Development: Canada's Search for Solutions*. 2nd edn. Toronto: University of Toronto Press.

———. 1999. *Governing from the Centre: The Concentration of Power in Canadian Politics*. Toronto: University of Toronto Press.

———. 2003. 'Regional Development: A Policy for All Seasons'. In F. Rocher and M. Smith, eds. *New Trends in Canadian Federalism*. 2nd edn. Peterborough: Broadview Press.

———. 2008. *Court Government and the Collapse of Accountability in Canada and the United Kingdom*. Toronto: University of Toronto Press.

Saywell, J. 2002. *The Lawmakers: Judicial Power and the Shaping of Canadian Federalism*. Toronto: University of Toronto Press.

Scharpf, F.W. 1988. 'The Joint-Decision-Making Trap: Lessons from German Federalism'. *Public Administration* 66: 239–78.

———. 1996. 'Negative and Positive Integration in the Political Economy of European Welfare States'. In G. Marks, ed. *Governance in the European Union*. London: Sage.

———. 1997. *Games Real Actors Play: Actor-Centered Institutionalism in Policy Research*. Boulder, CO: Westview Publishing.

———. 1999. *Governing in Europe: Effective and Democratic?* Oxford: Oxford University Press.

———. 2006. 'The Joint-Decision Trap Revisited'. *Journal of Common Market Studies* 44, 4: 845–64.

Schneiderman, D. 1999. *The Quebec Decision: Perspectives on the Supreme Court Ruling on Secession*. Toronto: J. Lorimer.

Scott, F.R. 1951. 'Centralization and Decentralization in Canadian Federalism'. *Canadian Bar Review* 29, 10: 1095–125.

———. 1959. *Civil Liberties and Canadian Federalism*. Toronto: University of Toronto Press.

Senate. 2002. *The Effectiveness and Possible Improvements to the Present Equalization Policy*. Ottawa: Senate of Canada.

Sharman, C. 1990. 'Parliamentary Federations and Limited Government: Constitutional Design and Redesign in Australia and Canada', *Journal of Theoretical Politics* 2, 2: 205–30.

———. 1994. 'Discipline and Disharmony: Party and the Operation of the Australian Federal System'. In C. Sharman, ed. *Parties and Federalism in Australia and Canada*. Canberra: Federalism Research Centre, Australian National University.

Shearer, R. 1985. 'Regionalism and International Trade Policy'. In J. Whalley, ed. *Canada–United States Free Trade*. Toronto: University of Toronto Press.

Simeon, R. 2006 [1972]. *Federal–Provincial Diplomacy: The Making of Recent Policy in Canada*. Toronto: University of Toronto Press.

———. 1990. 'Why Did the Meech Lake Accord Fail?'. In R. L. Watts and D.M. Brown, eds. *Canada: The State of the Federation, 1990*. Kingston: Institute of Intergovernmental Relations, Queen's University.

————, and D. Cameron. 2002. 'Intergovernmental Relations and Democracy'. In Bakvis and Skogstad, eds (2002).

————, and A. Nugent. 2008. 'Parliamentary Canada and Intergovernmental Canada: Exploring the Tensions'. In Bakvis and Skogstad, eds (2008).

————, and I. Robinson. 1990. *State, Society, and the Development of Canadian Federalism*. Toronto: University of Toronto Press.

Simmons, J.M. 2004. 'Securing the Threads of Cooperation in the Tapestry of Intergovernmental Relations: Does the Institutionalization of Ministerial Conferences Matter?'. In J.P. Meekison, H. Telford, and H. Lazar, eds. *Canada: The State of the Federation, 2002: Reconsidering the Institutions of Canadian Federalism*. Kingston: Institute of Intergovernmental Relations, Queen's University.

————. 2005. 'Executive Federalism after Charlottetown: Understanding the Role of Non-Governmental Actors'. PhD, University of Toronto.

————. 2008. 'Democratizing Executive Federalism: The Role of Non-Governmental Actors in Intergovernmental Agreements'. In Bakvis and Skogstad, eds (2008).

Simpson, J. 2001. *The Friendly Dictatorship*. Toronto: McClelland and Stewart.

————, M. Jaccard, and N. Rivers. 2007. *Hot Air: Meeting Canada's Climate Change Challenge*. Toronto: McClelland and Stewart.

Skogstad, G. 2003. 'Who Governs? Who Should Govern? Political Authority and Legitimacy in Canada in the Twenty-First Century', *Canadian Journal of Political Science* 36, 5: 955–73.

Smiley, D.V., ed. 1978. *The Rowell–Sirois Report: An Abridgement of Book I of the Royal Commission Report on Dominion–Provincial Relations*. Toronto: Macmillan of Canada.

————, 1979. 'An Outsider's Observations of Federal–Provincial Relations among Consenting Adults'. In R. Simeon, ed. *Confrontation and Collaboration: Intergovernmental Relations in Canada Today*. Toronto: Institute of Public Administration of Canada.

————. 1980. *Canada in Question: Federalism in the Eighties*. Toronto: McGraw-Hill Ryerson.

————. 1987. *The Federal Condition in Canada*. Toronto: McGraw-Hill Ryerson.

————, and R.L. Watts. 1985. *Intrastate Federalism in Canada*. Toronto: University of Toronto Press.

Smith, D.E. 1985. 'Party Government, Representation and National Integration in Canada'. In P. Aucoin, ed. *Party Government and Regional Representation in Canada*. Toronto: University of Toronto Press.

————. 1995. 'Bagehot, the Crown and the Canadian Constitution'. *Canadian Journal of Political Science* 28, 4: 619–35.

Smith, J. 1983. 'The Origins of Judicial Review in Canada'. *Canadian Journal of Political Science* 16, 1: 115–34.

————. 1988. 'Canadian Confederation and the Influence of American Federalism'. *Canadian Journal of Political Science* 21, 3: 443–63.

————. 1998. *The Meaning of Provincial Equality in Canadian Federalism*. Anonymous, ed. Kingston: Institute of Intergovernmental Relations, Queen's University.

———. 1999. 'Responsible Government and Democracy'. In F.L. Seidle and L. Massicotte, eds. *Taking Stock of 150 Years of Responsible Government in Canada*. Ottawa: Canadian Study of Parliament Group.

———. 2002a. 'Informal Constitutional Development: Change by Other Means', In Bakvis and Skogstad, eds (2002).

———. 2002b. 'Atlantic Canada at the Start of the New Millenium'. In H. Telford and H. Lazar, eds. *Canada: The State of the Federation 2001: Canadian Political Culture(s) in Transition*. Montreal: McGill–Queen's University Press.

———. 2004. *Federalism, Canadian Democratic Audit*. Vancouver: University of British Columbia Press.

———. 2005. 'Institutionalism in the Study of Canadian Politics: The English-Canadian Tradition'. In A. Lecours, ed. *New Institutionalism: Theory and Analysis (Studies in Comparative Political Economy and Public Policy)*. Toronto: University of Toronto Press.

Soroka, S.N. 2002. *Agenda-Setting Dynamics in Canada*. Vancouver: University of British Columbia Press.

Sproule-Jones, M. 1975. *Public Choice and Federalism in Australia and Canada*. Canberra: Centre for Research on Federal Financial Relations, ANU.

———. 1993. *Governments at Work: Canadian Parliamentary Federalism and Its Public Policy Effects*. Toronto: University of Toronto Press.

Statistics Canada. 2008. 'Aboriginal Peoples in Canada in 2006: Inuit, Metis and First Nations, 2006 Census'. Ottawa: Public Works and Government Services.

Stevenson, D., and R. Gilbert. 2005. 'Coping with Canadian Federalism: The Case of the Federation of Canadian Municipalities'. *Canadian Public Administration* 48, 4: 528–51.

Stevenson, G. 1989. *Unfulfilled Union: Canadian Federalism and National Unity*. Toronto: Gage.

Stoney, C., and K. Graham. 2008. 'Creatures of the Provinces? The Impact of the Federal Government on Municipalities and Urban Affairs'. Paper presented at the Canadian Political Science Association Annual Meeting, Vancouver, BC.

Swinton, K. 1992. 'Federalism under Fire: The Role of the Supreme Court of Canada'. *Law and Contemporary Problems* 55, 1: 121–45.

———. 1995. 'Courting Our Way to Economic Integration: Judicial Review and the Canadian Economic Union'. *Canadian Business Law Journal* 25, 1: 280–304.

Taylor, C. 1992. *Multiculturalism and "The Politics of Recognition"*. Princeton, NJ: Princeton University Press.

———. 1993. *Reconciling the Solitudes: Essays on Canadian Federalism and Nationalism*. G. Laforest, ed. Montreal: McGill–Queen's University Press.

Taylor, M. 1978. *Health Insurance and Canadian Public Policy*. Montreal: McGill–Queen's University Press.

Telford, H. 2003. 'The Federal Spending Power in Canada: Nation-Building or Nation-Destroying?'. *Publius* 33, 1: 23–44.

Ter-Minassian, T., ed. 1997. *Fiscal Federalism in Theory and Practice*. Washington, DC: International Monetary Fund.

Thomas, D.M. 1997. *Whistling Past the Graveyard: Constitutional Abeyances, Quebec, and the Future of Canada*. Toronto: Oxford University Press.

Tinbergen, J. 1965. *International Economic Integration*. 2nd edn. Amsterdam: Elsevier.

Tomblin, S. 1995. *Ottawa and the Outer Provinces: The Challenge of Regional Integration in Canada*. Toronto: J. Lorimer.

Trebilcock, M.J. 1987. 'Federalism and the Canadian Economic Union'. In H. Bakvis and W.M. Chandler, eds. *Federalism and the Role of the State*. Toronto: University of Toronto Press.

Treff, K., and D. Perry. 2005. *Finances of the Nation: A Review of Expenditures and Revenues of the Federal, Provincial, and Local Governments of Canada*. Toronto: Canadian Tax Foundation.

Trudeau, P. 1968a. 'Federal Grants to Universities'. In Trudeau (1968b).

——— 1968b. *Federalism and the French Canadians*. Toronto: Macmillan of Canada.

Tully, J. 1995. *Strange Multiplicity: Constitutionalism in an Age of Diversity*. Cambridge: Cambridge University Press.

———. 2000. 'A Just Relationship between Aboriginal and Non-Aboriginal Peoples of Canada'. In C. Cook and J. Lindua, eds. *Aboriginal Rights and Self-Government: The Canadian and Mexican Experience in North American Perspective*. Montreal: McGill–Queen's University Press.

Tuohy, C. 1992. *Policy and Politics in Canada: Institutionalized Ambivalence*. Philadelphia: Temple University Press.

Turpel, M.E. 1993. 'The Charlottetown Discord and Aboriginal Peoples' Struggle for Fundamental Political Change'. In K. McRoberts and P. Monahan, eds. *The Charlottetown Accord, the Referendum, and the Future of Canada*. Toronto: University of Toronto Press.

Valiante, M. 2002. 'Legal Foundations of Canadian Environmental Policy: Underlying Values in a Shifting Landscape'. In D. VanNijnatten and R. Boardman, eds. *Canadian Environmental Policy: Context and Cases*. 2nd edn. Toronto: Oxford University Press.

VanNijnatten, D. 2002. 'Getting Greener in the Third Mandate? Renewable Energy, Innovation and the Liberals' Sustainable Development Agenda'. In G.B. Doern, ed. *How Ottawa Spends 2002–03: The Security Aftermath and National Priorities*. Toronto: Oxford University Press.

Vernon, R. 1988. 'The Federal Citizen'. In R. Olling and M. Westmacott, eds. *Perspectives on Canadian Federalism*. Scarborough: Prentice Hall.

Vojnovic, I. 1998. 'Municipal Consolidation in the 1990s: An Analysis of British Columbia, New Brunswick and Nova Scotia'. *Canadian Public Administration* 41, 2: 239–83.

Waite, P.B., ed. 1963. *The Confederation Debates in the Province of Canada, 1865*. Toronto: McClelland and Stewart.

Watts, R.L. 1999a. *Comparing Federal Systems*. 2nd edn. Kingston and Montreal: McGill–Queen's University Press.

———. 1999b. *The Spending Power in Federal Systems: A Comparative Study*. Kingston: Institute of Intergovernmental Relations, Queen's University.

———. 2005. 'Comparing Forms of Federal Partnerships'. In D. Karmis and W. Norman, eds. *Theories of Federalism*. Houndsmills: Palgrave Macmillan.

————. 2008. *Comparing Federal Systems.* 3rd edn. Kingston: Institute of Intergovernmental Relations, Queen's University.

Webber, J. 1994. *Reimagining Canada: Language, Culture, Community and the Canadian Constitution.* Montreal: McGill–Queen's University Press.

Weiler, P.C. 1974. *In the Last Resort: A Critical Study of the Supreme Court of Canada.* Toronto: Carswell/Methuen.

Wheare, K.C. 1963. *Federal Government.* 4th edn. London: Oxford University Press.

White, G. 2005. *Cabinets and First Ministers.* Vancouver: University of British Columbia Press.

Whyte, J. 1987. 'Federal Powers over the Economy: Finding New Jurisdictional Room'. *Canadian Business Law Journal* 13: 257–302.

————. 1990. 'The Impact of Internationalization on the Constitutional Setting'. Paper presented at the Think Globally: Proceedings of the 42nd Annual Conference of the Institute of Public Administration of Canada. Quebec City, QC.

Wilson, J. 1998. *Talk and Log: Wilderness Politics in British Columbia.* Vancouver: University of British Columbia Press.

Winfield, M., and D. Macdonald. 2008. 'The Harmonization Accord and Climate Change Policy: Two Case Studies in Federal–Provincial Policy'. In Bakvis and Skogstad, eds (2008).

Young, R. 1999. *The Struggle for Quebec.* Montreal: McGill–Queen's University Press.

Index